Charlemagne's Defeat in the Pyrenees

I0593003

Charlemagne's Defeat in the Pyrenees

The Battle of Rencesvals

Xabier Irujo

Routledge
Taylor & Francis Group

LONDON AND NEW YORK

First published in 2021 by Amsterdam University Press Ltd.

Published 2025 by Routledge
4 Park Square, Milton Park, Abingdon, Oxon OX14 4RN
605 Third Avenue, New York, NY 10158

Routledge is an imprint of the Taylor & Francis Group, an informa business

© X. Irujo / Taylor & Francis Group 2021

All rights reserved. No part of this book may be reprinted or reproduced or utilised in any form or by any electronic, mechanical, or other means, now known or hereafter invented, including photocopying and recording, or in any information storage or retrieval system, without permission in writing from the publishers.

Trademark notice: Product or corporate names may be trademarks or registered trademarks, and are used only for identification and explanation without intent to infringe.

ISBN: 9789463721059 (hbk)
ISBN: 9781041176718 (pbk)
ISBN: 9781003692232 (ebk)
NUR 684

Cover illustration: Roland's death. Detail of the stained-glass window of Charlemagne in the Chartres cathedral representing the hero blowing the oliphant asking for help and trying to break his sword against the rock right before dying. Dr Stuart Whatling, used with permission.

Cover design: Coördesign, Leiden

DOI: 10.5117/9789463721059

Every effort has been made to obtain permission to use all copyrighted illustrations reproduced in this book. Nonetheless, whosoever believes to have rights to this material is advised to contact the publisher.

For Product Safety Concerns and Information please contact our EU representative:
GPSR@taylorandfrancis.com
Taylor & Francis Verlag GmbH, Kaufingerstraße 24, 80331 München, Germany

Table of Contents

Preface

Abstract
Distinguishing between myth and reality has been the greatest challenge in writing this book. The image of Roland in the Basque oral
tradition is quite different from the noble courtier of literature and the
image of Charlemagne diverges from the Frankish chronicles written
in the monasteries of northern Europe. While the Frankish tradition
exalted its heroes, the Basque oral tradition, largely unknown to English
readers, had a very different interpretation of the events. Charlemagne
and Roland represent bringers of war, foreign paladins ignorant of the
customary law of the Basques and their way of life. This book is based
entirely on original historical sources, contemporaneous with the
events, translated from the original Latin by the author, some presented
in English for the first time. The author has also examined the terrain
exhaustively, enabling him to provide a totally new image of the battle
and its consequences.

Keywords: Rencesvals, Way of Saint James, Epic traditions, historiography,
Charlemagne, Roland

This book examines the events that took place in the Pyrenean pass of
Errozabal (Rencesvals) on August 15, 778.[1] Not only a mere battle, Errozabal
is also the most dramatic episode of a historical event that affected Vasconia,
the land of the Basques, for almost the entire eighth century. Indeed, the
battle was not an isolated military incident but part of a complex military
and political process that began after the Muslim conquest of the Iberian
Peninsula in 711 and culminated with the creation of the Kingdom of
Pamplona in 824.

---

1   The battle of Rencevals is known under a variety of different names, Rencevals (French and
English), Roncevalles (Spanish), and Errozabal (Basque). The original Basque term has been
preferred. However, it should be remembered that the names are interchangeable.

Irujo, X., *Charlemagne's Defeat in the Pyrenees: The Battle of Rencesvals*. Taylor & Francis, 2021
DOI 10.5117/9789463721059_PRE

Following the penetration of Islam into Europe, the Visigothic Kingdom of Toledo—the traditional rival of Vasconia since its formation in the early sixth century—suddenly disappeared in the early eighth century, giving rise to a new political landscape. Indeed, when Tariq ibn Ziyad crossed the Strait of Gibraltar into the Iberian Peninsula, the Visigoth King Rodrigo was in the vicinity of Pamplona leading a new campaign to punish the Basques. Therefore, the Basques viewed the collapse of the Visigothic order with caution, but not without a certain satisfaction and even optimism.

The course of the eighth century would pit Vasconia between East and West, forcing its rulers and people to cope with the ambitions of the Christian kings of the north and the impetuous expansionism of the Caliphate of Damascus in the south. Between 714 and 732 Franks and Basques allied against Islam, but after the defeat at Poitiers the situation changed. Pepin the Short, having deposed Chilperic III in 751, became king of the Franks and, taking advantage of the weakness of Vasconia under Waiofar, wrested Aquitaine from the Basques after a bloody eight-year war (760-768), which culminated in the Basque ruler's murder at the hands of Pepin's assassins.

In 768, Charlemagne inherited from his father Pepin not only a crown, but also a political project. Pepin's war with the Lombard Kingdom had allied him with Rome, giving way to the dream of a Christian Empire. And the collapse in 750 of the Umayyad dynasty in Damascus led to the Frankish expansion to the south. Abd al-Rahman, last survivor of the Umayyad dynasty, established an emirate in al-Andalus in 755 but faced a serious challenge from the Muslim *walis* (governors) of the Ebro valley, who took advantage of the power vacuum to free themselves from the yoke of the central power.

The relative weakness of the Basque Kingdom, the desire to stop the Muslim advance to the north, and, finally, the project of creating a Western Christian Empire as the heirs of the Roman Empire, convinced Charlemagne to propose in the Paderborn Diet of 777 the creation of the *Marca Hispanica*. This was a political venture with a certain religious streak, the genesis of the Early Medieval Crusades. However, the first aim of the Marca Hispanica was the conquest and pacification of Vasconia. It was then that Charlemagne crossed the Pyrenees. The year was 778.

The consequences of the Carolingian defeat affected not only the Basque Country but the whole of the Western political picture. Charlemagne had to cope with new uprisings in Saxony in the autumn of that year and was forced to undertake a political and administrative reform of the Frankish Kingdom and its newly acquired possessions in Aquitaine and Lombardy. The defeat did not enhance the emirate, which, despite embarking on a punitive campaign on Vasconia in 781, was unable to capitalize on its victory. As regards the Basque Country, their victory cemented the alliance between the Banu Qasi, Islamized southern Basques, and the mountain leaders, including Eneko, the father of the first king of Pamplona, Eneko Aritza.

While Charlemagne abandoned the idea of creating the Marca Hispanica after the 778 defeat, his son Ludovico, who became king of Aquitaine, resumed the project twenty years later and, between 797 and 812, succeeded in dominating the lands of the Basques east of the Pyrenees. After the uncertain outcome of the campaign of 812 and the disaster of the third battle of Errozabal in 824, the empire definitively abandoned the project of creating a Marca Hispanica comprising the whole Pyrenean range and replaced the original dream with a less ambitious *Marca Gothica* limited to the eastern Pyrenees.

In the shadow of these political and military vicissitudes and after fighting three battles in the pass of Errozabal, the Kingdom of Pamplona arose around the figure of Eneko Aritza, whose father had fought in the first Rencesvals.

The Battle of Errozabal is one of the most important military events of the reign of Charlemagne. Since it was one of the few defeats of the imperial army this singular episode inspired one of the earliest and most famous epic poems in Western Europe. And, even more than its impact on literature and, by extension, European culture, Errozabal also had profound political repercussions.

Distinguishing between myth and reality in the eighth century has been my greatest challenge in writing this book. The few surviving historical sources have been strongly imbued with fantastic elements through the passage of time, and the literary sources have distorted reality through the incorporation of hyperbolic elements. However, we owe to these literary texts the memory of those men whom history made warriors and literature heroes. While we expect prudence, zeal, and respect for historic events—and the suffering they cause—from our chroniclers, we must never deny the pleasure of reading our history, the history of humankind, written as literature as was done nearly a thousand years ago by the master Turoldus.

And if this is true for all our Medieval history, then it is even more so in the case of the events that took place here in the Pyrenees on August 15, 778, 1,240 years ago. The Basques have lived with the legend of Rencesvals for over a millennium. The ancient marketplace of the kings of Navarre in Lizarra/Estella, city of my grandparents and great-grandparents, has a capital—the crowning head of a column—that shows a fragment of Charlemagne's legend. There eight hundred years ago a stonemason named Martinus carved a depiction of the single combat between Roland and Ferracutus that, according to legend, occurred at the gates of Naiara (Najera), the burial place of the kings of Navarre.

On the left side of the capital, Ferracutus rides to meet his rival wearing a large round shield bearing a star, the city's symbol. The giant protects his body with a heavy coat of mail, made of iron, which gave him his name, Ferracutus, the Iron Chainmail Colossus. And hefted to his left there should be a long lance bearing his banner. On the capital's front, Ferracutus, left, unwinds a long turban, which picks up, blowing in the scene's violent wind to create a long veil. Roland confronts him, also wearing chain mail and carrying a triangular shield bearing the cross of his faith. The crash of the two heroes is brutal: Ferracutus's spear is broken on impact with Roland's shield, while the impact of Roland's pike at Ferracutus's navel sends the giant reeling, losing his stirrups and elevating his legs almost to his waist. Ferracutus does not, however, drop his shield.

On the capital's right face, Roland and Ferracutus continue the fight on foot. Roland bears his huge triangular shield, which protects practically all of him from the giant's mace which is brandished overhead. Ferracutus by contrast has no shield and has lost his turban, which allows the master Martinus the opportunity to fully represent the fierce warrior: He screams, with his mouth wide open, and has long hair and a thick beard, which is as curly as those of the stained-glass figures of Charlemagne in the Chartres cathedral. The giant arches back as if building momentum to hit Roland, while the latter, rising from his knees, tries unsuccessfully to stick his knife in to Ferracutus's iron chest.

Everyone in Lizarra/Estella knows that Roland could only unseat Ferracutus by wrenching his thick, curly black beard and could only kill him—through divine intercession—by plunging his dagger into Ferracutus's navel, the chainmail giant's only weak point. Even then he did not manage to kill the colossus, who, mortally wounded and imploring Mohammed, was assisted to Naiara's gates. Here Martinus did allow a little license. On the front of the capital, in the background, he sculpted Ferracutus on the ground, decapitated, the image of the biblical giant Goliath.

Beyond the royal market in Lizarra/Estella, which is a rare and beautiful example of the non-religious European Romanesque, climbing the steep stairs to the austere church of San Pedro de la Rua, built in the twelfth century, we see another capital that tells the same story; this time Ferracutus's spear breaks while Roland unseats the giant from his horse.

Early on, epic poems sung in romance language were produced, which exalted Roland and the rest of the Frankish warriors in legend. A beautiful example of this tradition can be found in the *Roncesvalles navarro* that includes Charlemagne's speech before the body of his nephew Roland, in the stained-red fields of Rencesvals, the Errozabal of the Basques. These hundred verses were written by an educated official of the court of Charles III *El Noble*, King of Navarre, who may have known the kingdom well enough as he walked it to complete the 1366 census.

But while the Frankish epic tradition exalted their sons killed in Errozabal, the Basque oral tradition forged a quite different interpretation from that of the poets of the *Camino de Santiago* (the Way of Saint James). In the eyes of this tradition, Roland represents the bearer of war, a paladin belonging to a foreign court ignorant of the customary law of the Basques and their way of life; as Basque mothers say, they do not want their sons to be soldiers. Xabier Diharce's poem 'Orreaga' reflects this view. The author, writing in exile under the pseudonym of Iratzeder, whose brother was killed fighting the Nazi occupation, compares the arrival of the troops of the Reich and the events that took place in Errozabal. He raises his voice against all those cases in which a man has sought to impose a political project by force of arms, beyond reason and the rights of peoples and their lives:

The beech is the most beautiful trees of the black forest
On the mountains of Rencesvals goes the soul of the Basques:
Between wars and gales still standing along the centuries
Mature beech stands silently in the future of Europe.
Some warriors, eager to slaughter, thirst for blood and fire,
Wishing to crush the Europeans have been here.
If Mount Ibañeta could talk about them
It would first mention Roland and Charlemagne.
Would have liked to behead, rob and oppress the heart
And all the people, make everyone vassal.
But the Basque people, always alert, have managed to rise,
So that in these mountains man continues being man, with head high.
Poised to breach our borders, pushed on by violence,
When will the Basque soul will fly like the eagle?
When will free men come out of Rencesvals?
As wise and earnest as Azpilikueta?
The mountain stream jumping from the mountain is so beautiful...
Sons of the Fatherland, drink with all your heart the spirit of your fathers!
Lift up the front and sing all at once, the War of the Basques
So that hearing our cry, all of Europe will arise.[2]

2   Diharce, Jean Mari, "Orreagako mendi gainetan", *Eguna*, 4th year, No. 269, 1989, p. 26.

Near my parents' house in Altzuza is the hill of Altzuzate, a natural stronghold that protects Pamplona's access from Esteribar, which is where Charlemagne began his retreat through the port of Zize, before being ambushed in Errozabal by the Basques. And just 24 kilometres east of Altzuza, in Urrotz, there is a block of stone, three feet long, that Roland launched from the heights of Erro, more than 20 kilometres away, when he was about to die. As in the case of Ezpeleta, the legend says Roland missed because as he was preparing to launch a huge boulder, he slipped on some cow dung. But he seized the stone with such force it bears the imprint of his fingers.

Visitors may still see the hoof prints of Roland's steed Veillantif, in Gainekoleta, from when the hero fought, mortally wounded on the Zize pass. As recounted by Jose Maria Satrustegi, Roland covered with a jump the 13 kilometres separating Astobizkar from Luzaide, later known as Valcarlos, where the stone was engraved with the horse's hoof at Loulone.

The Roland of the Basque oral tradition is quite different from the noble courtier. But both the Roland of the *Chanson* and the Roland who threw rocks from the heights of Erro are legendary figures, twelve centuries from their historical reality. Equally, the Charlemagne of the Frankish chronicles which were written in the monasteries of northern Europe close to the court of Aachen, is far from the person who should have been Charles, the son of Pepin the Short and Bertha, the queen with the goose-foot. The tribulated emperor who could hear the best men of his army, his and his father's friends, dying while fleeing in terror was behind the legendary Frankish warrior; he was also the man who took on an empire's fate, who decided the life and death of the kingdom's inhabitants and the fates of surrounding nations.

And it was these same Basques who erected a hermitage in honour of the soldiers who were there defeated and killed and gave the name of *Valcarlos* (Charles's valley) to the town that hosted the emperor that terrible night of August 15, 778. The twelfth-century pilgrim Aymeric Picaud bequeathed to us the first and most startling description of the place where the battle took place and where Charlemagne prayed to Saint James before his troops descended on Pamplona, the strongest city of the Basques:

In the land of the Basques, on the road to Santiago, there is a very high mountain called Zize pass, either because this is the entrance to Hispania, or because said mountain is the transport route from one land to the other, and the rise is eight miles [thirteen kilometres] and the descent it also eight. In fact, its height is such that seems to touch the sky. He who ascends there seems to be able to reach heaven with his hand. From its summit you can see the sea in Brittany and the western sea [...]. On top of this mountain there is a place called the Cruz de Carlos, because in this place, with axes and pickaxes, hoes and other tools Charlemagne opened a path to go to Hispania with his armies and for the first time erected a cross and kneeling in the face of Galicia, he prayed to God and Santiago. Therefore, kneeling, pilgrims usually pray in this place looking towards Santiago and they all stick their crosses so that there they can be counted in thousands. And so, this is the place to raise the first prayer to Santiago.[3]

The present book is based entirely on original sources, contemporaneous with the events, many of which were published in the *Monumenta Germaniae Historica* collection and have been translated from Latin, Romance, or Basque by the author. Some of these contemporary sources are here first presented in English, mainly Latin and Arabic sources and fragments of the Basque tradition recounting the battle. There is no other geographical study of the battle's locale. For ten years I have studied the terrain from Altzuzate to the Pyrenean Zize pass, taking photographs and measurements along the way, exploring the topography of the battlefield and walking the road that the Carolingian army traversed more than one thousand years ago.

3   Rialle, Girard De; Vinson, Julien (eds.), *Revue de Linguistique et de Philologie Comparée* 15 (Maisonneuve de Cie, Libraires-éditeurs, 1882), 14–15. An English version may be found in Melczer, William (ed.), *The Pilgrim's Guide to Santiago de Compostela* (New York: Italica Press Inc., 1993). For this passage see pp. 93–94.

1.   Precedents of the Battle

Abstract

This chapter examines the creation of the Emirate of Cordoba under Abd al-Rahman I and King Charles' call for the Paderborn Diet in 777. The purpose of the 778 campaign launched by the Frankish king was not to fire up a crusade against Islam but to create a *march* in the Pyrenees, a vassal domain of the Frankish Kingdom bounded by the 600-kilometer (373-mile) old Roman road connecting Pamplona and Girona. Indeed, sources indicate that King Charles negotiated terms with the Muslim rulers of the Ebro valley and there was no offer on the part of the Muslim emissaries to embrace the Christian faith. However, the religious aspect provided a suitable and effective casus belli and the literary tradition presented this military adventure as the first European crusade.

Keywords: Charlemagne, crusade, *Marca Hispanica*, Paderborn, Pamplona, Islam

The Paderborn Diet, 777

Charlemagne became king of the Franks in 768 when he reached the age of 21.[1] As custom dictated, the kingdom was divided between the two brothers (*divisio regnorum*), and Charles ruled with his seventeen-year-old brother

---

1   According to the date of birth (747) given by the *Annales Pitaviani* (Et ipso anno fuit natus Karolus rex). See *Annales Petaviani*, in Pertz, Georg Heinrich (ed.), *Monumenta Germaniae Historica* (MGH), SS, I, Hannover, 1826, pp. 10-11. Despite this record the date of birth of Charlemagne is questioned by various authors who place his birth in 742. In Pertz, Georg Heinrich (ed.), *Annales et chronica aevi Carolini*, Monumenta Germaniae Historica (MGH), SS, I, Hannover, 1826, p. 10. Acording to the *Annales Salisburgenses* Charlemagne was born in 742. In Pertz, Georg Heinrich (ed.), *Annales et chronica aevi Carolini*, Monumenta Germaniae Historica (MGH), SS, I, Hannover, 1826, p. 89. The *Annales Sancti Emmerammi Ratisponensis Minores* date Charlemagne's birth in 743.

Irujo, X., *Charlemagne's Defeat in the Pyrenees: The Battle of Rencesvals.* Taylor & Francis, 2021

DOI 10.5117/9789463721059_CH01

Carloman.[2] Carloman died in 771 as the dispute between brothers was intensifying, and Charles became the only heir of the kingdom left by Pepin. In 778, at the age of 31, Charles envisioned the *renovatio Romanorum imperii*, the restitution of the Roman Empire, a dream inherited from his father. The new king successfully started the first set of military campaigns of his reign between 770 and 776. In the southeast, in the year 770, Charles crushed the insurrection of Hunald II who, after the death of Pepin in 768, tried to restore the duchy of Aquitaine under the protection of Lupus II, Prince of Vasconia.[3] In the northeast, the emperor's troops entered Saxony (*Carlus Saxoniam bello adgressus*) and, after crossing the rivers Eder and Diemel, they arrived in the vicinity of Eresburg (*Eresburgum castrum*), about 40 kilometres south of Paderborn, adding these areas to the Frankish domain.[4] In the south, Charlemagne started two campaigns against Lombardy (in 773-774 and 776) as a result of which he incorporated these territories under vassalage to the empire. Desiderio was divested, and Charlemagne took the iron crown and adopted the title of *rex Langobardorum* that he later passed to his son Pepin (781-810).[5]

The diet (*Campus Martius* or *Placitum Generalis*)[6] was held annually at the beginning of the spring, between March and May, in different places designated by the king in the winter. The Campus Martius met for two main reasons: *auxilium et consilium*. *Auxilium* meant, in essence, to gather the troops needed in order to address the annual military campaign. The *Regnum Francorum* was organized as a massive military apparatus, strongly hierarchical and subject to a severe military code. Thus, at the beginning of the year the military forces that would undertake the yearly campaign met to accomplish the goal determined by the king or imposed

---

2   Carloman was born in 751. In Richter, Gustav; Kohl, Horst, *Annalen der deutschen Geschichte im Mittelalter, von der Gründung des fränkischen Reichs bis zum untergang der Hohenstaufen: mit fortlaufenden Quellenauszügen und Literaturangaben*, Verlag der Buchhandlung des Waisenhauses, Halle, 1885, vol. 2, p. 29.

3   Holder-Egger, Oswald (ed.), *Einhardi Vita Karoli Magni,* Monumenta Germaniae Historica (MGH), SSRG, Hannover & Leipzig, 1911, p. 7. See also, Kurze, Friedrich (ed.), *Annales regni Francorum (741–829) qui dicuntur Annales Laurissenses maiores et Einhardi*, Monumenta Germaniae Historica (MGH), SSRG, VI, Hannover, 1895, pp. 29-30.

4   Kurze, Friedrich (ed.), *Annales regni Francorum (741–829) qui dicuntur Annales Laurissenses maiores et Einhardi*, Monumenta Germaniae Historica (MGH), SSRG, VI, Hannover, 1895, pp. 32-34.

5   Holder-Egger, Oswald (ed.), *Einhardi Vita Karoli Magni,* Monumenta Germaniae Historica (MGH), SSRG, Hannover & Leipzig, 1911, p. 8-9. See also, Kurze, Friedrich (ed.), *Annales regni Francorum (741–829) qui dicuntur Annales Laurissenses maiores et Einhardi*, Monumenta Germaniae Historica (MGH), SSRG, VI, Hannover, 1895, pp. 35-36.

6   The annals also refer to the diet as *Martiuscampus* or simply *Conventus Francorum*.

by circumstances during the winter. While at first the Campus Martius met in March, they later convened in May (*Campus Maius*), apparently because the weather conditions were more favourable.[7] The grass was already grown in May, and therefore it was easier and cheaper to feed the workhorses and the rest of the draft animals used during the strenuous marches of hundreds or even thousands of kilometres.[8] Usually the Franks prepared for prolonged military campaigns that could span anywhere from two to four months. Sometimes, as happened in 775, the military campaigns took place simultaneously in several theatres of operation during the same season. The *liberi homines* subject to conscription (*auxilium*) came to the call of the imperial *missi* (*missus dominicus* or 'emissaries' of the king).[9] To fail in the call of duty or fail to disburse the tax stipulated in lieu of service in these cases was punished, as this was one of the main services in the life of a free man.[10]

Consilium connoted the introduction and approval of matters of political, military, and ecclesiastical nature, all activities linked to the central administration of the Carolingian realm. One of the key points on the agenda was the inspection of the troops and the military equipment that the civilian (*dux*) and religious authorities had to contribute for the campaign.[11] From this perspective, the diet reflected the hierarchy of the Frankish

7   Also referred to as *Magicampus*, *Magi Campus*, *Maiscampus* or, *Meienfeld*. These Frankish warriors' assemblies were also known as *Conventus Francorum*.

8   As recorded in the Annales Petaviani, Pepin the Short first convened the Campus Maius in Nevers in 763, although it is considered that the first Campus Maius took place in 755. However, it appears that these assemblies met at the beginning of the spring, often after the celebration of Easter. Perry, Walter C., *The Franks: From their First Appearance in History to the Death of King Pepin*, Longman, Brown, Green, Longmans, and Roberts, London, 1857, p. 335.

9   While the *missi* existed previously it was not until 802, the date of the approval of the *Capitulare missorum generale*, that the emperor reorganized the empire by dividing it into administrative units called *misaticae*. Under the *Capitulare missorum generale* 'the most serene and most Christian lord emperor Charles has chosen from his noblemen the wisest and most prudent men, also various archbishops and bishops, abbots and venerable and pious laymen, and have sent them across his kingdom and, along with them, all classes of persons mentioned in the following chapters will live according to the law ('secundum legem rectam liveth concessit'). Full text in its original Latin version in Reich, Emil, *Select Documents Illustrating Medieval and Modern History*, P.S. King & Son, London, 1905, pp. 297-300. See also another translation into English of the complete original text of the *Capitulare missorum generale* in Ogg, Frederic A., *A Source Book of Mediaeval History: Documents Illustrative of European Life and Institutions from the German Invasion to the Renaissance*, American Book Company, New York, 1908, pp. 134-141.

10   As stated in the capitulary of 808: '67.' In Migne, Jacques P., *Patrologiae cursus completus. Operum beati Caroli Magni Imperatoris*, Paris, 1862, p. 562.

11   Collins, Roger, *Charlemagne*, University of Toronto Press Ltd., Toronto and Buffalo, 1998, p. 22.

administration, so that while most civil and religious personalities were present, the assembly offered the king the means of sounding his will and resolving differences or disputes among nobles who had expressed their dissatisfaction.

The Campus Martius also provided the opportunity to celebrate religious ceremonies and royal rituals. The excellent diplomatic relations that the Frankish leaders had managed to establish with the Papacy by adopting the observance of Christian rites, allowed the emperor to imbue with divine authority the origin of the temporal power of the *rex Francorum*, who was crowned under the title of *Dei Gratia Francorum Rex*.

The celebration of the Campus Martius was conducted with pomp and circumstance. As referred in the *Annales Laurissenses* and, according to tradition, on the first day of the celebration the king, seated on his throne and surrounded by the army, received the offerings of the people in the presence of the seneschal (*maior domus* or *domus regiae maior*).[12] However, the diet of 777 (*Magi Campus ad Paderbruna*) was unique for several reasons but mainly because for the first time it was held in the newly conquered Saxony, thus providing the *Conventus Francorum* a singular political character. The town of Paderborn is located about 300 kilometres northeast of the imperial seat of Herstal, captured after a long war that began five years before, in 772. It was not therefore one more annual assembly but was conceived as the council that would end the wars in Westphalia, thus asserting definitive control of the Frankish over Saxony and instituting the authority of Charlemagne on their principals.

The diet was therefore prepared for methodically; as if it were a stage set, a wooden palace was erected on the site where the event would take place. The Frankish sources mention scenic arrangements as the collective baptism of the pagan chieftains in the presence of high ecclesiastical dignitaries and the blessing of the papal nuncio; the chroniclers did not avoid drawing a parallel between the *rex Francorum* and John the Baptist.[13] The annals

12   The participation of ecclesiastical dignities in the Campus Martius was always relevant. In 751, Pepin the Short, the imperial palace's seneschal, and yearning for the throne, asked Pope Zachary for the license to call himself 'king' because the person who held the title and sat on the throne during the assemblies was not a king. Thus, Pepin was proclaimed king and Childeric was tonsured and confined in a monastery as we read in the original Latin version of the *Annales Laurissenses Menores*. In Pertz, Georg Heinrich (ed.), *Annales et chronica aevi Carolini*, Monumenta Germaniae Historica (MGH), SS, I, Hannover, 1826, p. 116.

13   As recorded in the *Petau Annals*: '777.' In King, P. D., *Charlemagne: Translated Sources*, P. D. King, Lambrigg, Kendal, Cumbria, 1987, p. 151. The *Annales Mosellani* also registered the baptisms: '777. Charles held the assembly of the Franks – the Mayfield, that is in Saxony, at Paderborn, and an immense multitude of pagan Saxons were baptised there. From the death

also mention the placement of the foundation stone and the consecration of the church that became the seat of the Paderborn Bishopric, dependent on the one at Wursburg.[14]

Also, the ceremony of the oath of allegiance to the king mentioned by the *Annales Mettenses Priores* and the *Annales Regni Francorum* was conducted in a theatrical way, highlighting that Widukind was isolated, out of his own land and away from his Saxon compatriots. Charlemagne thus received 'triumphant but generous' (*Victor et Triumphator atque semper Augustus*) the delegation of the Saxon chieftains who succumbed on behalf of his vassals to his rule after years of bloody struggle.[15]

Finally, the reception of a Muslim delegation in Paderborn made up of the *walies* or governors of some of the mayor cities of the Ebro valley in al-Andalus was not exempt from theatricality. The chronicles mention that 'some Saracens from Hispania also came to this assembly, among them Ibn al-Arabi and Deiuzef [Yusuf] that in Latin is said Joseph and his son and son in law'.[16] However, the annals do not agree about the Muslim envois who went to Paderborn. The *Annales qui dicuntur Annales Laurissenses maiores et Einhardi* include in the list of deputies the son and son in law of Yusuf al Fihri.[17] However, the *Annales Regni Francorum* recorded that Sulayman ibn Yaqzan ibn al-Arabi *cum aliis Sarracenis sociis suis* assisted the diet without specifying their names.[18] The *Annales Mettenses Priores* instead mention

of pope Gregory to this present year makes 172 years.' In King, P. D., *Charlemagne: Translated Sources*, P. D. King, Lambrigg, Kendal, Cumbria, 1987, p. 133.

14 Simson, Bernhard von (ed.), *Annales Mettenses Priores*, Monumenta Germaniae Historica (MGH), SSRG, X, Hannover & Leipzig, 1905, pp. 65-66. See another English version in King, P. D., *Charlemagne: Translated Sources*, P. D. King, Lambrigg, Kendal, Cumbria, 1987, p. 151.

15 The *Annales Regni Francorum* also recorded the events in Kurze, Friedrich (ed.), *Annales regni Francorum (741–829) qui dicuntur Annales Laurissenses maiores et Einhardi*, Monumenta Germaniae Historica (MGH), SSRG, VI, Hannover, 1895, p. 48. See also another English version in King, P. D., *Charlemagne: Translated Sources*, P. D. King, Lambrigg, Kendal, Cumbria, 1987, p. 79.

16 Kurze, Friedrich (ed.), *Annales regni Francorum (741–829) qui dicuntur Annales Laurissenses maiores et Einhardi*, Monumenta Germaniae Historica (MGH), SSRG, VI, Hannover, 1895, p. 48. See also another English version in King, P. D., *Charlemagne: Translated Sources*, P. D. King, Lambrigg, Kendal, Cumbria, 1987, p. 79.

17 Kurze, Friedrich (ed.), *Annales regni Francorum (741–829) qui dicuntur Annales Laurissenses maiores et Einhardi*, Monumenta Germaniae Historica (MGH), SSRG, VI, Hannover, 1895, p. 48. See also another English version in King, P. D., *Charlemagne: Translated Sources*, P. D. King, Lambrigg, Kendal, Cumbria, 1987, p. 79.

18 Kurze, Friedrich (ed.), *Annales regni Francorum (741–829) qui dicuntur Annales Laurissenses maiores et Einhardi*, Monumenta Germaniae Historica (MGH), SSRG, VI, Hannover, 1895, pp., 49 & 51. The *Annales Einhardi* also mention *Ibn al-Arabi* in Pertz, Georg Heinrich (ed.), *Annales et chronica aevi Carolini*, Monumenta Germaniae Historica (MGH), SS, I, Hannover, 1826, p. 159.

that some Muslim leaders went to Paderborn, but only mention Sulayman ibn al-Arabi and Ibn Yusuf.[19] In the same vein, the Saxon poet[20] and the *Annales Tiliani* mention that 'ad eundem placitum venientes Saraceni de partibus Spaniae, hii sunt Ibinalarabi et filius Denizesi, qui et latine Ioseph nominatur'.[21] The *Einhardi Fuldensis Annales* only mention the presence of *Ibinalarabi*[22] and the *Annales Lauricenses* reveal that 'etiam ad eundem placitum venerunt Sarraceni de partibus Hispaniae, hii sunt Ibinalarabi et filius Deiuzefi, qui et latine Ioseph nominatur, similiter et gener eius'.[23] As regards the Muslim sources, *Kitab al-bayan* registers the attendance of Sulayman ibn al-Arabi,[24] governor of Barcelona and Girona, and of Hussain ibn Yahya al-Ansari, governor of Zaragoza.[25]

The chronicles allow us, therefore, to establish with certainty the presence of ibn Sulayman al-Arabi, *wali* of Barcelona and Girona in Paderborn ('Qui praefectus Barcinonae Gerundaeque fuisse videtur')[26] and, with less certitude, the attendance of Hussain ibn Yahya al-Ansari, *wali* of Zaragoza. Also, most of the annals mention the son, Kasmin ibn Yusuf, and son-in-law of Yusuf al Fihri, who was the emir of Cordoba until it was overthrown by Abd al-Rahman I in 755 and later assassinated in 760.

---

19   Some Saracen princes from Hispania attended this meeting: 'Ibinalardi [Sulayman al-Arabi] and Withseui [Kasmin ibn Yusuf] that is said Joseph in Latin. And they and their vassals were surrendered to King Charles [...] And the king celebrated the Nativity of the Lord in the city they call Dotiacus [Douzy] and Easter in Aquitaine, in the village called Cassinaghilo [Chasseneuil].' In Simson, Bernhard von (ed.), *Annales Mettenses Priores*, Monumenta Germaniae Historica (MGH), SSRG, X, Hannover & Leipzig, 1905, pp. 65-66. See another English version in King, P. D., *Charlemagne: Translated Sources*, P. D. King, Lambrigg, Kendal, Cumbria, 1987, p. 151.

20   Pertz, Georg Heinrich (ed.), *Annales et chronica aevi Carolini*, Monumenta Germaniae Historica (MGH), SS, I, Hannover, 1826, p. 234.

21   Pertz, Georg Heinrich (ed.), *Annales et chronica aevi Carolini*, Monumenta Germaniae Historica (MGH), SS, I, Hannover, 1826, pp. 220.

22   Pertz, Georg Heinrich (ed.), *Annales et chronica aevi Carolini*, Monumenta Germaniae Historica (MGH), SS, I, Hannover, 1826, pp. 349.

23   Pertz, Georg Heinrich (ed.), *Annales et chronica aevi Carolini*, Monumenta Germaniae Historica (MGH), SS, I, Hannover, 1826, pp. 157-158.

24   Mentioned as *Ibinalardi* or *Ezirlabio*.

25   The *Kitab al-bayan* or *Libro de la fabulosa historia de los reyes de al-Andalus y Marruecos* (Book of the fabulous history of the kings of al-Andalus and Morocco) and *Los anales del Magreb y de Hispania* (Annals of the Mogreb and Hispania), among other Muslim sources, mention Hussain ibn Yahya al-Ansari as governor of Zaragoza. See Fagnan, Edmond (ed.), *Histoire de l'Afrique du Nord et de l'Espagne intitulée Al-Bayano'l-Mogrib*, vol. 2, Imprimerie Orientale, Argelia, 1904, p. 90 ; Ibn al-Athir, *Annales du Maghreb & de l'Espagne traduites et annotées par Edmond Fagnan*, Typographie Adolphe Jourdan, Alger, 1898, pp. 128-129 & 141.

26   Simson, Bernhard von (ed.), *Annales Mettenses Priores*, Monumenta Germaniae Historica (MGH), SSRG, X, Hannover & Leipzig, 1905, p. 66.

The *Enhardi Fuldensis Annales*, the *Annales Laurissenses*, the *Chronicon Moissiacense*, and the *Annales Tiliani* also mention Abu Taur,[27] *wali* of Huesca (Weschka) by virtue of the role played by the latter during the campaign of 778, but do not identify him as being present in Paderborn.[28] His absence in the chronicles supports the idea that, although he may have acted in collusion with the *walies* of Barcelona and Zaragoza, Abu Taur did not travel to Saxony.

The *walies* who attended the imperial diet had to be highly motivated to travel 2,000 kilometres from Zaragoza to Paderborn via Barcelona. In any case, the alliance, which, because of the distances and the state of the roads at the time must have been forged at least a year earlier, was difficult to seal because it combined many and varied interests.

While the chronicles are silent about the imperial designs, the events that took place in the spring and summer of 778 indicate that once Charlemagne had subdued the Saxons in the northeast (beyond the rivers Ruhr and Lippe) and the Lombards in the south (beyond the Alps), he grasped the possibility of expanding the influence of his kingdom beyond the Pyrenees to contain the Muslims south of the river Ebro. The armies of the Emirate of Cordoba had not broken into Septimania through the Pertus passage since their defeat at the hands of Pepin the Short and the subsequent occupation of Narbonne *c.* 757. The weakness of the emirate granted Charlemagne the possibility of taking the initiative and, crossing the line into aggressiveness, sealing an agreement with the Muslim governors opposed to Abd al-Rahman I, which would enable him to establish Frankish garrisons in the Iberian Peninsula.

Along with the military and political submission of Saxony, this project was most probably the main topic of discussion at the imperial assembly of 777. The *Marca Hispanica* was conceived by the new king as a vassal domain of the Frankish Kingdom encompassing the southern hillside of the Pyrenees, bonded through the 600-kilometer (373-mile) old Roman road connecting Pamplona in the west with Girona in the east. The execution of this ambitious project meant to revive the armed confrontation with the Emirate of Cordoba and, thus, was only possible through the subjugation of

27 Also named Abu Tawr or *Habitauro, Abitauro, Abutauro* and *ibi Taurus* by the Frankish chroniclers.

28 Pertz, Georg Heinrich (ed.), *Annales et chronica aevi Carolini*, Monumenta Germaniae Historica (MGH), SS, I, Hannover, 1826, p. 349. See also the *Annales Laurissenses* in Pertz, Georg Heinrich (ed.), *Annales et chronica aevi Carolini*, Monumenta Germaniae Historica (MGH), SS, I, Hannover, 1826, p. 158. Regarding the reference to *Abu Taur* in the *Annales Tiliani* and in the *Chronicon Moissiacense* see Pertz, Georg Heinrich (ed.), *Annales et chronica aevi Carolini*, Monumenta Germaniae Historica (MGH), SS, I, Hannover, 1826, pp. 220 & 296.

the Basques on both sides of the Pyrenees and the acquiescence of the *walies* of the main cities in the area.[29] On the other hand, maintaining the Muslim cities under vassalage was both politically and strategically demanding.

The attendance of the *walies* of the Ebro valley at Paderborn has led to the conclusion that they were in agreement and that, consequently, the Muslim cities of the Ebro valley were facing the emirate. Attendance of envoys from Damascus was not feasible since the caliphate was undergoing a crisis and, above all, it was incompatible with the interest of the *walies* since it involved full submission to the Abbasid Empire. Similarly, in the light of events, it is hardly credible that the *walies* of Zaragoza and Barcelona were willing to surrender to the vassalage of a Christian prince. The fact that the *wali* did not need military assistance from Charlemagne to the point of paying the price of their independence had been demonstrated in the battlefield. Sulayman ibn al-Arabi had defeated 'Abd al-Rahman ibn Habib al-Fihri (nicknamed al-Siqlabi), and Hussain ibn Yahya al-Ansari had withstood the siege of Zaragoza, defeated the forces of the emir and captured their general, Ta'iaba ibn 'Obeyd.

The caliph aimed to overthrow the Umayyad emir, restore the Abbsid order in al-Andalus, and subdue the territory to the vassalage of Baghdad. However, the defeat of al-Siqlabi had foreclosed the possibility of starting a new military campaign in the short or even medium term.

Finally, there was no Basque delegation to the diet. Given that the creation of the western division of the Marca Hispanica was only possible by subduing the Basques at both sides of the Pyrenees, we must conclude that the Basques constituted, along with the Emirate of Cordoba, the main enemies of the alliance. In this context, the Dux Vasconum Lupus II played a key strategic role, as the old Roman road Ab Asturica Burdigalam crossed Vasconia from north to south and, logically, the submission of the Peninsular Vasconia would be made more feasible by controlling and even counting on the cooperation of the continental Basques. But none of the chronicles mention Basque delegates from either side of the Pyrenees in Paderborn.

The Saxon poet recorded in the *Annales de Gestis Caroli Magni* that the Muslim leaders surrendered to some extent to the emperor.[30] The Muslim

29   From the moment when the first forces of the Caliphate of Cordoba crossed the Pyrenees through Pertus in 718 until the expulsion of the last Muslim detachments in Narbonne *c.* 757, the Frankish Kingdom was at war with Islam. From that year until 777 the area had twenty years of relative peace.

30   Pertz, Georg Heinrich (ed.), *Annales et chronica aevi Carolini*, Monumenta Germaniae Historica (MGH), SS, I, Hannover, 1826, pp. 234.

historian Abu al-Hassan Ali ibn Muhammad ibn Muhammad, known as Ali 'izz ad-Din ibn al-Athir al-Jazari, who wrote his chronicle four centuries after the events, agreed with the Christian authors that the *walies* in Paderborn paid tribute to Charlemagne in exchange for military assistance to confront the power of the Emir of Cordoba Abd-al-Rahman I, 'the falcon of al-Andalus'.[31] At a distance of 1,000 kilometres (621 miles) and with the insurmountable barrier of the Pyrenees between them, the allegiance to Charlemagne would be more easily negotiable (cheaper), more beneficial, and subtler than a pact with the emir of Cordoba or the caliph of Baghdad. On the other hand, there were precedents. In 759 the governor of Barcelona had offered the submission of his city to Pepin the Short in exchange for protection against the emir of Cordoba and, in 765 the Frankish Kingdom had sent ambassadors to Baghdad.[32] Finally, the subsequent establishment of the *Marca Gothica* or *Gothia* also indicates that the provisions adopted in Paderborn were not far from what was recorded by al-Athir.[33]

While the chronicles do not mention it and, although we assume that the *walies* were independent from each other, it is not possible to define exactly what kind of political relationship and what military or administrative ties existed among them. On the other hand, we must also explain why, once the deal with the Muslim leaders was sealed in Paderborn, Charlemagne planned and organized such an expensive military campaign involving the conscription of two armies ('Hispaniam quam maximo poterat belli apparatu adgreditur')[34] and facing a 3,000-kilometres march (1,864 miles). The author of the *Vita Karoli Magni* points out the obvious: The king arranged such a formidable force because he was going to start a military campaign in Hispania ('Hispaniam quam maximo poterat belli apparatu adgreditur');[35] once war against the emirate south of the Ebro River was unnecessary, the only enemy of the alliance were the Basques.

31 Ibn al-Athir, *Annales du Maghreb & de l'Espagne traduites et annotées par Edmond Fagnan*, Typographie Adolphe Jourdan, Alger, 1898, pp. 128-129.

32 Bury, John B.; Brooke, Zachary N., *The Cambridge Medieval History*, Macmillan, 1913, vol. 2, pp. 604-606.

33 The events that took place subsequently indicate that the conciliation of interests was impossible to get and that the submission of the Balearic Islands (799), or the capitulation and control of Barcelona (801), Tarragona (809) and Tortosa (811) was only possible after military occupation and by maintaining garrisons headed by Frankish counts.

34 Holder-Egger, Oswald (ed.), *Einhardi Vita Karoli Magni,* Monumenta Germaniae Historica (MGH), SSRG, Hannover & Leipzig, 1911, p. 12.

35 Holder-Egger, Oswald (ed.), *Einhardi Vita Karoli Magni,* Monumenta Germaniae Historica (MGH), SSRG, Hannover & Leipzig, 1911, p. 12.

In order to ensure the success of the military operations, the Frankish forces needed to capture and control the main trans-Pyrenean roads—the ancient Roman roads communicating the cities of Girona, Barcelona, Zaragoza, and Pamplona along the Ebro valley—and to keep the forces of the emirate south of the river Ebro. When 'Abd al-Rahman sent his troops to the north against Zaragoza, the forces of Sulayman ibn al-Arabi confronted and stopped them. It follows from here that it was not the task of the emperor's army to confront the troops of the emir. In other words, the control of the old Roman road along the Ebro valley was to be beforehand secured by the *walies*. The imperial troops were disposed to capture and control the south-Pyrenean Vasconia, which explains why the king himself led the army that penetrated through Errozabal. Possibly the force that crossed the Pyrenees through Pertus (in the east) was not as large as the first army, since its main task was limited to accepting the vassalage of Girona, which had been prearranged in Paderborn, recognizing the territory, and preventing the penetration of an enemy army from the southeast boundary of the Frankish Kingdom.

Quite possibly Hussain ibn Yahya al-Ansari offered Charlemagne military assistance to secure the control of the main routes of the expedition south of the Pyrenees, from the south bank of the river Ebro as it passes through Tudela until Zaragoza. The same assistance would be provided by Sulayman ibn al-Arabi in the east; the control of the gate of Pertus and the way to Zaragoza. The control of the trans-Pyrenean routes was also necessary given that these were the only means of retreat. Charlemagne was at great risk when penetrating so far south, about 1,500 kilometres (932 miles) from Herstal, leaving Saxony at the mercy of a possible attack by Widukind.

The capture and subsequent control of Pamplona was granted to Charlemagne. In any event, this is the most controversial point of the plan, and whatever the agreement was on the capture and control of Pamplona, the disagreement between Hussain ibn Yahya al-Ansari and the emperor motivated al-Ansari to refuse to open the doors of Zaragoza, leaving Charlemagne at the mercy of an attack of the forces of the emir and his ally Sulayman ibn al-Arabi in the hands of the Frankish king.

Last but not least, Charlemagne had to take into account the religious aspect of the campaign because a league with a number of Muslim governors, even if it was an alliance against the emirate, required a major diplomatic effort in relation with the Papacy.

The *Marca Hispanica*: A New Political Project

The purpose of the campaign launched by Charlemagne in 778 was not to fire up a crusade against Islam. As far as the sources indicate, there was not on the part of the Muslim emissaries any offer in the sense of embracing the Christian faith. Although the *Annales Regni Francorum* do not explicitly mention the Marca Hispanica until 797 ('Barcinona a civitas in limite Hispanico sita')[36] and do not mention a 'committees marcae Hispanicae' until 822,[37] as noted in the previous chapter, the expedition was the first attempt to create the Marca, that is, an attempt to apply in Iberia the same political system that had provided such good results in Transalpine Lombardy in 774. This plan required the subjugation of the Basques who were not Muslims, and also the sealing of an alliance with the Muslim governors of the Ebro valley.[38] However, the religious aspect provided a suitable and effective casus belli.

The Marca Hispanica was not different from other *marcae* of the regnum Francorum, such as the Marca Britannica,[39] the Marca Baioariorum,[40] the Marca Foroiuliensis,[41] and the Marca contra Saxones or Marca contra esclavos.[42] It was similar to the Roman concept of *limes*.[43] Characteristic of a borderland, a *marca* was a heavily militarized administrative unit headed

36 Kurze, Friedrich (ed.), *Annales regni Francorum (741–829) qui dicuntur Annales Laurissenses maiores et Einhardi*, Monumenta Germaniae Historica (MGH), SSRG, VI, Hannover, 1895, p. 101.

37 Kurze, Friedrich (ed.), *Annales regni Francorum (741–829) qui dicuntur Annales Laurissenses maiores et Einhardi*, Monumenta Germaniae Historica (MGH), SSRG, VI, Hannover, 1895, p. 158.

38 After fifty years of Muslim domination of the southern areas of the Basque Country (714-778) there were islamized Basques in the city of Tudela and surrounding areas.

39 The Annales Regni Francorum mention the Marca Britanniae under Count Wido in Kurze, Friedrich (ed.), *Annales regni Francorum (741–829) qui dicuntur Annales Laurissenses maiores et Einhardi*, Monumenta Germaniae Historica (MGH), SSRG, VI, Hannover, 1895, p. 108.

40 The *Annales Regni Francorum* mention Tassilo as dux of the *marca Baioariorum*. In Kurze, Friedrich (ed.), *Annales regni Francorum (741–829) qui dicuntur Annales Laurissenses maiores et Einhardi*, Monumenta Germaniae Historica (MGH), SSRG, VI, Hannover, 1895, pp. 84 & 89.

41 The *Annales Regni Francorum* mention the '*comitem et marcae Foroiuliensis e praefectum*'. See Kurze, Friedrich (ed.), *Annales regni Francorum (741–829) qui dicuntur Annales Laurissenses maiores et Einhardi*, Monumenta Germaniae Historica (MGH), SSRG, VI, Hannover, 1895, p. 149.

42 Kurze, Friedrich (ed.), *Annales regni Francorum (741–829) qui dicuntur Annales Laurissenses maiores et Einhardi*, Monumenta Germaniae Historica (MGH), SSRG, VI, Hannover, 1895, pp. 36 & 149.

43 In fact, Pierre de Marca named it '*Limes Hispanicus*'. See Marca, Pierre de, *Marca Hispanica sive Limes Hispanicus, hoc est geographica & historica descriptio cataloniae, ruscinonis, &*

by a count or *comites* with broad powers and a strong military contingent and, as a consequence, rigidly hierarchical. The *Comites marcae Hispanicae* would report directly to the *rex Francorum*, who under the right of conquest accumulated the titles of possession of these territories: *rex langobardorum*, *rex Aquitaniae*, *rex Vasconiae*, or in our case, *rex Hispaniae*. The marcae therefore constitute the *limes* or external territories of the Carolingian Empire in opposition to the Frankish territories of the kingdom itself, namely Austrasia, Neustria, and Burgundy.

From this perspective, the campaign of 778 does not differ in relation to the rest of the campaigns promoted by Charlemagne. Building an empire required subduing all those nations that, like the Lombards, Saxons, Bavarians, Avars, Slavs, Bretons, Basques, and Aquitans, were not Frankish and did not want to be part of the empire. That meant living in a constant state of war. And thus it is recorded in the *Annales Regni Francorum* that the regnum Francorum knew only three years of peace in the first thirty-two years of rule of Charlemagne: 777 (preparation of the campaign against the Basques), 781 (coronation of Charlemagne's son in Rome), and 790 (*Hoc anno nullum iter exercitale a rege factum*), most likely a result of the inability to undertake a military campaign due to the episodes of famine and scarcity recorded that year. In general, since 769—when Charlemagne stormed Aquitaine—until the end of his reign in 813 (forty-four years), a total of fifty-two major military campaigns were held.[44] The victims of these military operations were primarily the Saxons (approximately seventeen major campaigns), the Avars (seven wars), the Muslims (seven campaigns), the Lombards (approximately six campaigns), and finally, the Bavarians, the Veneti, the Slavs, and the Bretons (two campaigns each). The *Annales Regni Francorum* recorded two large campaigns against the Basques before the coronation of Charlemagne in Rome in 801; however, with the beginning of the new century, the number of campaigns led by Ludovico against the Basques—in his role of king of Aquitaine—increased dramatically, especially after 803.

---

circumiacentium populorum, ed. by É. Baluze, Paris, 1688. See also, Sholod, Barton, *Charlemagne in Spain: The Cultural Legacy of Roncesvalles*, Librairie Droz, Genève, 1963, pp. 44-46.

44   Lewis, David L., *God's Crucible: Islam and the Making of Europe, 570 to 1215*, W. W. Norton & Company, New York, 2008, p. 312. Some authors consider that his reign started after the death of his brother Carloman in 771 and, therefore, it is common to read that his reign lasted for 42 or 43 years. See also Van Ness Myers, Philip, *A History of Rome*, Ginn & Company, Boston, 1904, p. 257; *Life and times of Charlemagne*, The Religious Track Society, London, 1799, p. 46-48.

Without being exhaustive, these are the most significant military operations referred to in the *Annales Regni Francorum*: 770 (Fronsac, Vasconia),[45]
772 (Irminsul, Saxony),[46] 773 (siege of Pavia, Lombardy), 774 (capture of Pavia,
Lombardy), 775 (Westphalia, Saxony),[47] 775 (Lombardy),[48] 776 (capture of
Eresburg, Saxony),[49] 776 (Lombardy),[50] 778 (burning of Pamplona, Vasconia), 778 (Saxony),[51] 779 (subduing of Eastphalia, Angria, and Westphalia,
Saxony),[52] 780 (collective baptisms, Saxony),[53] 782 (massacre of Verden on

45 Kurze, Friedrich (ed.), *Annales regni Francorum (741–829) qui dicuntur Annales Laurissenses maiores et Einhardi*, Monumenta Germaniae Historica (MGH), SSRG, VI, Hannover, 1895,
pp. 29-30.

46 Charlemagne crossed the rivers Diemel and Eder and near Heresburg, probably in the
Teutoburg forest, and destroyed Irminsul, the sacred *omnisustentante* tree of the Saxons (*'idolum
Saxonum, quod vocahatur Irminsul, destruit'*). The destruction of symbols, palaces, temples,
and shrines is one of the constants of the emperor's campaigns. The *Annales regni Francorum*
recorded the event. See Kurze, Friedrich (ed.), *Annales regni Francorum (741–829) qui dicuntur
Annales Laurissenses maiores et Einhardi*, Monumenta Germaniae Historica (MGH), SSRG, VI,
Hannover, 1895, p. 34.

47 Kurze, Friedrich (ed.), *Annales regni Francorum (741–829) qui dicuntur Annales Laurissenses
maiores et Einhardi*, Monumenta Germaniae Historica (MGH), SSRG, VI, Hannover, 1895, p. 42.

48 Kurze, Friedrich (ed.), *Annales regni Francorum (741–829) qui dicuntur Annales Laurissenses
maiores et Einhardi*, Monumenta Germaniae Historica (MGH), SSRG, VI, Hannover, 1895, p. 42.

49 The *Annales qui dicuntur Annales Laurissenses maiores et Einhardi*, registered the capture of
Eresburg: *Cui vix Alpes transgresso occurrernnt, qui nuntiarent, Eresburgum castrum a Saxonibus
expugnatum ac praesidium Francorum, quod in eo posuerat, expulsum*. Kurze, Friedrich (ed.),
Annales regni Francorum (741–829) qui dicuntur Annales Laurissenses maiores et Einhardi,
Monumenta Germaniae Historica (MGH), SSRG, VI, Hannover, 1895, p. 45.

50 *Tunc domnus Carolus rex Italiam ingressus est partibus Foroiulensium pergens*. Kurze,
Friedrich (ed.), *Annales regni Francorum (741–829) qui dicuntur Annales Laurissenses maiores
et Einhardi*, Monumenta Germaniae Historica (MGH), SSRG, VI, Hannover, 1895, p. 42.

51 Widukind took advantage of Charlemagne's campaign in the south to attack from the north
in Saxony. See Kurze, Friedrich (ed.), *Annales regni Francorum (741–829) qui dicuntur Annales
Laurissenses maiores et Einhardi*, Monumenta Germaniae Historica (MGH), SSRG, VI, Hannover,
1895, p. 52.

52 The campaign was promoted to crush the rebellion led by Widukind; after crossing the rivers
Rhine and Lippe (*'Ad confluentes Lippae et Rheni'*), the king suppressed the rebellion. See Kurze,
Friedrich (ed.), *Annales regni Francorum (741–829) qui dicuntur Annales Laurissenses maiores
et Einhardi*, Monumenta Germaniae Historica (MGH), SSRG, VI, Hannover, 1895, p. 54.

53 Kurze, Friedrich (ed.), *Annales regni Francorum (741–829) qui dicuntur Annales Laurissenses
maiores et Einhardi*, Monumenta Germaniae Historica (MGH), SSRG, VI, Hannover, 1895, p. 56.
But the Frankish kings were not branded tyrants in virtue of the occupation campaigns against
Saxony or other nations in various parts of the empire, but rather because of their attitude towards
certain ecclesiastical dignitaries as Hincmar, Archbishop of Reims (845-882), who because of
the financial disagreements with Carlos Martel referred to him as *'non rex sed tyrannus'*. See
Story, Joanna (ed.), *Charlemagne, Empire and Society*, Manchester University Press, Manchester,
2005, p. 13.

the Aller, Saxony),[54] 783 (campaign against Saxony),[55] 784 (simultaneous campaigns—*auxiliante Domino domnus Carolus, filius magni regis Caroli, victor extitit una cum Francis, multis Saxonibus s*—, Saxony),[56] 785 (baptism of Widukind, Saxony),[57] 785 (capture of Girona and Urgel—*Orgellis*, Marca Gothica), 786 (campaign against Britania),[58] 787 (campaign against Arechis (*Areghisus*), Benevento),[59] 788 (campaigns in Lombardía and Avaria),[60] 789 (campaign against the Slaves),[61] 791 (campaigns in Panonia and Avaria),[62] 792 (conspiracy of Pepin, son of Charlemagne, Lombardy),[63] 793 (uprising in Westphalia, Eastphalia and Nordalbingia, Saxony),[64] 794 (Campaign and

---

54   The approval of the *Capitulatio de partibus saxoniae* in 782 resulted in a new insurrection in Saxony. One of the most dramatic consequences of the war was the execution of about 4,500 prisoners of war at the hands of the imperial army after the battle of Suntel. While it is difficult to estimate the level of repression of the imperial army and the subsequent military campaigns led by Charlemagne in the area, some authors estimate that nearly a quarter of the population of Saxony was affected by these dissuasive measures. Cawthorne, Nigel, *Military Commanders: The 100 Greatest Throughout History*, Enchanted Lion Books, New York, 2004, p. 55. The *Annales qui dicuntur Annales Laurissenses maiores et Einhardi*, records 4,500 deaths: '*Tunc orones Saxones iterum convenientes subdiderunt se sub potestate supradicti domni regis et reddiderunt omnes malefactores illos, qui ipsum rebellium maxime terminaverunt, ad occidendum IIII D.*' In Kurze, Friedrich (ed.), *Annales regni Francorum (741–829) qui dicuntur Annales Laurissenses maiores et Einhardi*, Monumenta Germaniae Historica (MGH), SSRG, VI, Hannover, 1895, p. 62.

55   Kurze, Friedrich (ed.), *Annales regni Francorum (741–829) qui dicuntur Annales Laurissenses maiores et Einhardi*, Monumenta Germaniae Historica (MGH), SSRG, VI, Hannover, 1895, p. 64.

56   Kurze, Friedrich (ed.), *Annales regni Francorum (741–829) qui dicuntur Annales Laurissenses maiores et Einhardi*, Monumenta Germaniae Historica (MGH), SSRG, VI, Hannover, 1895, p. 66.

57   The symbol of the submission of the Saxons, Widukind was baptized in Attigny: '*Et ibi [Attiniacum] baptizati sunt supranominati Widochindus et Abbi una cum sociis eorum; et tunc tota Saxonia subiugata est.*' In Kurze, Friedrich (ed.), *Annales regni Francorum (741–829) qui dicuntur Annales Laurissenses maiores et Einhardi*, Monumenta Germaniae Historica (MGH), SSRG, VI, Hannover, 1895, p. 70.

58   Kurze, Friedrich (ed.), *Annales regni Francorum (741–829) qui dicuntur Annales Laurissenses maiores et Einhardi*, Monumenta Germaniae Historica (MGH), SSRG, VI, Hannover, 1895, p. 72.

59   Kurze, Friedrich (ed.), *Annales regni Francorum (741–829) qui dicuntur Annales Laurissenses maiores et Einhardi*, Monumenta Germaniae Historica (MGH), SSRG, VI, Hannover, 1895, p. 74.

60   Kurze, Friedrich (ed.), *Annales regni Francorum (741–829) qui dicuntur Annales Laurissenses maiores et Einhardi*, Monumenta Germaniae Historica (MGH), SSRG, VI, Hannover, 1895, p. 82.

61   Kurze, Friedrich (ed.), *Annales regni Francorum (741–829) qui dicuntur Annales Laurissenses maiores et Einhardi*, Monumenta Germaniae Historica (MGH), SSRG, VI, Hannover, 1895, p. 85.

62   Kurze, Friedrich (ed.), *Annales regni Francorum (741–829) qui dicuntur Annales Laurissenses maiores et Einhardi*, Monumenta Germaniae Historica (MGH), SSRG, VI, Hannover, 1895, p. 88.

63   The *Annales qui dicuntur Annales Laurissenses maiores et Einhardi* records the insurrection. See Kurze, Friedrich (ed.), *Annales regni Francorum (741–829) qui dicuntur Annales Laurissenses maiores et Einhardi*, Monumenta Germaniae Historica (MGH), SSRG, VI, Hannover, 1895, p. 91.

64   Kurze, Friedrich (ed.), *Annales regni Francorum (741–829) qui dicuntur Annales Laurissenses maiores et Einhardi*, Monumenta Germaniae Historica (MGH), SSRG, VI, Hannover, 1895, p. 93.

deportations, Saxony),[65] 795 (campaign in Saxony),[66] 796 (campaign against Eric de Friuli and insurrection in Avaria),[67] 796 (uprising in Angria—*et ipse quidem Saxonia ex magna parte vastata ad hiemandum Aquasgrani revertilur*—Saxony),[68] 797 (new deportations, Saxony),[69] 797 (capture of Barcelona, Catalunya, or Marca Gothica),[70] 798 (deportations, Saxony),[71] 799 (pirates in the Balearic Islands),[72] 800 (Pope Leo's restitution and imperial coronation, Rome),[73] 800 (siege of Barcelona, Marca Gothica), 801 (siege of Barcelona, Marca Gothica),[74] 804 (insurrection in Nordalbingia, Saxony),[75] 805 (campaign against the Slaves),[76] 808 (uprising in Denmark),[77]

65   To achieve the subjugation of Saxony Charlemagne ordered the deportation of 7,000 people. The *Annales qui dicuntur Annales Laurissenses maiores et Einhardi* records the insurrection and the campaign. See Kurze, Friedrich (ed.), *Annales regni Francorum (741–829) qui dicuntur Annales Laurissenses maiores et Einhardi*, Monumenta Germaniae Historica (MGH), SSRG, VI, Hannover, 1895, p. 95.

66   Kurze, Friedrich (ed.), *Annales regni Francorum (741–829) qui dicuntur Annales Laurissenses maiores et Einhardi*, Monumenta Germaniae Historica (MGH), SSRG, VI, Hannover, 1895, p. 96.

67   Kurze, Friedrich (ed.), *Annales regni Francorum (741–829) qui dicuntur Annales Laurissenses maiores et Einhardi*, Monumenta Germaniae Historica (MGH), SSRG, VI, Hannover, 1895, p. 98.

68   Kurze, Friedrich (ed.), *Annales regni Francorum (741–829) qui dicuntur Annales Laurissenses maiores et Einhardi*, Monumenta Germaniae Historica (MGH), SSRG, VI, Hannover, 1895, p. 98.

69   The emperor ordered the deportation of one in three households or families. See Kurze, Friedrich (ed.), *Annales regni Francorum (741–829) qui dicuntur Annales Laurissenses maiores et Einhardi*, Monumenta Germaniae Historica (MGH), SSRG, VI, Hannover, 1895, p. 100.

70   Kurze, Friedrich (ed.), *Annales regni Francorum (741–829) qui dicuntur Annales Laurissenses maiores et Einhardi*, Monumenta Germaniae Historica (MGH), SSRG, VI, Hannover, 1895, p. 100.

71   In this case the emperor ordered the deportation of about 1,600 leaders: 'Los *Annales Regni Francorum* registran la campaña: *Rex collecto exercitu de Haristalli ad locum, qui Mimda dicitur, perrexit; et facto consilio in desertores arma corripuit et totam inter Albim et Wisuram Saxoniam populando peragravit*.' In Kurze, Friedrich (ed.), *Annales regni Francorum (741–829) qui dicuntur Annales Laurissenses maiores et Einhardi*, Monumenta Germaniae Historica (MGH), SSRG, VI, Hannover, 1895, p. 102.

72   Kurze, Friedrich (ed.), *Annales regni Francorum (741–829) qui dicuntur Annales Laurissenses maiores et Einhardi*, Monumenta Germaniae Historica (MGH), SSRG, VI, Hannover, 1895, pp. 105 & 108.

73   Kurze, Friedrich (ed.), *Annales regni Francorum (741–829) qui dicuntur Annales Laurissenses maiores et Einhardi*, Monumenta Germaniae Historica (MGH), SSRG, VI, Hannover, 1895, p. 112.

74   Kurze, Friedrich (ed.), *Annales regni Francorum (741–829) qui dicuntur Annales Laurissenses maiores et Einhardi*, Monumenta Germaniae Historica (MGH), SSRG, VI, Hannover, 1895, p. 112.

75   Kurze, Friedrich (ed.), *Annales regni Francorum (741–829) qui dicuntur Annales Laurissenses maiores et Einhardi*, Monumenta Germaniae Historica (MGH), SSRG, VI, Hannover, 1895, p. 118.

76   Kurze, Friedrich (ed.), *Annales regni Francorum (741–829) qui dicuntur Annales Laurissenses maiores et Einhardi*, Monumenta Germaniae Historica (MGH), SSRG, VI, Hannover, 1895, p. 120.

77   Kurze, Friedrich (ed.), *Annales regni Francorum (741–829) qui dicuntur Annales Laurissenses maiores et Einhardi*, Monumenta Germaniae Historica (MGH), SSRG, VI, Hannover, 1895, p. 125.

809 (campaign against the Frisians, Frisia),[78] 809—811 (capture of cities in the Marca Gothica),[79] 810 (campaign in the Veneto),[80] 810—811 (three military campaigns in Albia, Panonia, and Britania),[81] 812 (expedition against Wilzos),[82] and 813 (campaigns in Denmark, Septimania, and Mallorca).[83]

Pepin the Short (751-768) had acted similarly, although his campaigns focused mainly on Saxony, Aquitaine, and Lombardy. Years without military campaigns were rare during the reign of Pepin, and in most of these cases the reason is the preparations for engaging in a longer war. This explains, for example, the absence of military campaigns in 758 and 759, which were followed by the destructive campaign waged against Aquitaine between 760 and 768.[84]

The Carolingian Empire's administrative and political system revolved around a heavily militarized and essentially on a war footing structure. The campaigns were overwhelmingly, if not entirely, campaigns for expansion of territory. Neither the strategy nor the policy, the means, or the level of repression that followed leads to the assumption that these military campaigns were defensive or preventive wars. To find an enemy became a political necessity.[85]

Occupation campaigns were usually accompanied by looting, burning of fields for agriculture, destruction of towns, mass evacuations, and sometimes the slaughter of prisoners of war or non-combatants. The adoption in 789 of the *Admonitio generalis* reflects the repressive character and, thus, punitive nature of the royal policy. The same is true as for the Capitularies,

---

78   Kurze, Friedrich (ed.), *Annales regni Francorum (741–829) qui dicuntur Annales Laurissenses maiores et Einhardi*, Monumenta Germaniae Historica (MGH), SSRG, VI, Hannover, 1895, p. 129.
79   The *Annales Regni Francorum* mention *Osca* (Huesca), *Caesaraugusta* (Zaragoza) and *Dertosam* (Tortosa) in Kurze, Friedrich (ed.), *Annales regni Francorum (741–829) qui dicuntur Annales Laurissenses maiores et Einhardi*, Monumenta Germaniae Historica (MGH), SSRG, VI, Hannover, 1895, p. 125.
80   Kurze, Friedrich (ed.), *Annales regni Francorum (741–829) qui dicuntur Annales Laurissenses maiores et Einhardi*, Monumenta Germaniae Historica (MGH), SSRG, VI, Hannover, 1895, p. 130.
81   Kurze, Friedrich (ed.), *Annales regni Francorum (741–829) qui dicuntur Annales Laurissenses maiores et Einhardi*, Monumenta Germaniae Historica (MGH), SSRG, VI, Hannover, 1895, p. 135.
82   *Expeditio facta ad Wilzos, et ab eis obsides accepti.* Kurze, Friedrich (ed.), *Annales regni Francorum (741–829) qui dicuntur Annales Laurissenses maiores et Einhardi*, Monumenta Germaniae Historica (MGH), SSRG, VI, Hannover, 1895, p. 137.
83   These campaigns were not started by the *regnum Francorum*. See Kurze, Friedrich (ed.), *Annales regni Francorum (741–829) qui dicuntur Annales Laurissenses maiores et Einhardi*, Monumenta Germaniae Historica (MGH), SSRG, VI, Hannover, 1895, p. 139.
84   Bachrach, Bernard S., *Early Carolingian Warfare: Prelude to Empire*, University of Pennsylvania Press, Philadelphia, 2001, p. 26.
85   Wilson, Derek A., *Charlemagne*, Random House, Inc., New York, 2006, p. 46.

especially those approved for the control of certain areas of the empire like the *Capitulatio de partibus saxoniae* of 782, the *Capitulare Saxonicum* of 797 or the *Lex Saxonum* of 803. The *Capitulatio de partibus Saxoniae*, published immediately after the conquest of Saxony and worded in order to subjugate the population, pays particular attention to the religious aspects (mass conversion processes). In essence, the Capitularies were conceived to impose religious uniformity on the imperial domains and thus assimilate the people beaten at the battlefield through a process of acculturation.[86]

The 797 *Capitulare Saxonicum* are less brutal, eliminating the death penalty for various transgressions that applied under the *Capitulatio* of 782. Other clauses regulated the taxation (*litus*) for the maintenance of the clergy; fines for those who avoided baptism, for the transgression of the laws of marriage, and for the practice of pagan rites. Another clause prohibits the Saxons from holding public assemblies not authorized by a *missus dominicus*.[87]

While it is true that the campaigns of conquest and expansion (*occupatio*) led by the emperor were caused essentially by economic and military factors, the official propaganda endeavored to give these wars a religious and civilizing purpose. Also, the Carolingian cultural 'renaissance' was founded upon the association of the concepts *civilization* and *Christianity*. From their civilizing character the Frankish kings obtained the title of *Triunphator* and from their religious character that of *Christiannisumus*. Obviously, in light of the Frankish chronicles, the subjugated peoples were

86   The *Capitulatio de partibus Saxoniae* was characterized by its extreme severity with regard to criminal law. Death was the penalty for most religious crimes (*morte moriatur*). If someone killed a bishop or a priest or a deacon, he also must pay with his life. If anyone broke into a church, stole something with violence or by stealth from it or set a church on fire, they should be put to death. If someone in contempt of the Christian faith rejected the holy Lenten and ate meat, they should die (but it was in hands of the priest to find out if this person was forced by necessity to eat meat). Anyone who was considered to be deceived by the devil (*diabolo deceptus crediderit*) and thus followed pagan rites or ate human flesh should pay with his life. If a Saxon rejected baptism they should die; if a person persisted in maintaining hostility toward the Christians, they should die and, in general, anyone who was considered to be unfaithful to the king, would suffer the death penalty. However, the *Capitulatio* added that anyone who had committed these capital crimes who confessed his or her crimes to a priest and was willing to undergo penance, this person should be excused from the death penalty under the protection of the priest. Complete Latin edition in Ferdinand, Walter (ed.), *Corpus iuris germanici antiqui*, Impensis G. Reimeri, Berlin, 1824, vol. 2, pars 1, pp. 104-109. A complete translation into English of the *Capitulatio de partibus Saxoniae* is in Loyn, Henry Royston; Percival, John, *The Reign of Charlemagne: Documents on Carolingian Government and Administration*, St. Martin's Press, New York, 1976, pp. 51-52.

87   Stubbs, William, *The Constitutional History of England, in its Origin and Development*, Clarendon Press, Oxford, 1891, p. 49.

distinguished by their *barbarism* and *paganism*, which, in virtue of the duality of Christianity/civilization, came to be equivalent terms. In this sense, we read in the *Vita Karoli Magni* that 'none of the wars initiated by the Franks was held so persistently and with such hardness or cost as the one led against the Saxons who, like most of the Germanic peoples, were a fierce people, devil worshipers, hostile to our religion and people who did not consider a dishonour the transgression of human or divine laws'.[88]

Occupatio was the means of acquiring property or lands that did not belong to anyone, or *res nullius*. The only way to get a property right on vacant lands was to take possession of them.[89] In light of the right of conquest of the eighth century, it did not matter too much if the territory acquired was empty or belonged to a barbarous (uncivilized) or pagan (non-Christian) people, since in either case it would be considered *terra nullius*. Thus, due to the fact that the civilizing or Christianizing character of a military campaign was the key factor to obtaining the right of conquest over the captured domain, the Church took a decisive role in determining what was and what was not legitimately acquired by *occupatio*; in other words, the Papacy determined to some extent the legitimacy of the military campaigns held by the emperor and, in this sense, the collaboration of the successive Carolingian kings with the Papacy became crucial, such as in the case of the mutual assistance of Pepin the Short and Pope Adrian I and the later understanding of Charlemagne and Pope Leo III.

Religious imagery was the genesis of what would later culminate with the conception of the Holy Roman Empire and of Charlemagne as most Christian (*Christianissimus rex*) Emperor (*Romanorum Imperator*).[90] After the coronation of the emperor in 800, under the formula 'Carolo augusto, a Deo coronato magno et pacifico imperatori Romanorum, vita et victoria', the capitulary of 802 ('Capitulare Primum anni DCCCII sive capitula data Missis Dominicis; anno secundo Imperii')[91] referred to the new emperor as 'Serenissimus et Christianissimus domnus imperator Karolus'.[92] In this

---

88   Holder-Egger, Oswald (ed.), *Einhardi Vita Karoli Magni,* Monumenta Germaniae Historica (MGH), SSRG, Hannover & Leipzig, 1911, p. 9.

89   Lee, Guy C., *Historical Jurisprudence: An Introduction to The Systematic Study of The Development of Law,* Macmillan, London, 1911, p. 237.

90   His son Ludovico Pio (Louis the Pious) would also hold the title of *Ludovicus Magnus Rex Christianissimus.*

91   Complete Latin edition in Ferdinand, Walter (ed.), *Corpus iuris germanici antiqui,* Impensis G. Reimeri, Berlín, 1824. Volume 2, pars 1, pp. 157-161.

92   Reich, Emil, *Select Documents Illustrating Medieval and Modern History,* P.S. King & Son, London, 1905, pp. 297.

sense, the conquest of Lombardy in 773/74 led to a political and diplomatic transformation of the relations with the Papacy. Four years later, the religious aspect of the campaign in 778 was to turn the *Marca Hispanica* into a unique political project, with a religious element lacking in previous military campaigns undertaken by Charlemagne, since it meant confronting Islam.

Classical historiography on Charlemagne in general or in particular on the events that took place in 778 typically refer to the Basques as being converted to Christianity; however, the reality in the Basque eighth century was much more complex.[93] While the continental Basques (inhabitants of the ancient Roman Aquitaine)[94] were intensely Christianized and, as a consequence, also the *vasconum princeps* were all Christians, the reality was quite different among the peninsular Basques. North of the Christianized areas of Pamplona, Deierri, and Araba, the original religion of the Basques was still predominant in the late eighth century. This religion was most likely shared with the Basques north of the Pyrenees living in the area that extended until Sobrarbe and Ribagorza to the east. On the other side, the southern area of the peninsular Vasconia, covering a large area along the river Ebro between Pancorbo and Gallur was deeply Islamized. Therefore, three religions coexisted in Vasconia in 778 although the native pagan religion was the most widespread. After the creation of the Kingdom of Pamplona in 824, Christianity was rapidly spread over the northern valleys, and thus we can infer that only by the eleventh century the Christian religion was the followed by most of the Basques on both sides of the Pyrenees.

In any case, the creation of the *Marca Hispanica* had the necessary elements to be presented in the form of a political project marked by a strong religious character. Charlemagne took the necessary diplomatic measures in order to justify the conquest and thus convert the annexation campaign into a crusade or even into a preventive campaign against the Muslim pirates and the expansion of the Emirate of Cordoba, which had waged a war in Septimania in 718 when troops, led by Al-Hurr ibn Abd al-Rahman al-Thaqafi, penetrated into the area for the first time (in the time of Charlemagne's grandfather Charles Martel). War in Septimania would not end until the conquest of Narbonne by Pepin the Short (Charlemagne's father) in 757.

93 Bard, Rachel, *Navarra: The Durable Kingdom*, University of Nevada Press, Reno, 1982, p. 13.
94 According to Julius Caesar (*The Gallic War*) Gaul was divided in to three areas populated by peoples speaking different languages, holding diverse institutions and living under various laws. Aquitaine, or Vasconia, stretching between the rivers Garonne and the Pyrenees, was one of these three territories. See Allen, J. H.; Allen, W. F.; Hudson, Henry P. (eds.), *Caesar's The Gallic War*, Ginn & co., Boston, 1891, p. 2.

Charlemagne had agreed to travel to Rome on Easter Day (April 14)[95] 778 to have his son Carloman baptized by Pope Adrian I (772-795).[96] However, after the celebration of the Paderborn diet in 777 the emperor decided to undertake the military campaign and, as the *Codex Carolinus* records, Charlemagne received the blessing of Pope Adrian I in May 778, when the expedition was already underway.[97] The blessing, like the later crowning, granted the emperor the legitimacy to proclaim the divine origin of his temporal power over the *Marca Hispanica* and other parts of his kingdom under the formula 'Karolus divina ordinante providentia rex'.[98] Under the doctrine of *terra nullius* that would later lead to the political concept of the crusades, the papal blessing subsequently gave rise to the falsification of a document, the *Donatio Constantini*, by which the Pope reserved his temporal authority over the territories not yet Christianized. Under this authority, the Pope would delegate to Christian kings the right to occupy and control the lands conquered or occupied by force. In practice, Charlemagne held the military and political power, but the papal authorization endowed divine authority onn his royal power, all of which is condensed in the following formula: 'Karolus, gratia Dei regnique francorum rector, et devotus sanctae ecclesiae defensor atque adjustor in ómnibus apostolicae sedis.'[99]

Subsequent to these events and with the purpose of conferring a religious character on the campaign, the legend of Charlemagne's crusade was exploited. According to the legend, the apostle James appeared in a dream to Charlemagne and told him that, following the Milky Way, he should occupy Galicia (the northern peninsular coast or the Way of Saint James) to liberate his tomb from Muslim rule. This legend was represented in the

---

95   King identifies 19 April 778 as Easter day. See King, P. D., *Charlemagne: Translated Sources*, P. D. King, Lambrigg, Kendal, Cumbria, 1987, p. 344.

96   Charlemagne's son would be finally baptized by Pope Adrian I in 781 under the name of Pepin.

97   Pope Adrian's letters to Charlemagne of May 778 are contained in the *Codex Carolinus*, a collection of about 100 letters between various Frankish kings and different popes between 739 and 791, which was compiled in 791. Unfortunately, the compilation only collects the letters written by the Papacy. For the original Latin edition of the *Codex Carolinus* see Dümmler, Ernestus et alia (eds.), *Epistolae Merowingici et Karolini Aevi*, Monumenta Germaniae Historica (MGH), EPP. III, Berlin, 1892, pp. 469-657. The May 778 letters (numbered 60 and 61) are on pp. 585-589. See also, Haller, Johannes, *Die Quellen Zur Geschichte der Entstehung des Kirchenstaates*, Druck und Verlag von B. G. Teubner, Leipzig & Berlin, 1907, pp. 77-238. The May 778 letters (numbered 60 and 61) are on pp. 192-197.

98   Böhmer, Johann F.; Mühlbacher, Engelbert, *Die Regesten des Kaiserreichs unter den Karolingern, 751-918*, Innsbruck Wagner'schen Universitätsbuchhandlung, Innsbruck, 1908, Volume 1, Part 3, p. 85.

99   Dabbs, Jack A., *Dei Gratia in Royal Titles*, Mouton, The Hague, 1971, p. 8.

ninth scene of the stained-glass window of the Chartres cathedral relating the 778 expedition of Charlemagne in twenty-two scenes, as narrated in the *Codex Calixtinus* written by Pseudo Turpin. Not only the legendary tales but also the Frankish historiography would underline the religious character of the campaign of 778. In this sense the *Annales Mettenses* recorded that 'in the year of the Incarnation of our Lord 778, King Charles, moved by the entreaties and lamentations of the Christians who were in Hispania under the servitude of the cruel Saracens, came with his army to Hispania'.[100]

The diffusion of the campaign's religious character also gave rise to the legend of the *Oriflamme* or banner of St. Denis (*signum Karoli Magni*), which was allegedly given by Pope Adrian I to Charlemagne as a symbol of the crusade against the infidel.[101]

---

100 Simson, Bernhard von (ed.), *Annales Mettenses Priores*, Monumenta Germaniae Historica (MGH), SSRG, X, Hannover & Leipzig, 1905, p. 66. For an English version, see King, P. D., *Charlemagne: Translated Sources*, P. D. King, Lambrigg, Kendal, Cumbria, 1987, p. 152.
101 Spiegel, Gabrielle M., *The Past as Text: The Theory and Practice of Medieval Historiography*, The Johns Hopkins University Press, Baltimore (MD), 1999, pp. 154-162.

2. The Campaign of 778

Abstract

This chapter discusses in detail the development of the military expedition of 778 against the Basques with emphasis on the events that took place in Pamplona and Zaragoza between spring and summer of that year. The author provides a detailed description of the itinerary of the two Frankish armies that entered the Iberian Peninsula and the chronology of the march from April to August 778. This chapter is divided into four sections. The march on Vasconia by the Carolingian army at the beginning of the campaign in the spring of 778, the siege and capture of the city of Pamplona in June 778, the infructuous siege of Zaragoza in July and the final retreat and destruction of Pamplona by King Charles in August 778.

Keywords: Charlemagne, 778, Pamplona, Zaragoza, Islam

Vasconia was a vast territory enclosed between the courses of the rivers Garonne in the north and Ebro in the south. The research of the toponymy carried out to the present day confirms that within the limits of the most inaccessible areas of the Pyrenees, Vasconia extended to the river Noguera in Ribagorza and the episode of Uthman ibn Naissa (*Munuza*) in 732 shows that the area of influence of the Basques went as deep as to Cerdanya.[1] Unfortunately, the historical sources did not identify the leaders who defeated the Frankish army, but the first king of Pamplona, Eneko Aritza (*c.* 770-852), was count of Bigorre and Sobrarbe, which confirms the presence of Basque warlords in Ribagorza before the beginning of the ninth century.

However, this immense territory bound by cultural and linguistic ties was not unified under a single central power directly linked to one *princeps*

---

1   Flórez, Enrique, *España sagrada*, vol. 8, Real Academia de la Historia, Madrid, 1869, pp. 310-311. See also, Ximenez de Rada, Rodrigo, *Historia Arabum*, cap. XIII in Buckler, Francis W., *Harunu'l-Rashid and Charles the Great*, The Mediaeval Academy of America, Cambridge (Mass.), 1931, p. 6.

Irujo, X., *Charlemagne's Defeat in the Pyrenees: The Battle of Rencesvals*. Taylor & Francis, 2021
DOI 10.5117/9789463721059_CH02

vasconum but was rather composed of various territories ruled by warlords united by shared interests and common enemies (*foederati*), which explains the crystallization of various political units after the coronation of the first king of Pamplona in 824. Basque cities also had their own administration linked by federative ties to the rest of Vasconia.

As consigned by the Frankish chronicles, Lupus II was the *princeps vasconum* for a peaceful period of between ten and thirty years, from *c.* 767 or 769 to *c.* 778, or even 801.[2] There is no mention in the chronicles of any *princeps vasconum* until 801, when the chronicles make reference to the son of Lupus II, Sancho I Lupus, as taking part in the siege of Barcelona.[3] In the peninsular Vasconia, which had started to be known as Navarre by various historical sources,[4] several Basque warlords or *buruzagis* were mentioned, probably the ones who led the troops that ambushed

---

2   The *Annales Regni Francorum*, the *Annales Laurisensses* and the *Annales Mettenses Priores* all mention '*Lupus Wasconum Princeps*' and the *Einhardi Vita Karoli Magni* mentions '*Lupus dux Wasconum*' in 769. See Simson, Bernhard von (ed.), *Annales Mettenses Priores*, Monumenta Germaniae Historica (MGH), SSRG, X, Hannover & Leipzig, 1905, p. 56. And, Holder-Egger, Oswald (ed.), *Einhardi Vita Karoli Magni*, Monumenta Germaniae Historica (MGH), SSRG, Hannover & Leipzig, 1911, p. 7. Charles Higounet points that Hunald II, who had taken up arms against Charlemagne to restore the independence of the Duchy of Aquitaine after Pepin the Short's death in 768, was the leader of the Basques during the Battle of Errozabal. See Higounet, Charles, *Bordeaux pendant le haut moyen age*, Fédération historique du Sud-Ouest, Bordeaux, 1963, p. 27.

3   *Capta est Barcinonam civitas*. Kurze, Friedrich (ed.), *Annales regni Francorum (741–829) qui dicuntur Annales Laurissenses maiores et Einhardi*, Monumenta Germaniae Historica (MGH), SSRG, VI, Hannover, 1895, p. 116. However, the *Annales Regni* do not mention Lupus who appears in the *Chronicle of Ernoldo Nicello* (*Ermoldus Nigellus*):

> *Haec rex: atque Lupus fatur sic Santio contra,*
> *Santio, qui propriae gentis agebat opus,*
> *Wasconum princeps, Caroli nutrimine fretus,*
> *Ingenio atque fide qui superabat avos:*
> *'Rex, censura tibi, nobis parece necesse est,*
> *Haustus consilii cujus ab ore fluit.*
> *Si tamen a nostris agitur modo partibus haec res,*
> *Parte mea, testor pax erit atque quies'.*

In Migne, Jacques-Paul (ed.), *Patrologiae cursus completus*, Garnier, Paris, 1864, vol. 105, p. 579. See also, Alzog, Johannes B., *Historia eclesiástica o adiciones a la Historia general de la Iglesia*, Librería Religiosa, Barcelona, 1855, vol. 2, pp. 514-517.

4   The Frankish chroniclers gave the generic name of Navarrese to all Basques south of the Pyrenees (*Annalis dicuntur Egginhard* or *Einhardi Annales, Annales Regni Francorum, Poetae Saxonis Annalium de Gestis Caroli Magni Imperatoris Libri Quinque, Annales Mettenses Priores*) and two centuries later the *Codex Calixtinus* also mentions the Navarrese.

Charlemagne in Errozabal. The Arab chroniclers mention that during the campaign of retribution against the Basques and insurgent Muslims that took place in 781, just three years after the Battle of Errozabal, the Basques had a leader named Eneko (*Enneco*), probably brother-in-law of Ximen the Strong. Ibn Hayyan and Ibn Hazm say that Eneko died in 820.[5] Eneko must have governed in Pamplona and its surrounding region, and certainly had to hold a relevant political and social role among the peninsular Basques since he fathered Eneko or *Enneco Ennecones*, who was called *Wannaqo ibn Wannaqo* by Arab chroniclers[6] and nicknamed Aritza (*oak* or *the strong* in Basque), the first king of Pamplona, who was crowned in 824 and reigned until 852.[7] The Muslim sources also refer to Ximen the Strong, of the Ximena family (Ibn Hayyan called him Shemen al Agra)[8] as ruling over an area that roughly corresponds with the current Deierri, around Lizarra.[9] The Muslim

---

5   Estornés Lasa, Bernardo, *Historia General de Euskal Herria. 476-824 época vascona*, in *Enciclopedia General Ilustrada del País Vasco*, vol. 2, Auñamendi, Donostia, 1981, pp. 274-276.

6   Enneco Ennecones is the transliteration into Latin of the Basque name Eneko Enekoitz meaning 'Eneko son of Eneko'. Eneko was also identified in the chronicles as *Enneco Ennequez*. There are also other variants such as *Uneko, Wanko, Wennkoh, Induon*, and *Endeka*. See Estornés Lasa, Bernardo, *Historia General de Euskal Herria. 476-824 época vascona*, in *Enciclopedia General Ilustrada del País Vasco*, vol. 2, Auñamendi, Donostia, 1981, pp. 274-276.

7   Ibn Hayyan gave him the nickname of 'the Basque' and Ibn Hazm named him 'Aritza'. Évariste Lévi Provençal argued that Eneko was the father of King Enneco Ennequez or Eneko Enekoitz in the original Basque language (Iñigo Íñiguez or Íñigo Arista in Spanish), whose father, in any case, certainly was called Eneko. See Estornés Lasa, Bernardo; Lévi-Provençal, Évariste, *Eneko "Arista", fundador del reino de Pamplona y su época: un siglo de historia vasca, 752-852*, Ekin, Buenos Aires, 1959, pp. 9-11. See also, Estornés Lasa, Bernardo, *Historia General de Euskal Herria. 476-824 época vascona*, in *Enciclopedia General Ilustrada del País Vasco*, vol. 2, Auñamendi, Donostia, 1981, pp. 284-286; Ibn al-Athir, *Annales du Maghreb & de l'Espagne traduites et annotées par Edmond Fagnan*, Typographie Adolphe Jourdan, Alger, 1898, pp. 129-130. 'Abd al-Rahman III, Emir of Cordoba was a sixth-generation descendant of Eneko Aritza.

8   Estornés Lasa, Bernardo; Lévi-Provençal, Évariste, *Eneko "Arista", fundador del reino de Pamplona y su época: un siglo de historia vasca, 752-852*, Ekin, Buenos Aires, 1959, pp. 11-12 & 20.

9   Following sanction of the code of laws of Estella in c. 1076 Lizarra was called Stella (Estella), the city of the star. According to the *Codex Calixtinus*, Estella is a city where the bread is good, the wine excellent is plenty of meat and fish, and is rich in all kinds of delicacies. The original Latin version is in Fita y Colomer, Fidel; Vinson, Julien, *Le codex de saint-Jacques-de-Compostelle*, Maisonneuve et Cie, Paris, 1882, p. 5. For another English version see Melczer, William, *The Pilgrim's Guide to Santiago de Compostela*, Italica Press Inc., New York, 1993, p. 86. Also, around the same time Peter the Venerable: 'There is in Hispania a noble and famous city that in virtue of its location and the fertility of the lands that surround it as well as for the large number of people that inhabit it, is far superior to other cities around (*quibus rebús próxima castella exsuperat*).' Bouthillier, Denise (ed.), *Petri Cluniacensis Abbatis De miraculis libri duo*, Brepols, Turnhout, 1988, p. 86.

chroniclers also recorded Ibn Belaskot, the 'son of Belasko', who controlled in 781 an area extending between the regions between Pamplona and Lizarra.[10]

Finally, the chronicles also record the lineage of the Banu Qasi, whose patriarch Fortun ibn Qasi, father Musa ibn Fortun ibn Qasi, married the widow of Eneko Aritza and controlled the area around the city of Tudela, which was occupied sporadically by the Frankish army in the campaign of 778.[11]

Family ties binding the aforementioned leaders suggest that these Basque principals acted together, confronting a common enemy. On the other hand, the incorporation of Deierri and the region of Lizarra to the Kingdom of Pamplona after the coronation of Eneko Aritza in 824 also leads to the conclusion that beyond family ties, these lands were also associated by political ties. Moreover, the chronicles do not record any rising or commotion before or after the establishment of the Kingdom of Pamplona and, as stated above, all these territories and their leaders were incorporated by *promissio fidei* to the crown of Pamplona under the figure of a single *Rex Pampilonensis*.

As we have already noted, outside the borders of Vasconia, Asturias was ruled by Silo (774-783). Pope Adrian I (from 772 until his death in 795) headed the Papacy. 'Abd al-Rahman I was the emir of Cordoba and Muhammad ibn Mansur al-Mahdi (775-785) was the caliph of Baghdad.

March on Vasconia

In the spring of 778 (late March or early April), after placing garrisons at selected points along the border with Saxony, Charlemagne launched the military expedition to take possession of the Muslim cities and occupy the region of Pamplona, and as recorded in the *Vita Karoli Magni*, crossed the Pyrenees 'with the greatest war machine he had'.[12] Also, the *Annales Mettenses Priores* underlined the scale of the emperor's armies recording

10   Lafuente Alcántara, Emilio (ed.), *Ajbar Machmua (Colección de tradiciones), Crónica anónima del siglo XI*, Real Academia de la Historia, Madrid, 1867, p. 105. See also Codera, Francisco, *Discursos leídos ante la Real Academia de la Historia en la recepción*, Impresor de los Señores Rojas, 1879, pp. 72-73.

11   Bard, Rachel, *Navarra: The Durable Kingdom*, University of Nevada Press, Reno, 1982, pp. 20-22. See also, Settipani, Christian, *Noblesse du Midi Carolingien: Études Sur Quelques Grandes Familles d'Aquitaine et de Languedoc du IXe au XIe Siècles*, Prosopographica et Genealogica, Oxford, 2004, p. 102.

12   Holder-Egger, Oswald (ed.), *Einhardi Vita Karoli Magni,* Monumenta Germaniae Historica (MGH), SSRG, Hannover & Leipzig, 1911, p. 12.

that 'all Hispania shuddered at the countless legions'.[13] The *Chronicon Moissiacense* also detailed that it was a grand army.[14] But while all the sources recorded a major force, they are not explicit on this point, and the question about the number of troops recruited for this campaign remains a matter of debate.[15]

In connection with the chronicles, three fundamental aspects reveal that this was a considerable force. First, the chronicles consistently record that there was no military campaign in 777, suggesting that the emperor focused his energies, resources, and time on the submission of Saxony, which culminated in the diet of Paderborn, and organizing the campaign of 778, which also was forged in the diet of 777. As pointed out in the previous chapter, most military campaigns were organized in the winter months, and very few years are recorded in which no campaign was held. All this suggests that the preparations for 778 demanded an additional effort that prevented the conduction of a campaign in 777. In addition, as revealed by the sources, the army was composed of Frankish mercenaries, as well as nearly all peoples subjugated by the emperor: Bavarians, Lombards, Burgundians, Septimanians, and even Muslims *et coniugentes*.[16] Interestingly, the sources do not mention Basques or Aquitanians among the king's troops. Finally,

13   Simson, Bernhard von (ed.), *Annales Mettenses Priores*, Monumenta Germaniae Historica (MGH), SSRG, X, Hannover & Leipzig, 1905, p. 66. For an English version, see King, P. D., *Charlemagne: Translated Sources*, P. D. King, Lambrigg, Kendal, Cumbria, 1987, p. 152.

14   In the original Latin: '*Et in anno 778 congregans Karolus rex exercitum magnum, ingressus est in Spania, et conquisivit civitatem Pampelonam. Et ibi Taurus, Saracenorum rex, venit ad eum, et tradidit civitates quas habuit, et dedit ei obsides fratrem suum et filium.*' In Pertz, Georg Heinrich (ed.), *Annales et chronica aevi Carolini*, Monumenta Germaniae Historica (MGH), SS, I, Hannover, 1826, p. 296.

15   There are several general accounts of the battle but it is necessary to highlight the first detailed account of the battle provided by Bernardo Estornés Lasa. See Estornés Lasa, Bernardo, *Historia General de Euskal Herria. 476-824 época vascona*, in *Enciclopedia General Ilustrada del País Vasco*, vol. 2, Auñamendi, Donostia, 1981, pp. 207-281. See also, Jimeno Jurio, José María, *¿Dónde fue la batalla de Roncesvalles?*, Institución Príncipe de Viana, Iruñea/Pamplona, 1974. And, Mombert, Jacob Isidor, *A History of Charles the Great (Charlemagne)*, D. Appleton & Co., New York, 1888, pp. 154-165.

16   The *Annales Laurissenses* and the *Annales Regni Francorum* state: '*Ibique venientes de partibus Burgundiae et Austriae vel Baioariae seu Provinciae et Septimaniae et pars Langobardorum.*' In Kurze, Friedrich (ed.), *Annales regni Francorum (741–829) qui dicuntur Annales Laurissenses maiores et Einhardi*, Monumenta Germaniae Historica (MGH), SSRG, VI, Hannover, 1895, p. 50. As for the *Annales Laurissenses* and the *Annales Tiliani* see Pertz, Georg Heinrich (ed.), *Annales et chronica aevi Carolini*, Monumenta Germaniae Historica (MGH), SS, I, Hannover, 1826, pp. 158 & 220. The *Annales Mettenses Priores* also reveals the diversity of the Carolingian army: '[D]e Austria, Burgundia, Bavaria seu Provincia et Langobardia.' In Simson, Bernhard von (ed.), *Annales Mettenses Priores*, Monumenta Germaniae Historica (MGH), SSRG, X, Hannover & Leipzig,

the army marched in two columns, and both went through a potentially hostile territory from which it follows that both should have been, separately, of a significant size.

As pointed out by Bernard S. Bachrach,[17] based on the calculations of David Herlihy,[18] north of the Alps the Carolingian Kingdom had a total population of about eight million people, and nearly two million men were of an age for the performance of war service (between 15 and 55.) Given that the kingdom was divided into approximately 600 or 700 counties and calculating that no more than 4 percent of men of military age were called to the annual service (a very conservative estimate), it follows that the king could potentially raise an army of 100,000 men in the same military station. In any event, considering the economic cost of a draft of 100,000 men and taking into consideration the logistical requirements of such a force, Bachrach concludes that the imperial army could not have had a total of over 10,000 men. Karl F. Werner agreed with these numbers and, based on similar demographics as Bachrach concluded that the Carolingian Empire at the end of Charlemagne's reign could recruit up to a total of approximately 100,000 foot soldiers and 36,000 horsemen.[19] In the same vein, accepting the figures given by Werner, Philippe Contamine is of the opinion that only on rare occasions, as in the campaign of 796 against the Avars, would Charlemagne have arranged an army of more than 15,000 or 20,000 troops.[20] Jan F. Verbruggen has estimated that the Carolingian army could have reached a total of 10,000 ground troops and 3,000 horsemen.[21] John F. Haldon argues that from the tenth to the twelfth centuries, an army could well reach up to 20,000 troops, but he considers that these figures are a bit high for an armed force of the eighth

1905, p. 66. For an English version of the aforementioned sources see King, P. D., *Charlemagne: Translated Sources*, P. D. King, Lambrigg, Kendal, Cumbria, 1987, p. 66.

17   Bachrach, Bernard S., *Early Carolingian Warfare: Prelude to Empire*, University of Pennsylvania Press, Philadelphia, 2001, pp. 59-60.

18   Herlihy, David, "Demography", in Strayer, Joseph R., *Dictionary of the Middle Ages*, Volume 4, Charles Scribner's Sons, New York, 1984, pp. 139-140.

19   Werner, Karl F., "Heeresorganisation und Kriegsführung im Deutschen Königreich des 10 und 11 Jardhunderts", *Ordinamenti Militari in Occidente nell'alto medioevo*, Settimane di Studio del Centro Italiano di Studi sull'alto medioevo 15, Spoleto, 1968, pp. 791-856.

20   Contamine, Philippe, *War in the Middle Ages*, Basil Blackwell, Oxford, 1984, pp. 25-26.

21   Verbruggen, J. F., *The Art of Warfare in Western Europe During the Middle Ages: From the Eighth Century to 1340*, The Boydell Press, Woodbridge, 2001, pp. 5-9. See also, Verbruggen, Jan F., "L'Armée et la stratégie de Charlemagne", in Braunfels, Wolfgang (ed.), *Karl der Grosse, Lebenswerk und Nachleben*, L. Schwann, Dusseldorf, 1965, vol. 1, pp. 420-436.

century.[22] Hans Delbrück believed that the Carolingian armies count with contingents from 5,000 up to 10,000 men.[23] And, in similar terms, Ferdinand Lot[24] and François-Louis Ganshof[25] believe that the number of troops of a Carolingian army could hardly exceed 10,000 men. Finally, Guy Halsall, based on estimates of Timothy Reuter, argues that in the eighth century an army of over 10,000 men would be very difficult to train, pay, and maneuver.[26]

There is therefore a difference of opinion, but most authors agree on several points. Virtually all authors agree that the figure of 100,000 potential recruits is acceptable in the light of demographic studies of the Frankish Kingdom during Charlemagne's reign, although most agree that the organization of an army of such size would be quite ineffective and extremely costly. Arnold H. M. Jones[27] and Averil Cameron[28] have asserted that between the third and the fifth centuries the Roman Empire was able to recruit up to 400,000 troops scattered in the various theatres of operations over the vast territory controlled by the Roman administration. And in fact, according to the data provided by Jones, imperial records of the fifth century show allocations for nearly 650,000 men (both active and in the reserve),[29] while the armies recruited for particular campaigns rarely exceeded 20,000 men, as noted earlier, mainly due to the financial and logistical difficulties involved. Sources point to a decline in the number of active troops down to no more

22 Haldon, John F., *Warfare, State and Society in the Byzantine World, 565-1204*, Routledge, London, 2003, p. 106.

23 Delbrück, Hans, *History of the Art of War: Within the Framework of Political History*, Greenwood Press, Westport (Conn.), 1985, vol. 3, pp. 22-23.

24 Lot, Ferdinand, *L'art militaire et les armées au Moyen Age en Europe et dans le Proche Orient*, Payot, Paris, 1946, pp. 412-435.

25 Ganshof, François-Louis, *The Carolingians and the Frankish Monarchy*, Longman, London, 1971. See also, Ganshof, François-Louis, "L'armee sur les carolingiens", *Ordinamenti Militari in Occidente nell'alto medioevo*, Settimane di Studio del Centro Italiano di Studi sull'alto medioevo 15, Spoleto, 1968, pp. 109-130.

26 Halsall, Guy, *Warfare and Society in the Barbarian West (450-900)*, Routledge, London & New York, 2003, pp. 119-133; Reuter, Timothy, "The Recruitment of Armies in the Early Middle Ages: What Can We Know?", in Nørgård Jørgensen, Anne; Clausen, Birthe L. (eds.), *Military Aspects of Scandinavian Society in a European Perspective AD 1-1300*, Copenhagen, 1997, pp. 32-37.

27 Jones, Arnold H. M., *The Later Roman Empire, 284-602: A Social Economic and Administrative Survey*, John Hopkins University Press, Baltimore, 1986, pp. 607-686. Especially, pp. 679-686.

28 Cameron, Averil, *The Later Roman Empire (284-430)*, Harvard University Press, Cambridge, 1998, pp. 33-35.

29 Jones, Arnold H. M., *The Later Roman Empire, 284-602: A Social Economic and Administrative Survey*, John Hopkins University Press, Baltimore, 1986, p. 684.

than 150,000 men during Justinian's era (483-565),[30] but Jones assumes that these estimates are moderately low.[31]

Another source for calculating the number of troops of Charlemagne's army is the *Epitoma rei militaris* of Flavius Vegetius Renatus, a source of great value to the knowledge of the military art and organization of the fourth-century Roman army. The extraordinary diffusion of the work throughout the Middle Ages suggests that it was well known in the eighth century.[32] According to the *Epitoma* and the records of the Roman imperial troops of the fifth century, a *legio* had a total of about 6,100 infantry troops (*pedites*) and 726 cavalry (*equites*) commanded by a *primus pilus* or first centurion who in turn was under the command of a *minor tribunus*. The command of the *legio* was in the hands of the *tribunus maior*, directly designated by the emperor. The smallest unit of the *legio* was the *contubernium*, a section of about ten men who shared the same tent under the command of a *decanus*.[33] Ten *contubernia* comprised a *centuria* (about 110 men) commanded by a *centurion* (60 per legion). Six centuries made a *cohors* (about 555 men on average)[34] and about ten cohorts formed a *legio*. Vegetius states that not all cohorts were identical in size, but the first cohort (*prima cohors*),[35] consisting of experienced troops, was double that of the others (about 1,100 men or *cohors miliaria*) and that, therefore, there were 66 riders for each

30   One of the main sources for the calculation of military contingents of the Roman Empire at the beginning of fifth century is the *Notitia Dignitatum*. It is a valuable document that, while it does not contain staff numbers and, therefore, does not allow us to assess accurately the total size of the Roman army of the period, it still allows us to estimate that in the early fifth century the Roman army had over 400,000 men distributed all across the empire in units of less than 20,000 troops. See Seeck, Otto (ed.), *Notitia dignitatum. Accedunt notitia urbis Constantinopolitanae et latercula provinciarum*, Berlin, 1876. In the opinión of Peter J. Heather it is extremely difficult to estimate the size of the army, although it may be established in light of the sources that it had about 435,000 men in the Diocletian era (284-305). See Heather, Peter J., *The Fall of the Roman Empire: A New History of Rome and the Barbarians*, Oxford University Press, New York, 2006, pp. 63-64.

31   Jones, Arnold H. M., *The Later Roman Empire, 284-602: A Social Economic and Administrative Survey*, John Hopkins University Press, Baltimore, 1986, p. 684.

32   There is an excellent bilingual edition by Leo F. Stelten (1990). See Vegetius Renatus, Flavius, *Epitoma rei militaris*, Peter Lang, New York, 1990. There is also an older edition, Vegetius Renatus, Flavius, *Epitoma rei militaris*, Peter Lang, Leipzig, 1869.

33   Webster, Graham, *The Roman Imperial Army of the First and Second Centuries A.D.*, University of Oklahoma Press, Norman, 1998, pp. 169-172.

34   And not 666 as was expected according to Vegetius' own calculations, since not all cohorts and centuries had the same number of troops.

35   Vegetius Renatus, Flavius, *Epitoma rei militaris*, Peter Lang, New York, 1990, pp. 72-79 & 124-129.

cohort, and twice that, 132, in the first cohort.[36] The smallest unit of cavalry was the *turma* composed of 32 riders led by a *decurio*.

As indicated by the few sources we have,[37] the *primus pilus* and the *tribunus* mentioned by Vegetius, had been replaced in the eighth century by the counts (*comes*) and dukes (*dux*) gathered around the *rex Francorum* in the Campus Martius. The counts were in charge of the direct recruitment of troops that were under their orders in the battlefield. The differences with the Roman system are obvious. The Carolingian army was not a stable military body but the result of an annual draft (*hostem*) of free men (*liberi homines*) and their servants in the context of a late Medieval society. However, there is no doubt that the Carolingian military units knew, in a similar fashion to the Roman armies, an administrative division and, consequently, a hierarchy of ranks. The *Epistola De Ordine Palatii* mentions the *ministeralii*,[38] officers of the military expeditions, as well as the *capitanei*, commanders of the units of the *exertitus Francorum* mentioned in the third article of the *Memoratorium de Exercitu in Gallia Occidentali Praeparando* of 807.[39]

The *comitatus* or military unit assigned to the count, who in turn answered to the *dux*, was the nuclear unit of the army.[40] The figure of around 7,000 troops, including cavalry, for a Carolingian army of the late eighth century is assumable and within the limits of a conservative estimate for most of

---

36 Southern, Pat, *The Roman Army: A Social and Institutional History*, ABC-CLIO, Santa Barbara (Cal.), 2006, pp. 99-105. Based on the data provided by Vegetius, see Vegetius Renatus, Flavius, *Epitoma rei militaris*, Peter Lang, New York, 1990, pp. 72-79 & 124-129.

37 *De ordine palatti* (On the Administration of the Court) is a treatise written by Hincmar, Archbishop of Reims, in 882 on the occasion of the coronation of Carloman. The author has suggested that the book was composed following the treaty written by Adalhard, Charlmagne's advisor and Abbot of Corbie, but this has not been yet confirmed. *De ordine palatti* and the Carolingian *Capitularia* (especially the *Capitulare de villis*, the *Capitulare missorum generale* or *Capitulare Aquisgranense*, the *Capitularia missorum specialia* and the *Capitulare missorum de exercitu promovendo*, among others *Capitularia regnum Francorum*) allow us to establish the guidelines of the Carolingian army's administration. While these works do not address the organization of the army in particular, the strongly hierarchical structure of the Carolingian administration allows us to establish the outlines of the organization of the *exercitu regis Caroli*. See Hincmar, *Epistola De Ordine Palatii*, F. Vieweg Librairie Éditeur, Paris, 1883.

38 Hincmar, *Epistola De Ordine Palatii*, F. Vieweg Librairie Éditeur, Paris, 1883, p. 68.

39 Boretius, Alfredus (ed.), *Capitularia Regum Francorum*, Monumenta Germaniae Historica (MGH), Leges, Hannover, 1883, vol. 1, p. 135.

40 Stephen S. Evans has studied the institution of the *comitatus* in light of historical and literary sources from the Middle Ages and the administrative and institutional practices on which this peculiar form of military organization was based, closely linked to the social structure of the time but also rooted in the Roman military structure. See Evans, Stephen S., *The Lords of Battle: Image and Reality of the Comitatus in Dark Age Britain*, Boydell Press, Woodbridge, 1998.

the aforementioned authors, and it is also in the line of the figures given by Vegetius for a *legio* (6,100 *pedites* and 726 *equites*). This same approximate figure of 10,000 men is maintained by the author of *Knyghthode and Bataile*, a fifteenth-century verse paraphrase of Flavius Vegetius Renatus's treatise *De re militari*.[41]

We must add to this figure the auxiliary troops in charge of the baggage and the presence of all the assistants who accompanied the army during the military campaigns: carriers, carpenters, blacksmiths, painters, teachers, specialists in building bridges and mounting war machines.[42] An expeditionary force of the size of a legion required about 520 beasts to carry the impedimenta.[43] Bachrach's calculations are not far from what follows from Julius Caesar's campaign in the Gaul. This author believes that an army of about 20,000 men (two legions) required a minimum of a kilo of ground wheat per man-day; for a march of twenty days, this implies a total of 400 tons of ground wheat, which in turn would require 800 wagons pulled by 1,600 workhorses.[44] On that basis, we may set the size of each of the columns in the campaign of 778 as at least the approximate size and general characteristics of a Roman legion. Indeed, each of the four military units sent by Charlemagne against the Saxons in 774 was referred to as a *legio* in the *Annales Mettenses Priores*.[45] In sum, following Vegetius we may thus conclude:

> [I]n the course of minor wars legions led by a praetor and junior officers, auxiliary forces, that is, 10,000 soldiers on foot and 2,000 cavalry, should be sufficient. But if the enemy force is expected to be considerable, a consul should be sent in command of a force of 20,000 ground troops and

---

41   Dyboski, R.; Arend, Z. M. (eds.), *Knyghthode and bataile: A XVth Century Verse Paraphrase of Flavius Vegetius Renatus' Treatise "De re militari"*, The Early English Text Society, London, 1935, p. 40.

42   Vegetius Renatus, Flavius, *Epitoma rei militaris*, Peter Lang, Leipzig, 1869, pp. 82-83.

43   Allen, J. H.; Allen, W. F.; Hudson, H, p. (eds.), *Caesar's The Gallic War*, Ginn & co., Boston, 1891, p. 99.

44   Bachrach, Bernard S., *Early Carolingian Warfare: Prelude to Empire*, University of Pennsylvania Press, Philadelphia, 2001, p. 237. See also, Bachrach, Bernard S., "Animals in Warfare in Early Medieval Europe", *Septimane*, vol. XXXI, 1983, pp. 707-764. Bachrach based his data on Ober, Josiah, "Hoplites and Obstacles", in Hanson, Victor (ed.), *Hoplites: The Classical Greek Battle Experience*, Rotledge, London & New York, 1989, pp. 173-196. See also, Goldsworthy, Adrian K., *The Roman Army at War 100 B.C.-A.D. 200*, Clarendon Press, Oxford, 1996, pp. 287-296; Roth, Jonathan P., *The Logistics of the Roman Army at War (264 BC – AD 235)*, E.J. Brill, Leiden, 1999.

45   Simson, Bernhard von (ed.), Annales Mettenses Priores, Monumenta Germaniae Historica (MGH), SSRG, X, Hannover & Leipzig, 1905, p. 62.

4,000 horsemen. And if an innumerable multitude of the most savage nations rose up in arms, then, in extreme necessity, two leaders with two armies should be sent with the following provision: 'Let both consuls or one of them consider how to do something to prevent any damage to the republic.'[46]

However, it should be noted that historical sources provide very little specific data and, as a consequence, in the absence of more sources and archaeological finds or an assessment based on contemporary chronicles, references to the actual size of the Carolingian army in 778 are approximate.[47]

The *Annales Regni Francorum*, the *Annales Laurissenses*, and the *Annales Mettenses Priores*, among other sources, state that Charlemagne celebrated Christmas in 777 in Duziaco (Douzy) near Sedan, less than 200 kilometres south of Herstal. As Charlemagne had done before on several occasions, such as in the campaigns against the Lombards in 773 or against the Saxons in 794, the Frankish army was divided into two columns.[48] The king himself led the main army or legion to Pamplona commanding troops from Neustria and penetrated in the peninsula from the west, through the Zize pass in Errozabal. A second legion 'of similar size' composed of troops from Austrasia, Burgundy, Lombardy, Bavaria, and Provence crossed the Pyrenees from the east, through Pertus, arriving in Girona and Barcelona.[49] From there they would continue westwards to find the troops commanded by the emperor

46 Vegetius Renatus, Flavius, *Epitoma rei militaris*, Peter Lang, Leipzig, 1869, pp. 65-66. See also a bilingual edition in Vegetius Renatus, Flavius, *Epitoma rei militaris*, Peter Lang, New York, 1990, p. 125.

47 For example, the *Annales qui dicuntur Annales Laurissenses maiores et Einhardi*, recorded the death of 4,500 prisoners of war at the hands of the Franks after the battle of Suntel in 782 in what is known as the slaughter of Verden, on the shores of the river Aller. These figures, which should be handled with caution, allow us to estimate the average size of the Saxon forces in 782 and also, given the superior financial might and the higher population density of the Frankish Kingdom, let us estimate Charlemagne's army's strength. See Kurze, Friedrich (ed.), *Annales regni Francorum (741–829) qui dicuntur Annales Laurissenses maiores et Einhardi*, Monumenta Germaniae Historica (MGH), SSRG, VI, Hannover, 1895, p. 62.

48 *Annales Regni Francorum*, in Kurze, Friedrich (ed.), *Annales regni Francorum (741–829) qui dicuntur Annales Laurissenses maiores et Einhardi*, Monumenta Germaniae Historica (MGH), SSRG, VI, Hannover, 1895, p. 94. In the 787 campaign against the Bavarians and in the campaigns of the years 791 and 796 against the Avars, Charlemagne's army was divided into three columns, and, in the case of the campaign against the Saxons in 774, in to four army bodies. In all these cases the main reason was strategic but also answered to standard logistical problems.

49 Simson, Bernhard von (ed.), *Annales Mettenses Priores*, Monumenta Germaniae Historica (MGH), SSRG, X, Hannover & Leipzig, 1905, p. 66. Another English version is in King, P. D., *Charlemagne: Translated Sources*, P. D. King, Lambrigg, Kendal, Cumbria, 1987, p. 152.

at the gates of Zaragoza.[50] As the author of the *Annales Mettenses Priores* put it, 'all Hispania shuddered at the countless legions'.[51]

When the expedition led by the king came to Cassinogilum (Aquitaine),[52] they stopped to celebrate Easter. Resurrection Sunday 778 was held on Sunday April 14.[53] There are about 550 kilometres (342 miles) from Douzy to Cassinogilum (following the Reims-Troyes-Auxerre-Bourges-Cassinogilum route),[54] which represents a one-month trip. If we consider that the king

---

50   The *Annales Regni Francorum* also recorded it in Salrach i Marés, Josep M., *El procés de formació nacional de Catalunya: (segles VIII-IX)*, Edicions 62, 1978, p. 132.

51   Simson, Bernhard von (ed.), *Annales Mettenses Priores*, Monumenta Germaniae Historica (MGH), SSRG, X, Hannover & Leipzig, 1905, p. 66. Another English version is in King, P. D., *Charlemagne: Translated Sources*, P. D. King, Lambrigg, Kendal, Cumbria, 1987, p. 152.

52   While it is logical to consider that the Cassinogilum mentioned by the chroniclers is the current Chasseneuil located about 28 km south of Châteauroux (in the via Lemovicensis), there are differing views on what city it is. The *Annales Regni Francorum* and the *Annales Laurissenses* mention 'Cassinogilo', the *Annales Mettenses Priores* 'Cassinaghilo', and the *Eginhardi Annales* refer to 'Cassinoilum'. The chronicles also refer to this place as 'Cassinoildum' which has led to several disquisitions as there is a town named Casseuil on the banks of the river Garonne north east of La Réole and, likewise, a third Casseneuil on the north bank of the river Lot (Olt in Occitan) near Villeneuve-sur-Lot. While not very feasible, the possibility that the town mentioned in the chronicles is the current Casseuil located on the north bank of the river Garonne is more plausible, since it is located in the via Lemovicensis, between Perigueux and Bazas. See the original Latin versión of the *Annales Mettenses Priores* in Simson, Bernhard von (ed.), *Annales Mettenses Priores*, Monumenta Germaniae Historica (MGH), SSRG, X, Hannover & Leipzig, 1905, p. 66. The *Annales Regni Francorum* and the *Annales qui dicuntur Einhardi* record the same event ('*et celebravit natalem Domini in villa quae dicitur Dotciacum, et pascha in Aquitania in villa Cassinogilo*'). See Kurze, Friedrich (ed.), *Annales regni Francorum (741–829) qui dicuntur Annales Laurissenses maiores et Einhardi*, Monumenta Germaniae Historica (MGH), SSRG, VI, Hannover, 1895, pp. 50-51. The *Annales Laurissenses* also mention it: '*Et celebravit natalem Domini in villa quae dicitur Dotciacum, et pascha in Aquitania, et in villa Cassinogilo.*' The *Einhardi Annales* also record it: '*Idcirco rex, peracto memorato conventu, in Gallia reversus, natalem Domini in Dutciaco villa, pascha vero in Aquitania apud Cassinoillum celebravit.*' For the *Annales Laurissenses*, the *Einhardi Annales* and the *Annales Tiliani*, see Pertz, Georg Heinrich (ed.), *Annales et chronica aevi Carolini*, Monumenta Germaniae Historica (MGH), SS, I, Hannover, 1826, pp. 158 & 220.

53   During the Council of Arles (314) it was established that all Christendom was to celebrate Easter on the same date, which should be set by the Pope. A few years later, the Council of Nicaea (325) decided that the date would be calculated at Alexandria and communicated to Rome and, from there, the Pope would transmit it to the rest of the Christendom. In 525 Dionysius Exiguus unified the calculation of Easter according to the Alexandrian computation. While the calculation is quite complex, it is only necessary to consider two fundamental issues: Easter Day should be a Sunday. And, this Sunday has to be the first after the first full moon (or Paschal full moon) of the spring in the northern hemisphere (the equinox may take place from March 19 to 21.) If the Paschal full moon falls on a Sunday, then Easter will be held on the following Sunday.

54   Assuming that this is the current Chasseneuil, the nearest town from Douzy of the three possible candidates (Chasseneuil, Casseuil or Casseneuil).

was in Cassinogilum on April 14, then we deduce that the army left Douzy in the first half of March; an early date to start a campaign.

While the king's army may have marched faster during this first phase of the campaign – the roads were better and it was not a hostile territory – it is likely that the various army units from Neustria converged in Cassinogilum and that from there they together undertook the rest of the campaign. With impedimenta, an advancing army of those proportions would have been much slower. In fact, the Latin word *impedimenta* comes precisely from the supposed delay caused by the need for an army to drag up the carts carrying the supplies.[55] A legion was called *legio impedita* when carrying baggage and when without, *legio expedita*.

There is some agreement on the distances that an army of these characteristics could cover daily. Based on the information given by contemporary sources, it is possible to establish that the legions were moving at a rate of 7 to 20 kilometres per day (4-13 miles per day), depending of course of various fundamental factors such as the terrain, the state and quality of the driveways, the nature of the territory, the presence of enemy troops, the weather, and the condition of the army (with or without impedimenta). Given these factors, sources record exceptionally marches without baggage up to 30 kilometres (approximately 19 miles) in one day. Caesar recorded in his *Commentarii de Bello Gallico* a march of 29 kilometres (approximately 18 miles) in Gaul only to force his troops to load their equipment themselves to avoid dragging a convoy of supply wagons.[56] This record matches the details given by Vegetius about the 52-kilometer (32-mile or 20 Roman miles) march exercises that the legionaries had to do three times a month while carrying equipment of about 19.5 kilos.[57] Centuries after, the author of *Knyghthode and Bataile* ratified this *antiqua consuetudo*.[58]

Procopius (*History of the Wars*) records marches of up to 10 or 12 kilometres per day (approximately 6 or 7 miles a day) for seven consecutive days with infantry, cavalry, and baggage.[59] The same view is shared by Bachrach

---

55 Plural of *impedimentum* (meaning 'burden'). From the Latin verb *impedire* meaning 'to delay', or literally 'to chain the feet'.

56 Holmes, Thomas R., *Caesar's Conquest of Gaul*, Macmillan, London, 1903, p. 89.

57 Vegetius Renatus, Flavius, *Epitoma rei militaris*, Peter Lang, New York, 1990, p. 50.

58 Dyboski, R.; Arend, Z. M. (eds.), *Knyghthode and bataile: A XVth Century Verse Paraphrase of Flavius Vegetius Renatus' Treatise "De re militari"*, The Early English Text Society, London, 1935, p. 22.

59 Haldon, John F., *Warfare, State and Society in the Byzantine world, 565-1204*, Routledge, London, 2003, p. 165.

who, based on data from the campaigns against Aquitaine led by Pepin the Short between 760 and 768, concludes that an army could advance in good condition and for a week at a rate of 14 kilometres per day (approximately 9 miles).[60] Guy Halsall has estimated that a force of the eighth century of two legions composed of approximately 20,000 men, with a caravan of supplies, similar in size and structure to Charlemagne's, could hardly move at a top speed of 16 kilometres per day (or 10 miles a day).[61] John F. Haldon has estimated that an army advancing under favorable conditions, both climatic and orographic, could march even at a maximum rate of 20 kilometres per day (about 12 miles a day) while dragging the supply train.[62] In fact, marches of up to 30 km (20 Roman miles or 18.5 miles today) have been recorded, but only in exceptional condition with no baggage, only for a few days, and usually at the expense of many beasts of burden.[63] King Basil II, having left Istanbul with approximately 40,000 men to relieve Aleppo, covered a distance of 891 kilometres (or approximately 557 miles) that normally took 60 days (15 kilometres per day) in 20 (an average of 44.5 kilometres per day). However, only 17,000 men arrived. Horses and oxen need about a day of rest for every six days of march.[64]

After celebrating Easter in Cassiloginum, Charlemagne left his wife Hildegard, who was pregnant with their sixth child. On April 16, Tuesday,[65] she gave birth to twins, Lothar and Clovis, the future Ludovico Pio (Louis

---

60 Bachrach, Bernard S., *Early Carolingian Warfare: Prelude to Empire*, University of Pennsylvania Press, Philadelphia, 2001, p. 221.

61 Halsall, Guy, *Warfare and Society in the Barbarian West (450-900)*, Routledge, London & New York, 2003, p. 131.

62 Haldon, John F., *Warfare, State and Society in the Byzantine world, 565-1204*, Routledge, London, 2003, p. 165.

63 Michael Prestwich provides concrete examples of the movement of troops in the eleventh and fourteenth centuries; based on contemporary documents, the data provided is entirely consistent with those outlined above: Marches between 11 and 24 km per day (approximately 7 and 15 miles per day). See Prestwich, Michael, *Armies and Warfare in the Middle Ages: The English Experience*, Yale University Press, New Haven, 1999, pp. 190-191. The data provided by Philippe Pollute also matches these figures (15 km a day on average over 900 km for an entire army of the fourteenth century). See Contamine, Philippe, *War in the Middle Ages*, Basil Blackwell, Oxford, 1984, p. 225. See also, Nicholson, Helen, *Medieval Warfare: Theory and Practice of War in Europe 300-1500*, Palgrave Macmillan, London & New York, 2004, p. 125. Lastly, Bachrach also mentions the loss of beasts of burden due to marching excessively. See Bachrach, Bernard S., *Merovingian Military Organization, 481-751*, University of Minnesota Press, Minneapolis, 1972, p. 58.

64 Holmes, Thomas R., *Caesar's Conquest of Gaul*, Macmillan, London, 1903, pp. 165-166.

65 McMahon Sheehan, Michael (ed.), "Aging and the Aged in Medieval Europe", *Papers in Mediaeval Studies*, 11, PIMS, 1990, p. 92.

the Pious).[66] To reach Pamplona, Charlemagne's troops had to cross the river Garonne, penetrate the Duchy of Gascony, a potentially hostile territory and, crossing the Pyrenees, cover the 600 kilometres separating Cassinogilum from Pamplona. As recorded in the *Vita Hludowici imperatoris*, Charlemagne certified the neutrality of the *princeps vasconum* Lupus II by a covenant and hostage-taking.[67]

The fifth book of the *Codex Calixtinus*, *Guide du Pèlerin* de Aimery Picaud, refers in the first chapter to the four main routes to access Pamplona, and only two of them connected Pamplona with Cassinogilum: the via Lemovicensis and the via Turonensis.[68] Although the pilgrimage to Santiago acquired popularity and was universalized some centuries later, the first of the aforementioned routes, known as *voie limousine* or *voie de Vézelay* by Francophone pilgrims, was one of the main branches of the *Camino de Santiago* and one of the most important trading routes in this part of Europe since the Roman occupation of Gaul.[69]

66 Hildegard (758-783), the daughter of Count Gerold of Vinzgouw and Emma of Alamannia, was the second wife of Charlemagne, to whom she was married in 771. They had nine children:
1. Carolus (772 or 773-811), Count of Maine from 781 and King of the Franks with Charlemagne from 800.
2. Adelaide (born in 773 or 774).
3. Pepin (777-810), baptized Carloman and later rechristened with the name of Pepin in Rome, was king of Italy from 781.
4. Hruodrud (777-810).
5. Ludovico Pio or Louis the Pious (born in 778), King of Aquitaine from 781, and emperor from 813 to 840.
6. Lothair, Louis's twin brother, wo died at the age of two years in 780.
7. Bertha (779-823?).
8. Gisela (781-808?).
9. Hildegarde (782-783?).

67 Tremp, Ernst (ed.), *Astronomus. Das Leben Kaiser Ludwigs* (*Vita Hludowici imperatoris*), Monumenta Germaniae Historica (MGH), SSRG, LXIV, Hannover, 1995, p. 286.

68 Vielliard, Jeanne, *Le guide du pèlerin de Saint-Jacques de Compostelle: texte latin du XIIe siècle*, Librairie Philosophique J. Vrin, Paris, 2004, p. 4. See the English edition by William Melczer in Melczer, William (ed.), *The Pilgrim's Guide to Santiago de Compostela*, Italica Press Inc., New York, 1993, p. 85.

69 It is unlikely that the army entered Bordeaux – it is not recorded by the sources – thus following the old Roman road that connected this city with the Pyrenees. This road, called *via Turonensis* by the pilgrims, runs from Bordeaux to the south, until Baiona (Bayonne). In Akitze (Aquis or Dax), a secondary branch of the way led through Orthez to Donibane Garazi and, finally, to Ibañeta. In any case, both along the the *via Lemovicensis* or the *via Turonensis*, it is certain that the army arrived at Ostabat where these two roads converged. From there the army entered Donibane Garazi and then, travelling across the Pyrenees through Ibañeta reached Pamplona from the north.

Most likely, from Cassinogilum the army continued along the main road or *via Lemovicensis*, which is also the shorter way. This pathway linked Limoges and Perigueux along 600 kilometres, crossing the river Garonne and the former *via Aquitania* (Narbonne-Toulouse-Bordeaux), which extends into Vasconia towards Pamplona.[70] The most common passes across the Garonne were Langon, La Réole, or Marmande, all on the road to Bazas, which was a common point along the way. It is therefore very likely that the meeting with the delegation of Lupus II took place in one of these four locations, before crossing the Garonne, which in turn, as we have mentioned above, reinforces the thesis that the Cassinogilum mentioned by the sources is not the current Chasseneuil, but Casseuil, near La Réole.

Already in Vasconia, on the south bank of the river Garonne, the *via Lemovicensis* ran according to Aymeric Picaud's pilgrims' guide[71] for 190 kilometres (119 miles) through Bazas, Mont de Marsan, Orthez, Ostabat[72] until Donibane Garazi.[73] The journey would take no less than 15 days to cover:[74]

> Then, crossing the Garonne, is the territory of Bordeaux, with excellent wine and rich in fish, but speaking a rustic language [Basque substrate]. It has been noted that the inhabitants of Saintes speak a rustic language, but those of Bordeaux even more. Then, in three exhausting days, you

70   Vielliard, Jeanne, *Le guide du pèlerin de Saint-Jacques de Compostelle: texte latin du XIIe siècle*, Librairie Philosophique J. Vrin, Paris, 2004, p. 2.

71   *The Pilgrims' Guide* by Aymeric Picaud is the Liber V of the *Codex Calixtinus*. Sometimes it is called Liber IV due to the fact that in the eighteenth century one of the books that comprised the *Codex Calixtinus* was ripped and the guide thus became the fourth book of the codex. It is a fundamental source for the study of the route crossed by the Carolingian army in 778, as it describes in detail the journey from Donibane Garazi (Saint-Jean-Pie-de-Port) to Pamplona.

72   In Ostabat, an important crossroad on the road since it was the converging point of three of the main routes of the western Pyrenees, the *via Podense*, the *via Turonense* and the *via Lemovicense*, which was the one followed by the emperor's army.

73   Coordinates:
Lat.: 43° 9' 50.396" N. Lon.: 1° 14' 10.621" W.
UTM: x = 643,383 m. y = 4,780,623 m
Altitude: 300 m.

74   Picaud's *Pilgrims' Guide* is not a reliable source when it comes to the steps or days in to which the way is divided. In some cases the author records days of up to 97 km (Jaca-Monreal) or 69 km (Gares / Puente la Reina-Naiara / Najera) travel that in the best case a pilgrim would cover in no less than three or two long march days respectively. In the present case, Picaud states that the way from Saint Michel to Pamplona (approx. 70 km) can be covered in two days, which may be true for an athletic pilgrim but absolutely impossible for a *legio impedita* dragging a supply train through the port of Zize.

have to cross the Landes of Bordeaux. This is a countryside lacking everything, from bread to wine, meat, fish and, water springs; sparsely populated, flat, and sandy, although abundant in honey, millet, maize, and pigs. If, by chance, you cross this region in the summer, you should carefully protect your face from the huge flies, commonly called wasps or horseflies, of which there are plenty. And if you do not look carefully where you step, you will sink quickly to your knees in the sea sand that covers everything. Once you have traversed this territory you come into the Basque Country, rich in white bread and excellent red wine, woods, meadows, rivers, and healthy water springs. The Basques are light word talkers, blabbermouth, jokers, libidinous, drunkards, gluttons, scruffy and devoid of gems, but well used to war and distinguished for their hospitality to the needy. They have the habit of eating without a table, sitting around the fire, and drinking from the same vessel. They eat and drink a lot, dress badly, and lie together indecently, the servants with the master and mistress, on some straw in the dirt.[75]

In the foothills of the Zize pass, Picaud describes the inhabitants of the northern slopes of the Pyrenees, who he called 'Basques'. Picaud's *Pilgrims' Guide* offers certainly a prejudiced image of these people. In any case, the note is extremely interesting, as it reflects the image that the author had of Vasconia, an image of an uncivil land, full of thugs and skilled warriors, one that authors like Jimeno Jurio believe comes from the battle of Errozabal and the subsequent oral and written literature:[76]

Then, nearby the Zize pass, you arrive in the Basque Country, with the city of Baiona [Bayonne] on the coast in the north. This is a barbarous region, forested, mountainous, lacking bread and wine and all kinds of food except for apples, cider and milk that constitute the only relief. In this country, i.e., near the Zize pass, in the towns of Ostabat, Saint-Michel

---

75 Rialle, Girard de; Vinson, Julien (eds.), *Revue de Linguistique et de Philologie Comparée*, vol. 15, Maisonneuve de Cie, Libraires-éditeurs, 1882, pp. 11-13. Also in a bilingual Latin-French edition in Vielliard, Jeanne (ed.), *Le guide du pèlerin de Saint-Jacques de Compostelle: texte latin du XIIe siècle*, Librairie Philosophique J. Vrin, Paris, 2004, pp. 18-20. There is also an excellent English version in Melczer, William (ed.), *The Pilgrim's Guide to Santiago de Compostela*, Italica Press Inc., New York, 1993. For this specific part see, pp. 90-91. An abridged Spanish version is in Orella, José Luis, *Historia de Euskal Herria*, Volume 1, Txalaparta, Tafalla, 2003, pp. 253-260.
76 Jimeno Jurio, José María, *¿Dónde fue la batalla de Roncesvalles?*, Pamiela, Iruñea/Pamplona, 2004, pp. 134-136.

and Donibane Garazi [Saint-Jean-Pied-de-Port], the collectors of tolls are so heinous that they deserve the utmost condemnation since, armed with two or three yards, they approach the pilgrims and force them to paying unfair taxes. And if the pilgrim refuses to pay what they ask for, they beat him, threaten him and search him and even take away his bag from him. People in this land are fierce, as fierce, untamed and barbaric as the land they live on. Their faces are fierce and their language is barbarous and they terrorize anyone who behold them. Legally they can only tax the merchants so whatever they charge the pilgrims and travelers is illegal. When the rate of something is four or six coins, they charge eight or twelve, that is, twice.[77]

In line with the description of the inhabitants north of the Pyrenees, the Basques south of the range, generically called Navarrese by the author, are described in these terms:

> After this valley is the country of Navarre, rich in bread, wine, milk, and cattle. The Navarrese and the Basques look alike in meals, clothing, and language, but the Basques are whiter than the Navarrese [...] As anyone can notice, they dress badly, and they eat and drink inadequately too, since the Navarrese have the habit of eating together at home, servants and masters, mixing all dishes in one only pan, and they do not use spoons, but eat with their hands, and all drink from the same jug. Also, hearing them talk their barbarous tongue reminds me of the barking of the dogs. They call God *urcia*; the mother of God *andrea Maria*; bread is *orgui*; wine is *ardum*; meat is *aragui*; fish, *araign*; home, *echea*; the owner of the house is called *Iaona*; woman, *andrea*; church, *elicera*; priest, *belaterra*, meaning 'beautiful land'; wheat is *gari*; water, *uric*; king, ereguia; and Santiago, Iaona domne iacue. They are a barbarian people, different in customs and nature from all other people, extremely evil, black, messy, wicked, perverse, treacherous, disloyal, lascivious, drunken, aggressive, fierce and savage, ruthless and reprobate, impious and rude, cruel, quarrelsome, devoid of any virtue, and used to all vices and iniquities; as iniquitous as the Getas and the Saracens and

77   Rialle, Girard de; Vinson, Julien (eds.), *Revue de Linguistique et de Philologie Comparée*, vol. 15, Maisonneuve de Cie, Libraires-éditeurs, 1882, p. 13. Another English version is in Melczer, William (ed.), *The Pilgrim's Guide to Santiago de Compostela*, Italica Press Inc., New York, 1993. For this specific passage see, pp. 91-92. An abridged version in Spanish is in Orella, José Luis, *Historia de Euskal Herria*, Volume 1, Txalaparta, Tafalla, 2003, pp. 253-260.

total enemies of our Gallic nation. For a miserable coin, a Basque or a
Navarrese would kill a Frenchman, given the opportunity. In some of
their regions, in Bizkaia and Araba for example, the Navarrese, while
heating themselves, show their parts to each other, man to woman and
woman to man. In addition, the Navarrese incestuously fornicate with
the livestock. Also, it is said that the Navarrese put on the haunches
of their mares or mules some protection, so no one but the owner can
access them. Men also lustfully kiss the vulva of their wives and their
mules. Therefore, educated people cannot but reprove the Navarrese.
However, they are considered brave in the battlefield, zealous at work,
compliant when paying tithes and, persevering in their offerings to the
altar. Whenever the Navarrese go to church, they bring bread, wine,
wheat, or any other offering for God.[78]

At Donibane Garazi, Picaud directs the pilgrims through the ancient Roman
road leading from Saint-Michel (in the vicinity of Donibane Garazi) through
the Pyrenean crests to Bizkarreta-Gerendiain and from there to Pamplona
in a two-day march:[79]

After the Zize pass, the most relevant populations that we found along
the way to the basilica of St. James in Galicia are the following: first, the
village of Saint Michel lies at the foot of the Zize pass in the northern
part of Vasconia; after passing through the summit of the mountain
pass, we reach Roland's hospital; then the village of Rencesvals [Auritz];
Bizkarreta is immediately thereafter and, from there, Larrasoaña and
then Pamplona [Iruñea].[80]

However, the Carolingian army would need about five hard march days
at a strenuous average rate of about 13 kilometres per day (roughly 8
miles a day) to cover the 65.6-kilometer (41-mile) road lined with three

---

78 *Liber Quartus S. Jacobi Apostoli*, in Rialle, Girard de; Vinson, Julien (eds.), *Revue de Linguis-tique et de Philologie Comparée*, vol. 15, Maisonneuve de Cie, Libraires-éditeurs, 1882, pp. 16-18. For another English version see Melczer, William (ed.), *The Pilgrim's Guide to Santiago de Compostela*, Italica Press Inc., New York, 1993. For this passage see, pp. 94-95. An abridged version in Spanish is in Orella, José Luis, *Historia de Euskal Herria*, Volume 1, Txalaparta, Tafalla, 2003, pp. 253-260.

79 Vielliard, Jeanne, *Le guide du pèlerin de Saint-Jacques de Compostelle: texte latin du XIIe siècle*, Librairie Philosophique J. Vrin, Paris, 1984, p. 5.

80 Vielliard, Jeanne, *Le guide du pèlerin de Saint-Jacques de Compostelle: texte latin du XIIe siècle*, Librairie Philosophique J. Vrin, Paris, 1984, p. 6.

mountain passes separating Donibane Garazi from Pamplona.[81] Once the army reached the hill of Ibañeta in two days,[82] they had to camp on the plain of Errozabal, around the town of Auritz.[83] The next day they would camp in the plain of Bizkarreta-Gerendiain. The army would cover the approximately 10 km (6.2 miles) between Bizkarreta and Zubiri in another day descending through the old road of the Erro pass and,[84] from there, the 21.6 km (13.4 m) from Zubiri to Pamplona along the Esteribar valley in another two days. After traveling 1,200 kilometres (745 miles) from Douzy to Pamplona in approximately three months, Charlemagne's army reached the gates of Pamplona in early June 778,[85] as described by the author of the *Vita Hludowici*:

> There he carried out what was dictated by his conscience and the op-
> portunity and decided to cross the rough Pyrenees and enter Hispania
> to aid with the help of Christ the church that underwent the bitter yoke
> of the Saracens. This mountain, so high that almost touches the sky,
> terrible for the roughness of the rocks, even sinister for the thick forests,
> almost prevented owing to the narrowness of the road, or rather simple

81 Approximately, a hard two-day ascending march to the summit of about 11 km and 14 km respectively, and four days descent of 9 km, 8 km, 10 km and 13 km respectively. Charlemagne likely reach the vicinity of Pamplona on the sixth day of the march after leaving Donibane Garazi.

82 Coordinates:
   Lat.: 43° 1' 16.813» N. Lon.: 1° 19' 23.718" W.
   UTM: x = 636,629 m. y = 4,764,634 m.
   Altitude: 1.062.

83 Coordinates:
   Lat.: 42° 59' 25.386" N. Lon.: 1° 20' 4.889" W.
   UTM: x = 635,765 m. y = 4,761,178 m
   Altitude: 890 m.

84 Coordinates:
   Lat.: 42° 56' 10.542" N. Lon.: 1° 30' 6.121" W.
   UTM: x = 622,257 m. y = 4,754,911 m
   Altitude: 536 m.

85 As indicated, following the 550 km of the Douzy-Reims-Troyes-Auxerre-Bourges-Cassinogilum route, Charlemagne would have completed about 45 days on the road. From here, and despite it being a wide enough road through a predominantly flat terrain, the Carolingian army would have required no less than 45 days (at an average of 12 km a day) to cover the 550 km road from Limoges to Donibane Garazi (Limoges-Périgueux-Cassinogilum-Bazas-Mont de Marsan-Orthez-Ostabat-Donibane Garazi). Finally, Charlemagne needed another five days to cover the 75 km road between Donibane Garazi and Pamplona through Erozabal. In total, a march of some 1,200 km was completed in about 95 days (12.63 km per day), including mandatory rest days for the beasts of burden.

path, not just the passage of an army, but the one of a simple detachment. With Christ's favor could he happily cross it since the king's generous spirit ennobled by God did not want to be any less than Pompey, nor less courageous than Anibal who at one time, undergoing many hardships and losses, overcame the hostility of these places.[86]

Meanwhile, the second army crossed the Pyrenees along the ancient Roman *via Domitia* connecting Nimes and the Pyrenees. From the *Summum Pyrenæum*,[87] the army followed the *via Augusta* or the *via Herculea* leading to Gerunda (Girona), Barcino (Barcelona), Ilerda (Lleida) and, following the Roman road along the Ebro valley to Caesaraugusta (Zaragoza), leaving Osca (Huesca) on the north.

Siege and Capture of Pamplona

Charlemagne's army arrived in Pamplona before the cereal from the fields around the city was harvested and were thus able to starve the otherwise strongly defended city into submission.[88] Starvation was a common tactic to bring a city to the point of surrender. The besieging army surrounded Pamplona, blocking all routes whereby it might have been resupplied with food and water. Also, the collected cereal could be used for the maintenance of the Carolingian troops. The data provided by the estimates of the march of Charlemagne's army from Douzy to Pamplona matches with this need, since the season for the collection of cereal in the region of Pamplona takes place in late June. Leaving early March from Douzy, the emperor came to Pamplona in early or mid-June 778.

---

86 Tremp, Ernst (ed.), *Astronomus. Das Leben Kaiser Ludwigs* (*Vita Hludowici imperatoris*), Monumenta Germaniae Historica (MGH), SSRG, LXIV, Hannover, 1995, pp. 286-288.

87 Also known as *Col de Panissars*, a few kilomters to the west of the current Pertus pass.

88 Name given to the old city in honor of Pompey the Great. The pre-Roman town was called Iruñea ('the city') in Basque. The chronicles record different names for the city, among them, *Pampalona* and *Pampalonia* (*Annalium Petavianorum Pars Secunda*), *Pampalona* (*Annales Nazariani y Annales Laurissenses Minores*), *Pampilona* (*Annales Regni Francorum, Annales Laurissenses y Einhardi Fuldensis Annales*), *Pampilone* (*Reginonis Chronicon*), *Pompelone* (*Einhardi Annales y Annales qui dicit Einhardi*), *Pampelona* (*Chronicon Moissiacense*).
   Coordinates:
   Lat.: 42° 49' 15.076" N, Lon.: 1° 38' 24.490" W.
   UTM: x = 611,168 m; y = 4,741,903 m.
   Altitude: 430-450 metres in the urban centre of the 8th century.

As related by the Saxon poet, 'reaching Pamplona, which happens to be a noble stronghold of the Navarrese, he took it by force'.[89] However, it should have not been easy to capture the city since the description given by the *De Laude Pampilone* indicates that the walled city was built by the Romans in stone, and that it was large:[90]

This is a providential place, made and chosen by God, found by man, as full of water springs as there are days in a year. It is always possible to get water from these wells so no one, urged by the need of water, needs to supply from the other, since there is plenty for everyone. Rising colossal, the towers of the city walls are 63 feet thick and 84 ft. high.[91] The surrounding wall has one thousand dextras.[92] It has 67 towers. The Lord, in His mercy, endowed the city with innumerable relics of martyrs and their prayers saved them unharmed among barbarous nations and enemies. As told by an ancient tradition, thanks to these attentive prayers and the many merits of the martyrs an angelic light shines over the city. If men slept during the vigils of the martyrs, they were awakened by the cries of the stones. For them it was always a victorious place, adorned with virtues. Pamplona is a good stronghold, locked within three corners, with three front doors and four rear entrances, neighboring the port.[93]

89   The Saxon poet's *Annales de Gestis Caroli Magni Libri V*: '*Insidias eius summo sub vertice montis tendere Wascones ausi.*' In Pertz, Georg Heinrich (ed.), *Annales et chronica aevi Carolini*, Monumenta Germaniae Historica (MGH), SS, I, Hannover, 1826, p. 234.

90   *De Laude Pampilone* is a manuscript written in Latin that provides a description of Pamplona while praising its Christian essence. This document is included in the *Codex de Roda* dated to the late tenth century. However, it is hard to date, and according to some authors this is a document of the fourth century. See Larrañaga, Koldo, "Glosa sobre un viejo texto referido a la historia de Pamplona: el De laude Pampilone", *Príncipe de Viana*, 55, Nº 201, 1994, pp. 137-148.

91   If we calculate 31.5 cm per foot, the dimensions of the towers would be 2 metres wide (6.3 feet) by 2.65 metres tall (8.4 feet). On the other hand, the text does not reveal whether the towers were built of stone or, as is more likely, were made of wood and supported on stone walls. The study based on the ancient walls shows that the walls were 1.3 to 1.65 metres wide, so it fits the description given by the poem. See Tudanca, Juan M., *Evolución socioeconómica del alto y medio Valle del Ebro en época bajoimperial romana*, Gobierno de La Rioja, Instituto de Estudios Riojanos, Logroño, 1997, p. 369.

92   One dextra corresponds to 4.4 metres, from which it follows that the calculation is very exaggerated as the archaeological remains allow us to see that the perimeter of the city had 1,650 metres.

93   Original and Spanish translation are in Larrañaga, Koldo, "Glosa sobre un viejo texto referido a la historia de Pamplona: el De laude Pampilone", *Príncipe de Viana*, 55, Nº 201, 1994, pp. 138-139. The original Spanish translation was taken from Elizalde, Ignacio, *Navarra en las literaturas románicas, Edad Media*, Institución Príncipe de Viana, Iruña/Pamplona, 1977. vol. 1, pp. 26 y ss. See also a second translation by José M. Muruzabal in Muruzabal, José M., "Nuevos

The various archaeological excavations and studies on the Medieval city show that Pamplona would have covered an area of about 150,000 square metres (15 hectares), and the walls would have had a perimeter of approximately 1,600 metres, so that while the description of *De Laude Pampilone* seems slightly exaggerated, it matches quite well the data provided by the archaeological examination. Furthermore, excavations carried out in Curia street in 1856 unearthed a Roman mosaic with a large graphical representation of the towers crowning the walls of Pamplona.[94]

While we have no direct data on the siege and capture of Pamplona, sources indicate that the city resisted for some time the onslaught of the Carolingian troops before it was finally subdued by Charlemagne. The only account of the events that took place in the vicinity of Pamplona and southern Vasconia during the campaign of 778 are included in the *Historia Caroli Magni et Rotholandi*, a twelfth-century literary text included in the *Codex Calixtinus*.[95] Based on the story told in the *Historia Caroli Magni et Rotholandi*, the reliquary of Aachen, the *Karlsschrein*, dated to the early thirteenth century, contains a metal relief of the siege of Pamplona (*Pampelun*) representing the Frankish camp with its tents around the city of the Basques and various Frankish soldiers killed by projectiles thrown from the top of the walls by the defenders of the city, while a divine hand from above subsides one of the towers of the wall.[96] Also, based on the *Historia Caroli Magni et Rotholandi*, the eleventh scene of one of the stained glass windows of Chartres cathedral represents Pamplona resisting the siege for three months, and Charlemagne knelt at the sight of his army, imploring God to intercede for him. The twelfth scene of the window shows how, after one of the towers of the city walls collapsed, Charlemagne entered Pamplona.

But, beyond the fantasy of the *Historia Caroli Magni et Rotholandi* and based on historical sources, the city was besieged and taken by the Frankish troops. Virtually all sources record the capture of the place by force.

datos sobre el origen del reino de Navarra", *Espacio, Tiempo y Forma. Serie III. Historia Medieval*, 7, 1994, pp. 43-44.

94   Blázquez, José María, *Mosaicos romanos de Navarra*, Instituto Español de Arqueología del Consejo Superior de Investigaciones Científicas, Madrid, 1985, pp. 54-58. See also, Jimeno Jurio, José María, *Historia de Pamplona y de sus lenguas*, Txalaparta, Tafalla, 1995, p. 26.

95   Wrongly attributed to Bishop Turpin of Reims, the chronicle focuses on the campaign against Pamplona. For a recent edition of the original Latin version, see Jones, Cyril M., *Historia Karoli Magni et Rotholandi: ou, Chronique du Pseudo-Turpin*, Slatkine, Genève, 1972.

96   Dated to between 1200 and 1215. Schramm, Percy E.; Mütherich, Florentine, *Denkmale der deutschen Könige und Kaiser: Ein Beitrag zur Herrschergeschichte von Karl dem Grossen bis Friedrich II, 768-1250*, Prestel, Munich, 1962, p. 188 et seq.

Besides the *Annales de Gestis Caroli Magni*, the *Annales Regni Francorum qui dicuntur Einhardi*, the *Einhardi Annales*, the *Annales Mettenses Priores*, the *Annales Nazarianorum continuatio alteri Laureshemnsium parti subiicitur*, the *Annales Petaviani*, and the *Chronicon Moissiacense* states: 'And he conquered Pamplona'.[97] The Saxon poet also makes reference to the capture of Pamplona in the *Annales de Gestis Caroli Magni*, and describes it as 'a noble stronghold of the Navarrese'.[98] Therefore, although suggestive, the thesis that the city was held by the Muslims at the arrival of Charlemagne is difficult to sustain.[99]

The ideal place to make a breach in the walls and penetrate through them was the city's southern flank. Flat, devoid of steep slopes and slightly elevated (450 metres), it certainly offered an unbeatable location to set up camp and rush the siege. The northern slope by contrast, between the south bank of the river Arga and the city walls, offered a steep 20-meter drop that, added to the height of the walls, made of it an almost insurmountable barrier.

Without knowing how long it took to Charlemagne to capture Pamplona nor whether the Muslim troops led by Abu Taur helped the Franks breaking the siege of the city (which is very plausible, as other Muslim contingents had sieged and taken the city before), the *Annales Laurissenses Minores* and the *Chronicon Moissiacense* record that the king spent some days there after he received Abu Taur, *wali* of Huesca, in Pamplona, and after giving his brother and his son as hostages, led him to Zaragoza.[100]

The *Annalium Petavianorum Pars Secunda* also report that Charlemagne received Sulayman ibn Yaqzan ibn al-Arabi, governor of Barcelona and

---

97   In the original Latin: '[E]t conquisivit civitatem Pampelonam.' In Pertz, Georg Heinrich (ed.), *Annales et chronica aevi Carolini*, Monumenta Germaniae Historica (MGH), SS, I, Hannover, 1826, p. 296.

98   Pertz, Georg Heinrich (ed.), *Annales et chronica aevi Carolini*, Monumenta Germaniae Historica (MGH), SS, I, Hannover, 1826, pp. 234.

99   'In Spain, Abu Taber emerges from Min. (a) 778 as governor of Huesca; my suggestion in King, p. 13, that he might also have ruled Pamplona is based on nothing more substantial than the fact that Mos. 778 reports him to have come there to offer hostages to Charles and that the city was in Muslim hands later in the century but is not ruled out by·city of the Navarrans' in Rev. 778': King, P. D., *Charlemagne: Translated Sources*, P. D. King, Lambrigg, Kendal, Cumbria, 1987, p. 48.

100 Pertz, Georg Heinrich (ed.), *Annales et chronica aevi Carolini*, Monumenta Germaniae Historica (MGH), SS, I, Hannover, 1826, p. 296. The *Annales Laurissenses Minores* also recorded the event in Pertz, see Georg Heinrich (ed.), *Annales et chronica aevi Carolini*, Monumenta Germaniae Historica (MGH), SS, I, Hannover, 1826, p. 118. See also, the *Annales Nazariani* in Pertz, Georg Heinrich (ed.), *Annales et chronica aevi Carolini*, Monumenta Germaniae Historica (MGH), SS, I, Hannover, 1826, p. 31.

Girona, in Pamplona.[101] Similarly, the *Poetae Saxonis Annales de Gestis Caroli Magni Imperatoris Libri Quinque*, the *Annales Laurissenses*, the *Einhardi Annales*, the *Enhardi Fuldensis Annales*, the *Reginionis Chronicon*, and the *Annales Tiliani* suggest that both Frankish armies met, as planned, in front of Zaragoza. Without making any reference to the fact the city of Zaragoza did not open the doors to the king nor denying that some Muslim troops could have come to Pamplona, they indicate that some Muslim leaders paid tribute to Charlemagne in Zaragoza,[102] implying that the city finally submitted, which was not the case.[103]

Likewise, the thirteenth stained glass window of Chartres—following the *Historia Caroli Magni et Rotholandi*—relates that, being in Pamplona, Charlemagne ordered a church to be built in honor of Santiago. Without granting historical veracity to the note, the sources consistently emphasize that Charlemagne stopped for some time in the city after taking it by force. The *Chanson de Roland* also reads the same.[104] Historians and literary critics agree to translate the passage as 'I [Roland] have conquered for you [Charlemagne] Pamplona and Miranda de Arga; I have taken Valtierra and the land of Pina, Balaguer, Tudela and the Sierra of Sivil'.[105] Furthermore, the *Chanson* mentions 'Kordr' or 'Cordres',[106] which is translated as 'Cortes'. All these places are located south of the peninsular Vasconia (except Balaguer, which is 27 kilometres northeast of Lleida, and Pina de Ebro,

---

101 Pertz, Georg Heinrich (ed.), *Annales et chronica aevi Carolini*, Monumentae Germaniae Historica (MGH), SS, I, Hannover, 1826, p. 16.

102 For the *Annales Laurissenses* see, Pertz, Georg Heinrich (ed.), *Annales et chronica aevi Carolini*, Monumentae Germaniae Historica (MGH), SS, I, Hannover, 1826, p. 158. For the *Einhardi Annales* see, p. 159. For the *Annales Tiliani*, p. 220. For the *Annalium de Gestis Caroli Magni Imperatoris*, p. 234. For the *Enhardi Fuldensis Annales*, p 349. For the *Reginionis Chronicon*, p. 559.

103 Pertz, Georg Heinrich (ed.), *Annales et chronica aevi Carolini*, Monumentae Germaniae Historica (MGH), SS, I, Hannover, 1826, pp. 234.

104 Burgess, Glyn S., *The Song of Roland*, Penguin Classics, London, 1990, p. 170.

105 Regarding the translation of the toponyms mentioned in the *Chanson de Roland* see Aebischer, Paul, *Rolandiana et Oliveriana: Recueil d'études sur les chansons de geste*, Librairie Droz, Genève, 1967, pp. 235, 243 & 259-260; Aebischer, Paul, *Textes norrois et littérature française de moyen âge*, Librairie Droz, Genève, 1972, p. 54. See also, Boissonnade, Prosper, *Du nouveau sur la chanson de Roland: la genèse historique, le cadre géographique, le milieu, les personnages, la date et l'auteur de poème*, Honore Champion, Paris, 1923; Sholod, Barton, *Charlemagne in Spain: The Cultural Legacy of Roncesvalles*, Librairie Droz, Genève, 1963, pp. 167-169. See also, Bédier, Joseph (ed. and tr.), *La Chanson de Roland, publiée d'àpres le manuscrit d'Oxford et traduite*, Piazza, Paris, 1937. And, Lot, Ferdinand, *Études sur les légendes épiques françaises*, Honore Champion, Paris, 1958; Jenkins, Thomas A., *La Chanson de Roland, Oxford version, edition, notes and glossary by T. Atkinson Jenkins*, D. C. Heath, Boston, 1924; Burgess, Glyn S., *The Song of Roland*, Penguin Classics, London, 1990, p. 170.

106 Burgess, Glyn S., *The Song of Roland*, Penguin Classics, London, 1990, p. 167.

40 kilometres southeast of Zaragoza, both on the road of the second army that approached Zaragoza from the east).[107] All of them (except the sierra of Sivil, located northeast of Huesca, ruled by Abu Taur)[108] are places located on the road from Pamplona to Zaragoza, which necessarily had to be controlled to ensure the passage of the troops and to maintain the communication between Pamplona, Zaragoza and Girona open and secured.

At the Gates of Zaragoza

The most direct and busiest route between Pamplona and Zaragoza was the old Roman road that connected Pamplona with Gracurris (nearby Alfaro), Allabone (Alagon), and Caesaraugusta (Zaragoza) covering approximately 200 kilometres (124 miles). Not considering the time consumed capturing the aforementioned cities (Cortes, Valtierra, Monjardín, and Tudela), the Carolingian army would have taken two long weeks to reach Zaragoza from Pamplona. Thus, it is possible that after four months of campaigning, the armies met at the gates of Zaragoza by mid-July.

However, the city did not open the gates to Charlemagne.[109] The eleventh-century Mozarabic Chronicle records that the governor of Zaragoza simply refused to open the gates of the city.[110]

According to the version of *Al-Kamil fi al-Tarikh* (*The Complete History*) by Abu al-Hassan Ali ibn Muhammad ibn Muhammad (Ali 'Izz al-Din Ibn

---

107 Besides the above mentioned the *Karlamagnús saga* also mentions Montgardig that has been identified as Monjardín.

108 It is not unreasonable to think that in the context of the campaign of 778, Abu Taur undertook a punitive operation against the Basques in northern Huesca, a military operation that the Muslims led by Abd al-Malik had already attempted in the campaign of 732-734. Also, years later, in 824, Ludovico Pio's forces commanded by counts Aeblus and Aznar would be defeated by the Basques and their allies in the vicinity of Jaca.

109 Ibn al-Athir, *Annales du Maghreb & de l'Espagne traduites et annotées par Edmond Fagnan*, Typographie Adolphe Jourdan, Alger, 1898, pp. 128-129.

110 Lafuente Alcántara, Emilio (ed.), *Ajbar Machmua (Colección de tradiciones), Crónica anónima del siglo XI*, Real Academia de la Historia, Madrid, 1867, p. 103. See also, *Coloquios de Roncesvalles*, Institución Príncipe de Viana, Iruñea/Pamplona, 1956, p. 42. The same text is in Codera, Francisco, *Discursos leídos ante la Real Academia de la Historia en la recepción*, Impresor de los Señores Rojas, 1879, p. 72. Ibn al-Athir simply recorded that Sulayman resorted to Charlemagne and promised to deliver the city and Ta'laba to him; but when the emperor came to him, he only gave Ta'laba to him and refused to open the gates of the city. See Estornés Lasa, Bernardo, *Historia General de Euskal Herria. 476-824 época vascona*, in *Enciclopedia General Ilustrada del País Vasco*, vol. 2, Auñamendi, Donostia, 1981, p. 202.

al-Athir al-Jazari), Hussain ibn Yahya al-Ansari, *wali* of Zaragoza, refused to render the place because in his opinion he had never promised allegiance to the Frankish king. The version by the Muslim chronicler Ibn al-Athir is more explicit than the Mozarabic Chronicle of the eleventh century, and contradicts it; al-Athir states that Hussain ibn Yahya al-Ansari did not promise obedience to Charlemagne but to Sulayman ibn al-Arabi, governor of Barcelona and Girona.[111] This suggests that Hussain ibn Yahya al-Ansari, governor of Zaragoza was somehow subordinated to Sulayman ibn al-Arabi. The chronicler al-Athir also says that Hussain gave Ta'iaba ibn 'Obeyd [Ta'laba ibn 'Ubayd] to Charlemagne as a pledge, who was captured when leading the army sent by Abd al-Rahman I to besiege and occupy Zaragoza, and in exchange for whom Charlemagne could ask a good ransom.[112]

Following the Frankish sources, we must assume that the Muslim envoys had agreed in Paderborn to hand the keys of the cities of Girona, Barcelona, and Zaragoza (and perhaps also Huesca)[113] to Charlemagne. It is therefore difficult to explain the sudden change in attitude of the governor of Zaragoza Hussain ibn Yahya al-Ansari. While the chroniclers are not at all explicit about it, it seems in fact that Hussein was somehow dependent of Sulayman ibn al-Arabi, probably under a treaty of protectorate or vassalage, which would explain the promise made by the latter to Charlemagne in Paderborn and the subsequent decision of the king to arrest him and take Sulayman with him back to the court. The *Annales qui dicuntur Annales Laurissenses maiores et Einhardi* record that Ibn al-Arabi 'cum aliis Sarracenis sociis suis' went to the diet held in Paderborn, which leads us to think that he was the single most powerful warlord or the main leader of the region.[114] The *Einhardi Fuldensis Annales* record

111 Recorded as *Ibinalardi* or *Ezirlabio*.

112 Estornés Lasa, Bernardo, *Historia General de Euskal Herria. 476-824 época vascona*, in *Enciclopedia General Ilustrada del País Vasco*, vol. 2, Auñamendi, Donostia, 1981, p. 202. See also, Menéndez Pidal, Ramón, *La Chanson de Roland y el neotradicionalismo*, Espasa-Calpe, Madrid, 1959, p. 470.

113 No historical source gives definite information on this point. It is reasonable to assume that Charlemagne would not undertake a campaign on the Ebro valley facing the Emirate of Cordoba without the support of the leaders of the main strongholds of the area. For this reason, we can conclude that the decision of al-Ansari was taken later and took Charlemagne by surprise.

114 Kurze, Friedrich (ed.), *Annales regni Francorum (741–829) qui dicuntur Annales Laurissenses maiores et Einhardi*, Monumenta Germaniae Historica (MGH), SSRG, VI, Hannover, 1895, p. 49 & 51. The *Annales Einhardi* also recorded it in Pertz, Georg Heinrich (ed.), *Annales et chronica aevi Carolini*, Monumenta Germaniae Historica (MGH), SS, I, Hannover, 1826, p. 159.

only the presence of Sulayman at the diet and give the title of *praefectus Caesaraugustae* to him.[115] Instead, the Arab chronicles record Hussain ibn Yahya al-Ansari as governor of Zaragoza.[116] It is thus difficult to know whether the ties among the Muslim leaders of Girona and Zaragoza resulted from a stable political agreement or were simply a relationship of economic and military dependence, which seems more plausible in light of the Arab chronicles.

Hussain's refusal to open the doors of Zaragoza is even more difficult to explain considering that it was a last-minute decision, since otherwise Sulayman would not have come to Charlemagne to offer himself. On the other hand, it should be noted that Sulayman had to go through Zaragoza to reach Pamplona from Girona; hence Hussain's decision must have been taken when both Frankish armies were approaching Zaragoza.[117] It is probable that the attitude of Charlemagne in Pamplona did alarm al-Ansari and that the Muslim leader considered that Zaragoza would suffer the same fate as the later. While historical sources do not comment about the order to destroy Pamplona, literary sources agree in describing the Carolingian troops sacking a number of places, looting and dragging away a rich treasure. Cities like Cortes and Tudela were not in the hands of the Basques but rather controlled by Islamized Basques or mixed populations of Muslims and Islamized Basques. This hypothesis is also supported by the fact that Hussain offered money to Charlemagne, indicating that he did not face him and, to some extent, sought to appease the king by offering him some compensation.

The most plausible explanation is that the attitude of the troops of King Charles at Pamplona induced Hussain ibn Yahya al-Ansari, *wali* of Zaragoza, to fear that his city would suffer the same fate as Pamplona. In addition, the geopolitical situation of al-Ansari had improved markedly in the months between the conclusion of the Paderborn diet in spring and the winter of 777. Al-Ansari had defended the city of Zaragoza against the troops sent by the emir of Cordoba Abd al-Rahman in the autumn of 777 and had even

---

115 Pertz, Georg Heinrich (ed.), *Annales et chronica aevi Carolini*, Monumenta Germaniae Historica (MGH), SS, I, Hannover, 1826, pp. 349.

116 Fagnan, Edmond (ed.), *Histoire de l'Afrique du Nord et de l'Espagne intitulée Al-Bayano'l-Mogrib*, vol. 2, Imprimerie Orientale, Argelia, 1904, p. 90. See also, Ibn al-Athir, *Annales du Maghreb & de l'Espagne traduites et annotées par Edmond Fagnan*, Typographie Adolphe Jourdan, Alger, 1898, pp. 128-129 & 141.

117 The *Annalium Petavianorum Pars Secunda* record that Charlemagne received Sulayman ibn al-Arabi in Pamplona. See Pertz, Georg Heinrich (ed.), *Annales et chronica aevi Carolini*, Monumenta Germaniae Historica (MGH), SS, I, Hannover, 1826, p. 16.

captured the commander of the besieging army, Ta'iaba ibn 'Obeyd.[118] This crushing victory over the troops of the emir allowed al-Ansari to become king of Zaragoza and the adjacent lands without undergoing the 'protection' of Charlemagne and, above all, without the payment of such military 'assistance'.

The Arab historian Al-Athir says that in order to satisfy Charlemagne, al-Ansari gave Ta'iaba ibn 'Obeyd [Ta'laba ibn' Ubayd] to him, for which he could ask a good ransom. The *Annales Mettenses Priores* and the *Annales Tiliani* mention that the king received presents from Ibn al-Arabi and Abu Taur (*obsidibus receptis ab Abinolarbi et Apotauro*). Meanwhile the *Annales Petaviani* and the *Annales Nazarianorum continuatio alteri Laureshemnsium parti subiicitur* exaggerate the facts and state that the Frankish king took al-Ansari himself to Herstal, thus suggesting that the Franks had conquered Zaragoza, something that the rest of the Frankish and Muslim chronicles belie.

It is logical to assume that Charlemagne decided not to place the city under siege. The siege of Pavia in 773-774 had lasted ten months, and the Carolingian troops did not have the necessary machinery to undertake a siege of the magnitude required to take a city like Zaragoza since the king simply had not planned for it in advance.[119] Also, Hussain's attitude would probably have moved Charlemagne to rethink the whole political picture since the *Marca Hispanica* required a stable and solid control of the main cities of the Ebro valley and the unwavering political position of the Muslim rulers. In fact, subsequent historical events indicate that, after the military and political failure of the 778 campaign, the construction of the so-called *Marca Gothica* between 785 and 800 was only possible by virtue of the conquest and capture of the main Muslim cities of the area and the subsequent transfer of the political and military control of these places to Frankish governors.

---

118 Lafuente Alcántara, Emilio (ed.), *Ajbar Machmua (Colección de tradiciones), Crónica anónima del siglo XI*, Real Academia de la Historia, Madrid, 1867, p. 103. See also, *Coloquios de Roncesvalles*, Institución Príncipe de Viana, Iruñea/Pamplona, 1956, p. 42; Codera, Francisco, *Discursos leídos ante la Real Academia de la Historia en la recepción*, Impresor de los Señores Rojas, 1879, p. 72; Estornés Lasa, Bernardo, *Historia General de Euskal Herria. 476-824 época vascona*, in *Enciclopedia General Ilustrada del País Vasco*, vol. 2, Auñamendi, Donostia, 1981, p. 202; Chalmeta Gendrón, Pedro, *Invasión e islamización: la sumisión de Hispania y la formación de al-Andalus*, Universidad de Jaén, Jaén, 2003, p. 368.

119 The weather should be taken into account. The average maximum temperature in July in Zaragoza is 33° Celsius (91.4° Fahrenheit). However, in July 2015, the temperature in Zaragoza rose to 44.5° Celsius (112.1° Fahrenheit).

Furthermore, the situation worsened. The emir of Cordoba sent reinforce-
ment troops and occupied the area nearby Barcelona, closing the Carolingian
army's path of retreat through the eastern Pyrenees. Contrary to *Chronicon
Moissiacense*, the *Annales Mettenses Priores*, or the *Annales Petaviani* record,
Charlemagne did not order a retreat when the news of Widukind's rebellion
in Saxony reached him, a notification he would not have received by his
arrival in Auxerre.[120] Moreover, none of the Frankish chronicles record a
siege of Zaragoza, and most of them do not even mention explicitly the
physical presence of the emperor before the city, which we primarily know
about through the Arab sources or the Mozarabic Chronicle of the eleventh
century.[121] The *Annales Regni Francorum* and the *Vita Karoli Magni* do
not mention anything at all, and the *Annales qui dicuntur Einhardi*, the
Annales Mettenses Priores, and the *Annales Laurissenses* simply record that
Charlemagne crossed the river Ebro and received Sulayman ibn al-Arabi
and Abu Taur, governor of Huesca, under vassalage.[122]

   Thus, probably before 5 August, after no more than a week in front of the
gates of Zaragoza, both columns retreated to Pamplona, where they arrived
ten or fifteen days later, during the first week of August. Most likely they

---

120 McKitterick, Rosamond, *Charlemagne: The Formation of a European Identity*, Cambridge
University Press, Cambridge, 2008, p. 223. The event was also recorded in the *Chronicon Moissiacense* in King, P. D., *Charlemagne: Translated Sources*, P. D. King, Lambrigg, Kendal, Cumbria,
1987, p. 152. Albeit less explicitly, the *Annales de Petau* record that Charlemagne received the
news of the rebellion of Widukind while he was campaigning in Hispania: 'Meanwhile, the
Saxons rebelled, mobilized an army and moved quickly on the banks of the river Rhine. The
Saxon have burned cities and had set fire to the city that the Franks had built on the banks
of the river Lippe'. King, P. D., *Charlemagne: Translated Sources*, P. D. King, Lambrigg, Kendal,
Cumbria, 1987, p. 152. As for the *Annales Mettenses Priores* see Simson, Bernhard von (ed.),
Annales Mettenses Priores, Monumenta Germaniae Historica (MGH), SSRG, X, Hannover &
Leipzig, 1905, p. 67.
121 Lafuente Alcántara, Emilio (ed.), *Ajbar Machmua (Colección de tradiciones)*, *Crónica anónima
del siglo XI*, Real Academia de la Historia, Madrid, 1867, p. 103. See also, *Coloquios de Roncesvalles*,
Institución Príncipe de Viana, Iruñea/Pamplona, 1956, p. 42; Codera, Francisco, *Discursos leídos
ante la Real Academia de la Historia en la recepción*, Impresor de los Señores Rojas, 1879, p. 72;
Estornés Lasa, Bernardo, *Historia General de Euskal Herria. 476-824 época vascona*, in *Enciclopedia
General Ilustrada del País Vasco*, vol. 2, Auñamendi, Donostia, 1981, p. 202.
122 Kurze, Friedrich (ed.), *Annales regni Francorum (741–829) qui dicuntur Annales Laurissenses
maiores et Einhardi*, Monumenta Germaniae Historica (MGH), SSRG, VI, Hannover, 1895, p. 51.
The *Annales Mettenses Priores* record the following: '*Coniunxerunt autem se uterque exercitus
ad Cesaraugustam munitissimam urbem; in qua expeditione obsidibus receptis ab Abinolarbi et
Apotauro.*' In Simson, Bernhard von (ed.), *Annales Mettenses Priores*, Monumenta Germaniae
Historica (MGH), SSRG, X, Hannover & Leipzig, 1905, p. 67. As for the *Annales Laurissenses*, see
Pertz, Georg Heinrich (ed.), *Annales et chronica aevi Carolini*, Monumenta Germaniae Historica
(MGH), SS, I, Hannover, 1826, p. 158.

followed the same route they took to Zaragoza, through the old Roman road that connected Zaragoza, Allabone, Gracurris, and Pompaelo.

Retreat and Destruction of Pamplona

Charlemagne therefore decided to retreat but, aware of the danger, demanded a reward and the delivery of hostages to ensure that the army would not be attacked on the way back. Sources agree that he took with him Sulayman ibn al-Arabi and Kasmin ibn Yusuf; however, Ibn al-Athir narrates that, 'when Carlos left the Muslim territory and believed himself safe' upon entering Vasconia, probably somewhere between Tudela and Pamplona, 'Matruh and Aishun, Suleyman's children, fell on top of him with his troops and freed their father. They returned together to Zaragoza, allied with al-Hussain and continued the revolt against Abd al-Rahman I.'[123]

On their way through Pamplona, Charlemagne ordered the destruction of the city ('Pampilonam urbem destruit').[124] The *Vita Karoli Magni* only records that Charlemagne retreated to Errozabal 'salvo et incolomi'.[125] The *Annales Mettenses Priores* records that 'the mighty city of Pamplona was captured and later destroyed'.[126] The same thing is recorded by the *Annales Regni Francorum*,[127] the *Annales Tiliani*,[128] and the *Annales Laurissenses*.[129]

123 Estornés Lasa, Bernardo, *Historia General de Euskal Herria. 476-824 época vascona*, in *Enciclopedia General Ilustrada del País Vasco*, vol. 2, Auñamendi, Donostia, 1981, p. 236. See also, *Coloquios de Roncesvalles*, Institución Príncipe de Viana, Iruñea/Pamplona, 1956, pp. 51 & 57; Menéndez Pidal, Ramón, *La Chanson de Roland y el neotradicionalismo*, Espasa-Calpe, Madrid, 1959, p. 192.

124 *Einhardi Fuldensis Annales*, in Pertz, Georg Heinrich (ed.), *Annales et chronica aevi Carolini*, Monumenta Germaniae Historica (MGH), SS, I, Hannover, 1826, p. 349.

125 Holder-Egger, Oswald (ed.), *Einhardi Vita Karoli Magni*, Monumenta Germaniae Historica (MGH), SSRG, Hannover & Leipzig, 1911, p. 12.

126 In the original Latin: '*Pampilona firmissima civitate capta atque destructa.*' In Simson, Bernhard von (ed.), *Annales Mettenses Priores*, Monumenta Germaniae Historica (MGH), SSRG, X, Hannover & Leipzig, 1905, p. 67.

127 *Pampilona destructa*, in Kurze, Friedrich (ed.), *Annales regni Francorum (741–829) qui dicuntur Annales Laurissenses maiores et Einhardi*, Monumenta Germaniae Historica (MGH), SSRG, VI, Hannover, 1895, p. 50.

128 *Pampalonia distructa*, in Pertz, Georg Heinrich (ed.), *Annales et chronica aevi Carolini*, Monumenta Germaniae Historica (MGH), SS, I, Hannover, 1826, pp. 220-221.

129 *Pampilona distructa*, in Pertz, Georg Heinrich (ed.), *Annales et chronica aevi Carolini*, Monumenta Germaniae Historica (MGH), SS, I, Hannover, 1826, p. 158. The *Petri Bibliothecarii Historia Francorum Abbreviata*, that follows the aforementioned sources, records that in 778, '*Carlus in Hispania Pampilonem destruxit*'. Pertz, Georg Heinrich (ed.), *Annales et chronica aevi Carolini*, Monumenta Germaniae Historica (MGH), SS, I, Hannover, 1826, p. 417. The *Regionionis*

The *Annales de Gestis Caroli Magni* of the Saxon poet, the *Einhardi Annales*, and the *Annales qui dicuntur Einhardi* are more explicit and state that the king, understanding that the city could not be controlled and preserved and in order to prevent a rebellion, decided to tear down its walls and marched to the north through the passage of Errozabal.[130] The Saxon poet also narrates in laconic verses that the troops of Charlemagne 'returned to Pamplona, and razed its walls, so it did not rebel'.[131]

Neither the destruction of a city nor the demolition of such thick walls is an easy task; it is not something that can be carried out in the short span of a few days. Considering that Pamplona was again a walled city just a few decades later, we may deduce that the order was limited to burning and looting the city, without conducting a thorough demolition of the walls.

In any case, the order to destroy Pamplona indicates that Charlemagne was aware of the failure of the expedition before undertaking the passage through the Pyrenees. The king understood that the walled city would be used against his troops; that is, Pamplona had been taken by force, but the Basques had not been subjugated and his Muslim partners were not as faithful and reliable as he had thought. It also indicates that the king was aware that after his departure not even a garrison would be able to keep the control over the city and its region, or on the road that ran towards the continental Vasconia across the Pyrenees.

Following Aymeric Picaud's *Pilgrims' Guide*, there is a significant distance between Pamplona and Errozabal plain, ascending to where the town of Auritz is located, on a flatter area, among forests. Indeed, there are 40.4 kilometres and two strong mountain passes in between these two places, with a difference in height of 457 metres. It is therefore very difficult to suppose that the army could get through this difficult stretch of mountain in less than four stages:[132]

Chronicon records the same: '*Eiectis, itaque Sarraceni de Pampilona, murisque eiusdem civitatis dirutis, Vasconibusque subiugatis, in Franciam revertitur.*' In Pertz, Georg Heinrich (ed.), *Annales et chronica aevi Carolini*, Monumenta Germaniae Historica (MGH), SS, I, Hannover, 1826, p. 559.

130 The *Annales qui dicuntur Einhardi*, in Kurze, Friedrich (ed.), *Annales regni Francorum (741–829) qui dicuntur Annales Laurissenses maiores et Einhardi*, Monumenta Germaniae Historica (MGH), SSRG, VI, Hannover, 1895, p. 51. The *Einhadi Annales* record the same event, see Pertz, Georg Heinrich (ed.), *Annales et chronica aevi Carolini*, Monumenta Germaniae Historica (MGH), SS, I, Hannover, 1826, p. 159.

131 Pertz, Georg Heinrich (ed.), *Annales et chronica aevi Carolini*, Monumenta Germaniae Historica (MGH), SS, I, Hannover, 1826, pp. 234.

132 Picaud's *Guide* claims that a pilgrim could cover in a single day the 35 kilometres from Pamplona to Bizkarreta (Erro), crossing in his way two severe mountain passes, the Arre pass and the Erro pass. Undoubtedly, this was virtually impossible to walk in a single day for an

1. 13.5 kilometres (8.4 miles) from Pamplona to Zuriain. Elevation: 50 metres (ascent from 436 metres to 484 metres).
2. 8 kilometres (5 miles) from Zuriain to Zubiri. Elevation: 52 metres (ascent from 484 metres to 536 metres).
3. 10.3 kilometres (6.4 miles) from Zubiri to Bizkarreta. Elevation: 246 metres (ascent from 536 metres to 782 metres).
4. 8.6 kilometres (5.3 miles) from Bizkarreta to Auritz (on the esplanade of Errozabal). Elevation: 111 metres (ascent from 782 metres to 893 metres).

After completing the ascension, the Carolingian army needed to complete two further days of sharp decline to cross the Pyrenees: 14.1 kilometres (8.76 miles) from Auritz to Luzaide through the strategic hill of Ibañeta with a maximum altitude of 694 metres (ascension from 890 metres to 1,062 metres),[133] and then finally overcome the 14-kilometer (8.7-mile) descent to Luzaide (368 metres). Additionally, the army would have to cover 11 kilometres more until reaching Donibane Garazi beyond the Zize pass.

In sum, after abandoning Pamplona to the flames, on the morning of 11 August, Sunday, the Frankish army rushed through the road along the Esteribar Valley to Zubiri and spent the night in the forecourt of Zuriain. The next day the army faced a second march to Zubiri, on the slopes of Erro pass, after making a journey of about 21 kilometres in two days (13 miles). Following the Picaud's *Pilgrim's Guide*, the following day (Tuesday 13), the army ascended the Erro pass, and the troop would camp after a hard 10-kilometer (6.2-mile) march an ascension, all along the road linking Lintzoain, Bizkarreta, and Mezkiritz, at the foothills of the mountain pass.

The next morning, 14 August, Wednesday, the army ascended from Bizkarreta through the Mezkiritz pass until the plain of Errozabal, around Auritz, completing an uphill march of 8.6 kilometres (5.3 miles). On Thursday 15 August, the army was to undertake the journey that connects Auritz with Luzaide, a difficult and convoluted mountain descent from Ibañeta hill to Luzaide for approximately 14 kilometres (8.7 miles). According to the

---

army of the magnitude of the Carolingian army. See Vielliard, Jeanne, *Le guide du pèlerin de Saint-Jacques de Compostelle: texte latin du XIIe siècle*, Librairie Philosophique J. Vrin, Paris, 1984, p. 6.

133 Coordinates:
  Lat.: 43° 5' 35.469» N. Lon.: 1° 18' 4.718» W
  UTM: x = 638,256 m. y = 4,772,649 m
  Altitude: 368 metres.

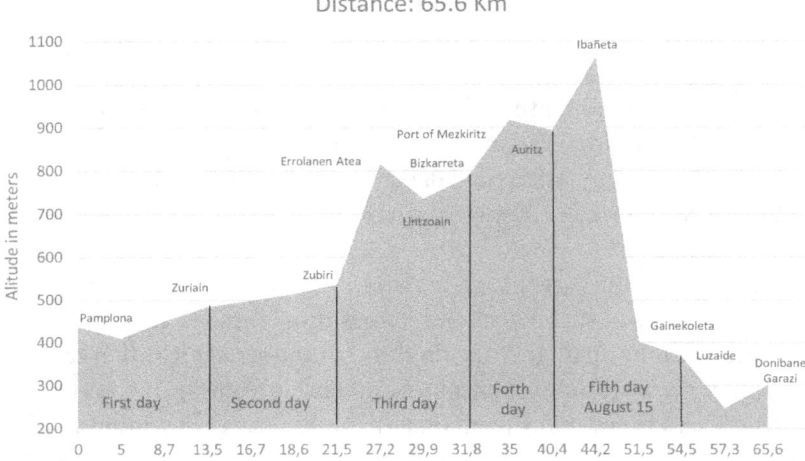

Graphic altimetry in scale of Charlemagne's route along the Pyrenees.

Pilgrims' Guide, Charlemagne was forced to stay overnight in Luzaide, so the town was named after him Valcarlos, the town in Charlemagne's valley.[134]

As the *Annalium de Gestis Caroli Magni* records, the Basques harassed the Frankish army along their way from Pamplona to the north (towards Errozabal) in successive but reduced waves, continually pursuing and pushing their enemy into the Ibañeta funnel where, according to the Saxon poet, the Basques undertook a new and decisive assault (*proelia temptant nova*).[135]

134 *Liber Quartus S. Jacobi Apostoli*, in Rialle, Girard de; Vinson, Julien (eds.), *Revue de Linguistique et de Philologie Comparée*, vol. 15, Maisonneuve de Cie, Libraires-éditeurs, 1882, p. 15. See an English version in Melczer, William (ed.), *The Pilgrim's Guide to Santiago de Compostela*, Italica Press Inc., New York, 1993. For this episode see, p. 93.

135 Pertz, Georg Heinrich (ed.), *Annales et chronica aevi Carolini*, Monumenta Germaniae Historica (MGH), SS, I, Hannover, 1826, p. 234. See also, Jimeno Jurio, José María, *¿Dónde fue la batalla de Roncesvalles?*, Diputación Foral de Navarra, Institución Príncipe de Viana, Iruñea/ Pamplona, 1974, p. 31.

3. The Battle of Errozabal in Light of the Frankish Sources

Abstract

This chapter describes the military operation, marches, fights and outcome of King Charles' venture in August 778 with a detailed description of the route and the location of the Carolingian army's defeat. It therefore provides a comprehensive description of the action in the light of Medieval historical sources including a wide-ranging description of the characteristics of both armies, numbers and relative position in the battlefield, weaponry and clothing, and the strategic factors leading to the collapse of the Carolingian army and the resultant massacre in the Pyrenees. Based on original historical sources and a careful study of the terrain with the help of the Rangers of the Government of Navarre and expert archaeologists of the region, this is one of the most accurate and detailed description of the battle ever written.

Keywords: 778, Rencesvals, Errozabal, Charlemagne, Roland, Eneko

The Frankish historical sources present serious problems of interpretation. The chronicles did not record the events of the campaign against Vasconia in 778 during Charlemagne's life, and the chroniclers who wrote immediately after the emperor's death recorded the episode from a subjective standpoint. For instance, Eginhard states in the *Vita Karoli Magni* that 'Charlemagne crossed the Pyrenees, obtained the capitulation of all places and castles that stood in his way, and returned with his army safe and unharmed',[1] which is far from accurate. The author sought to avoid any mention of the failure of the campaign of 778, omitted any reference to the battle, obviated the events that took place at the gates of Zaragoza and avoided any reference to the

---

1 *Salvo et incolomi exercitu revertitur*, in Holder-Egger, Oswald (ed.), *Einhardi Vita Karoli Magni*, Monumenta Germaniae Historica (MGH), SSRG, Hannover & Leipzig, 1911, p. 12.

Irujo, X., *Charlemagne's Defeat in the Pyrenees: The Battle of Rencesvals*. Taylor & Francis, 2021
DOI 10.5117/9789463721059_CH03

events around Pamplona, which ultimately led to the order of destruction of the city and the final withdrawal of the Carolingian troops from Vasconia.

Virtually all the major sources converted failure into victory. In this sense, the Frankish sources strove to emphasize the actual submission of the Basques, which contradicts the events that took place in Errozabal. The *Annales Mettenses Priores*, the *Annales Laurissenses*, the *Einhardi Fuldensis Annales*, and the *Reginionis Chronicon* record that, once the Hispanics,[2] the Basques,[3] and the Navarrese[4] capitulated, the king returned victorious to his country.[5] The *Annales Regni Francorum* also records that Charlemagne returned to his country after having subdued the Basques,[6] and the *Annales Tiliani* and the *Annales Regni Francorum* also record that after having confronted the Basques, Charlemagne returned to France.[7] Only a few sources such as the *Annales Sangallenses Baluzii* record that the campaign was a failure, *ibi dispendium habuit grande.*[8]

Charlemagne's defeat at Errozabal has been the cause of rivers of ink to flow, but in fact the Frankish army was already defeated and in retreat when the king gave the order to burn Pamplona. The Saxon poet specifies that the Basques fought a battle 'once again' in Errozabal ('and they attempted

---

2   Muslims.

3   Basques from continental Vasconia.

4   Basques from peninsular Vasconia.

5   The *Annales Mettenses Priores* record that: *'Hispanis, Wasconibus et Nabarris subiugatis, victor in patriam reversus est.'* In Simson, Bernhard von (ed.), *Annales Mettenses Priores*, Monumenta Germaniae Historica (MGH), SSRG, X, Hannover & Leipzig, 1905, p. 67. The *Annales Laurissenses* state: *'Pampilona distructa, Hispani Wascones subiugatos, etiam et Nabarros, reversus in partibus Franciae.'* Pertz, Georg Heinrich (ed.), *Annales Laureshamenses, Alamannici, Guelferbytani et Nazariani*, Monumenta Germaniae Historica (MGH), SS, I, Hannover, 1826, p. 158. The *Einhardi Fuldensis Annales*: *'Wasconibus et Nabarris subactis revertitur in Franciam.'* In Pertz, Georg Heinrich (ed.), *Annales et chronica aevi Carolini*, Monumenta Germaniae Historica (MGH), SS, I, Hannover, 1826, p. 349. The *Reginionis Chronicon*: *'Vasconibusque subiugatis, in Franciam revertitur.'* In Pertz, Georg Heinrich (ed.), *Annales et chronica aevi Carolini*, Monumenta Germaniae Historica (MGH), SS, I, Hannover, 1826, p. 559.

6   *'Hispani Wascones subiugatos, etiam et Nabarros, reversus in partibus Franciae':* D'Abadal i de Vinyals, Ramon, *Catalunya Carolingia. El Domini Carolingi a Catalunya*, Barcelona, 1986, p. 44.

7   *Annales Regni Francorum:* *'Hispani Wascones subiugatos, etiam et Nabarros, reversus in partibus Franciae.'* In Kurze, Friedrich (ed.), *Annales regni Francorum (741–829) qui dicuntur Annales Laurissenses maiores et Einhardi*, Monumenta Germaniae Historica (MGH), SSRG, VI, Hannover, 1895, p. 50.

8   In the original Latin: *'778. Hoc anno domnus rex Karlus perrexit in Spania, et ibi dispendium habuit grande.'* Pertz, Georg Heinrich (ed.), *Annales et chronica aevi Carolini*, Monumenta Germaniae Historica (MGH), SS, I, Hannover, 1826, p. 63.

to fight again');[9] that is, Franks and Basques had fought for the control of Pamplona and the route that connected the city to the southern boundary of Vasconia, on the road to Zaragoza. The destruction of Pamplona was the result of Charlemagne's inability to create the *Marca Hispanica*, beyond the Pyrenees.

In line with the above, Astronomus Limosinus's *Vita Hludowici Pii imperatoris* and the *Reginionis Chronicon* confuses Muslims with Basques.[10] The chroniclers try to describe Charlemagne's campaign in terms of a crusade against Islam, but the Arabic chronicles of the period do not mention the battle of Errozabal, which reveals that no Muslim warlord participated in that struggle and that they did not even have accurate news of what had happened.

Furthermore, the Frankish sources leave open several key aspects, such as the specific names of the warlords who led the Basques in the battlefield and a complete record of the Frankish leaders who lost their lives there. In some cases these omissions are covered by other secondary sources, but unfortunately in other cases only comprehensive archaeological surveys or the possible discovery of new sources can fill the gaps still surrounding this episode.

The eighteenth window of the Chartres cathedral depicts Charlemagne riding through Ibañeta, which took place on Thursday, 15 August, 778. The exact date of the battle was established by Ernst Dümmler in an manuscript discovered by Weflin-Trall in the National Library in Paris containing the epitaph of Agiardo or Eggihard (*Aggiardus*), seneschal of the emperor's palace ('and he was the first at the king's court'), one of the warriors killed in the battle.[11] The Latin manuscript sets the date of his death, 'die XVIII Kalendas septembrias', that is, 15 August.[12] However, we must bear in mind that this is sensu stricto the date of the Palatine's death, and that the sources

---

9   The Saxon poet's *Annales de Gestis Caroli Magni Libri V*: '*Insidias eius summo sub vertice montis tendere Wascones ausi*.' In Pertz, Georg Heinrich (ed.), *Annales et chronica aevi Carolini*, Monumenta Germaniae Historica (MGH), SS, I, Hannover, 1826, p. 234.

10   The *Vita Hludowici Pii imperatoris* mentions that, '*ad Hispaniam pergere laborantique ecclesiae sub Sarracenorum acerbissimo iugo Christo fautore suffragari*'. In Tremp, Ernst (ed.), *Astronomus. Das Leben Kaiser Ludwigs (Vita Hludowici imperatoris)*, Monumenta Germaniae Historica (MGH), SSRG, LXIV, Hannover, 1995, p. 286. The *Reginionis Chronicon*: '*Eiectis itaque Sarracenis de Pampilona, murisque eiusdem civitatis dirutis, Vasconibusque subiugatis, in Franciam revertitur*.' Pertz, Georg Heinrich (ed.), *Annales et chronica aevi Carolini*, Monumenta Germaniae Historica (MGH), SS, I, Hannover, 1826, p. 559.

11   As will be discussed later, the battle did not take place in one day only, but most probably extended through the five-day march of the Carolingian army over the Pyrenees.

12   Dümmler, Ernst; Strecker, Karl; Traube, Ludwig, *Poetae Latini aevi Carolini*, Monumenta Germaniae Historica (MGH), Berlin, 1881, vol. 1, pp. 109-10.

mention that the Basques 'attacked again' when the Carolingian army went into the Zize pass ('nova proelia temptant').

Taking this date as the day of the attack at the Zize pass, Charles would have left Pamplona on 11 August, Sunday, and as already noted, after four days of hard marching, most probably camped on the plain of Errozabal on Wednesday, 14 August. The next day, on Thursday, 15 August, 778, the Frankish army departed from Errozabal and headed through Ibañeta and towards Donibane Garazi along the Zize pass. The Saxon poet conveniently set the end of the battle at sunset, which, together with the prevailing panic and disarray of the troops, prevented the king from avenging the death of his paladins and from recovering his treasure. The poet avoids making any mention of the king's flight leaving his army behind at the mercy of the enemy and abandoning his treasure. However, as we gather from reading the *Annales de Gestis Caroli Magni Libri V*, the battle probably began immediately after the Carolingian army left Pamplona, and, given the magnitude of the battle, it likely was prolonged by at least one or several days after the 'tumultuous' attack that took place in Ibañeta on Thursday, 15 August.[13]

The Frankish chronicles provide only three accurate dates for the entire 778 campaign. The first one is Sunday 14 April, the date of the celebration of Easter in Cassinogilum. The second is the date of Eggihard's death, and the third key date is provided by sources is October 778, when the chroniclers locate, with some margin of error, Charlemagne in the vicinity of Herstal, specifically in the town of Gôdene (Godinne).[14] These are the only three dates that allow us to frame the campaign chronologically.

The contemporary historical sources do not mention Errozabal or the Zize pass. They just state that once Pamplona was devastated, the Carolingian army went into the Pyreenean forests ('Pyrinei saltum ingressus est'), that the army was ambushed at the hilltop of the Pyrenees ('summitate'), and that in that mountain the king lost his army ('in eodem Mount'). Einhard's *Vita Karoli Magni* simply mentions the chain or passage connecting both sides of the Pyrenees (Pyrinei iugo) and the Saxon poet only mentions that the Basques engaged in combat 'at the foot of these mountains' summit' ('sub vertex montis').

---

13   Pertz, Georg Heinrich (ed.), *Annales et chronica aevi Carolini*, Monumenta Germaniae Historica (MGH), SS, I, Hannover, 1826, p. 234.

14   Estornés Lasa, Bernardo, *Historia General de Euskal Herria. 476-824 época vascona*, in *Enciclopedia General Ilustrada del País Vasco*, vol. 2, Auñamendi, Donostia, 1981, p. 272. See also, Ganshof, François-Louis, "Une crise dans le règne de Charlemagne. Les années 776 et 779", in Roth, Charles; Gilliard, Charles (eds.), *Mélanges d'histoire et de littérature offerts à Monsieur Charles Gilliard, professeur honoraire de l'Université de Lausanne, à l'occasion de son soixante-cinquiéme anniversaire*, F. Rouge & Cie., Lausanne, 1944, p. 137.

The first mention of Errozabal (Rozaballes) and, more specifically, of the Zize pass (Portum Sicera)[15] as the location of the battle is recorded in the *Nota Emilianense* from the eleventh century,[16] discovered in 1954 by Damaso Alonso in the monastery of San Millán de la Cogolla, Rioja, which specifies that 'as the army passed through the Zize pass, Roland was killed in Errozabal at the hands of the Saracens'.[17]

The *Chanson de Roland* (stanza 44, line 584) also locates the events of the battle in Zize:

'Good Knight Guenes' said King Marsiliun
'How can I kill Roland?'
Guenes responds: 'I'm going to tell you,
The king will go to the vast Zize pass,
He will leave behind his rear;[']'[18]

And by mouth of Malprimis de Brigal, *who runs faster on foot than on a horse*, the Chanson also mentions Errozabal (Rencesvals) in stanza 71, line 892:

Along with Marsiliun he screams very high:
'I will risk my life in Errozabal,
If I meet Roland, I'll kill him!'[19]

15   The *Zize* pass that the Latin sources record as *Portus Sicera, Sizer* or *Cisera* and the Muslim chroniclers as *Bort-Jezar* or *Schzezar*. Picaud's *Pilgrims' Guide* (or *Liber V* of the *Liber Sancti Jacobi*) also mentions the *Cisera* pass on the hills of Donibane Garazi (*Saint-Jean-Pie-de-Port* in French).

16   It may be dated between 1065 and 1075.

17   In the original Latin: '*Deinde placuit ad regem, pro salutem hominum exercituum, ut Rodlane, belligerator Fortis, cum suis posterum ueniret. At ubi exercitum portum di Sicera transiret, in Rozaballes a gentibus sarracenorum fuit Rodlane occiso.*' Alonso, Dámaso, *La primitiva épica francesa a la luz de una nota emilianense*, Revista de Filología española, 37, Madrid, 1953, pp. 1-94. Also in Alonso, Dámaso, *La primitiva épica francesa a la luz de una nota emilianense*, Consejo Superior de Investigaciones Científicas, Madrid, 1954. The first mention in Berganza, Francisco, *Antigüedades de España, propugnadas en las noticias de sus reyes, en la crónica del real monasterio de San pedro de Cerdeña, en historias, cronicones y otros instrumentos, manuscritos, que hasta ahora no han visto la luz pública*, Francisco de Hierro, Madrid, 1721, vol. 2, p. 560. See also, Frappier, Jean, *Les Chansons De Geste Du Cycle De Guillaume D'orange: Le Couronnement De Louis, Le Charroi De Nîmes, La Prise D'orange*, Société d'Edition d'Enseignement Supérieur, Paris, 1955, p. 78 ; Menéndez Pidal, Ramón, *La Chanson de Roland et la tradition épique des Francs*, Librairie Picard, Paris, 1960, p. 390.

18   Stanzas 56 and 210 also record the Carolingian army crossing the Pyrenees through Zize, in Müller, Theodor, *La Chanson de Roland: nach der Oxforder Handschrift*, Verlag der Dieterichschen Buchandlung, Göttingen, 1863, p. 35.

19   *Rencesvals* is mentioned fifteen times in the *Chanson* in stanzas 72 (line 901), 73 (line 912), 74 (line 923), 75 (line 934), 76 (line 944), 77 (line 963), 78 (line 985), 165 (line 2225), 181 (line

Jimeno Jurío recorded the form 'Rocidevalles' in texts of the twelfth century and the variants 'Ronçasvailles', 'Roncesvailles', and 'Roncesvalles' between the thirteenth and fifteenth centuries.[20] 'Rencesvals', 'Rozaballes', or 'Roncesvalles' (in Spanish) is the romance version of the original Basque toponym 'Errozabal', which literally means 'the plain of Erro'.[21] Errozabal is a 5-square-kilometer meadow slightly inclined from north (900 metres) to south (870 metres) where the town of Auritz is located (890 metres high). This is the only point where an army could have camped on the evening of Wednesday, 14 August, and the only wide esplanade along the road to organize a good defense around the main camp.

The Frankish chronicles also suggest that the ambush took place in the narrow Ibañeta pass, at about 4.5 kilometres north of the town Auritz, the only access to the tortuous descent into Luzaide. They do not specify any further. The Ibañeta hill, 1,062 metres high, is the bridge that connects both sides of the Pyrenees and was a key strategic point in the *Ab Asturica Burdigalam* Roman road. As we shall see, the whole battle revolved around the control of this hill, as this was the only gateway to the northern slopes of the Pyrenees.

Beyond Ibañeta, the 10.5-kilometer rough descent to Luzaide opens, along which the slaughter took place. With a very steep slope, the track has a vertical drop of 694 metres between Ibañeta and Luzaide, especially leaning over the first 7.2 kilometres downhill, until Gainekoleta, 402 metres high.[22] Four hundred years after the battle, in the twelfth century, Luzaide was already known as Valcarlos, the valley in which the emperor lost his army.

While all historical sources indicate that the battle was fought at Errozabal, along the road connecting Erro with Luzaide, opinions differ among historians in this regard, since there were two roads between Auritz and Donibane Garazi. The first one, the Zize pass, is a 27-kilometer long winding road surrounded by forests, reaching 1,062 metres in Ibañeta, connecting both locations through Luzaide and along a moderate slope

---

2483), 184 (line 2516), 195 (line 2716), 200 (line 2791), 203 line 2854), 204 (line 2855) and 246 (line 3412). In Müller, Theodor, *La Chanson de Roland: nach der Oxforder Handschrift*, Verlag der Dieterichschen Buchhandlung, Göttingen, 1863, p. 56.

20   Jimeno Jurio, José María, *Nafarroako toponimia eta mapagintza / Toponimia y cartografía de Navarra*, vol. 35, Nafarroako Gobernua, Iruñea, 1996, p. 225.

21   Errozabal > Rozaval > Rozavalles > Rocidevalles > Roncesvalles > Rencesvals

22   Coordinates:
     Lat.: 43° 4' 6.390» N. Lon.: 1° 18' 21.583» W.
     UTM: x=637,930 m. y=4,769,894 m.
     Altitude: 402 metres.

leading to Donibane Garazi. The ancient road did not run exactly along the current motorway but a little further down the valley, parallel to the existing pilgrim's path. The second road, 35 kilometres in length, ascending to 1,400 metres, follows the crests of the Pyrenean picks and, with a strong but short climb descends to Saint-Michel and Donibane Garazi.

There are three basic reasons to believe that Charlemagne's army did not go by the second path.

All contemporary sources describing the battle agree that it was an ambush;[23] undoubtedly the second route was not suitable for an ambuscade, since it runs along the highest peaks of the mountain chain and, as a consequence, any attack on this route is bound to occur bottom-up, eliminating any advantage to the attacker. Sources agree that 'the Basques descended from top of the mountain',[24] swooping down onto the army, indicating attack from higher positions. They add that 'the Franks had against them their position that was worse than that of the Basques'.[25] The Saxon poet also says that first 'the Basques shot dead the [Frankish] warriors with their projectiles, launched from the height of the hills'.[26]

The road following the crests of the Pyrenean picks is completely devoid of the trees and forests mentioned by the sources. Einhard writes in the *Vita Karoli Magni* that 'the Basques ambushed them because the thicket

23   The version of the *Annales Regni Francorum qui dicuntur Einhardi* in Kurze, Friedrich (ed.), *Annales regni Francorum (741–829) qui dicuntur Annales Laurissenses maiores et Einhardi*, Monumenta Germaniae Historica (MGH), SSRG, VI, Hannover, 1895, p. 53. The *Vita Karoli Magni* of Einhard: '*Wasconesh in summi montis vertice positis insidiis.*' In Holder-Egger, Oswald (ed.), *Einhardi Vita Karoli Magni,* Monumenta Germaniae Historica (MGH), SSRG, Hannover & Leipzig, 1911, p. 12. The *Einhardi Annales*: '*In cuius summitate Wascones insidiis conlocatis.*' In Pertz, Georg Heinrich (ed.), *Annales et chronica aevi Carolini*, Monumenta Germaniae Historica (MGH), SS, I, Hannover, 1826, p. 159. The Saxon poet's *Annales de Gestis Caroli Magni Libri V*: '*Insidias eius summo sub vertice montis tendere Wascones ausi.*' In Pertz, Georg Heinrich (ed.), *Annales et chronica aevi Carolini*, Monumenta Germaniae Historica (MGH), SS, I, Hannover, 1826, p. 234.

24   Holder-Egger, Oswald (ed.), *Einhardi Vita Karoli Magni,* Monumenta Germaniae Historica (MGH), SSRG, Hannover & Leipzig, 1911, p. 12.

25   The *Einhardi Annales* and the *Annales Regni Francorum qui dicuntur Einhardi* mention that the *iniquitate locorum* was a factor against the Frankish warriors. See Pertz, Georg Heinrich (ed.), *Annales et chronica aevi Carolini*, Monumenta Germaniae Historica (MGH), SS, I, Hannover, 1826, p. 159. For the *Annales Regni Francorum qui dicuntur Einhardi* see Kurze, Friedrich (ed.), *Annales regni Francorum (741–829) qui dicuntur Annales Laurissenses maiores et Einhardi*, Monumenta Germaniae Historica (MGH), SSRG, VI, Hannover, 1895, p. 53.

26   The Saxon poet's *Annales de Gestis Caroli Magni Libri V* states: '*Missilibus primo sternunt ex collibus altis.*' In Pertz, Georg Heinrich (ed.), *Annales et chronica aevi Carolini*, Monumenta Germaniae Historica (MGH), SS, I, Hannover, 1826, p. 234.

forest at that place was suitable for it'.[27] The Saxon poet also says that the Basques were able to 'breakaway quickly through the winding roads of the vast forest'.[28] Finally, Astronomus Limosinus's *Vita Hludowici Pii imperatoris* also mentions the thick and shady forest along the road.[29] Finally, the *Annales de Gestis Caroli Magni* indicate very accurately that the attack occurred when, on his return, 'he reached the innermost region of the Pyrenees, when he was marching through the narrow gorges that open between the hills'.[30] Astronomus Limusinus's *Vita Hludowici Pii imperatoris* also records that the passage, from which one could touch the sky, runs through dark and shady forests through a very narrow path.[31] These descriptions do not match with the path along the ridges, where there is no narrow gorge to cross, or where there are no trees and, therefore, no shady roads.

Finally, the second route is 4 kilometres (2.48 miles) longer than the first and rises 300 metres more than the latter, which makes it a more difficult route to access, particularly for an army of about 20,000 men with impedimenta, that is, dragging a long caravan of supplies.

Everything thus indicates that the army was following the old Roman road called *Via Ab Asturica Burdigalam*, connecting Auritz with Donibane Garazi through Luzaide. This is the view of Bernardo Estornés[32] and José M. Jimeno.[33] Joseph Moret, chronicler of the Kingdom of Navarre, also has affirmed in the *Annales del Reyno de Navarra* that Charlemagne retreated through Luzaide and not along the so-called 'high road' through the Lepoeder and Bentartea passes.[34] Contrary to this thesis, Ramón Menéndez Pidal,[35]

27   Holder-Egger, Oswald (ed.), *Einhardi Vita Karoli Magni,* Monumentae Germaniae Historica (MGH), SSRG, Hannover & Leipzig, 1911, p. 12.

28   Pertz, Georg Heinrich (ed.), *Annales et chronica aevi Carolini*, Monumentae Germaniae Historica (MGH), SS, I, Hannover, 1826, p. 234.

29   Tremp, Ernst (ed.), *Astronomus. Das Leben Kaiser Ludwigs* (*Vita Hludowici imperatoris*), Monumentae Germaniae Historica (MGH), SSRG, LXIV, Hannover, 1995, pp. 286 & 288.

30   Pertz, Georg Heinrich (ed.), *Annales et chronica aevi Carolini*, Monumentae Germaniae Historica (MGH), SS, I, Hannover, 1826, p. 234.

31   Tremp, Ernst (ed.), *Astronomus. Das Leben Kaiser Ludwigs* (*Vita Hludowici imperatoris*), Monumentae Germaniae Historica (MGH), SSRG, LXIV, Hannover, 1995, pp. 286 & 288.

32   Estornés Lasa, Bernardo, *Historia General de Euskal Herria. 476-824 época vascona*, in *Enciclopedia General Ilustrada del País Vasco*, vol. 2, Auñamendi, Donostia, 1981, pp. 207-281.

33   Jimeno Jurio, José María, *¿Dónde fue la batalla de Roncesvalles?*, Pamiela, Iruñea/Pamplona, 2004. In toto.

34   Moret, Joseph, *Annales del Reyno de Navarra*, Imprenta de Martín Gregorio de Zavala, Pamplona, 1684, p. 188.

35   Menéndez Pidal also stated that there was no Roman road passing through Zize. Indeed, there was no material evidence of the existence of a Roman road through the Zize pass or the foothills of Astobizkar (*Camino de Santiago*) but rather two unpaved roads. However, the last

Ramón Abadal,[36] and André Burger[37] held that the battle took place on the other side of Ibañeta hill, that is, about 3 kilometres (2 miles) away on the east side, along the Arrañosin cliff connecting Auritz with Astobizkar hillside, beside the *Camino de Santiago*.

Essentially, Menendez Pidal, Abadal, and Burger argue that there was not a Roman road passing through Zize and, as a consequence, the debate about the place of the battle has been about the existence of this route. However, this statement was not based on evidence, and the few sources available indicate otherwise. As noted by Jimeno Jurio, based on research completed between 1968 and 1969, when the new chapel of San Salvador in Ibañeta was built in 1965 archaeologists found a fragment of a votive altar and other materials from Roman times in the area. According to Jimeno Jurio, these pieces show that the port of Zize was in use in Roman times.[38] Furthermore, in 2013 a group of historians and archaeologists discovered the remains of the ancient Roman road through Luzaide. The aforementioned *Nota Emilianense* mentions the *Portum Sicera*, and the *Kaiserchronik* of the twelfth century mentions *Karlestal* or Charles's Valley. Aymeric Picaud is also very precise when stating that many people passed through the port Zize and specifies that this was the path traced by Charlemagne's troops because 'many pilgrims going to Santiago who are not willing to climb the mountain ridges go down this path [the Zize pass]'.[39]

The presence of Roman remains in Ibañeta is an important indication of the existence of the Zize pass, but recently Juan M. Txoperena, a member of Aranzadi Society of Sciences, has provided new evidence of the existence of a Roman road that connected Errozabal with Donibane Garazi. Txoperena has located two milestones in Ibañeta. As Txoperena explains, 'these milestones, as the ones previously found in Aurizberri, may be dated to the late Roman Empire; one of them is devoted to Galerius (293-305 A.D.) before he received the title of Augustus in May 305 and the other has not

archaeological discoveries have demonstrated that indeed it did exist. Menéndez Pidal, Ramón, *La Chanson de Roland y el neotradicionalismo*, Espasa-Calpe, Madrid, 1959, p. 206.

36   Abadal, Ramón, "La expedición de Carlomagno a Zaragoza: el hecho histórico. Su carácter y significación", *Coloquios de Roncesvalles*, Institución Príncipe de Viana, Iruñea/Pamplona, 1956, pp. 39-71.

37   Burger, André, "Le champ de bataille de Roncevaux dans la Chanson de Roland", *Coloquios de Roncesvalles*, Institución Príncipe de Viana, Iruñea/Pamplona, 1956, pp. 105-111.

38   Jimeno Jurio, José María, *Nafarroako toponimia eta mapagintza / Toponimia y cartografía de Navarra*, vol. 35, Nafarroako Gobernua, Iruñea, 1996, p. 225.

39   Rialle, Girard de; Vinson, Julien (eds.), *Revue de Linguistique et de Philologie Comparée*, vol. 15, Maisonneuve de Cie, Libraires-éditeurs, 1882, p. 15. Another English version in: Melczer, William (ed.), *The Pilgrim's Guide to Santiago de Compostela*, Italica Press Inc., New York, 1993, p. 93.

yet been dated since the epigraphy is very run down and only retains some letters, but it also seems to be datable to the early fourth century, similar to those of Aurizberri. Approximately half way down the Zize pass a number of padded blocks from a Roman bridge were located, recycled in a culvert of the current road, built around 1881.[40]

The existence of Roman padded blocks and milestones that marked the Roman roads indicating the distances is very substantial evidence of the existence of a pass through Zize in 778. If we add to this the discovery of archaeological remains from that time, both in Errozabal and in the Zize pass, the hypothesis that the battle did indeed take place in this route becomes very difficult to refute.[41]

Additionally, Menendez Pidal, Abadal, and Burger argued that to lead the army through the depths of the Zize pass was not a correct strategic decision and that therefore Charlemagne never would have taken it. However, the historical data and the final result of the battle reveal that the emperor did indeed take the wrong decision. Althought not likely, it is possible that, given the size of the army, the Arrañosin cliff was part of the scenario of secondary fights on the day of the battle.

Apart from the archaeological evidence, the sources themselves mention a passage of narrow, wooded mountain and stress that the Basques were launched on the columns of the French army *from above* when those were *clearing narrow passes opening between its hills*. This description fits perfectly with the passage of Zize and can rule out the theory that the battle took place in the *high road* since an ambush on that road is quite impracticable and the description does not fit the narrative of the contemporary chroniclers.

The location of the battle in the port of Zize is also present in literature and later traditions that owe their origin to the historical events leading up to the legend. The overwhelming majority of these literary sources suggest that the battle took place around Ibañeta between the plain of Errozabal and Luzaide.

Other authors place the battle in other locations, distant from Errozabal. Antonio Ubieto, based on data provided by the *Chanson de Roland*, located the battle in the Somport pass, about 30 kilometres (18.6 miles) north of Jaca, where some time after the battle the monastery of Siresa was located. In the author's opinion, the oral tradition confused the original toponym Siresa and transformed it into Sizer or Sizera. Moreover, this mountain

40   Letter by Juan M. Martínez Txoperena to the author. September 24, 2015.
41   Martínez Txoperena, Juan Mari, "La batalla de Orreaga y la participación de los nativos", *Megalitos Pirenaicos. Arqueología y megalitismo en el Pirineo Occidental*, August 2014.

pass is also known in French *port de Aspe,* and one of the manuscripts of the *Chanson de Roland* twice mentions the *porz d'Aspre*.[42] In any case, this hypothesis contradicts all the historical sources and the subsequent oral and written tradition, and clashes with the historical evidence indicating that Charlemagne went to the Saltus Pyrinei once Pamplona was destroyed. There are about 142 kilometres from Pamplona to Somport (through Jaca), while there are only, as I have indicated, 44.2 kilometres (27.5 miles) from Pamplona to Ibañeta (through Auritz). On the other hand, the Jaca region, extremely mountainous and controlled by the Basques in 778, was the location of several battles in which the Muslim troops of Abd al-Malik were defeated in 732-734. Venturing further north through the corridor that ascends from Jaca to Somport would have been extremely risky, even for an army like Charlemagne's. Finally, the second (812) and third (824) battles of Errozabal took place in the Zize pass, which suggests that this was the place of the 'first' battle and the route chosen by the Frankish troops to cross the Pyrenees.

In short, there is no archaeological or strong documentary evidence to locate the battle in the 'high road' or in any place other than the port of Zize.

All contemporary historical sources referred to a battle between Franks and Basques. The mention of Saracens in the battle is literary and chronologically posterior to the events and, consequently, does not have historiographical basis. Arab sources did not even record the battle because it was of no concern since no Muslim forces participated in it.

Furthermore, the sources do not refer to the Basques as *Navarrii* (Navarrese or Basques south of the Pyrenees) or *Hispani Wascones* (Peninsular Basques), as they do in other passages concerning events in Peninsular Vasconia before or after 778. The *Annales Regni Francorum* and the *Annales Laurissenses* mention that Charles subjugated the Basques of Spain and Navarre (*Hispani Wascones subiugatos, etiam et Nabarros*). The *Einhardi Fuldensis Annales* mention Basques and Navarrese or peninsular and continental Basques (*Wasconibus et Nabarris*), and the *Annales Mettenses Priores* mention Basques, Navarrese, and Spaniards (*Hispanis, Wasconibus et Nabarris subiugatis*). Similarly, while the Saxon poet mentions that Pamplona was 'a noble city of the Navarrese' (*nobile castrum esse Navarrorum*), that is, of the peninsular Basques, with regard to the battle the author only mentions the 'perfidious Basques'. The reference to *Wascones* in general seems to imply that troops of continental Vasconia participated in the battle.

---

42   Ubieto, Antonio, "La derrota de Carlomagno y la Chanson de Roland", *Hispania*, 23, Madrid, 1963, pp. 3-28. See also, Ubieto, Antonio, *La Chanson de Roland y algunos problemas históricos*, Anubar, Zaragoza, 1985.

Indeed, the participation of troops from continental Vasconia supports the idea of 'treachery' and 'betrayal' that, from the perspective of the Frankish chroniclers, underlies the battle. And indeed, the sources do not mention Lupus II Otsoa after this date. It should be recalled that, as the Astronomus Limusinus states in the *Vita Hludowici Pii imperatoris*, Otsoa had to surrender several of his own family members to King Charles as hostages as a guarantee of his loyalty (*'Lupo principe se et sua eius nutui dedente'*) before Charles undertook a punitive expedition through his own kingdom, which Otsoa would have very reluctantly accepted with the sole intention of keeping peace among their two kingdoms.[43]

As noted, sources suggest that Charlemagne's army was ambushed. In fact, any point along the 33 kilometres (20.5 miles) separating Zubiri from Luzaide is optimal for an ambush.[44] Already in Errozabal, the Carolingian army was at the mercy of the enemy. It was three exhausting marching days from Pamplona, after having undertaken two hard mountain passes and still facing two more grueling days of 14 kilometres (8.7 miles) and 11 kilometres (6.8 miles), respectively, to reach Donibane Garazi through the meandering descent along the Zize pass. But, fundamentally, the road also did not have forks or splits where the troops could find escape routes. Their only escape was the path running through the dense wooded hillsides flanking both sides of the road.

On the other hand, it is important to remember that the Saxon poet mentions the Basques having attacked the Carolingian army earlier in its course across the road between Pamplona and Errozabal. This makes perfect sense considering that it would be simple for very lightly armed and reduced units to undertake small attacks all along the way, leading to the widespread panic described by the Frankish chroniclers. Although it has been established that the date of the battle is Thursday, 15 August, this date only marks the day when the main attack took place, the day of Eggihard's death. The actual battle began when the Carolingian army left Pamplona around 11 August and, given the size of the army, would not end until at least one or several days after Thursday, 15 August.

Although the Carolingian army was originally composed of two legions, or about 20,000 men, by August we should assume the army would have

---

43   Tremp, Ernst (ed.), *Astronomus. Das Leben Kaiser Ludwigs (Vita Hludowici imperatoris)*, Monumenta Germaniae Historica (MGH), SSRG, LXIV, Hannover, 1995, pp. 286 & 288.

44   Basing his study on literary sources, Robert Fawtier concluded that literary authors, following the Frankish chronicles, presented the battle as an ambush. See Fawtier, Robert, *La Chanson de Roland: étude historique*, E. de Boccard, Paris, 1933.

been somewhat reduced. The king's army had left garrisons at the cities of the eastern Pyrenees it had passed through which had pledged allegiance to the Frankish king; mainly in Girona and Barcelona. Additionally, we should also substract from the original contingent the casualties that might have taken place during the campaign.

An army of such size moving through such a narrow road occupies a large area. Considering the size of the army and the narrow path, the battle could have not taken place only at the Ibañeta hill but necessarily all along the Errozabal plain (where the troops had camped), the Ibañeta hill, and all along the Zize pass through the rough road that descends from Ibañeta to Luzaide, all of which represents an extension of about 14 kilometres in length (approximately 9 miles), consistent with the data provided by the Frankish chroniclers. As Einhard relates, 'when the army was marching in a long line, as required by the narrowness of the road, the Basques ambushed them'.[45] This explains why the Saxon poet specifies that the combat took place when the Carolingian troops were 'marching through the narrow gorges that open between the hills'.[46] The 'narrow gorges'[47] (in plural) may refer to the two different passes of Erro and Ibañeta along the way from Pamplona to Auritz.

The path was so narrow that the troops literally had to penetrate through Ibañeta hill into the Zize pass in a straight line, which certainly favored the ambush. The road was not more than four metres wide at its widest point, and most likely, in most sections would be much narrower. In 877, King Basilio I, leading an army of approximately 8,000 men, had to cross the mountain range of Anti-Taurus through the Koukousos (Cappadocia) gorge to Germanikeia (Kahramanmaras);[48] the column covered a distance of about 8 kilometres and, at a speed of 3 kilometres per hour, the vanguard was about 2 hours from the rear.[49] A force of 5,000 horsemen marching in rows of two occupy an area of approximately 6 kilometres (about 4 miles) of road; if we add the baggage carts, the distance doubles.[50] An army like

---

45   Holder-Egger, Oswald (ed.), *Einhardi Vita Karoli Magni,* Monumenta Germaniae Historica (MGH), SSRG, Hannover & Leipzig, 1911, p. 12.

46   Pertz, Georg Heinrich (ed.), *Annales et chronica aevi Carolini*, Monumenta Germaniae Historica (MGH), SS, I, Hannover, 1826, p. 234.

47   Pertz, Georg Heinrich (ed.), *Annales et chronica aevi Carolini*, Monumenta Germaniae Historica (MGH), SS, I, Hannover, 1826, p. 234.

48   Or simply Maras, in current Turkey.

49   Haldon, John F., *Warfare, State and Society in the Byzantine world, 565-1204*, Routledge, London, 2003, p. 165.

50   Halsall, Guy, *Warfare and Society in the Barbarian West (450-900)*, Routledge, London & New York, 2003, p. 131.

that of Charlemagne, which was composed of two legions and a long train of provisions, would move in a column several kilometres long, so that when the head was coming to Gainekoleta, the rear would still be in the vicinity of Errozabal, about 17.5 kilometres (nearly 11 miles) away, separated by the two slopes of a mountain pass, and about four hours walk from the avant-garde of the army.

As the Saxon poet explains, the first attack came from the height of the hills flanking the road where an ambush is easy to undertake, 'the aggressors shot dead the Frankish warriors with their projectiles, launched from the height of the hills'.[51] And indeed, the highest point of the road is Ibañeta hill. In line with the aforementioned sources, Ibañeta hill, being the single retreat gateway of the French army and the highest point of the battlefield, may have become the hottest place of the battle and the key strategic position whose control was going to determine the victory in battle.

Taking advantage of attacking from the heights of the northeast slope of Mount Girizu (the left side of the road that descends through the Zize pass) and from the northwest slope of Ibañeta (the right flank), known as Otezilo (or Otezulo),[52] the main attack occurred when the army was stretched along an extended line and therefore helpless and unable to perform any maneuver. The Basques, hidden in the leafy beech forests of the hillsides flanking the road, let the forefront of the army pass through Ibañeta, before attacking while the central body of the army was marching down through Zize, with the rear sloping up toward Ibañeta hill through Otezilo creek, and the vanguard approached Gainekoleta.

The main attack surprised the Franks. The Saxon poet says that 'at this attack, the army panicked; soldiers [were] disconcerted by the tumultuous and sudden attack'.[53] The *Annales qui dicuntur Einhardi* also notes that the Basques 'sow[ed] great disorder in the whole army'.[54] The surprise effect in such circumstances must have had a devastating impact on the Frankish warriors, whose sole purpose that day was to take control of Ibañeta hill in order to escape towards Luzaide and beyond the Pyrenees, to Donibane Garazi.

---

51   Pertz, Georg Heinrich (ed.), *Annales et chronica aevi Carolini*, Monumenta Germaniae Historica (MGH), SS, I, Hannover, 1826, p. 234.

52   Literally meaning gorse hollow (*Ulex europaeus*).

53   Pertz, Georg Heinrich (ed.), *Annales et chronica aevi Carolini*, Monumenta Germaniae Historica (MGH), SS, I, Hannover, 1826, p. 234.

54   In the original Latin: '[T]otum exercitum magno tumultu perturbant.' In Kurze, Friedrich (ed.), *Annales regni Francorum (741–829) qui dicuntur Annales Laurissenses maiores et Einhardi*, Monumenta Germaniae Historica (MGH), SSRG, VI, Hannover, 1895, pp. 51 & 53.

The main sources for the study of the battle, Einhard's *Vita Karoli Magni*, the Saxon poet's *Annales de Gestis Caroli Magni Libri V*, the *Einhardi Annales*, and the *Annales Regni Francorum qui dicuntur Einhardi* do not mention a plain attack on the rear but clearly state that the attack focused on the back of the caravan of supplies and the guard that was shielding it, thus affecting the entire Carolingian army.

The *Einhardi Annales* and the *Annales qui dicuntur Einhardi* record that the attack fell on the rear ('extremum agmen') but also highlight that this first attack threw 'the entire army' into disarray ('totum exercitum magno tumulto perturbant').[55] 'Extremum agmen' has been commonly translated as 'rear', but the chronicler is referring to the 'end of the line of march', since the more orthodox expression to refer to the rear in Latin is 'novissimum agmen', which is the term used by Einhard in the *Vita Karoli Magni*. In this context 'agmen' literally means an army on the move. The vanguard in Latin was named 'primum agmen' and the central body of the army was referred to as 'medium agmen'.

Einhard insisted on this fact, reporting that, indeed, the attack was launched on 'the back part of the caravan of provisions' ('extremam impedimentorum partem') and then emphasizing that this attack also fell on the troops that preceded it covering up the rear army ('et eos qui, novissimi agminis incedentes subsidio, praecedentes tuebantur') that therefore formed part of the main body of the army.[56] Also, the *Annales de Gestis Caroli Magni Libri V* are very explicit in specifying that the king marched at the head of the vanguard, leaving behind 'the rest of the army engaged in transporting the baggage, which hindered their march, making it slower'.[57] That is, the attack focused on the back of the royal caravan ('prostrate populi regalis') due to the fact that 'the king had already pressed forward' ('rex iam praecessit') at the head of the vanguard 'and the rest of the army followed him from behind' ('tardumque remanserat agmen').

The legend forged by the *Chanson de Roland* and supported in the earlier tradition emphasizes that the attack affected only the rear. Indeed, the notion that the attack took place on the rear is of literary origin. The *Chanson de Roland*, to avoid describing the king retreating, leaving their

---

55 Kurze, Friedrich (ed.), *Annales regni Francorum (741–829) qui dicuntur Annales Laurissenses maiores et Einhardi*, Monumenta Germaniae Historica (MGH), SSRG, VI, Hannover, 1895, pp. 51 & 53.

56 Holder-Egger, Oswald (ed.), *Einhardi Vita Karoli Magni*, Monumenta Germaniae Historica (MGH), SSRG, Hannover & Leipzig, 1911, pp. 12-13.

57 Pertz, Georg Heinrich (ed.), *Annales et chronica aevi Carolini*, Monumenta Germaniae Historica (MGH), SS, I, Hannover, 1826. P. 234.

troops behind, helpless, turned 'the rest of the army' into 'the rear', which is partly true, since, as I have explained, the attack focused throughout that part of the army located 'behind the forefront'. However, arguing that the Basques only attacked 'the rear guard' is difficult to sustain and, as we have seen, contradicts the historical sources that clearly indicate that the attack affected 'the whole army' and specify that only the king was at safe, at the forefront, beyond the epicentre of the struggle.

On the other hand, it is difficult to presume that if the majority of the paladins of the king died in battle, including the seneschal, the attack took place only on the rear. Even less credible is the fact that the baggage and, most importantly, the real treasure, marched in the rear.

The formation of the troop is particularly important and, depending on the terrain, the position, and whether the enemy is ready to attack, the army must march in a certain formation, intended to cope in the best possible way with an attack. For example, an army marching through a wide and flat land at war could acquire the formation called *agmen quadratum* or *quadrato agmine*, which basically allowed the army to defend itself from all positions irrespective of the origin of the attack. The formations referred to as *quadratum agmen* and *agmen munitum* were square or rectangular formations whose sides were shielded by the cavalry and light infantry, thus protecting the interior where the baggage train and the most vulnerable sections of the army marched, including the standing command. One of the advantages of marching in *agmen munitum* formation was that the army could advance, defend itself, and protect the baggage at the same time. It was basically a way of marching in battle formation. Troops moving in *quadratum agmen* formation could, in addition to the above, go on the attack.[58]

However, general conditions and, more often, orography, often prevented armies from using such quadrangular formations. Through a narrow mountain pass, an army was bound to stretch over several kilometres, which amounted to an adoption of an *agmen pilatum* or stretched, elongated formation, adapted to a narrow path. The *agmen iustum* or *agmen pilatum* is basically one of the most common formation schemes for an army marching through particularly difficult or narrow places, such as the Zize pass. Some authors suggest that the word *pilatum* comes from the Latin word *pila* meaning 'pillar' or 'column' that logically refers to an elongated formation.

58   Pérez Castro, Lois C., "Los agmina romanos y los significados de pilatvm agmen y qvadrato agmine", Emerita. Revista de Lingüística y Filología Clásica (EM), LXXIV 1, january-June 2006, pp. 1-16.

Other authors argue that *pilatum* derives from the Latin word *pilo* meaning 'stacked' or 'compact'. In any case, this formation scheme is characterized by its vulnerability, since an army marching along a narrow road flanked by trees located at a short distance from the line of march and whose layout offers an abrupt slope, both along the road itself and perpendicular to the march, is fully exposed.

The adoption of this formation required extraordinary organization, and a precise coordination between the various parts of the army, which would be communicated by, for instance, various musical instruments.

It is also unlikely that the baggage train with the supplies was transported in the rear.[59] The *Annales de Gestis Caroli Magni* reports that the king was marching ahead with the leading part of the army and that the rest of the army were engaged in transporting the baggage which hindered the march, slowly following behind.[60] But this version contradicts the *Vita Karoli Magni*, recording that the Basques attacked the tail end of the train of supplies (*extremam impedimentorum partem*) and also the main army body. Furthermore, the *Vita Karoli Magni* does not mention that the baggage train was carried on the rear. In line with the above, the *Annales Regni Francorum qui dicuntur Einhardi* also report that the Basques attacked on the rear but also underline that the attack affected the entire army, except of course the forefront. In sum, the chronicler never mentions that the baggage train travelled in the rear but indicates that the attack came on the back of the supply train that in general was transported in the middle of the formation, protected on both flanks.

Actually, most military treatises of the period, including illustrations and narratives on military strategy, indicate that the baggage train should go in the centre, flanked on both sides.[61] Most authors are clear in this respect. In any other case, but mainly when marching through hostile territory, the impedimenta must be transported in the centre of the formation, or even close to the vanguard.[62] The *Strategikon* of Emperor Maurice, written in

---

59 Merwin, William S., *The Song of Roland*, Random House, Inc., New York, 2001, p. XII.

60 Pertz, Georg Heinrich (ed.), *Annales et chronica aevi Carolini*, Monumenta Germaniae Historica (MGH), SS, I, Hannover, 1826, p. 234.

61 Connolly, Peter, *Greece and Rome at War*, Prentice-Hall Inc., Englewood Cliffs (NJ), 1981, p. 46.

62 Vegetius Renatus, Flavius, *Epitoma rei militaris*, Peter Lang, New York, 1990, p. 139-147. See also, Holmes, Thomas R., *Caesar's Conquest of Gaul*, Macmillan, London, 1903, p. 53; Dennis, George T., *Maurice's Strategikon: Handbook of Byzantine Military Strategy*, University of Pensilvannia Press, Philadelphia, 1984, p. 99; Haldon, John F., *Warfare, State and Society in the Byzantine world, 565-1204*, Routledge, London, 2003, p. 156.

the late sixth century, and the *Tactica* of Leo VI the Wise, written around 895-908, agree that the baggage train has to travel between the vanguard and the rearguard. The author of the *Tactica* specifies in chapter 9 (*De exercitus itinere* or on the march of the armies) and, especially, in chapter 10 (*De Tuldo, id est, impedimentis* or on the train of provisions) that the baggage train shall march in the centre of the army, flanked and protected by units especially designed and trained for this task (*'in omni itinere, hostibus imminentibus, in medio exercitus tui tuldum habeas'*).[63] Also, the aforementioned Vegetius records in the *Epitoma rei militaris*:

> [F]irst, the cavalry must lead the way. Then, foot soldiers, the train of provisions, pack horses, soldiers' slaves and vehicles must be assembled in the centre so that the infantry and light cavalry remain in the rear. Because if it is true that sometimes a surprise attack may fall on the forefront of an army on the march, most often it occurs on the rear. The baggage train must be escorted on either side by a group of armed men, because attackers usually attack from both sides. However, it should be taken into account that the part that is believed to be attacked by the enemy shall be reinforced with very carefully selected and equipped cavalry troops using light weapons and with infantry and archers positioned on the opposite side [of the assailants]. But in case the enemy rushes everywhere, it is better to be prepared on all sides. To avoid too much damage from the sudden confusion of the attack, soldiers must be forewarned and mentally prepared, with the weapons in their hands, as they may be startled by a sudden danger. In contrast, it is not easy to terrify them when they foresee the danger. The veterans often take diligent precautions to prevent the soldiers from becoming disorganize in battle, or the servants, sometimes injured and sometimes overwhelmed with dread, or the beasts of burden, which also can be alarmed by the noise. Precautions were also taken so that the army, more dispersed or more packed than necessary, did not disrupt itself and thereby benefit the enemy. And, therefore, as an example for the soldiers, the baggage train was also organized in accordance with certain rules. Thus, some men were chosen among the servants, whom they called *galearii*, adequate and qualified by experience, entrusted with taking care of no less than two hundred packhorses and slaves. Instructions were given to them so they knew when they should pick up the luggage in accordance to the

---

63   Migne, Jacques-Paul (ed.), *Patrologiae cursus completus*, Apud Garnier Fratres et J.-P. Migne Successores, Paris, 1863, vol. 107, p. 791 & 790.

signals. But soldiers on the front line are separated of the baggage train by a large space, unless, being too clustered, the baggage train becomes a hindrance in the battlefield.[64]

This way of organizing the march of an army is a standard argument repeated in the military strategy manuals of the fifth, sixth, and seventh centuries as well as in later written manuals, in the eleventh and twelfth centuries.[65] Moreover, in some cases the king marched behind the baggage train, in the central part of the army, since this is the safest area of the formation.[66] Thus, the chroniclers represent Charlemagne crossing the Alps in the centre of the formation during the campaign of Pavia (Lombardy) in the campaign of 773 and 774.[67] The fifteenth century *Knyghthode and Bataile* describes it in the following way:

In a maner himself betrayeth he,
Whos taken is by negligence thespie;
Forthi be war, and quickly charge hem se
On euery side, and fast ayeyn hem hye;
Horsmen beforn eke euer haue an eye;
On vch an half footmen, and cariage
Amydis is to kepe in the viage.[68]

The only exception to this rule occurred when an army penetrated into hostile territory or when an army adopted combat formation and, therefore,

---

64 Vegetius Renatus, Flavius, *Epitoma rei militaris*, Peter Lang, New York, 1990, p. 142.

65 Haldon, John F., *Warfare, State and Society in the Byzantine world, 565-1204*, Routledge, London, 2003, p. 156. There are different editions of the *Tactica* in Latin and Greek, among them *Leonis imperatoris Tactica*, Typis Regiae Universitatis Scientiarum Budapestinensis, Budapest, 1922. From this point of view the Constitutio IX *De exercitus itinere* (pp. 767-787) and the Constitutio X *De Tuldo id est, impedimentis* (pp. 787-791) are particularly interesting. See also a bilingual edition in Migne, Jacques-Paul (ed.), *Patrologiae cursus completus*, Apud Garnier Fratres et J. P. Migne Successores, Paris, 1863, vol. 107.

66 Haldon, John F., *Warfare, State and Society in the Byzantine World, 565-1204*, Routledge, London, 2003, p. 156.

67 When Henry W. Longfellow (1807-1882) poetically described in *Tales of a Wayside Inn (Part Third. Poet's Tale; Charlemagne)* the capture of Pavia by Charlemagne's troops in the campaigns of 773 and 774; he placed the emperor in the army centre ('All who went before him, beside him, and behind him, his whole host, were armed with iron'). Indeed, the fact that the king did not march at the head of the troop is the leitmotiv of the poem and the leading cause of Desiderio's embarrassment. See Hutton, Edward, *The Cities of Lombardy*, Macmillan Co., New York, 1912, pp. 149-151.

68 Dyboski, R.; Arend, Z. M. (eds.), *Knyghthode and bataile: A XVth century verse paraphrase of Flavius Vegetius Renatus' treatise "De re militari"*, The Early English Text Society, London, 1935, p. 50.

expected to meet the enemy head-on, in which case the supply train should logically go in the rear.[69] Also, when oblivious to the danger, an army crossed its own territory in which other sources of food could easily be found the supply train could also go at the rear. But, as noted in Maurice's *Strategikon*, which along with Vegetius's work was widely disseminated at the time, when an army crossed gorges or areas of extreme difficulty in hostile territory, the impedimenta was placed in the centre of the formation.[70] The author further states that such impedimenta must be guarded by a strong contingent of well-trained foot troops (*milites*) under the command of a leader of confidence, which coincides with the legend representing Roland in charge of the same.

In line with Vegetius's writing, there was indeed a special body of servants in charge of organizing the baggage train, the *lixae*.[71] This crowd of officers, bartenders, merchants (*mercatores*), stable lads to take care of the animals, and soldier attendants also were responsible for packing and driving the train of supplies. These and other servants are referred to under the generic term of *lixae*. The *Capitularia Regnum Francorum* stipulated in great detail what the characteristics of the carts carrying the supplies should be and even what were the provisions that they had to carry: flour, wine, bacon, and, in general, *abundant* food; sharpening stones for the weapons, axes, cranes and machines to drag and to hook; tools for blacksmithing and carpentry, as well as everything needed to repair fabrics and leathers.[72] Article 64 of the *Capitulare de Villiis* also stipulated that these wagons—usually single axis since these were more manageable in the field[73]—should have a minimum capacity and comply with very precise requirements:[74] 'The cars that come with our army, i.e., the war chariots, shall be well assembled, and their covers

---

69   Dennis, George T., *Maurice's Strategikon: Handbook of Byzantine Military Strategy*, University of Pensilvannia Press, Philadelphia, 1984.

70   Dennis, George T., *Maurice's Strategikon: Handbook of Byzantine Military Strategy*, University of Pensilvannia Press, Philadelphia, 1984, p. 101.

71   In Roman times many of these *lixae* were slaves and were called *calones*. Delbrück, Hans, *History of the Art of War within the Framework of Political History: The Middle Ages*, Greenwood Press, Westport (CT), 1982, p. 298.

72   Loyn, Henry Royston; Percival, John, *The Reign of Charlemagne: Documents on Carolingian Government and Administration*, St. Martin's Press, New York, 1976. See also, Halsall, Guy, *Warfare and Society in the Barbarian West (450-900)*, Routledge, London & New York, 2003, p. 150.

73   Moreover, two-axle wagons, lacking direction, were more difficult to handle and too often the wooden wheels were broken because of this lack of mobility and had to be repaired.

74   Halsall, Guy, *Warfare and Society in the Barbarian West (450-900)*, Routledge, London & New York, 2003, p. 149. See also, *Capitulare de Villiis*, in *Introduction to Contemporary Civilization in the West*, Columbia University Press, London & New York, 1961, pp. 326-334.

must be of good quality, with fur on top and stitched so that if there is need to go across deep rivers, they can pass through without getting water in them and thus preventing the provisions to spoil and arriving safely to the other shore. Also, we want each cart to bring twelve measures of flour for our consumption, and in those transporting wine, twelve measures of wine. And each cart shall be fitted with a shield, a spear, a bow and a quiver.'[75] As stated above, the custody of the supply train was assigned to agile and skilled light foot troops.[76]

The main reason for placing the baggage carts in the centre was security. In this sense, David Nicolle states that one of the main missions of the Muslim cavalry of the twelfth and thirteenth centuries was precisely to separate the army from the baggage train since an army deprived of their source of supply was at the mercy of the enemy.[77] Another key reason to locate the baggage train in the centre was that, if we consider that an army on the march covered several kilometres of road, the head of the army could reach the camp several hours before the rear, so it was important that carts with kitchen items and urgent food were already set when the last man arrived in the camp. To transfer the impedimenta to the rear would delay the march for hours. Julius Caesar notes in the *Commentarii de Bello Gallico* how the baggage was kept in the centre of the camp when they camped in Neuf-Mensil.[78]

On the other hand, pulling these carts (literally hundreds of carts dragged by more than one thousand horses and other beasts of burden) was not a simple task and the road was practically unusable after the march of the troops, which dropped all kinds of spoils on their path. The movement of these heavy carts would be much slower if the busy roads were dirty; as a consequence, the baggage train would march immediately after the forefront, both as a security measure and for convenience, especially when marching through a narrow trail.

It is also very doubtful that Charlemagne decided to place the treasure in the rearguard. As pointed out by Caesar in the *Commentarii de Bello Gallico*, the treasure supplied credit and honor and represented the success or failure of an expedition, so it was usually transported in the safest

75 *Capitulare de Villiis*, in *Introduction to Contemporary Civilization in the West*, Columbia University Press, London & New York, 1961, p. 333.

76 Haldon, John F., *Warfare, State and Society in the Byzantine world, 565-1204*, Routledge, London, 2003, p. 156.

77 Nicolle, David, *God's Warriors: Crusaders, Saracens and the Battle for Jerusalem*, Osprey Publishing, Oxford, 2005, p. 126.

78 Holmes, Thomas R., *Caesar's Conquest of Gaul*, Macmillan, London, 1903, p. 53.

part of the expedition, along with the leader.[79] In line with the historical chronicles and the *Chanson de Roland*, losing the booty to the enemy was considered an affront that threatened the honor of the troops and the king himself.

The battle of Errozabal has remarkable similarities with the disaster of Aduatuca in 54 B.C. described by Caesar. The narrowness of the road and the heavy impedimenta forced the Romans to march in an excessively long line that was attacked at several points from a wooded area, to which we must add in the case of Errozabal the slope that flanked the road and the narrowness of the way.[80]

Following the narrative of the *Annales de Gestis Caroli Magni*, the strategy of the Basques consisted in dividing the Carolingian army into two halves, since the vangaurd led by Charlemagne marched ahead and faster than 'the rest of the army'.[81] Thus, it was essential to gain control of Ibañeta and consequently divide the Frankish army into two, north and south of that hill, while focusing the main attack on the army's central body that stretched along several kilometers, descending through Zize towards Luzaide at the mercy of the attackers placed in the eight balconies from which it is possible to attack from above and under the protection of the trees next to the road.

By means of this attack, the Basques won key strategic advantages. On the one side, as indicated by the sources, the vanguard headed by the king had marched ahead, faster than 'the rest of the army'.[82] This part of the Carolingian army (*primum agmen*) therefore did not suffer the bulk of the attack and was cut off from the rest. While most of the vanguard—where the king marched—had penetrated into Luzaide, the central part of the Carolingian army (*medium agmen*) fell into a trap from which it could hardly escape. The baggage travelled precisely in this section of the army (at the rearmost of the vanguard) guarded by the royal paladins, most of whom subsequently died in the battle. As mentioned by the sources, caught by surprise and tired after several gruelling marching days,[83] they were easily pushed to the opposite side of the attack, downhill, causing them to fall

79   Holmes, Thomas R., *Caesar's Conquest of Gaul*, Macmillan, London, 1903, p. 135.

80   Holmes, Thomas R., *Caesar's Conquest of Gaul*, Macmillan, London, 1903, p. 83.

81   Pertz, Georg Heinrich (ed.), *Annales et chronica aevi Carolini*, Monumenta Germaniae Historica (MGH), SS, I, Hannover, 1826, p. 234.

82   Pertz, Georg Heinrich (ed.), *Annales et chronica aevi Carolini*, Monumenta Germaniae Historica (MGH), SS, I, Hannover, 1826. P. 234.

83   In the original Latin: '*Militie cum lasso calles trascenderet artos.*' In Pertz, Georg Heinrich (ed.), *Annales et chronica aevi Carolini*, Monumenta Germaniae Historica (MGH), SS, I, Hannover, 1826, p. 234.

into the deep Errekabeltz hollow and, without any escape and prevented by their thick clothing and heavy weapons, massacred there.[84]

The vanguard, reaching Gainekoleta, was entirely prevented from relieving the rest of the army due to the narrowness of the road, which, once the attack started, soon became clogged with the damaged and abandoned carts and the chaos generated by the encounter. The baggage train with the supplies and the royal treasury acted as a buffer separating the two first sections of the army. Consequently, the only way for the vanguard to counterattack would have been to ascend through the wooded slopes of Errinsaroko malda, Legarxuri, and Gorosagar and advance along the hillside, through the forest, for about 10 kilometres (6.2 miles), something which was entirely impracticable.

Finally, the rearward forces (*extremum agmen*), which had not yet crossed Ibañeta when the main attack started, were on the plain of Errozabal at the mercy of the attackers with no path of retreat or means of shelter. The rear, on the way up to Ibañeta, harassed from the heights of Xoritegi on the left flank and from Dorrondoa on the right, advancing throughout the narrow Otezilo creek, did not have any other alternative but to move up in a thin line and ascend about 2 kilometres (1.2 miles) until Ibañeta to gain access to the Zize pass, the only outlet. Considering that the least qualified foot troops marched in the rear, it is likely that most of the victims found death in the ascent to Ibañeta precisely where the monastery stands today.

Indeed, coupled with the advantage of their position, the attack completely disrupted the communication between the various bodies of the Frankish army, since the rear, trapped south of Ibañeta, could not see what was happening along the Zize pass, and the sinuous descent road prevented the vanguard from seeing what was happening in Errekabeltz cliff; all of which may be the origin of the myth of Roland's Oliphant.

Such an ambush requires the mobilization of a well-trained and coordinated army. To gain control and subsequently close off Ibañeta hill to lock the rear of such a colossal army in Errozabal and then subsequently ambush its central body composed of well-trained veterans in the port of Zize requires extensive planning and a remarkable military organization. In fact, controlling Errozabal, Ibañeta, and consequently the western slope of the Zize pass from which the attack started (which forms a line running north through Zubibeltz, Saraundi, Legarzuri, Kaxtizarra, Etsaro, and Boloki) is only possible through organizing and executing an open battlefield combat. It is unthinkable that

---

84 Place names give an idea of the topographical features of the terrain. *Errekabeltz* (literally meaning Black creek) refers to the lack of light or shades through which the stream flows. *Luzaide* in turn refers to the narrowness of the valley.

the Frankish army went into the Zize pass without recognizing it and trying to gain control of the left (west) side of the road. Only after obtaining control of these slopes through direct open combat with the Franks could the Basques have ambushed and defeated the main body and the rear of King Charles' army. In short, it is quite impossible to think that this battle could have been won by simply placing some men on the western side of the Zize pass and throwing stones from their positions, thus avoiding a pitched battle with the Carolingian troops.

Some authors have expressed the opinion that the battle was just a 'skirmish'. The Latin word for skirmish is *velitatio*. For the same, light infantry soldiers were named *veles* or *velites* in the plural. Other Latin terms to refer to a skirmish are *concursatio, praecursio* or *pugnicula*. But the Frankish scribes did not use any of these terms; on the contrary, the Frankish chronicles refer to Errozabal as a 'certamen', a very common word in Latin texts that translates as *battle* or even *war*. In this sense, the expression *in certamine ipso* literally means 'in battle'. Perhaps one note distinguishing the Latin term *certamen* from other words referring to a battle or armed encounter—such as *acies, proelium, pugna*, or *dimicatio*—is that the Latin word *certamen* is used to refer to extensive armed clashes or battles in the broader context of war and, in some Medieval texts, the word is used to refer to war itself. Moreover, generally, *certamen* refers to a 'decisive battle'. As a consequence, I have found no version of the Latin sources translating *certamen* as 'skirmish' in any of the five languages that I have analyzed. But apart from a proper translation of the sources, the idea that the battle was nothing more than a skirmish contradicts the information provided by the chronicles about the way it was fought and the high mortality that it caused among the Franks.

The *Annales Regni Francorum qui dicuntur Einhardi* and the *Einhardi Annales* express without hesitation that the 'inequality of the ground' (*'iniquitate locorum'*) and 'the difference in the fighting technique' (*'genere inparis pugnae'*) caused the inferiority of the Franks 'in this battle' (*'in hoc certamine'*).[85] Einhard also states in the *Vita Karoli Magni* that the Basques managed to surprise the Carolingian troops by attacking from a higher position, 'pushing the Franks down the cliff'.[86] The scribe also

85   Kurze, Friedrich (ed.), *Annales regni Francorum (741–829) qui dicuntur Annales Laurissenses maiores et Einhardi*, Monumenta Germaniae Historica (MGH), SSRG, VI, Hannover, 1895, pp. 51-53.
86   In the original Latin: '*Wasconesh in summi montis vertice positis insidiis* [...] *desuper incursantes in subiectam vallem deiciunt.*' In Holder-Egger, Oswald (ed.), *Einhardi Vita Karoli Magni*, Monumenta Germaniae Historica (MGH), SSRG, Hannover & Leipzig, 1911, pp. 12-13.

underlines that the Basques literally jumped on the Carolingian army ('*desuper incursantes*') and therefore engaged in a close combat in which they enjoyed the advantage provided to them by their lighter dress and weapons ('*levites armorum*').

In fact, studying the battlefield in detail, one finds very few spots in the Zize pass from which stones may be thrown at an army marching through it; that is, there are very few points from which to attack without engaging in close combat. One of such places is Kaxtizarra opposite to Arroiaundieta, which literally means 'old castle'. At this point the river Luzaide twists and lies to the rock, which towers over 40 metres above the Zize pass, forcing travelers to march just below the cliff. This point is of great strategic value, since from the edge of the wall a small unit can easily and safely attack an army running through this mountain pass. As Juan Mari M. Txoperena showed me, place names at these particular points, such as 'harrespil' or 'pile of stones', reinforce the idea that these particular positions along the Zize pass were used in the past for this purpose.

As indicated, the road linking Ibañeta pass with Gainekoleta in the eighth century had a very steep slope (a gradient of 694 metres) and was unpaved. Moreover, this route was extremely narrow, less than 3 metres wide, and flanked on both sides by a lush beech forest that allowed attackers to throw spears and arrows from a certain height while protected by the trees. The road did not have branches or secondary pathways to escape through. In addition, over the first 7.2 kilometres (4.5 miles) the downhill track is flanked on its eastern side by a series of elevated positions unreachable by the enemy from which it is extremely easy to throw large stones or any kind of shells on to the road. Specifically, there are eight 'balconies' between Ibañeta and Gainekoleta strategically located 800 metres (half a mile) apart from each other: Gabarbide, Zubibeltz, Saraundi, Legarzuri, Kaxtizarra, Etsaro, Boloki, and Lapitze.

Kaxtizarra in particular offers a unique position from which to throw projectiles from a height of about 40 metres over an enemy passing that way. If we consider that the total length of the Carolingian army can be estimated at about 11 kilometres and that the path is 7.2 kilometres (4.5 miles), in line with what was recorded by the Frankish chroniclers, the attack affected the whole army, except the front part of the forward guard that was already approaching Luzaide and the back part of the rearguard, which was trapped on the southern slope of the Ibañeta pass, ascending through Otezilo creek.

Although the surprise factor and the ensuing chaos was decisive, another important element determined the Frankish defeat. The Carolingian army was not prepared to fight in such terrain. The *Annales de Gestis Caroli Magni Libri V* mention that the Basques, taking advantage of their dominant position in the battlefield, 'first' (*primus*) shot their projectiles (*missilibus*) from the height of the hills on the west side of the Zize pass (*ex collibus altis*). As Einhard indicates, 'the lightness of their weapons and the terrain helped the Basques at that time, and the Franks had against them the weight of their arms and the position, which was worse than the one of the Basques'.[87] The *Annales qui dicuntur Einhardi* and the *Einhardi Annales* also agree that 'the imbalance of the combat ground and the difference in the way they fought caused their [the Frankish warriors'] inferiority'.[88] In addition, the *Annales de Gestis Caroli Magni* indicate that 'the narrowness of the location placed the Franks in disfavoring conditions'.[89]

This first attack, sudden and massive ('subitoque tumultu'), caused a great panic among the ranks of the Carolingian army, which resulted necessarily in a close combat and the subsequent persecution of those seeking to flee the battlefield either into the woods or along the bank of the river Luzaide downstream where they were slaughtered.

With no possibility of calling for combat positions, horses and heavy armors were not useful in Errozabal and even posed many challenges, and the same is true of the heavy spears and long swords. All sources agree in describing a battle in which the Basque troops clashed in hand-to-hand combat with the Carolingian troops, since this was precisely the best advantage of the Basques, who, lightly armed, required less space to move and maneuver and possessed a much greater mobility across the extremely uneven terrain on which both armies had to fight that day.

With respect to the clothing, the *miles* or Frankish warriors were equipped with a heavy coat of mail called *bronie*[90] consisting of sewn metal plates

---

87   In the original Latin: '*Adiuvabat in hoc facto Wascones et levitas armorum et loci, in quo res gerebatur, situs, contra Francos et armorum gravitas et loci iniquitas per omnia Wasconibus reddiditm impares.*' In Holder-Egger, Oswald (ed.), *Einhardi Vita Karoli Magni,* Monumenta Germaniae Historica (MGH), SSRG, Hannover & Leipzig, 1911, pp. 12-13.

88   Kurze, Friedrich (ed.), *Annales regni Francorum (741–829) qui dicuntur Annales Laurissenses maiores et Einhardi,* Monumenta Germaniae Historica (MGH), SSRG, VI, Hannover, 1895, pp. 51 & 53. Los *Einhardi Annales,* in Pertz, Georg Heinrich (ed.), *Annales et chronica aevi Carolini,* Monumenta Germaniae Historica (MGH), SS, I, Hannover, 1826, p. 159.

89   Pertz, Georg Heinrich (ed.), *Annales et chronica aevi Carolini,* Monumenta Germaniae Historica (MGH), SS, I, Hannover, 1826, p. 234.

90   The *bronie* is mentioned up to ten times in the *Chanson de Roland* (first mention is in stanza 107, line 1372). See Müller, Theodor, *La Chanson de Roland: nach der Oxforder Handschrift,* Verlag der Dieterichschen Buchandlung, Göttingen, 1863, p. 86.

and, both underneath and over it, a single piece of fabric tied to the waist.[91] The warriors wore a heavy iron helmet on a thick leather hood covering the forehead, the cheeks, and the nose, leaving the eyes and the mouth uncovered.[92] The Carolingian body armor was technologically superior to the Roman 'lorica sqamata' that, in various forms, had been used in Europe until then. In 779 Charlemagne forbade the selling of chainmail so that the enemies could not use or imitate them.[93] Under section 7 of the *Capitulare Missorum* of 803, Charlemagne forbade his troops from selling such chainmail or *Brunias* to the merchants they met on their long campaign marches.[94]

Riders (*milites*) were armed with a round shield (*scutum*) and a long lance or pike (*lancea*), along with the sword (*gladius*) and foot soldiers or *miles*, carried a sword or an ax. There were archers, although it seems that Charlemagne did not have large units of archers until years later. The following letter written by Charlemagne to Abbot Fulrad giving the necessary instructions to attend the Mayfield reflects what each count should provide and how each should organize and arm his men:

> Let it be known to you that we have determined to hold our general as-
> sembly this year in the eastern part of Saxony, on the river Bode, at the
> place which is known as Strassfurt. Therefore, we enjoin that you come
> to this meeting-place, with all your men well armed and equipped, on
> the fifteenth day before the Kalends of July, that is, seven days before
> the festival of St. John the Baptist [June 24]. Come, therefore, so prepared
> with your men to the aforesaid place that you may be able to go thence
> well equipped in any direction in which our command shall direct; that

91   De Vries, Kelly, *Medieval Military Technology*, University of Toronto Press, Toronto, 1992, pp. 24 & 60-64. See also, Bennett, Matthew; Bradbury, Jim; DeVries, Kelly, *Fighting Techniques of the Medieval World: Equipment, Combat Skills and Tactics*, Macmillan, London, 2006, p. 82.

92   Schutz, Herbert, *Tools, Weapons and Ornaments: Germanic Material Culture in Pre-Carolingian*, Brill Academic Publishers, Leiden, 2001, pp. 120 & 161-164. See also, DeVries, Kelly, *Medieval Military Technology*, University of Toronto Press, Toronto, 1992, pp. 60-64.

93   Bachrach, Beranrd S., *Armies and Politics in the Early Medieval West*, Variorum, London, 1993. DeVries, Kelly; Smith, Robert D., *Medieval Weapons: An Illustrated History of Their Impact*, ABC-CLIO, Santa Barbara, 2007, pp. 72-75. See also, De Vries, Kelly, *Medieval Military Technology*, University of Toronto Press, Toronto, 1992, p. 60.

94   Boretius, Alfredus (ed.), *Capitularia Regum Francorum*, Monumenta Germaniae Historica (MGH), Leges, Hannover, 1883, vol. 1, p. 115. See also, Robinson, James Harvey (ed.), *Readings in European History*, Ginn & Co., Boston, 1904, vol. 1, pp. 137-139; Loyn, Henry Royston; Percival, John, *The Reign of Charlemagne: Documents on Carolingian Government and Administration*, St. Martin's Press, New York, 1976.

is, with arms and accoutrements also, and other provisions. Each equiped horseman will be expected to have a shield, a convenient lance, a sword, a dagger, a bow, and quivers with arrows; and in your carts shall be implements of various kinds, that is, axes, planes, augers, boards, spades, iron shovels, and other utensils that are necessary in an army. In the wagons there should also be supplies of food for three months, dating from the time of the assembly, together with arms and clothing for six months. And furthermore, we command that you see to it that you proceed peacefully to the aforesaid place, through whatever part of our realm your journey shall be made; that is, that you presume to take nothing except fodder, wood, and water. And let the followers of each one of your vassals march along with the carts and horsemen, and let the leader always be with them until they reach the aforesaid place, so that the absence of a lord may not give to his men an opportunity to do evil. Send your gifts, which you ought to present to us at our assembly in the middle of the month of May, to the place where the Emperor shall be such that on your march you are able in person to present these gifts of yours to us; we shall be greatly pleased. Be careful to show no negligence in the future if you care to have our favor.[95]

Consequently, although the clothing and weapons tended to be uniform, coats of mail, helmets, shields and swords, spears, and other weapons and equipment of the troops varied slightly, mainly for economic reasons. Some chainmail covered the warriors to the knee, while others only protected the shoulders; some shields were round, while others were oval and the weight, length, design, and quality of the weapons was also diverse.[96] A full equipment, including warhorse (*equus*) cost between 40 and 44 solidi, while the price of an ox was 2-3 solidi.[97] Vegetius notes that, apart from the clothes, a Legionnaire with his entire equipment hauled about 19.5 kilos.[98]

The Basques were, by contrast, very lightly armed. They wore neither helmet nor breastplate; as noted in Picaud's *Pilgrims' Guide* they wore leather

---

95 Ogg, Frederic A., *A Source Book of Medieval History: Documents Illustrative of European Life and Institutions from the German Invasion to the Renaissance*, American Book Company, New York, 1908, pp. 143-144.

96 DeVries, Kelly; Smith, Robert D., *Medieval Weapons: An Illustrated History of Their Impact*, ABC-CLIO, Santa Barbara, 2007, p. 72.

97 Bachrach, Bernard S., *Early Carolingian Warfare: Prelude to Empire*, University of Pennsylvania Press, Philadelphia, 2001, p. 63. And, Ganshof, François-Louis, "L'armee sur les carolingiens", *Ordinamenti Militari in Occidente nell'alto medioevo*, Settimane di Studio del Centro Italiano di Studi sull'alto medioevo 15, Spoleto, 1968, pp. 109-130.

98 Vegetius Renatus, Flavius, *Epitoma rei militaris*, Peter Lang, New York, 1990, p. 36.

skirts (*sayas*) and leather sandals (*abarcas*) covering the sole tied with leather strips. As the *Pilgrim's Guide* describes it, 'the Navarrese like the Scots dress black and short clothes, until the knee, and use a type of shoe that they call *abarcas* made of untanned leather, tied to the foot with straps and covering only the sole, exposing the rest. They wear black woolen cloaks coming down to the elbows with a shot similar to a cloak that they call *sayas*.'[99]

In line with the reference of the *Annales de Gestis Caroli Magni* regarding their projectiles, the *Pilgrims' Guide* mentions the *azkonak* or short spears of the Basques. These spears were extremely inexpensive weapons, made of wood and requiring only a minimum amount of metal (iron or copper) at the tip. Picaud also refers to the clothing of the eleventh-century Basques and the *irrintzis* or war cries performed by them: 'Wherever a Navarrese or a Basque goes, like a hunter he hangs a horn from his neck, and uses to taking two or three javelins with him, which they call auconas.[100] And when he comes back home he whistles like a kite. And when in hiding to capture a prey he wants to call his colleagues quietly, he sings like an owl or howls like a wolf.'[101]

This quote validates the reference given by Aimonio in the *Historia Francorum o Libri IV de gestis Francorum*, whereby Ludovico Pio, obeying his father who had named him *princeps* of Aquitaine after deposing Hunald, appeared before him dressed as a Basque, that is, with a short dress, with loose sleeves, the spurs sewn to the footwear, and carrying the *azkonas* in his hands.[102]

Everything outlined here explains the slaughter that the sources refer to.[103] The *Einhardi Annales* and the *Annales qui dicuntur Einhardi* are very explicit that 'most of the paladins that the king had appointed to lead his

99   *Liber Quartus S. Jacobi Apostoli*, in Rialle, Girard de; Vinson, Julien (eds.), *Revue de Linguistique et de Philologie Comparée*, vol. 15, Maisonneuve de Cie, Libraires-éditeurs, 1882, pp. 16-17. Another English version is in Melczer, William (ed.), *The Pilgrim's Guide to Santiago de Compostela*, Italica Press Inc., New York, 1993, p. 94. An abridged version in Spanish is in Orella, José Luis, *Historia de Euskal Herria*, Volume 1, Txalaparta, Tafalla, 2003, pp. 253-260.

100 The author committed a minor mistake when transcribing the original Basque 'azkona' ('azkonak' in plural). Hence, in Spanish, 'azcona'.

101 *Liber Quartus S. Jacobi Apostoli*, in Rialle, Girard de; Vinson, Julien (eds.), *Revue de Linguistique et de Philologie Comparée*, vol. 15, Maisonneuve de Cie, Libraires-éditeurs, 1882, p. 18. Another English version is in Melczer, William (ed.), *The Pilgrim's Guide to Santiago de Compostela*, Italica Press Inc., New York, 1993, p. 95.

102 *Historia Francorum o Libri IV de gestis Francorum*, book 5, cap. 2, in Estornés Lasa, Bernardo, *Historia General de Euskal Herria. 476-824 época vascona*, in *Enciclopedia General Ilustrada del País Vasco*, vol. 2, Auñamendi, Donostia, 1981, p. 255.

103 Zink, Michel, *Medieval French Literature: An Introduction*, Medieval & Renaissance Texts & Studies, Binghamton, N.Y, 1995, p. 24.

troops were killed in course of this battle'.[104] Einhard says that they were
thrown down to the bottom of the valley and there annihilated to the last
man;[105] Einhard continues that, among the many others who died in the
battle, were Eggihard (*Aggiardus*),[106] palace seneschal; Anselmus, palatine
of the court; and Hruodland or Roland,[107] prefect or marquess of the Breton
Marc ('*Hruodlandus Brittannici limitis praefectus*'). The *Annales de Gestis Caroli
Magni* also indicates that the Basques, victorious, caused many deaths;[108] the
Astronomus Limusinus does not provide the names of the Frankish heroes
dead in battle, for in his own words they were known by all ('*vulgata sunt*').[109]
The aforementioned Note of the monastery of San Millán, datable to around the
year 1065, does not mention Alselmus's and Eggihard's deaths but—following
the tradition of the *Historia Caroli Magni et Rotholandi*—does mention Beltran,
Ojier *of the short sword*, Guillermo *curved nose*, Oliver, and Bishop Turpin.

One of the questions that remains unanswered is the approximate death
toll and the possible location of archaeological remains that may help elu-
cidate this and other questions. We know from the Frankish sources that
mortality was very high and, from studying the topography of the place, it is
clear that there are not many suitable places to dig mass graves. Most probably corpses were thrown into caves or ravines, which are not uncommon
in this area. Based on the archaeological evidence, Joseph Moret, Chronicler
of the Kingdom of Navarre, indicated that much of the fighting took place
around the Ibañeta hill and the Errozabal plain, since in the mid-seventeenth
century it was common among the neighbors in the area to dig for remains
of battle and 'very often', 'human bones, iron spears, spurs and swords' and
even 'horns and clubs and other spoils' were found in Errozabal.[110] Traces of
the passage of the Carolingian army through Errozabal are still being found

104 In the original Latin version: '[P]*lerique aulicorum, quos rex copiis praejecerat, interfecti
sunt.*' In Kurze, Friedrich (ed.), *Annales regni Francorum (741–829) qui dicuntur Annales Laurissenses maiores et Einhardi*, Monumenta Germaniae Historica (MGH), SSRG, VI, Hannover, 1895,
pp. 51 & 53. The *Einhardi Annales* also state that, '*in hoc certamine plerique aulicorum, quos rex
copiis praefecerat*'. In Pertz, Georg Heinrich (ed.), *Annales et chronica aevi Carolini*, Monumenta
Germaniae Historica (MGH), SS, I, Hannover, 1826, p. 159.

105 Holder-Egger, Oswald (ed.), *Einhardi Vita Karoli Magni,* Monumenta Germaniae Historica
(MGH), SSRG, Hannover & Leipzig, 1911, pp. 12-13.

106 *Egiardo, Einhard, Eginardo o Eginhard.*

107 There are multiple variants of the same name: *Roldán, Rolando, Roland, Rollant, Orlando.*

108 Pertz, Georg Heinrich (ed.), *Annales et chronica aevi Carolini*, Monumenta Germaniae
Historica (MGH), SS, I, Hannover, 1826, p. 234.

109 Tremp, Ernst (ed.), *Astronomus. Das Leben Kaiser Ludwigs (Vita Hludowici imperatoris)*,
Monumenta Germaniae Historica (MGH), SSRG, LXIV, Hannover, 1995, pp. 286 & 288.

110 Moret, Joseph, *Annales del reyno de Navarra*, Imprenta de Martín Gregorio de Zavala,
Pamplona, 1684, p. 208.

today. Such is the case of the Carolingian sword and ax found in Baratzeko erreka and the spearhead found in the area.[111]

Moret states that the bodies of the victims of the battle were thrown into the pit known as Charemagne's hollow 'that today [in 1684] may be seen in the chapel of Sancti Spiritus'. The author confirms that, despite being 'so big and so deep' in the seventeenth century, it was still 'full of human bones'. According to Moret, some of these bodies were laid bare without being deposited in any urn or receptacle while others, possibly the remains of the most prominent dead, were deposited in 'boxes made of stone'. Based on his testimony, the council of the Orreaga monastery fired a priest who sold the largest bones at 'an ounce of silver the piece' to pilgrims who were travelling along the Way.[112]

The temple's architecture reinforces Moret's claim, as it is the oldest temple of the Orreaga complex, and the chapel of Sancti Spiritus is indeed a mortuary temple built on a pit or trench that served as an ossuary. It seems that the original chapel was square and that the vault was supported by thick masonry walls. Obviously, the original tomb could not have been built by King Charles, as he fled after the defeat and never returned to the site. On the other hand, the oldest parts of the present church cannot be dated to prior to the twelfth century and, like the rest of the buildings in the complex, has undergone several changes over time. In any case, an archaeological survey in depth to determine the chronology, nature, and quantity of human remains deposited there has not yet been conducted.

Picaud's *Pilgrims' Guide (Liber V)* explicitly states that Charlemagne sought refuge in Luzaide after the attack of the Basques, which fits perfectly with the events we have outlined above: 'Near this mountain, for more details, to the north, there is a valley called Valcarlos where Charles himself encamped with his army after his warriors were decimated in Errozabal.'[113] The *Historia Caroli Magni et Rotholandi (Liber IV)* also refers to this episode, placing Charlemagne in Valcarlos *(in valle Karoli)* when the attack occurs; according to the *Historia Turpini*, Charlemagne was 12.8 kilometres (8 miles) from the epicentre of the battle so the sound of Roland's oliphant was transported

111 Martínez Txoperena, Juan Mari, "La batalla de Orreaga y la participación de los nativos", *Megalitos Pirenaicos. Arqueología y megalitismo en el Pirineo Occidental*, August 2014.

112 Moret, Joseph, *Annales del reyno de Navarra*, Imprenta de Martín Gregorio de Zavala, Pamplona, 1684, p. 208.

113 *Liber Quartus S. Jacobi Apostoli*, in Rialle, Girard de; Vinson, Julien (eds.), *Revue de Linguistique et de Philologie Comparée*, vol. 15, Maisonneuve de Cie, Libraires-éditeurs, 1882, p. 15. Another English version is in Melczer, William (ed.), *The Pilgrim's Guide to Santiago de Compostela*, Italica Press Inc., New York, 1993, p. 93.

to him by angels.[114] And indeed, it is 10.3 kilometres (6.4 mi) from Ibañeta to Luzaide (exactly 12.8 kilometres or 8 miles to Arnegi where the narrow gorge ends) and, as already noted, Luzaide has been known as Valcarlos for centuries as a result of the events that took place that day.

The nineteenth scene of the stained-glass windows of the Chartres cathedral recreates the *Chanson de Roland* depicting the hero trying to blow his ivory horn and then trying unsuccessfully to break his sword against a rock to keep it from being taken by the enemy. It is known that olifants were used to give battle orders, mainly to organize the troops in combat.[115] It is interesting to note that tradition refers to the olifant trying to explain why Charlemagne did not turn back to help his seneschal and why the blowing of the horn and warning signs were disregarded or could not be attended by the emperor. There are countless references to olifants in the classical sources as well as some illustrations of the Carolingian period indicating that these instruments were used regularly, such as the Aachen cathedral treasury's reliquary. And not just by the Carolingians. The Aachen reliquary, in line with Picaud's observations on the clothing and weapons used by the Basques, illustrates them blowing their olifants from the towers of Pamplona.

Musicians playing trumpets in the Roman army and, in general all those who served as musicians regardless of the nature of the instrument they played, were generically called *aeneatores*. Among the *aeneatores*, Vegetius mentions the *tubicines*, the *cornicines*, and the *buccinatores*, who were responsible for giving the warning and training signs during marches and in battle with tubas, trumpets, or horns respectively.[116] They were an essential part of the Roman and Carolingian armies, and accordingly they enjoyed certain privileges among the troops and as Vegetius says, held high ranks. The *tubilustrium* or day of the military musicians was celebrated every year in Rome on 23 May. In any case, along with the acoustic signals or *signa*, Vegetius also mentions the *signa vocalia*, *signa semivocalia*, and *signa muta*, that is, a complex system of signs to enable the organization of the *exertitus* when marching and in combat. It is known, for example, that at the image of the Roman *legio*, the Frankish army carried *signiferi* or *draconarii* (banners), one of them representing the image of a dragon as

---

114 Castets, Ferdinand (ed.), *Turpini Historia Karoli Magni et Rotholandi*, Société pour l'Etude des Langues Romanes, Montpellier, 1880, p. 46.

115 Deriving from 'elephant' since the most expensive horns were made of ivory from the horns of this animal.

116 Vegetius Renatus, Flavius, *Epitoma rei militaris*, Peter Lang, New York, 1990, p. 76.

reproduced in the Aachen psaltery.[117] The *Epitoma rei militaris* also records the use of these or similar signs centuries later:

Vocal is oon, and that is mannys voys,
Semyvocal is trompe & clarioun
And pipe or horn; the thridde macht no noys,
And mute it hight or dombe, as is dragoun
Or thegil or thimage or the penoun,
Baner, pensel, pleasaunce or tufte or creste
Or lyuereys on shildir, arm or breste.[118]

Given their relevance, there were different calls for performing various maneuvers, and it is particularly interesting that, according to Vegetius, the olifant was played only in the presence of the emperor. The author explains:

[A] Legion has *tubicines* [trumpeters,] *cornicines* [cornet players] and *buccinatores* [the ones responsible for giving signals with the olifant]. The trumpeter calls soldiers to battle and also gives the signal to retreat. Soldiers and not flaggers are subject to the signals or calls of the *tubicines*. Thus, whenever the soldiers go out to perform some task, they obey the sound of the tubicines' trumpets; when the flaggers are going to move, the *cornicines* are the ones responsible for their sound signals; when a battle is being fought, both the *tubicines* and the *cornicines* call together their sound signals. The *classicum* is the sound made by the *buccinatores* with the olifant. This seems to be the sign of the emperor, as the classicum only sounds when the emperor is present, or when the death sentence of a soldier is announced, as this is only executed by order of the emperor. If the soldiers are on guard, or for carrying out farming or construction works, or any other work, or for training in the field, the activity begins only once the *tubicines* have made the right calls and cease when they give the signal again. However, when flaggers move, or have already moved, or are about to move, the *cornicines* give the signal. These signals are therefore observed in all exercises and during the marches, so that soldiers obey easier in battle and fight if commanders order them to do so, or stop or continue, or retreat. It is common sense that what has to

117   Vegetius Renatus, Flavius, *Epitoma rei militaris*, Peter Lang, New York, 1990, p. 77.
118   Dyboski, R.; Arend, Z. M. (eds.), *Knyghthode and bataile: A XVth Century Verse Paraphrase of Flavius Vegetius Renatus' Treatise "De re militari"*, The Early English Text Society, London, 1935, p. 47.

be done out of necessity in the battlefield should be done regularly in leisure time.[119]

There are several historical examples of the use of olifants in situations similar to those of that day in Errozabal. During the Third Crusade, when the army of Richard Coeur de Lion moved from Acre to Jaffa on 25 August, 1191, he was attacked from the rear and, alerted by his own riders, turned to help his troops.[120] And when Emperor Frederick Barbarossa was attacked while he marched on 3 May 1190 at the head of his rearguard through a narrow gorge in Asia Minor, Duke Frederick of Swabia was alerted and moved back to assist his king. In these cases and many others, as in the attack on the rearguard during the battle of Arsuf on 7 September, 1191, communication systems by sounds, flaggers, and messengers allowed the king to have some knowledge of what was happening.[121] In the present case, the Zize pass has an ideal acoustic space by virtue of the echo provided by the slopes of the mountains. From Gainekoleta and even from below, the troops in the vanguard could hear perfectly not only the sound of the olifants, but also the noise generated by the fight itself.

Charlemagne never returned either to assist his men or to recover their bodies. The defeat had an emotional and psychological impact on the emperor, 'as such a big misdeed remained unpunished, sad clouds cast over the mind of the king, who later recovered serenity in virtue of his many victories'.[122] The *Einhardi Annales* and the *Annales qui dicuntur Einhardi* record that 'the memory of the inflicted injury greatly overshadowed in the king's heart the remembrance of the feats happily performed in Hispania'.[123] Charlemagne barely left Herstal from September 778 to May 779, wondering why he had lost God's favor.[124] This explains, in turn, why the official chronicles omitted the event until the emperor's death.[125]

119 Vegetius Renatus, Flavius, *Epitoma rei militaris*, Peter Lang, New York, 1990, p. 102 & 104.

120 Nicolle, David; Hook, Christa, *The Third Crusade 1191: Richard the Lionheart, Saladin and the Struggle for Jerusalem*, Osprey Publishing House, Botley, 2006, pp. 52 & 58.

121 Nicholson, Helen, *Medieval Warfare: Theory and Practice of War in Europe 300-1500*, Palgrave Macmillan, London & New York, 2004, p. 127.

122 Pertz, Georg Heinrich (ed.), *Annales et chronica aevi Carolini*, Monumenta Germaniae Historica (MGH), SS, I, Hannover, 1826, p. 234.

123 Kurze, Friedrich (ed.), *Annales regni Francorum (741–829) qui dicuntur Annales Laurissenses maiores et Einhardi*, Monumenta Germaniae Historica (MGH), SSRG, VI, Hannover, 1895, pp. 51 & 53. The *Einhardi Annales* also record that, 'Cuius vulneris acceptio magnam partem rerum feliciter in Hispania gestarum in corde regis obnubilavit'. Pertz, Georg Heinrich (ed.), *Annales et chronica aevi Carolini*, Monumenta Germaniae Historica (MGH), SS, I, Hannover, 1826, p. 159.

124 King, P. D., *Charlemagne*, Rouledge, London & New York, 1986, p. 14.

125 King, P. D., *Charlemagne*, Rouledge, London & New York, 1986, p. 13.

Sources agree that the battle ceased at nightfall. Logically, inside a wooded valley, sunset causes reduced or poor visibility. Einhard reports that 'they killed to the last man, took the baggage and quickly dispersed hidden in the early evening shadows'.[126] The *Einhardi Annales* and the *Annales qui dicuntur Einhardi* state that 'they took the loot and the enemy immediately disappeared owing to their knowledge of the country'.[127] The *Annales de Gestis Caroli Magni* also mention that 'after this feat, the enemies quickly fled through the winding roads of the vast forest; they were very familiar with the peaks of the mountains, with the remote hideouts of the forests and the profound caves of the valley. The stampede, which prevented the search, and the night that came on them stopped [the Frankish warriors] from taking revenge."[128]

It is certainly unlikely that the Basques took the heavy loot over the course of the evening and just disappeared with it uphill into the forest. It should be noted that neither carts like those described in the *Capitularia Regnum Francorum* of 802-803 and Article 64 of *Capitulare de Villiis*, heavy armor, weapons of all kinds, tools, beasts of burden, nor any other valuables left by the vanquished army could have been dragged uphill through the wilderness.[129] But beyond the physical impossibility of pulling the impedimenta uphill, there was no reason for the Basques to disperse, having killed most of the paladins and causing the rest to flee in disorder to the north, and anticipating that the Frankish troops could not undertake a counterattack. As noted above, an attack against the Basques ascending along 15 kilometres (9.3 miles) through the wooded Zize pass from Luzaide to Ibañeta by penetrating the worst part of the gorge would have simply been a second tactical error, a further rush into full defeat.

Although the Frankish chronicles only mention the capture of Pamplona and suggest the looting of small villages along the road to Zaragoza, the chroniclers agree in mentioning a fabulous booty. The royal treasure probably consisted of the payments to Charlemagne of cities like Girona

126 Holder-Egger, Oswald (ed.), *Einhardi Vita Karoli Magni,* Monumenta Germaniae Historica (MGH), SSRG, Hannover & Leipzig, 1911, pp. 12-13.

127 Kurze, Friedrich (ed.), *Annales regni Francorum (741–829) qui dicuntur Annales Laurissenses maiores et Einhardi*, Monumenta Germaniae Historica (MGH), SSRG, VI, Hannover, 1895, pp. 51 & 53. See also, Pertz, Georg Heinrich (ed.), *Annales et chronica aevi Carolini*, Monumenta Germaniae Historica (MGH), SS, I, Hannover, 1826, p. 159.

128 Pertz, Georg Heinrich (ed.), *Annales et chronica aevi Carolini*, Monumenta Germaniae Historica (MGH), SS, I, Hannover, 1826, p. 234.

129 Loyn, Henry Royston; Percival, John, *The Reign of Charlemagne: Documents on Carolingian Government and Administration*, St. Martin's Press, New York, 1976. See also, Halsall, Guy, *Warfare and Society in the Barbarian West (450-900)*, Routledge, London & New York, 2003, p. 150.

in exchange for their allegiance and vassalage that had been stipulated previously in Paderborn. There were also the weapons, horses and the rest of the baggage and supplies abandoned by the Carolingian military in their flight. In addition, the knights themselves could be redeemed for cash or sold to the Muslims, as happened years later when the Counts Aeblus and Aznar were captured during the Third Battle of Errozabal in 824. In this sense, the death of seneschal *Aggiardus* and the prefect Roland is a singular and hard-to-explain episode, especially considering the high number of paladins who lost their lives in the battle. This suggests that following the destruction of Pamplona and the punitive transit of the Carolingian troops through Vasconia, the battle became particularly bloody.

Charlemagne's return to Herstal was immediate and expeditious. This suggests that the emperor left the baggage train, foot troops, and other obstacles along the way. Although the *Chronicon Moissiacense* indicates that news of the uprising in Saxony (the looting of Karlsburg and Rhineland) reached Charlemagne when he was in Hispania, the *Annales Loisiliani*, the *Annales Laurissenses*,[130] the *Annales Regni Francorum*,[131] the *Annales Tiliani*,[132] and the *Reginionis Chronicon*[133] indicate that the king became aware of the insurrection in Saxony in Auxerre (Autosiodorum).[134] Indeed, it was from Auxerre that the king ordered the *scara Francisca* to march against Widukind's troops in Saxony.[135] From this it follows that the initial rush was not due to the news of the uprising. It should be noted that, as the Astronomus Limosinus records, the emperor, making a detour, quite possibly to stop at the Abbey of Saint-Denis, went through Paris on his way to the *palatium* in Herstal, adding several days to his march.[136]

130 Pertz, Georg Heinrich (ed.), *Annales et chronica aevi Carolini*, Monumenta Germaniae Historica (MGH), SS, I, Hannover, 1826, p. 158.

131 Kurze, Friedrich (ed.), *Annales regni Francorum (741–829) qui dicuntur Annales Laurissenses maiores et Einhardi*, Monumenta Germaniae Historica (MGH), SSRG, VI, Hannover, 1895, p. 52.

132 Pertz, Georg Heinrich (ed.), *Annales et chronica aevi Carolini*, Monumenta Germaniae Historica (MGH), SS, I, Hannover, 1826, pp. 220-221.

133 Pertz, Georg Heinrich (ed.), *Annales et chronica aevi Carolini*, Monumenta Germaniae Historica (MGH), SS, I, Hannover, 1826, p. 559.

134 *Annales Regni Francorum*: '[E]t nunciatum est hoc domno regi Carolo ad Autosiodorum civitatem.' In Fawtier, Robert, *La Chanson de Roland: étude historique*, E. de Boccard, Paris, 1933, p. 153.

135 *Annales Regni Francorum*: '*Tunc praedictus domnus rex mittens scaram Franciscam, ut sub velocitate festinaret ad resistendos supradictos Saxones.*' In Erbe, Michael, *Quellen zur germanischen Bekehrungsgeschichte (5.-8. Jahrhundert)*, G. Mohn, Gütersloh, 1971, p. 67.

136 Tremp, Ernst (ed.), *Astronomus. Das Leben Kaiser Ludwigs (Vita Hludowici imperatoris)*, Monumenta Germaniae Historica (MGH), SSRG, LXIV, Hannover, 1995, p. 292. See also, Estornés Lasa, Bernardo, *Historia General de Euskal Herria. 476-824 época vascona*, in *Enciclopedia General Ilustrada del País Vasco*, vol. 2, Auñamendi, Donostia, 1981, p. 272.

Ganshof says that *Goddinga villa*, where the emperor confirmed the privilege of immunity to the Abbey of Saint-Denis in October 778, is the current Godinne or Gôdene on the right bank of the Meuse (Walloon province of Namur, *arrondissement* Dinant), on the road between Paris and Herstal, specifically some 80 kilometres (50 miles) southwest of Herstal and approximately 1,270 kilometres (790 miles) from Errozabal.[137] From the foregoing it follows that, at an average of about 27 kilometres (16.7 miles) a day and considering forced stopovers in various places like Chasseneuil, where he reunited with his wife, in about fifty days Charlemagne covered the 1,350 kilometres (839 miles) separating Errozabal from Herstal (following the way Errozabal-Chaseneuil-Auxerre-Paris-Herstal), where he arrived in mid-October 778.

This can only mean that the king traveled virtually alone, without any baggage train, fleeing after the defeat, and leaving his army behind when most likely the battle was not yet over.

Considering these facts, the rush to leave Vasconia could also be because Lupus II Otsoa, 'princeps feroces vasconum gentes', likely cooperated with the warlords who took part in the battle. Indeed, according to Ermoldus Nigellus (*In honorem Hludowici*) Otsoa's loyalty was in doubt.[138] However, the silence of the Frankish sources regarding the princeps of the Basques should not lead to us to conclude that Charlemagne ordered his assassination, or that he died or disappeared soon after the battle but rather simply that, in line with the Frankish historiography of the eighth century, there were no armed clashes between him and Charlemagne, and therefore the chroniclers do not mention him. In fact, there is no reference to the Basques or to Lupus Otsoa until many years later. The lack of sources is an indication that the control over Vasconia was nominal, especially after the military disaster of August 778.

Charlemagne never again set foot in Errozabal and never attempted a new offensive against Vasconia.

137 Ganshof, François-Louis, "Une crise dans le règne de Charlemagne. Les années 776 et 779", in Roth, Charles; Gilliard, Charles (eds.), *Mélanges d'histoire et de littérature offerts à Monsieur Charles Gilliard, professeur honoraire de l'Université de Lausanne, à l'occasion de son soixante-cinquiéme anniversaire*, F. Rouge & Cie., Lausanne, 1944, p. 137. See also, Thompson, James W., *The Dissolution of the Carolingian Fisc in The Ninth Century*, University of California Press, Berkeley, 1935, pp. 77 & 130.

138 Joseph F. Rabanis has demonstrated that the letter of Alaon mentioning the alleged betrayal of Lupus was a forgery of the seventeenth century. See Rabanis, Joseph F., *Les Mérovingiens d'Aquitaine: essai historique et critique sur la charte d'Alaon*, Durand, Paris, 1856, p. 119.

Figure 00

Carolingian army's itinerary in 778.

The king himself led the main army to Pamplona commanding troops from Neustria and penetrated into the Iberian peninsula from the west, through the Zize pass in Errozabal. A second legion of similar size composed of troops from Austrasia, Burgundy, Lombardy, Bavaria, and Provence crossed the Pyrenees from the east, through Pertus, arriving in Girona and Barcelona. From there they would continue westwards to meet the troops commanded by the emperor at the gates of Zaragoza.

Map made by the author.

Figure 01
The plain of Errozabal from Lepoeder.
Errozabal is the name of the esplanade around the town of Auritz that gives the name to the battle. From Orreaga, the path ascends to Ibañeta and then zigzags down through the Port of Zize to Luzaide. The path between Ibañeta and Luzaide is an ideal place to conduct an ambush. Photograph taken by the author.

Figure 02
Otezilo.
The way from Ibañeta to Orreaga.
Photograph taken by the author.

Figure 03
Representation of the siege and capture of Pamplona by King Charles.
One of the eight silver reliefs of Charlemagne's reliquary in Aachen represents the king on his knees and praying to Saint Gabriel while God's hand destroys the walls of Pamplona.
Dr Stuart Whatling, used with permission.

Figure 04
Representation of the siege and conquer of Pamplona by King Charles.
Detail of the stained-glass window of Charlemagne in the Chartres cathedral representing the capture of Pamplona by the Frankish army. The Basque watchman sounding the alarm is represented with curly hair in the Muslim way.
Dr Stuart Whatling, used with permission.

Figure 05
Representation of the legendary duel between Roland and Ferracutus.
Detail of the capital of the Medieval market building in Lizarra/Estella representing the legendary duel between Roland and the giant Ferracutus who falls backwards due to the impact of Roland's spear on his navel.
Photograph taken by the author.

Itinerary Iruñea - Donibane Garazi

First day: Iruñea - Zuriain, 13.5 km
Second Day: Zuriain - Zubiri, 8 km
Third day: Zubiri - Bizkarreta, 10.3 km
Forth day: Bizkarreta - Auritz, 8.6 km
Fifth day: Auritz - Luzaide, 14.1 km
Sixth day: Luzaide - Donibane Garazi, 11.1 km

Total, 65.6 km

Iruñea / Pamplona

Figure 06
Charlemagne's army's trail from Pamplona to Donibane Garazi.
It took six long days for the two legions to advance through the narrow path that connected Pamplona and Donibane Garazi.
Map made by the author.

Figure 07
Representation of Charlemagne's march after leaving Pamplona.
Detail of the stained-glass window of Charlemagne in the Chartres cathedral
representing the march of his army through the narrow mountain way. The image
represents the king speaking to Bishop Turpin.
Dr Stuart Whatling, used with permission.

Figure 08
Otezilo.
The way from Orreaga to Ibañeta.
Photograph taken by the author.

Figure 09
The Zize pass from Ibañeta.
The mountains that flank the Zize pass through the Pyrenees.
Photograph taken by the author.

Figure 10
The Zize pass from the way to Luzaide.
The Zize pass is the road to Luzaide through the Pyrenees. The Basques attacked from the heights of Girizu and pushed the Frankish army down to Errekabeltz creek.
Photograph taken by the author.

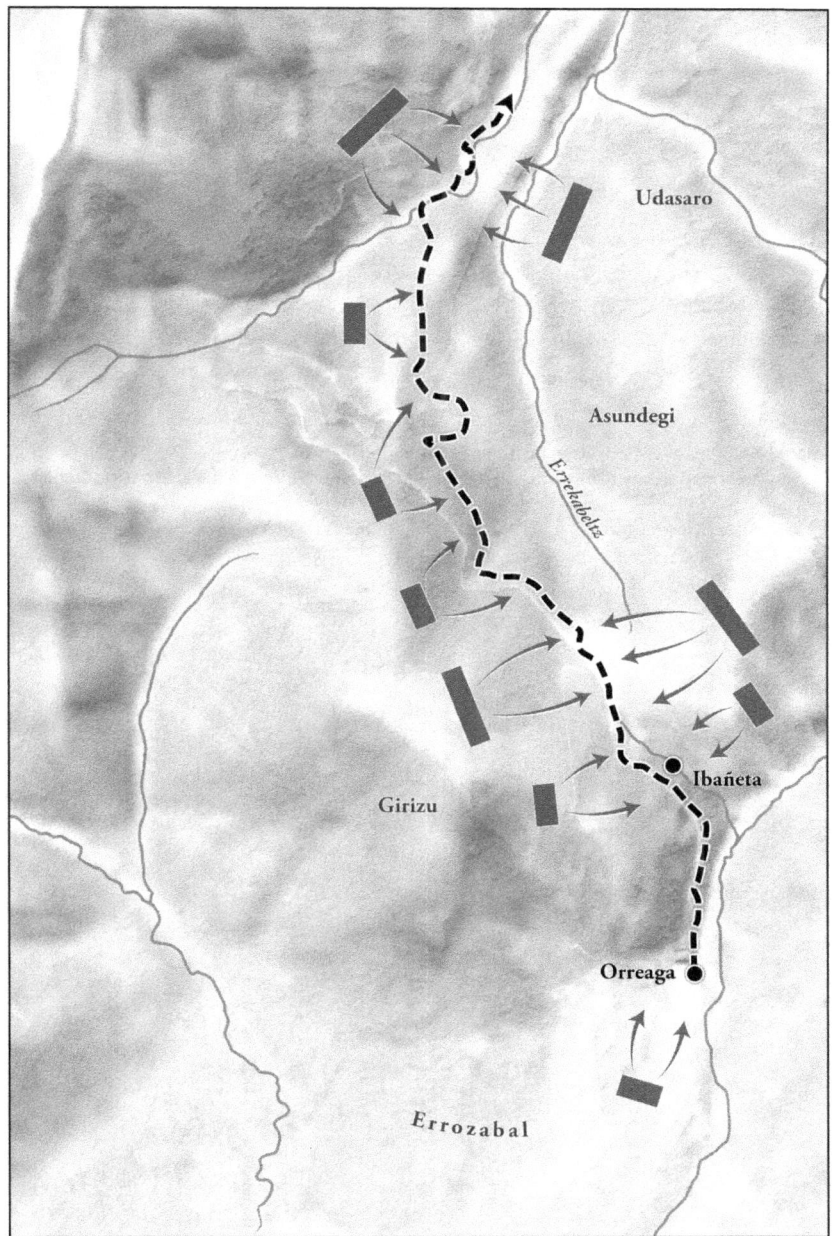

Figure 11
The battle of Errozabal.
Along the Zize pass the Basques attacked from the west and pushed the Frankish army down to
Errekabeltz creek all over the way from Ibañeta to Luzaide. Map made by Alvar Salom.

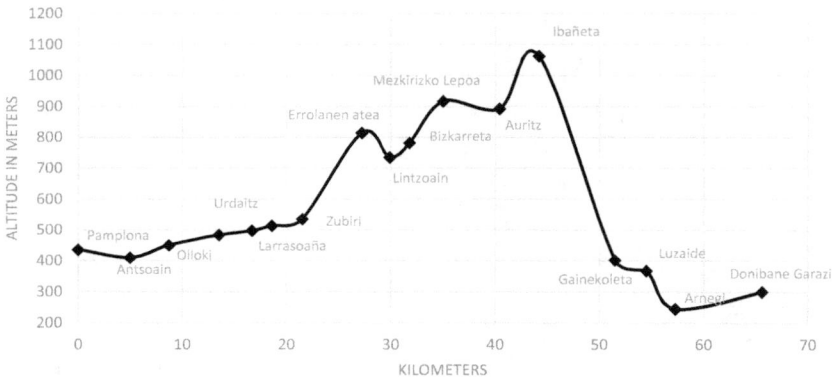

Figure 12
Graphic altimetry of the way from Pamplona to Donibane Garazi.
The way ascended slowly to Ibañeta and descended from there through the Zize pass to Donibane Garazi.
Graphic made by the author.

Figure 13
Legendary stone thrown by Roland from Ibañeta to Urrotz.
According to the legend, in the midst of the battle Roland took the stone and pitched it against the people of Urrotz but missed when he slipped and fell to the ground. There are other similar stones in different parts of the Basque Country which have been related to the same legend.
Photograph taken by the author.

Figure 14
The Zize pass from Ibañeta to Luzaide.
The way is less than 3.5 metres wide and flanked by beech trees.
Photograph taken by the author.

Figure 15
Kaxtizar.
Kaxtizar is a natural stronghold; the only place along the Zize pass from which stones could have been thrown over an army that marched through the way below.
Photograph taken by the author.

Figure 16
Roland's death.
Detail of the stained-glass window of Charlemagne in the Chartres cathedral
representing the hero blowing the oliphant asking for help and trying to break
his sword against the rock right before dying.
Dr Stuart Whatling, used with permission.

Figure 17
View of Errozabal from Ibañeta.
According to the legend Roland died as a hero and a conqueror, facing his opponents and looking
towards the lands that he had helped win.
Photograph taken by the author.

Figure 18
Monument to the battle of Errozabal in Orreaga.
There are four monuments dedicated to Roland and Charlemagne in Orrega. This monument
erected in commemoration of 1,200 years since the battle (778-1978) is currently the only
monument dedicated to the Basques who fought that day.
Photograph taken by the author.

4.   Consequences of the Battle

Abstract
This chapter focuses on the study of the political, economic and military consequences of the battle, both for the Frankish Kingdom and the Emirate of Cordoba, between 778 and 824. The disaster of Rencesvals abetted the revolt in Saxony and the decisions taken by King Charles after the battle suggest that he perceived the situation as critical. Without the spoils of war, the economic cost of the king's unsuccessful campaign fell on the royal coffers. Politically, one of the first measures taken by King Charles was the administrative reorganization of the Frankish Kingdom. However, one of the most important consequences was the definitive consolidation of the Kingdom of Pamplona under King Eneko Aritza, architect of the political alliances that led to the victory over the Frankish in 824, at the Third Battle of Rencesvals.

Keywords: Charlemagne, Ludovico Pio, Vasconia, Pamplona, Eneko Aritza

The physical absence of the Carolingian army coupled with the news of their defeat led to the insurrection of other subjugated peoples.[1] King Charles' defeat in the extreme south of the kingdom stimulated Widukind's uprising in Saxony[2] and, quite possibly, it also fueled the political upheaval in Aquitaine and Lombardy.[3] The *Enhardi Fuldensis Annales* records

---

1   *Einhardi Annales*, in Pertz, Georg Heinrich (ed.), *Annales et chronica aevi Carolini*, Monumenta Germaniae Historica (MGH), SS, I, Hannover, 1826, pp. 159.
2   Widukind's rebellion is recorded by many Frankish sources. Among these, see Kurze, Friedrich (ed.), *Annales regni Francorum (741–829) qui dicuntur Annales Laurissenses maiores et Einhardi*, Monumenta Germaniae Historica (MGH), SSRG, VI, Hannover, 1895, p. 48. See also, Simson, Bernhard von (ed.), *Annales Mettenses Priores*, Monumenta Germaniae Historica (MGH), SSRG, X, Hannover & Leipzig, 1905, p. 67; Kurze, Friedrich (ed.), *Annales regni Francorum (741–829) qui dicuntur Annales Laurissenses maiores et Einhardi*, Monumenta Germaniae Historica (MGH), SSRG, VI, Hannover, 1895, p. 52.
3   Verbruggen, J. F., *The Art of Warfare in Western Europe During the Middle Ages: From the Eighth Century to 1340*, Boydell & Brewer, Woodbridge, 1997, p. 282. See also, Ganshof, François-Louis, *The Carolingians and the Frankish Monarchy*, Longman, London, 1971, p. 18.

Irujo, X., *Charlemagne's Defeat in the Pyrenees: The Battle of Rencesvals*. Taylor & Francis, 2021
DOI 10.5117/9789463721059_CH04

that Widukind's uprising proved particularly bloody and resulted in the destruction of Karlsburg 'by iron and fire'.[4] And the repression was likewise brutal, with episodes of massive killings and deportations of population[5] over the course of several punitive military campaigns until the submission and baptism of the Saxon leader in 785.[6]

As François-Louis Ganshof has indicated, the disaster of Errozabal abetted the revolt in Saxony and produced a critical situation, from both a purely military perspective as well as from a political and economic one.[7]

As regards the economic consequences, the booty obtained from looting was one of the principal motivations for the Frankish annual military campaigns. As sources attest, the cost of the emperor's unsuccessful campaign fell on the royal coffer which was unable to count on the spoils of war. The sources record that upon his return to Herstal, the emperor had to face the additional economic burden of organizing a new army. We know also that on his way to Herstal he passed through Paris, most probably to stop in Saint-Denis and pay a visit to Abbot Fulrad, advisor of Pepin and Charlemagne from at least 750 until his death in 784. The urgency of the situation forced the emperor to go from Auxerre to Saint-Denis to request from the abbot political and spiritual guidance, as well as financial aid. This would explain why the emperor confirmed a few days later, in October 778, the privilege of immunity of the Abbey of Saint-Denis in the town of Gôdene.[8] Apart from

---

4   Pertz, Georg Heinrich (ed.), *Annales et chronica aevi Carolini*, Monumenta Germaniae Historica (MGH), SS, I, Hannover, 1826, pp. 349.

5   After the disaster of the Elbe River in the Battle of Suntelberg in 782, during which the constable and the chamberlain of the king were killed, 4,500 prisoners of war captured after the battle of Verden were executed by order of Charlemagne. Tens of thousands more were deported.

6   As recorded in the *Enhardi Fuldensis Annales*: '785. Widukind Saxo Attiniaci ad fidem Karoli venit, et baptizatus est, et Saxonia tota subacta.' In Pertz, Georg Heinrich (ed.), *Annales et chronica aevi Carolini*, Monumenta Germaniae Historica (MGH), SS, I, Hannover, 1826, pp. 350.

7   Ganshof, François-Louis, "Une crise dans le règne de Charlemagne. Les années 776 et 779", in Roth, Charles; Gilliard, Charles (eds.), *Mélanges d'histoire et de littérature offerts à Monsieur Charles Gilliard, professeur honoraire de l'Université de Lausanne, à l'occasion de son soixante-cinquième anniversaire*, F. Rouge & Cie., Lausanne, 1944, pp. 133-145. See also, King, P. D., *Charlemagne: Translated Sources*, P. D. King, Lambrigg, Kendal, Cumbria, 1987, pp. 48-49.

8   Ganshof, François-Louis, "Une crise dans le règne de Charlemagne. Les années 776 et 779", in Roth, Charles; Gilliard, Charles (eds.), *Mélanges d'histoire et de littérature offerts à Monsieur Charles Gilliard, professeur honoraire de l'Université de Lausanne, à l'occasion de son soixante-cinquième anniversaire*, F. Rouge & Cie., Lausanne, 1944, p. 137. See also, Thompson, James W., *The Dissolution of the Carolingian Fisc in The Ninth Century*, University of California Press, Berkeley, 1935, pp. 77 & 130.

the military disaster and the loss of a good part of his command, including the seneschal Eggihard, the *Chronicon Moissancense* refers to the year 779 as a year of shortages that caused high mortality among the Frankish population, which possibly fueled the financial crisis and the emperor's belief that this defeat was a divine punishment.[9]

Politically, the defeat even caused Charlemagne to recognize the possibility of losing the newly acquired territorial possessions of Aquitaine and Lombardy, which had been independent before the campaigns of 768 and 776, respectively, as well as the military control of Saxony itself. While it is difficult to establish to what extent the situation was critical, the actions taken by Charlemagne suggest that the monarch certainly perceived the situation as such and that therefore he undertook a series of military, political, and administrative measures to address the state of affairs.[10]

One of the first measures that Charlemagne adopted was the administrative reorganization of the Frankish Kingdom. The military occupation of Saxony was confirmed by the application of a purely military law, the Capitulary of Herstal (*Capitulare Haristallense*).[11] The legislative measures were adopted during the meeting held in March 779 in the Palace of Herstal, by means of *capitula* or epigraphs. The capitulary thus constitutes a collection of legal norms numbered from 1 to 23 by which the secular and ecclesiastical administration and the courts were reformed These legal codes were approved by Charlemagne himself by with the agreement of the *Concilium* or mixed assembly composed of secular and ecclesiastical authorities. From this date forward, the *Capitularia* – especially the first three (779, 789, and 794) – became the main form of legislation during Charlemagne's reign and were essentially designed to culturally and socially assimilate the people subjected to the Carolingian order.

Among other important legal dispensations, such as the *Capitulare episcoporum* (780?), *Capilulatio de partibus Saxoniae* (785), *Duplex legationis edictum* (789), *Breviarium missorum Aquitanicum* (789), *Pippini capitulare*

9   In the original Latin: '*In Francia vero fames magna et mortalitas facta est.*' In Pertz, Georg Heinrich (ed.), *Annales et chronica aevi Carolini*, Monumenta Germaniae Historica (MGH), SS, I, Hannover, 1826, pp. 296.

10   King, P. D., *Charlemagne: Translated Sources*, P. D. King, Lambrigg, Kendal, Cumbria, 1987, pp. 48-49.

11   Kroeschell, Karl (ed.), *Deutsche Rechtsgeschichte*, UTB, Köln, 2005, vol. 1, Pp. 73-74. Also in Boretius, Alfredus (ed.), *Capitularia Regum Francorum*, Monumenta Germaniae Historica (MGH), Leges, Hannover, 1883, vol. 1, p. 20.

(787) or Capitulary of Charlemagne, and *Pippini Capitulare Papiense* (787-788),[12] Charlemagne issued four other capitularies between the years 779 and 802.

In comparison to the later ones, the Capitulary of Herstal of 779 is a relatively brief document focusing on those aspects related to civil and religious order, designed to ensure the pacification of the territory, including the prohibition of creating *trustis* or armed groups without express permission of the king.

The *Admonitio Generalis* [General Admonition] of 23 March, 789, is an exhortation for organizing a new society arranged in 82 *capitula*. The *Admonitio* highlights the legal measures taken by the authorities—synods—and the palatine Carolingian tradition, including, for the first time, measures concerning the social and cultural field, for which reason it has been considered one of the most relevant political documents of the so-called *Carolingian Renaissance*. In any case, along with the Capitulary of Herstal, the new political document goes a step further and emphasizes the Christian and Catholic character of the Carolingian order. At the same time, it delegates to the monarch—legally converted into the *rector* of the kingdom of the Franks and the devoted defender of the Church—the responsibility for converting and leading his people as much in civil and military aspects as in religious matters, condemning all other religions, which are referred to as *pseudographia*.[13]

The Capitulary of Frankfurt (*Synodus Franconofurtensis*) of 794 was written primarily to deal with Christian religious movements considered heretical, such as adoptionism or iconoclasm.

In line with the previous ones, the *Capitulare de villis* [Programmatic Capitulary] of the year 800 [802?], written long after the campaigns against the Saxons and the Basques, considerably enlarges its objective and provides general administrative rules designed not only to control and assimilate the conquered areas, but to administer the vast Frankish Kingdom.

Unlike in Saxony, the king did not enforced *Capitularia* in Aquitaine. An armed rebellion in Aquitaine would have had a greater political impact throughout the Frankish Kingdom, especially if it had been in connection with or in conjunction with the rebellious movements of Widukind in Saxony. That explains why the policy promoted by Charlemagne in Aquitaine

---

12   All of them are compiled in Boretius, Alfredus (ed.), *Capitularia Regum Francorum*, Monumenta Germaniae Historica (MGH), Leges, Hannover, 1883, vol. 1, pp. 52-79.

13   Thatcher, Oliver J.; Schevill, Ferdinand, *Europe in the Middle Age*, Charles Scribner's Sons, New York, 1911, pp. 120-122.

was substantially more diplomatic and subtle. Possibly in the same 778 but surely three years later, in 781, after the meeting of Lippspringe and avoiding the issuance of specific *Capitularia* and without applying punitive measures to the principality of Aquitaine, Charlemagne appointed counts, dukes, and abbots of confidence in this territory and immediately adjacent areas. Most of them were of Frankish origin and most possibly very close to the court, and thus persons of great trust. As registered in the *Vita Hludowici imperatoris*:

> [N]ow, the very wise and cunning King Charles, knowing that a kingdom is like a body that will soon be affected by a condition, if it is not properly protected like a convalescent with certain medications and assistance, the advice and strength of the bishops was tried as needed. Abbots, counts, and many others generally called Vassi [vassals] by the Franks, were also established throughout the region of Aquitaine, who have among them as none others wisdom and strength as well as sly cunning. He entrusted them with the care of the kingdom since he considered them useful in securing the borders and in the management of the royal treasury.[14]

He first appointed Humbert as count of Bourges, Abbo as count of Poitiers, and Wigbod as count of Périgord. To Iterius he granted control of Auvergne, and to Bullus that of Velay. Chorso was transferred to Toulouse, and Sigwin to Bordeaux. Haimo maintained the care of the fortress of Albi, and Rotger that of Limoges. On Easter Monday of 781 the Pope crowned Charlemagne's son, Ludovico, who had conveniently been born on Aquitainian soil, granting him the title of king of Aquitaine, and thus attracting the favor of those Aquitainians who did not feel Frankish. At the same time, he did a similar thing with the Lombards. The Astronomer reveals how Ludovico, who was three years old, was taken to Aquitaine and crowned by the Pope.[15]

From the data provided by the Astronomer as well as by the *Breviarium missorum Aquitanicum* for the year 789, we can infer that the Kingdom of Aquitaine was built on a complex administrative structure that included the

---

14   Tremp, Ernst (ed.), *Astronomus. Das Leben Kaiser Ludwigs* (*Vita Hludowici imperatoris*), Monumenta Germaniae Historica (MGH), SSRG, LXIV, Hannover, 1995, pp. 290-292.

15   Tremp, Ernst (ed.), *Astronomus. Das Leben Kaiser Ludwigs* (*Vita Hludowici imperatoris*), Monumenta Germaniae Historica (MGH), SSRG, LXIV, Hannover, 1995, p. 294. The *Chronicon Moissiacense* also records the event in Pertz, Georg Heinrich (ed.), *Annales et chronica aevi Carolini*, Monumenta Germaniae Historica (MGH), SS, I, Hannover, 1826, p. 297.

four ecclesiastical provinces of Auch, Bourges, Bordeaux, and Narbonne. In this sense, the geographical boundaries of the new kingdom were broader than the former Basque Aquitaine. While the northern (Loire River), western (Atlantic Ocean), and southern (Garonne River) limits were maintained, Aquitaine widened its borders to the southeast toward the Mediterranean coast and the eastern Pyrenees. In fact, as the first and second chapters of the *Breviarium missorum Aquitanicum* note, these measures were reinstituted upon the measures established twenty years earlier by Pepin the Short after the conquest of Aquitaine. It should also be noted that, besides the organizational measures, the disposition number fifteen of the *Breviarium* refers to the prohibition of organizing armed bands (*'De truste non faciendo'*) in Aquitaine.[16]

Regarding Vasconia, the sources do not record any rebellion or administrative measures that would affect the Basque Kingdom of Lupus II Otsoa. Despite the insistence upon Frankish dominion over Vasconia ('Wascones subjugatos' in the *Annales Loiseliani* and *Annales Tiliani*, 'wasconibus subactis' in the *Annales Fuldensis* or 'subjugatis wasconibus' in the *Chronicle of Adonis*), the sources do not mention the presence of Frankish dukes or counts in Vasconia until the end of the eighth century, nor the payment of taxes, nor the sending of royal *missi* or *vassi* or the presence of any form of control or political, military or even administrative subjection to the Frankish Kingdom. Regarding peninsular Vasconia, the Arabic sources are very precise in referring to the Basque cheftains of southern Vasconia in the years immediately following the battle of Errozabal, as unbound to the Frankish Kingdom.[17] In fact, beyond the economic and even psychological translation of the military defeat of 778, and beyond the military and political turmoil that the Frankish monarch had to confront, the main political consequence of the disaster of Errozabal was the final crumbling of the political project of a Hispanic March covering the entire southern slope of the Pyrenees from east to west.

In this sense, Roussillon having submittted around the year 760, the campaign of 785 focused on taking Girona on the eastern side of the Pyrenees. Thirteen years later, the sources mention the taking of Urgell and Cerdanya and the capture of the fortress of Barcelona and its surroundings in 801. With these conquests, Charlemagne, who had been coronated in Rome

---

16   Boretius, Alfredus (ed.), *Capitularia Regum Francorum*, Monumenta Germaniae Historica (MGH), Leges, Hannover, 1883, vol. 1, p. 66.
17   James, Georg P. R., *France in the Life of Her Great Men: The History of Charlemagne*, J & J Harper, New York, 1833, p. 191.

in the year 800, managed to build the Gothic March, which constituted the eastern end of the original ambitious project of the Hispanic March. Between 798 and 802 the Frankish army made its way to Zaragoza following the course of the Ebro River to the west. But despite the *Annales Regni Francorum* stating that the Pamplonans had respected Frankish vassalage in 806,[18] subsequent events (the military expeditions of the years 812 and 824) provide evidence that the vassalage of the city of Pamplona to the Frankish Kingdom did not constitute a firm and prolonged commitment. Ensuing military campaigns were necessary to obtain the submission of the fortress of Pamplona, a project that would finally fail after the obstreperous defeat of 824.

The defeat of the Frankish forces in Errozabal in 778 also affected the Emirate of Cordoba, which feared not only the strength of the Muslim leaders of the Ebro valley, but also a possible Basque advance upon their lands south of the river Ebro, mainly in the mountains of modern Rioja and Burgos in which, as is evident in the place names of the region, the Basque language and ways of life were still preserved. Therefore, in 781 the Emir Abd-al-Rahman I undertook a punitive campaign against the Muslim *walies* of the Ebro valley and against the Basques.[19]

The events that took place in Vasconia between the First Battle of Errozabal in 778 and the third in 824 are very uncertain given that no great abundance of sources or of data about this crucial period of Basque history exists. On the other hand, it was a time of rapid change. Two monarchs, Mauregato (783-788) and Bermudo (788-791), succeeded to the Asturian throne until Alfonso II the Chaste returned and took possession of the throne in 791.[20] Alfonso II of Asturias, exiled from his land in 783, had taken refuge in the lands of Araba where his mother was born, remaining under Basque protection for about six years until 791. Abd-al-Rahman I (756-785/88) was succeeded on the throne of the Emirate of Cordoba by Hisham I (788-796), and he in turn by Al-Hakam ibn Hisham (796-822). In Baghdad three caliphs

---

18   Kurze, Friedrich (ed.), *Annales regni Francorum (741–829) qui dicuntur Annales Laurissenses maiores et Einhardi*, Monumenta Germaniae Historica (MGH), SSRG, VI, Hannover, 1895, p. 122.

19   Lafuente Alcántara, Emilio (ed.), *Ajbar Machmua (Colección de tradiciones), Crónica anónima del siglo XI*, Real Academia de la Historia, Madrid, 1867, p. 105. See also, Codera, Francisco, *Discursos leídos ante la Real Academia de la Historia en la recepción*, Impresor de los Señores Rojas, 1879, p. 72. Rusafa was a retirement villa on the outskirts of Cordoba, beyond the bridge over the Guadalquivir. See also, Codera, Francisco, *Estudios críticos de historia árabe española*, Editorial Maxtor, Valladolid, 2005, p. 226.

20   Gil Fernández, Juan, *Crónicas asturianas: Crónica de Alfonso III (Rotense y "A Sebastián"). Crónica albeldense (y "Profética")*, Universidad de Oviedo, Oviedo, 1985, p. 138.

succeed in a short lapse of thirty-four years: Muhammad ibn Mansur al-Mahdi (775-785), Abu Abdullah Musa ibn Mahdi al-Hadi (785-786), and Harun al-Rashid (786-809).

With respect to Vasconia, it is known that Lupus II Otsoa was succeeded at an uncertain date by his son Sancho I Lupus, whose relationship to Ludovico's Kingdom of Aquitaine or, in general, to the Carolingian Empire, escapes the sources. In any case, neither the *Vita Hludowici imperatoris* nor the *Annales Regni Francorum* mention Frankish counts in Vasconia until the revolt of Fedentiacus in 803. The sources also omit references to imperial *missi* in the domains of Sancho I Lupus, which leaves us to infer that although there was some link between the two kingdoms, it was not one of submission or vassalage, as happened in Saxony, Lombardy, or the neighboring Aquitaine.

On the other hand, the Astronomer recorded the conflict that took place between the recently appointed Count Chorso of Toulouse and the Basque chieftain Adeleric [Odalric] by 787. Chorso, to whom the *Vita Hludowici Imperatoris* indistinctly gives the titles *comes* and *dux Tolosanus*, 'attracted by the wiles of a Basque named Adeleric', falls into a trap from which he is only released after swearing to his captor. In order to remedy this situation, Ludovico and his noblemen, 'who managed the public affairs of the Kingdom of Aquitaine in Council',[21] organized a general assembly of the empire in a Septimanian location called Gotentod. Adeleric, despite having been summoned, did not agree to attend until the respective hostages were handed over to ensure his safety. Presents were even delivered to him, indicating that the affair had to be dealt with diplomacy to avoid a new armed conflict between the Franks and the Basques.

However, at that assembly the matter was apparently settled, and the next summer, possibly through the intercession of Charlemagne, Adeleric was called to Worms, where after being interrogated, he was condemned to exile. Chorso, for his part, 'because of his neglect has brought shame on the Frankish Kingdom', was deposed, and William was named in his place. The conviction of Adeleric generated unease among the Basques who, 'by nature fickle, were found to be very agitated by the punishment imposed upon Adeleric' who, while the sources do not describe it, should had been an envoy of 'the Basque prince'.[22] Only the diplomatic efforts of the new

21   Tremp, Ernst (ed.), *Astronomus. Das Leben Kaiser Ludwigs* (*Vita Hludowici imperatoris*), Monumenta Germaniae Historica (MGH), SSRG, LXIV, Hannover, 1995, pp. 296-300.
22   Tremp, Ernst (ed.), *Astronomus. Das Leben Kaiser Ludwigs* (*Vita Hludowici imperatoris*), Monumenta Germaniae Historica (MGH), SSRG, LXIV, Hannover, 1995, pp. 296-300.

Frankish Count of Toulouse, William (*Uuillelmus*), could avoid war. In order to seal and guarantee this uneasy peace, in that same year Ludovico called a new assembly in Toulouse, sending presents and messages of peace to Abu Taher (*Abu Taur*) and 'the rest of the neighbors of the Kingdom of Aquitaine'.

Starting in the first year of the new century, Ludovico, acting in a gradually more independent way with respect to his father, orchestrated the campaigns of subjection of the eastern side of the Pyrenees. At the diet convened in Toulouse in 801, the Ludovico introduced the project of the military campaigns upon the fortresses of Girona and Barcelona. The Basque *princeps* Sancho I Lupus, present at the assembly, objected and advised peace, saying, 'King, it is necessary to contain any censorship against your words because good advice flows from your mouth, but if the matter is referred to our judgement, I testify that, for my part, there will be peace and order'.[23]

Despite the objections of Sancho Lupus, the intervention in favor of the military operation of Count William of Toulouse inclined the balance in favor of war. The imperial armies composed of Aquitainians, Basques, Burgundians, and Septimanians entered the peninsula through the Pertus pass divided into several columns and were joined by small Muslim forces from fortresses along the Ebro valley in the vicinity of Barcelona. This army besieged the city, which withstood throughout the entire winter. The emirate responded by attacking throughout the south of Araba in order to force the Basques to divide their forces, but the Muslim troops under the command of Abd el-Malik and Abdul el-Karim were defeated. Barcelona finally surrendered in the spring of 801, remaining under the control of a Frankish count.

In reaction to the Frankish advance, in the summer of 801 Al-Hakam ibn Hisham sent a new army against southwestern Vasconia commanded by his own brother, Mu'awyba, who entered Araba along the river Zadorra toward Argantzun. However, upon arriving at the pass of Argantzungo haitzartea (called by the Arab chroniclers, *Fachch Argnsun*), the Muslim army was ambushed, suffering a severe defeat in September or October of that year. A good part of the commanders died in battle; Mu'awyba himself, who managed to flee with the rest of the Muslim column, perished shortly afterwards in Cordoba.

The emir immediately sent a second army led by Amrus ibn Yusuf, who had served under the command of Sulayman ibn al-Arabi. Yusuf directed his

23   Dulaurier, Édouard (ed.), *Histoire générale de Languedoc avec des notes et les pièces justifica-tives*, Édouard Privat Librairie Éditeur, Toulouse, 1876, vol. 2, p. 335.

forces against his hometown of Huesca, which he took by force, executing the governor Bahlul ibn Marzuq. From there he went toward Tudela, main city of the Banu Qasi, which he took possibly in the summer or autumn of 802, leaving his son Yusuf ibn Amrus in charge of it. Nevertheless, a coalition of Pamplonan Basques and Banu Qasi—whom the Arab chronicler generically called Franks—recaptured the fortress in 803, taking Yusuf himself as a prisoner. Yusuf was later taken to a place called by the Muslims *Kais Cliff* (*Çakhrat K'ays*), somewhere in the interior of Vasconia.[24] This event would lead to a subsequent campaign headed by Amrus ibn Yusuf that, starting this time from Zaragoza, entered Vasconia and took the fortress of *Çakhrat K'ays*, freeing his son.

The military campaigns upon the eastern Pyrenees and the Ebro valley as well as the violent campaigns of punishment of the emirate from the south upon Vasconia abetted and strengthened the alliance between the Basques and the Banu Qasi south of the Pyrenees, leading to further clashes with the Carolingian Empire to the north and the Emirate of Cordoba to the south. Thus, in 803 the Basque revolt broke out after the appointment of Luitardo as count of Fedentiacus, near Auch (current Fezensac) in northeastern Vasconia. The reaction of the Basques was very violent, to the point that several royal officials were imprisoned and killed, some of them on public pyres, but the Astronomer does not mention whether the count himself perished at the hands of the insurgents. Called before Ludovico and persuaded that their lives would be spared, some of the leaders of the revolt were imprisoned and burned alive, very possibly in Toulouse.[25]

The *Annales Regni Francorum* record that in 806, 'Navarrans and Pamplonans, who had separated themselves from the Saracens in previous years, were received under oath'.[26] The account is repeated in other Frankish sources such as the *Einhardi Annales*, the *Annales Tiliani*, and the *Reginionis Chronicon*.[27] But there was no vassalage whatsoever, as subsequent events

---

24   Ibn al-Athir, *Annales du Maghreb & de l'Espagne traduites et annotées par Edmond Fagnan*, Typographie Adolphe Jourdan, Alger, 1898, pp. 164-165.

25   Tremp, Ernst (ed.), *Astronomus. Das Leben Kaiser Ludwigs* (*Vita Hludowici imperatoris*), Monumenta Germaniae Historica (MGH), SSRG, LXIV, Hannover, 1995, p. 314.

26   In the original Latin: 'In Hispania vero Navarri et Pampilonenses, qui superioribus annis ad Sarracenos defecerant in fidem recepti sunt.' In Kurze, Friedrich (ed.), *Annales regni Francorum (741–829) qui dicuntur Annales Laurissenses maiores et Einhardi*, Monumenta Germaniae Historica (MGH), SSRG, VI, Hannover, 1895, p. 122.

27   Pertz, Georg Heinrich (ed.), *Annales et chronica aevi Carolini*, Monumenta Germaniae Historica (MGH), SS, I, Hannover, 1826, p. 193, 224 y 564 respectivamente.

prove, so that said oath ('in fides recepti') cannot be interpreted in terms of submission or surrender but rather as an alliance, especially if we take into account that there was no armed clash between the Basques of the southern Pyrenees and the Frankish Empire that would induce them to take an oath of vassalage. In fact, only six years later, after the death of the Basque *princeps* Sancho Lupus in 812, the Basques elevated his older brother, Semen Lupus, as *princeps*, who confronting Ludovico ruled Vasconia between the years 812 and 816.

Informed of the appointment of Semen Lupus, Ludovico organized a punitive campaign upon Vasconia, penetrating to the east upon Akitze (*Aquis* or *Dax*) where Semen Lupus promised submission. From here, as his aged father did thirty-four years before, he drove his forces through the Ibañeta Pass in Errozabal with the intention of approaching Pamplona from the north. The sources do not mention that the Frankish troops captured Pamplona and simply indicate that, after 'ordering everything as suited both the public and private interest', Ludovico decided to return to Toulouse through the pass of Errozabal. However, in order to avoid an ambush, he ordered the taking of as many women and children as he could capture to use them as human shields. So, despite the presence of hostile troops, no armed encounter of a greater scale occured. As the Astronomer Limosinus records:

> when spring arrived and he called his people to a general assembly, the rumor reached them that a certain Basque faction that had sur-rendered earlier had disloyally rebelled, for which reason the public interest advised responding in order to reprimand their contumacy. He proceeded therefore to organize and mobilize his army. He arrived at the city of Akitze (Aquis) and ordered that those who had incited the disloyalty present themselves before him. Since they refused to obey, he advanced and allowed the army to loot all their properties. Finally, when everything that seemed to belong to them had been destroyed, they came to him begging, and having lost everything, obtained the special grace of being forgiven. After overcoming the difficult passes of the Pyrenean Alps, he went down to Pamplona, staying there for as long as he wished, and arranging whatever seemed to him suitable for both public and private interest. But when he saw himself obliged to return through the same narrow mountain passes through which he had arrived, the Basques tried to implement their normal and innate habit of deception, but they were stopped by cunning, secured with prudence, and avoided with caution, because when one of them tried

to cause trouble, he was captured and hanged. And then almost all the women and children of the rest were captured, being conducted along with us even if it was necessary to trick them, so they could not cause any damage to the king or to the army.[28]

This campaign counted on the passive consent of the Emir of Cordoba Al-Hakam ibn Hisham, a natural enemy of the Basques. In fact, although the Hispanic March project was contrary to the interests of the emirate, a punitive campaign against the Basques like that of 812 did not cause the slightest interference with the Muslim order, which gained the weakening of a natural enemy. But beyond the political motivations, according to the records of the Frankish chroniclers, the defeat of Errozabal in 778 embittered the last years of the emperor. Perhaps his son wanted to pay him a last tribute since Charlemagne died soon after, in 814, when Ludovico inherited the title of emperor (*Karolus imperator obiit. Annus primus Hludowici imperatoris*).[29] As the *Chronicon Moissiacense* records, Pippin, son of Ludovico, received the crown of Aquitaine, so from that date on he had to deal with all matters related to Vasconia.[30]

Immediately after the crown of Aquitaine was in place, the first of a series of uprisings against the fragile Frankish order sprung up both to the north and south of the Pyrenees. The *Vita Hludowici Imperatoris* as well as the *Einhardi Annales* record the Basque revolt of 816, motivated by the deposition of the Frankish Count Sigwin (Siguinus), who had previously served as count of Bordeaux. As the Astronomer recorded, 'the citerior Basques [continental Basques], who live in the vicinity of the Pyrenees, with their usual instability, rebelled in mass. The cause of this uprising was that the emperor removed Count Sigwin from office as a punishment for his depraved habits, which were unbearable. Two expeditions were sufficient to subdue them, after which they repented and asked repeatedly for peace.'[31]

---

28 Tremp, Ernst (ed.), *Astronomus. Das Leben Kaiser Ludwigs (Vita Hludowici imperatoris),* Monumenta Germaniae Historica (MGH), SSRG, LXIV, Hannover, 1995, pp. 332-334.
29 *Annalium Alamannicorum Continuatio Augiensisen,* in Pertz, Georg Heinrich (ed.), *Annales et chronica aevi Carolini,* Monumenta Germaniae Historica (MGH), SS, I, Hannover, 1826, p. 49.
30 Pertz, Georg Heinrich (ed.), *Annales et chronica aevi Carolini,* Monumenta Germaniae Historica (MGH), SS, I, Hannover, 1826, p. 311.
31 Tremp, Ernst (ed.), *Astronomus. Das Leben Kaiser Ludwigs (Vita Hludowici imperatoris),* Monumenta Germaniae Historica (MGH), SSRG, LXIV, Hannover, 1995, p. 364. The *Einhardi Annales* also register the event in Pertz, Georg Heinrich (ed.), *Annales et chronica aevi Carolini,* Monumenta Germaniae Historica (MGH), SS, I, Hannover, 1826, p. 203.

But once Sigwin (Siguinus) was defeated, the Frankish sources record new uprisings in the subsequent years (*'wascones rebellaverunt contra imperatorum'*).[32] The Basques elected a native *princeps* in reaction to the attempt to name Frankish counts in Vasconia, Garsiminnicum, or Gartzia Eneko. He challenged Ludovico, who was forced to undertake a new military campaign to subdue the rebellion.[33] That same year the Basques had to deal with a military campaign organized by the emir who, taking advantage of the recent march against Pamplona and the uprisings in the north, initiated a new Saracen invasion 'against the enemy of Allah, Belask al-Yalashki' (Belasko, lord of Pamplona who was in control of the lands of southern Araba on the western edge of Vasconia). As the Arabic chronicler Ibn Hayyan records, the Muslim army, led this time by Abd al-Karim ibn al-Wahid ibn Mughit, went in the spring of that year through Pancorbo toward the town of Oron, 20 kilometres (12.4 miles) to the southwest of Argantzun, where he faced the Basques. The encounter between both forces dragged on for thirteen consecutive days until the Basques retreated north up the high bed of the river Zadorra, protected by the ridges and mountains that border the valley. The Muslims moved back toward the south. Several of the Basque leaders died in the battle, among them Gartzia ibn Lupus and Sancho, 'the greatest knight of Pamplona'.[34] As Ibn al-Athir reports, 'the fighting was resumed as fiercely as ever, but the Christians lost a lot of people both as dead and as prisoners. Those who could cross the river escaped death, but several of the princes and noblemen were taken prisoners. However, the Franks, encamped upon the bank, prevented our people from crossing the river, and they fought for thirteen consecutive days. But then the rains started, and the flow of the river increased, making the crossing of the river difficult. Abd al-Krim left on July 6, 816.'[35]

---

32 The *Chronicon Moissiacense* records a new rebellion in Vasconia in 815: '*Eadem anno Wascones rebellant contra imperatorem.*' In Pertz, Georg Heinrich (ed.), *Annales et chronica aevi Carolini*, Monumenta Germaniae Historica (MGH), SS, I, Hannover, 1826, p. 312. Also, the *Annales Aniani* –that has similarities to the *Chronicon Moissiacense*- register the rebellion.

33 As recorded in the *Chronicon Moissiacense*: 'Wascones autem rebelles Garsimirum super se in principem eligunt; sed in secundo anno vitam cum principatu amisit, quem fraude usurpatum tenebat.' In Pertz, Georg Heinrich (ed.), *Annales et chronica aevi Carolini*, Monumenta Germaniae Historica (MGH), SS, I, Hannover, 1826, p. 312.

34 Lévi-Provençal, Évariste; García Gómez, Emilio, "Textos inéditos del *Muqtabis* de Ibn Hayyan sobre los orígines del Reino de Pamplona", *Al-Andalus*, vol. 19, 1954, p. 297.

35 Ibn al-Athir, *Annales du Maghreb & de l'Espagne traduites et annotées par Edmond Fagnan*, Typographie Adolphe Jourdan, Alger, 1898, pp. 179-180. For versions of the battle written by the Muslim chroniclers Ibn Idhari, al-Makkari, Ibn Jaldum and al-Nuwairi see, Estornés Lasa,

After two years of military campaigns over northern Vasconia, Gartzia Eneko perished on the battlefield in 818, and the Basques elected another chieftain, Lupus III Zentulo, cousin or brother of the deceased, who ruled until 823 in a constant state of war, confronting the emperor ('*Wascones rebelles*').[36] As the Astronomer Limusinus describes it, 'in that time, Lupo, a Basque by the nickname Centulli, rebelled and presented battle to Count Werino of Auvergne and to Count Berenguer of Toulouse. In the course of the battle, along with many others, he lost his brother, Gersanum, and he saved his own life by retreating. Brought before the emperor, he was ordered to defend himself, and, found guilty, was condemned to exile.'[37]

By order of Emperor Ludovico, the Frankish troops penetrated in 819 under the command of his son Pippin into the northwestern part of Vasconia in order to suffocate the rebellion and, 'in such a way did they pacify that province, that after having eliminated the rebels it seemed that there did not remain in the rebellious zone a single insurgent'.[38] But only a year later the *Petri Bibliothecarii Historia Francorum Abbreviata* records a new Basque uprising.[39] And five years later, the emperor was forced to send new troops to Vasconia.

In 822 Al-Hakam ibn Hisham died, succeeded by his son Abd-al-Rahman II as head of the Emirate of Cordoba until 852. The first twenty years of the new emir's rule were marked by the wars against the Basque and Asturian

Bernardo, *Historia General de Euskal Herria. 476-824 época vascona*, in *Enciclopedia General Ilustrada del País Vasco*, vol. 2, Auñamendi, Donostia, 1981, pp. 329-331.

36   The *Chronicon Moissiacense* records the insurrection: '[*E*]*ius exercitus, quem miserat super Wascones rebelles, cum triumpho victoriae reversi sunt, occisis tyrannibus: et terra quievit.*' In Pertz, Georg Heinrich (ed.), *Annales et chronica aevi Carolini*, Monumenta Germaniae Historica (MGH), SS, I, Hannover, 1826, p. 313.

37   Tremp, Ernst (ed.), *Astronomus. Das Leben Kaiser Ludwigs (Vita Hludowici imperatoris)*, Monumenta Germaniae Historica (MGH), SSRG, LXIV, Hannover, 1995, p. 390. See also the *Einhardi Annales* in Pertz, Georg Heinrich (ed.), *Annales et chronica aevi Carolini*, Monumenta Germaniae Historica (MGH), SS, I, Hannover, 1826, p. 204.

38   The *Einhardi Annales* records the event in Pertz, Georg Heinrich (ed.), *Annales et chronica aevi Carolini*, Monumenta Germaniae Historica (MGH), SS, I, Hannover, 1826, p. 206. The *Vita Hludowici Imperatoris* also records the events in Tremp, Ernst (ed.), *Astronomus. Das Leben Kaiser Ludwigs (Vita Hludowici imperatoris)*, Monumenta Germaniae Historica (MGH), SSRG, LXIV, Hannover, 1995, p. 396. Finally, the *Einhardi Fuldensis Annales* also record that the Basques had been defeated: '*Pippinus, filius imperatoris, Wascones vicit ac subelit.*' In Pertz, Georg Heinrich (ed.), *Annales et chronica aevi Carolini*, Monumenta Germaniae Historica (MGH), SS, I, Hannover, 1826, p. 357.

39   *Pipinus, Huiudovici filius, Vascones vicit* [820], in Pertz, Georg Heinrich (ed.), *Annales et chronica aevi Carolini*, Monumenta Germaniae Historica (MGH), SS, I, Hannover, 1826, p. 417. However, it is necessary to consider that the chronicle could be referring to the rebellion that had taken place the previous year, in 819.

Christian princes in the north. The first offensive happened in 824, only two years after he ascended the throne, when coinciding with an offensive of the troops of Ludovico against Pamplona, Abd-al-Rahman II ordered an attack against Araba.

After a number of fruitless campaigns, in which the Basques had impeded the Muslim forces from penetrating into the plain of Gasteiz, in the heart of Araba, Abd al-Krim decided to advance from the east, from Calahorra, ascending to the north and very possibly penetrating over the plain of Gasteiz from Azazeta.[40] Busy as the Basques were fighting against the Frankish counts in Errozabal, the campaign, led again by Abd al-Krim, encountered practically no resistance:

> And in the year 208 (823-824) the raid on Araba and Al-Kile took place, which was led by Abd al-Krim ibn al-Wahid in the summer expedition, and camped on the Tseguer, and the armies of Islam joined him. And they proceeded around in a variety of ways trying to decide by which door they would enter into the house of Christianity, and agreed that it would take place through the door of Araba, since that door was the most dangerous for the enemy and the most impregnable for its owner. And they descended through a gorge which is called Djernik, behind which was a valley where the enemy had their stores and provisions. And the army attacked those plains and took them, and as for the provisions of those stores took them as well, causing besides the desolation of all the inhabited places and empty farm houses they found on their way. And the Muslims were profitable and triumphant. May Allah be praised.[41]

Once the zone had been sacked, the Muslim troops returned toward the south.

In the north, in the context of the campaigns of punishment headed by Pippin against Vasconia, Ludovico ordered a third advance on Pamplona. The sources do not mention the reason for this expedition, although, considering events prior to and immediately after the battle, it is possible that there was a new uprising. The expedition, ordered by the emperor, was led by Counts Aeblus and Aznar in the spring of 824. After arriving in Pamplona,

40 However, without more data than that provided by Arab sources, the plain that Ibn Idhari refers to could be the Trebiñu Valley.

41 Estornés Lasa, Bernardo, *Historia General de Euskal Herria. 476-824 época vascona*, in *Enciclopedia General Ilustrada del País Vasco*, vol. 2, Auñamendi, Donostia, 1981, p. 346. See also in the same source versions of the campaign provided by Muslim chroniclers Ibn al-Athir, al-Nuwairi, al-Makkari and, Ibn Jaldum (pp. 346 and 347).

the army returned toward Errozabal. In the context of the last campaigns for the creation of the Hispanic March, it is very possible that more than a punitive operation, the campaign had as its objective the subjection of the peninsular Basques through the establishment of a garrison in the city with the aid of some Basque faction from north of the Pyrenees. In any case, the expeditionary force entered the Zize pass where the Third Battle of Errozabal took place.

The defeat, of similar dimensions to that which had happened forty-six years earlier, turned out to be disastrous, the Franks being massacred to the last man ('capti sunt, et copiae cuas secum habere paene usque ad internicionem delatae').[42] Both counts, Aeblus and Aznar (Asinarius), fell prisoner at the hands of the Basques. The former was delivered to the new emir of Cordoba as a present, perhaps to appease Abd-al-Rahman and arrange a truce. On the other hand, Count Aznar, 'citerioris Wasconiae comes', was forgiven.[43] As the Astronomer records it in the *Vita Ludovicii Pii*:

> Counts Aeblus and Aznar were ordered to cross the top of the Pyrenees with large contingents of troops and to advance toward Pamplona. Once their assignment was accomplished there, they had to empirically verify by personal experience the known enmity of the inhabitants of the place. Surrounded, they ended up falling into the hands of their enemies, having lost all their troops. They sent Aeblus to Cordoba, to the king of the Saracens, while they forgave Aznar, to whom they were united by ties of blood.[44]

Apart from the military impact, the main political effect of the battle was the coronation of Eneko Aritza as king of the peninsular Basques. The constitution of the Kingdom of Pamplona obliged Ludovico to reverse his enterprise of subjecting Vasconia and finally dashed the ambitious political

42   Pertz, Georg Heinrich (ed.), *Annales et chronica aevi Carolini*, Monumenta Germaniae Historica (MGH), SS, I, Hannover, 1826, p. 213.

43   It is very possible that this Aznar was Count Aznar Galindo, Basque in origin but subject to the Franks, who was ousted from office in the county of Aragon for his son Gartzia Galindones the Bad, and died later at the hands of the Basques during the insurrection of 836.

44   Aznar was related to the Basque leaders Eneko Aritza and Musa ibn Fortun ibn Qasi, father of Musa ibn Musa, principal leaders of the Basque forces. See Tremp, Ernst (ed.), *Astronomus. Das Leben Kaiser Ludwigs (Vita Hludowici imperatoris)*, Monumenta Germaniae Historica (MGH), SSRG, LXIV, Hannover, 1995, p. 422. The *Annales Regni Francorum* also record the event in Kurze, Friedrich (ed.), *Annales regni Francorum (741–829) qui dicuntur Annales Laurissenses maiores et Einhardi*, Monumenta Germaniae Historica (MGH), SSRG, VI, Hannover, 1895, p. 166. The *Einhardi Annales* also recorded the battle in Pertz, Georg Heinrich (ed.), *Annales et chronica aevi Carolini*, Monumenta Germaniae Historica (MGH), SS, I, Hannover, 1826, p. 213.

project of the Hispanic March, recorded, among other sources, by the *Vita Karoli Magni*.[45] The victory likewise consolidated the alliance between the Islamicized Basques of the Banu Qasi clan and the Pyrenean Basques, who concentrated around the king of Pamplona, from Araba in the west to the County of Aragon in the east.

The victory also stimulated rebellious movements in the north of Vasconia, where, as the *Prudentii Trecensis Annales* records, Count Aznar was murdered in 836 trying to repress a new uprising in which, despite the objections of the emperor and of King Pippin of Aquitaine, he was replaced by his brother Sancho ('Sancius, comes Vasconiae'), elected by the Basques.[46] In 840 Ludovico died ('Hludowicus imperator obii'),[47] and his death initiated period of uncertainty for the empire.

45 Holder-Egger, Oswald (ed.), *Einhardi Vita Karoli Magni,* Monumenta Germaniae Historica (MGH), SSRG, Hannover & Leipzig, 1911, p. 18.

46 Pertz, Georg Heinrich (ed.), *Annales et chronica aevi Carolini*, Monumenta Germaniae Historica (MGH), SS, I, Hannover, 1826, p. 430.

47 *Annalium Alamannicorum Continuatio Augiensisen*, in Pertz, Georg Heinrich (ed.), *Annales et chronica aevi Carolini*, Monumenta Germaniae Historica (MGH), SS, I, Hannover, 1826, p. 49.

5. Impact of the Battle in the Medieval Tradition

Abstract

This chapter focuses on the magnitude of a historic episode that became a key literary and artistic topic of early medieval European art. It analyzes the characterization of the Frankish heroes as depicted in the epic poem *La Chanson de Roland* and in the *Historia Caroli Magni et Rotholandi*, and the interpretation of the battle by the master glassmaker who manufactured the exceptional stained-glass window of the Chartres cathedral, four centuries later. Chartres has been designated a World Heritage Site by UNESCO, which identifies the glass as 'the high point of French Gothic art'. It is fascinating to study how real characters became legendary heroes and how real, historic events became legends; especially interesting is the analysis of the intentions behind this conversion from reality into fantasy.

Keywords: Rencesvals, Roland, Charlemagne, Pamplona, Epic poetry, European Medieval literature.

No written chronicle during Charlemagne's lifetime ever mentioned the battle. In the first version of the *Annales Regni Francorum*, the chronicler stated only that 'Ibn al-Arabi, Abu Taher (*Abu Taur*), and a large number of Saracens turned over hostages [to Charlemagne], Pamplona was destroyed, the Basques of Hispania and the Navarrese were subdued and he returned to France'.[1]

---

1   Kurze, Friedrich (ed.), *Annales regni Francorum (741–829) qui dicuntur Annales Laurissenses maiores et Einhardi*, Monumenta Germaniae Historica (MGH), SSRG, VI, Hannover, 1895, p. 50. See also, D'Abadal i de Vinyals, Ramon, *Catalunya Carolingia. El Domini Carolingi a Catalunya*, Barcelona, 1986, p. 44; Thorpe, Lewis G. M. (ed.), *Einhard and Notker the Stammerer: Two lives of Charlemagne*, Penguin, London, 1969, p. 182. The *Annales Laurissenses* also omit mentioning the battle in Pertz, Georg Heinrich (ed.), *Annales et chronica aevi Carolini*, Monumenta Germaniae

Irujo, X., *Charlemagne's Defeat in the Pyrenees: The Battle of Rencesvals*. Taylor & Francis, 2021
DOI 10.5117/9789463721059_CH05

However, upon the emperor's death, the revised version of the *Annales Regni Francorum*—a version followed by Einhard—added important information, asserting that Charlemagne decided to turn around and withdraw through Errozabal ('regredi statuens Pyrinei saltum') where his forces suffered an ambush that affected his entire army ('totum exercitum magno tumulto perturbant').[2] The new version offers in addition a large amount of data, providing explanations about the reasons for the defeat and the impossibility of avenging the death of so many knights. Einhard decided to change the expression 'the entire army' ('totum exercitum') to the more circumspect 'the back part of the caravan of provisions' ('extremam impedimentorum partem') and he gave for the first time the names of three of the knights killed on the battlefield.[3]

In 840, the Astronomer also gave a detailed explanation of the events in the *Vita Hludowici Pii*, which underscores the fact that sixty years after the battle it continued to occupy the attention of the chroniclers to the extent that they were unable or refused to avoid describing it. All of which indicates that, in fact, it had been a significant military event, one that was subsequently going to inspire an epic romance three centuries later. Narratives of a person's historical deeds or those with a historical basis were precisely the stories that became legends and later literature by virtue of the interest they undoubtedly aroused among their audience.

The battle of Rencesvals provided four key ingredients to become one of the earliest and most successful legendary romances in Western Europe. Heroism, martyrdom, and the eternal struggle between good and evil are some of the legend's utmost appealing elements and, the plot, essentially a story of heroism, was endowed with the necessary ingredients to ensure its dissemination. From this perspective, the Carolingian peers embody the values of the literary heroes of the eleventh to thirteenth centuries (still in a state of gestation in the eighth century). These values were the possession of superlative courage and honor, talent, and strength; the glorification of violence for the sake of a just and necessary cause; the arrogance and self-sufficiency derived from the security of living subordinate to a purpose higher than life itself; the transcendence of life beyond death through action and

Historica (MGH), SS, I, Hannover, 1826, p. 158. See also, Salrach i Marés, Josep M., *El procés de formació nacional de Catalunya: (segles VIII-IX)*, Edicions 62, 1978, p. 132.

2   Kurze, Friedrich (ed.), *Annales regni Francorum (741–829) qui dicuntur Annales Laurissenses maiores et Einhardi*, Monumenta Germaniae Historica (MGH), SSRG, VI, Hannover, 1895, pp. 51 & 53.

3   Thorpe, Lewis G. M. (ed.), *Einhard and Notker the Stammerer: Two lives of Charlemagne*, Penguin, London, 1969, pp. 182-83.

memory; and, in general terms, a certain dehumanization that subordinates the self to action and, consequently, the individual to the course of history. This fact converts men into giants and magnifies their actions, which explains why one of the most favored literary resource in this epic is hyperbole, reinforced by adjectivization, repetition, alliteration, and parataxis.

The religious aspect is also present. Urban II, at the Council of Clermont in 1095, called for the First Crusade (1096-1099), and after the capture of Edessa in 1144, Bernard of Clairvaux proclaimed the need to undertake a Second Crusade. The oldest manuscript of all the preserved copies of the *Chanson de Roland* was written between 1140 and 1170, years before the capture of Jerusalem by Saladin in 1187 and consequently greatly influenced by the speeches of fervent Christian authors. The impact that the Crusades in general and the capture of Jerusalem in particular had in Western Europe probably induced the troubadours to transform Charlemagne's campaign into the crusade that originated the Camino de Santiago (Way of St. James).

The romance is set in a remote time, remote enough to forge an appropriate dimension for the characters and their actions and, at the same time, unknown to the general public. In any case, the historical background is one of the specific ingredients of the epic poems that, by means of the narration of a potentially real past, transported the public into a future also virtually possible and encouraged patriotic and pious feelings.

The mention of the heroes' journey through exotic countries in the face of distant civilizations and across strange lands was at the same time an essential ingredient of epic literature, in this case perfectly covered by the scenic backdrops provided by Vasconia and Hispania.

One of the first signs that the romance of Rencesvals was being widely spread is that it popularized the names of the Frankish heroes who lost their lives in that combat. The *Vita Pii Imperatoris Hludowicii*, written around 840 by the astronomer Limusinus, omitted mentioning the warriors who died in the battle because they were 'known by all' ('vulgata sunt').[4] Studies on Medieval onomastics have brought to light the popular tradition during the tenth century of baptizing brothers as Roland and Oliver, which shows that even at that time the narrative of the deeds of both heroes had far transcended the limits of history and even of literature itself.[5] Almost

4   Tremp, Ernst (ed.), *Astronomus. Das Leben Kaiser Ludwigs* (*Vita Hludowici imperatoris*), Monumenta Germaniae Historica (MGH), SSRG, LXIV, Hannover, 1995, pp. 286 & 288.

5   Lejeune, Rita, "La naissance du couple littéraire 'Roland et Olivier'", *Mélanges Henri Grégoire, Annuaire de l'Institut de philologie et d'histoire orientales et slaves*, Bruselas, 1950, pp. 371-401. See also, Horrent, Jules, *La Chanson de Roland dans les littératures française et espagnole au moyen âge*, Bibliothèque de la Faculté de Philosophie et Lettres de l'Université de Liège, Paris, 1951;

three hundred years after the *Vita Pii Hludowicii Imperatoris* was written, William of Malmesbury (*c.* 1080/1095-*c.* 1143) noted in *De Gestis Regnum Anglorum* (Chronicle of the Kings of England) that during the Battle of Hastings in 1066—that is, 288 years after the Battle of Errozabal—Taillefer chanted stanzas from the *Song of Roland* to rouse the soldiers:

> Then a song of Roland was begun, so that the man's warlike example would arouse the fighters.
> Calling on God for aid, they joined battle.
> Taillefer, who sang very well, rode on a swift horse before the duke singing of Charlemagne and Roland and Oliver and the knights who died at Roncevaux.[6]

The ballads sung by Taillefer, one of the many jugglers who partook of this tradition, most likely differed from those that have reached us by Turoldus's hand. Moreover, the language in which the referred passages and others before this were sung probably would to some extent or even essentially have varied from Turoldus's version. But despite the changes that a text that was transmitted orally for three centuries inevitably suffered, the story remained essentially the same.

Together with the *Chanson de Roland* and *Gormont et Isembart*, The *Chançun de Williame* (or *Chanson de Guillaume*) is one of the oldest epic poems in Medieval Europe, datable to around the first half of the twelfth century, although the first part of the poem may be older. This epic also described what happened on the beaches of Hastings:

> Lord William had a jongleur
> There was no finer Singer in all France
> Nor bolder swordsman in battle
> And he could recite songs from the epics
> About Clovis, the first emperor
> Who in sweet France believed in God, our Lord,
> And about his son, Flovent the bold,
> And about all kings who became famous

Aebischer, Paul, *Préhistoire et protohistoire du Roland d'Oxford*, Editions Francke, Berne, 1972, pp. 157-160.

6   Bowra, Cecil Maurice, *Heroic Poetry*, Macmillan, London, 1964, pp. 414. A second translation of this passage is in Stubbs, William (ed.), *Willelmi Malmesbiriensis Monachi De gestis regnum Anglorum. Libri Quinique, Historiae Novellae Libri III*, Her Majesty's Stationery Office (HMSO), London, 1887-89, p. 302.

Up to Pippin, the brave little fighter,
And Charlemagne and Roland, his nephew.[7]

The *Nota Emilianense* found in the Monastery of San Millán de la Cogolla, written sometime between 1054 and 1076,[8] also describes the campaign and mentions some of the heroes killed in the battle, but unlike the *Chanson de Roland* it does not include Eggihard (*Aggiardus*) in the list. It does mention others, which indicates that until the eleventh and mainly twelfth centuries the various versions of the story had not been captured in writing and thus did not crystallize, giving rise to local adaptations transmitted in various languages.[9] The importance of the *Nota Emilianense* lies in the fact that it is the first time that Rencesvals (Errozabal) is mentioned as the place of the battle.[10]

The tradition fostered from the early ninth century on would soon result in various compositions that included the romance of Rencesvals. One of the first variations of the story to be collected in writing was *Carmen de Prodicione Guenonis*,[11] or the *Song of the Betrayal of Ganelon*, a long poem

---

7   Tyler, Elizabeth Stearns, *La Chançun de Williame*, Oxford University Press, New York, 1919.

8   The note was initially published in 1721, but its publication went completely unnoticed. See Berganza, Francisco, *Antigüedades de España, propugnadas en las noticias de sus reyes, en la crónica del real monasterio de San pedro de Cerdeña, en historias, cronicones y otros instrumentos, manuscritos, que hasta ahora no han visto la luz pública*, Francisco de Hierro, Madrid, 1721, vol. 2, p. 560. Following this finding, it was republished in 1953, transcribed, translated and commented on by Damaso Alonso in Alonso, Dámaso, *La primitiva épica francesa a la luz de una nota emilianense*, Revista de Filología española, 37, Madrid, 1953, pp. 1-94.

9   Delbouille, Maurice, *Sur la genèse de la Chanson de Roland*, Palais des académies, Bruselas, 1954.

10   Alonso, Dámaso, *La primitiva épica francesa a la luz de una nota emilianense*, Revista de Filología española, 37, Madrid, 1953, pp. 1-94. Also in Alonso, Dámaso, *La primitiva épica francesa a la luz de una nota emilianense*, Consejo Superior de Investigaciones Científicas, Madrid, 1954. See also, Frappier, Jean, *Les Chansons De Geste Du Cycle De Guillaume D'orange: Le Couronnement De Louis, Le Charroi De Nîmes, La Prise D'orange*, Société d'Edition d'Enseignement Supérieur, Paris, 1955, p. 78; Menéndez Pidal, Ramón, *La Chanson de Roland et la tradition épique des Francs*, Librairie Picard, Paris, 1960, p. 390.

11   First edition in Michel, Francisque, *La Chanson de Roland ou de Roncevaux, du XIIe siècle*, Chez Silvestre libraire, Paris, 1837, pp. 228-242. Latin edition with some corrections on Michel's first edition is in Paris, Gaston B., P. (ed.), *Carmen de Prodicione Guenonis et la légende de Roncevaux*, Société des amis de la Romania, XI, 1882, pp. 465-518. English edition is in Livingstone, Arthur, "The Carmen de Prodicione Guenonis Translated into English, with Textual Notes", *The Romanic Review, a Quarterly Journal*, vol. 2, Columbia University Press, New York, 1911, pp. 61-79. See also bilingual French/Latin edition in Mortier, Raoul (ed.), *La Chronique de Turpin en les grandes chroniques de France, Carmen de Prodicione Guenonis, Ronsansvals*, Éditions de la Geste Francor, Paris, 1941, vol. 3, pp. 105 et seq.

of 479 verses composed, based on its language, style, and versification, in the beginning of the twelfth century (*c.* 1120).[12] The poem is found on pages 153-155 of the manuscript *Cottons Titus A. XIX* in the British Museum. Frantz Michel provided the first edition of *Carmen* in 1837 in his work *La Chanson de Roland ou de Roncevaux, du XIIe siècle* (The Song of Roland or of Roncesvalles, of the 12th century).[13]

With minor differences, the plot of *Carmen de Prodicione Guenonis* follows faithfully that of the *Song of Roland*. The action begins seven years after Charlemagne initially marched to Hispania and once he had conquered every fortress in his way, with the exception of Zaragoza. As Turoldus sings in the *Chanson*, at Roland's suggestion, Charlemagne decides to send a message to Marsilius, King of Zaragoza, delivered by his knight Ganelon. Ganelon is outraged because he thinks that Roland wants to see him dead, since Marsilius had already beheaded the two previous emissaries (Basil and Basan). Indeed, Charlemagne threatens King Marsilius, telling him that if he does not surrender Zaragoza, he will end up being 'less than no one, even less than that if that can be'.[14]

Actually, Ganelon's fears are real, and Marsilius is about to order his death, but the *wali's* beautiful wife saves the life of Charlemagne's messenger. On this point the *Carmen* differs from the *Chanson*, which does not mention the participation of Bramimonde ('la reine Bramimunde'),[15] wife of King Marsilius, in Ganelon's favor.[16]

---

12   Schlyter, Kerstin, *Les énumérations des personnages dans la Chanson de Roland: étude comparative*, C.W.K. Gleerup, Lund, 1974, pp 35-36.

13   Michel, Francisque, *La Chanson de Roland ou de Roncevaux, du XIIe siècle*, Chez Silvestre libraire, Paris, 1837, pp. 228-242.

14   Paris, Gaston B, p. (ed.), *Carmen de Prodicione Guenonis et la légende de Roncevaux, Société des amis de la Romania,* XI, 1882, p. 467.

15   She appears eight times in the *Chanson*. In stanza 50, when Bramimunde gives Guenes two collars for his wife: '[T]hey are of pure gold, inlaid with amethysts and hyacinths; worth more than all the treasures of Rome, your emperor never possessed so beautiful ones.' In stanzas 187 and 188 when crying after seeing the wounds of her husband King Marsiliun. In 197 which states that the Christian God has defeated the Muslims. In 201 after the defeat of Marsiliun. In 264 when on top of the tower along with 'the monks and priests of the false law', she watches the defeat of their king. In 265, in which, after her husband's death, she surrenders the ten largest towers and the fifty small ones to Charlemagne. In 267 Charlemagne takes her captive. And, in stanza 291 when having done justice, and appeased his great anger, the emperor converts Bramimunde to Christianity.

16   Paris, Gaston B, p. (ed.), *Carmen de Prodicione Guenonis et la légende de Roncevaux, Société des amis de la Romania,* XI, 1882, pp. 468-469.

Marsilius offers Ganelon all kinds of gifts, and he, blinded by rage and now also by ambition, plans his betrayal.[17] When Roland and his men, at the rearguard of the army, enter Errozabal, they are slaughtered. In line with later traditions, the author describes the Zize pass as a narrow mountain gorge 'surrounded by a steep and rugged mountain range, which is traversed by a terrible and fearsome valley'. Then, 'a terrible terror stops them there' and combat ensues in which all the heroes fall, one after the other. *Carmen* reproduces the scene in which Roland, under attack and in a fit of rage and panic, blows the olifant in an affront to Oliver, who tries to persuade the hero not to. In Oliver's view, to call for help was 'an intolerable ignominy, a perpetual dishonor, the greatest shame'.[18]

After the heroes' deaths on the battlefield, Charlemagne turns back and defeats Marsilius. Finally, diverging from the *Chanson*, at the end of the journey Ganelon is brought before the king and is punished right there for his betrayal. His hands and feet tied to four horses, he is pulled to pieces, 'and so his life ends'.

Around 1170 Konrad von Pfaffe composed a German version of the *Chanson de Roland* entitled *Rolandslied*.[19] The author complemented Christian themes with references to patriotic feelings, emphasizing by this means Charlemagne's feats in the framework of a religious crusade. As Kuno Francke has noted, religious fervor guides the actions of the hero in the German poem, who is portrayed as a crusader, a hero of the Old Testament. Charlemagne, having heard about the horrors of Muslim Hispania—where the Saracens worship idols and do not fear God—decides to rescue his people and 'throw paganism into the dark night of hell'. For an entire night the king remains fervently praying and the next morning he calls his twelve peers to him and informs them that they have been chosen to win the crown of martyrdom, which is 'as shiny as the morning star'. This version introduces new scenes, like the chess match that partially coincides with stanzas 8 to 11 of the *Chanson*. When the Muslim messengers approach Charlemagne to make a false offer, they find him playing chess. Without asking for him, the emissaries recognize the king by his fiery look. Three times the chief ambassador speaks to him, declaring the will of their master to accept Christianity. The emperor, his head bowed, listens in silence, until

---

17 Paris, Gaston B, p. (ed.), *Carmen de Prodicione Guenonis et la légende de Roncevaux*, Société des amis de la Romania, XI, 1882, pp. 470-471.

18 Paris, Gaston B, p. (ed.), *Carmen de Prodicione Guenonis et la légende de Roncevaux*, Société des amis de la Romania, XI, 1882, pp. 476-477.

19 Karl Bartsch's edition: Pfaffe, Konrad der, *Das Rolandslied*, F. A. Brockhaus, Leipzig, 1874.

he finally lifts his face and, as if moved by divine inspiration, bursts into praise of the Almighty.[20]

King Haakon Haakonarson or Haakon IV the Old of Norway (1217-1263) ordered the translation into Old Nordic[21] of a series of literary works including the *Chanson de Roland*, now entitled *Karlamagnús saga*.[22] This version of the epic is extremely interesting since the original version on which the translation was based is believed to have been an old copy of the *Chanson*, probably datable to the eleventh century. Divided into several parts, the first brings together a series of legendary interconnected pieces from which the original *Chanson de Roland* was probably originally drawn. This collection of texts includes, for example, a passage in which the origin of Ganelon's hatred is due to Roland's relationship with Geluviz, his second wife. Also of interest are the stories about the birth and youth of Roland, the origin of the sword Durandal, as well as the episodes regarding the capture of Pamplona (*Noples*)[23] and the account of the legend of St. Giles, in which Gisela,[24] having slept with her brother Charlemagne, conceived Roland and later retired to a convent. Charlemagne, penitent and contrite, tries to confess his dreadful sin to St. Giles, but in the end he finds himself unable to tell the hermit the truth. One day, as St. Giles celebrates mass, St. Gabriel appears to him and gives him a manuscript revealing the truth, prophesying that from this relationship a boy named Roland was to be born, and ordering that Gisela be married to Milon of Angleris. Charlemagne, conforming to the command, betrothed Gisela to Milon and named him duke of Brittany, which explains why Roland was later governor of this territory.[25]

20 Francke, Kuno, *Social Forces in German Literature: A Study in The History of Civilization*, Henry Holt & Co., New York, 1899, pp. 56-58.
21 Language formed from the eighth century from the old Germanic that gave rise to the family of the Scandinavian languages.
22 An edition in the original language is in *Karlamagnús saga*, C. R. Unger, Christiana, 1860. An edition of the original adapted to contemporary Icelandic is in Vilhjálmsson, Bjarni (ed.), *Karlamagnús saga og kappa hans*, Islendingasagnaútgáfan, Reykjavik, 1954 (3 vols.) There is an abridged French edition in Aebischer, Paul, *Textes norrois et littérature française de moyen âge*, vol. 1, Librairie Droz, Genève, 1954; Aebischer, Paul, *Textes norrois et littérature française de moyen âge*, vol. 2, Librairie Droz, Genève, 1972. An unabridged edition is in Aebischer, Paul, *Rolandiana Borealia. La "Saga af Runzivals bardaga" et ses dérivés scandinaves comparés à la Chanson de Roland. Essai de restauration du manuscrit français utilisé par le traducteur norrois*, Université de Lausanne. Publications de la Faculté des Lettres XI, Lausanne, 1954.
23 Duggan, Joseph J., *A Guide to Studies on the Chanson de Roland*, DS Brewer, London, 1976, p. 37.
24 The *Historia Caroli Magni et Rotholandi* names her Berta, confusing the real name of Charlemagne's sister (Gisela) with Berta, his mother's name.
25 Gabriele, Matthew; Stuckey, Jace, *The Legend of Charlemagne in the Middle Ages: Power, Faith, and Crusade*, Palgrave Macmillan, 2008, p. 5.

L'Entrée en Espagne is a manuscript of three hundred and four pages and approximately 20,000 verses dateable to the fourteenth century, with a great number of miniatures. The author was from Pavia, and the original contains numerous Italianisms. *L'Entrée en Espagne* presents new episodes and many variations on the original text, such as frequent allusions to the legend of the Round Table, including references to the Holy Grail not found in earlier Medieval traditions and moral digressions.[26]

The author states that he follows the chronicles of Turpin (*Historia Caroli Magni et Rotholandi*) but also those of Jean de Navarre and Gautier de Aragon, which allows him the opportunity to integrate new episodes into the text, thus generating more excitement for a narrative that had circulated throughout Western Europe for at least four centuries. With respect to the siege of Pamplona, the author mentions that it lasted several years and includes an interesting episode that would likewise be noted by the *Karlamagnús saga* regarding the taking and sacking of the fortress of Nobilis to the south of the river Garonne in continental Vasconia. According to both accounts, Charlemagne sent Roland to capture Nobilis, but he ordered the life of King Fulr to be spared. However, a massacre follows the attack by Roland's men, and Roland himself kills the king. When the fight ends, the slaughter is such that Roland's men seek to wash the bloodstained fields in order to deceive Charlemagne, but when the emperor arrives and realizes what has happened, he slaps Roland.[27]

There is a German version of the *Chanson* entitled *Ruolantes Liet* or *Rolandslied*,[28] based on an old version of the *Historia Caroli Magni et Rotholandi*. There is also a Dutch version from the beginning of the thirteenth century (*Roelantslied*),[29] a Welsh version known as *Ystorya Carolo Magno*,[30] and a later version of the romance in Occitan composed in the fourteenth

26 Limentani, Alberto, *"L'Entrée d'Espagne" e i signori d'Italia*, Antenore, Padua, 1992, p. 8.

27 Gautier, Léon, *L'Entrée en Espagne: chanson de geste inédite, renfermée dans un manuscrit de la Bibliothèque de Saint-Marc à Venise*, Techener, Paris, 1858, p.

28 Grimm, Wilhelm, *Ruolantes liet*, Göttingen 1838.

29 Gerritsen, Willem P.; Van Melle, Anthony G., *A Dictionary of Medieval Heroes: Characters in Medieval Narrative Traditions and Their Afterlife in Literature, Theatre and The Visual Arts*, The Boydell Press, Woodbridge, 2000, p. 235.

30 Williams, Robert, "The History of Charlemagne: A Translation of *Ystorya Carolo Magno* with a Historical and Critical Introduction", *Y Cymmrodor*, 20, 1907, pp. 1-219. See also, Powel, Thomas, *Ystorya de Carolo magno, From the Red Book of Hergest*, Honourable Society of Cymmrodorion, London, 1883; Duggan, Joseph J., *A Guide to Studies on the Chanson de Roland*, DS Brewer, London, 1976, p. 44.

or fifteenth century entitled *Ronsasvals*.[31] This version—of which only a few fragments have survived—is composed of 1,802 verses that cover the entire romance up to the death of Aude (Oliver's sister and Roland's lover), who collapses when the emperor gives her the news of the death of the latter (stanzas 268 and 269 of the *Chanson*)[32]. The incestuous relationship between Charlemagne and his sister is recorded in the Occitan version of the *Chanson* in which, before the body of Roland, Charlemagne says 'I am your father and your uncle at the same time, and you, dear sir, my nephew and my son'.[33]

The so-called *Navarrese Rencesvals,* a small fragment of 100 verses written in Romance that was copied on two pages inserted in a manuscript of 1366, is a piece of particular interest.[34] Datable to around the first third of the fourteenth century but possibly composed in the thirteenth century, the text records Charlemagne's emotional lament over the body of Roland and Turpin as well as the cries of Duke Aymond de Dordonne over the inert body of his son Rinalte Montauban, which concurs with stanzas 206 to 210 of the *Chanson* in the Oxford version. The fragment is entirely faithful to this version of the *Chanson* except for the fact that it depicts the heroes killed in the battle being decapitated, which can be explained by the juxtaposition on this point of the *Cantar de los Siete Infantes de Salas* (*Song of the Seven Princes of Salas*), in which Gonzalo Bustos, father of the seven decapitated brothers, weeps over their heads.[35]

In 1458 David Aubert compiled from preexisting fragments the *Chroniques et Conquestes de Charlemaine* (*Chronicles and Conquests of Charlemagne*), and in 1516 Ludovico Ariosto published an epic poem titled *Orlando Furioso*, introducing the romance to Italian Renaissance literature. Roland (Orlando)

31   Roques, Mario (ed.), "Ronsasvals, poème épique provençal", *Société des amis de la Romania*, XLVIII, 1922, pp. 311-314. This version of the poem has had two subsequent versions in Roques, Mario (ed.), "Ronsasvals, poème épique provençal", *Société des amis de la Romania*, LVIII, 1932, pp. 1-28 & 161-189. And, Roques, Mario (ed.), "Ronsasvals, poème épique provençal", *Société des amis de la Romania,* LXV, 1940-41, pp. 434-480.

32   Duggan, Joseph J., *A Guide to Studies on the Chanson de Roland*, DS Brewer, London, 1976, p. 43.

33   Cannone, Belinda; Orcel, Michel, *Figures de Roland*, Klincksieck, Paris, 1998, p. 37.

34   The text was reproduced and studied first by Ramón Menéndez Pidal in 1917. Menéndez Pidal, Ramón, "Roncesvalles, un nuevo cantar de gesta español del siglo XIII'", Revista de Filología Española, IV, Madrid, 1917, pp. 105-204. See also, Horrent, Jules, *Roncesvalles. Etude sur le fragment de cantar de gesta conservé à l'Archivo de Navarra (Pampelune)*, Société d'Edition 'Les Belles Lettres', Paris, 1951. Also an annotated reproduction of the poem in Riquer, Martín, *Chanson de Roland. Cantar de Roldán y el Roncesvalles Navarro*, Acantilado, Barcelona, 2003.

35   Riquer, Martín, *Chanson de Roland. Cantar de Roldán y el Roncesvalles Navarro*, Acantilado, Barcelona, 2003, p. 398.

is the central character of *Orlando Furioso* along with other legendary figures, but the story is set in a different context.

Dante, in the *Divine Comedy*, also mentions the defeat of Charlemagne. In Canto XXXI of the *Inferno*, Dante dedicates several verses to the 'painful defeat in which Charlemagne lost the fruits of his holy enterprise', alluding to the 12.8 kilometres (8 miles) from which, in the *Historia Caroli Magni et Rotholandi*, one could hear the echo of Roland's ivory horn.[36]

The tradition initiated in the Middle Ages has not stopped. In the nineteenth century a Basque poem was written dedicated to the deeds of their ancestors titled the *Song of Altabizkar*. As Webster Wentworth stated, the *Song* was released to the public for the first time in 1834, in a long article by Eugène Garay de Monglave, founder and permanent secretary of *L'Institut Historique*. The poem is uniquely written from the Basque point of view. The following is probably the first English translation from the original Basque version:

1

A cry has been heard
from amidst the Basque mountains
and the master of the house standing before his door
has cocked his ear and said:
'Who's there?
What do you want from me?'
And the dog who was sleeping at the foot of his master
has risen and filled with his barking
the environs of Altabizkar.

2

A crash is heard on the height of Ibañeta.
It approaches crashing against the rocks on the right and left.
It is the thunder of an army that is perceived from afar.
Our people have responded from the top of the mountains,
The call of the watchword has been heard,
And the master of the house sharpens his javelins.

36 Plumptre, Edward H., *The Commedia and Canzoniere of Dante Alighieri: Life of Dante. Hell. Purgatory*, W. Isbister Ltd., London, 1886, p. 156.

3

They are coming, they are coming, what a forest of spears!
Look how they float amidst those standards of all colours!
Sparks fly from their weapons!
How many are there? Son, count them well,
One, two, three, four, five, six, seven, eight, nine,
Ten, eleven, twelve, thirteen, fourteen, fifteen, sixteen,
Seventeen, eighteen, nineteen, twenty.

4

Twenty, and by the thousands still.
Time is lost in counting them
Let us get our vigorous arms closer.
Let us uproot those rocks, and throw them down the hill
upon their heads.
Let us crush them, wound them to death!

5

What did they want of our mountains, those men of the North?
Why have they come to disturb our peace?
When God made the mountains, he didn't want men
to cross them.
But the rocks tumble down upon them,
and crush the troops.
Blood flows in torrents,
Viscera quiver.
Oh! How many splintered bones!
What a sea of blood!

6

Flee, flee, those who still have strength and a horse!
Escape, King Charlemagne with your black feather and your red cape!
Your beloved nephew, the valiant Roland, lies there dead;
His courage served him for naught.
And now, Basques, let us leave these rocks, descend quickly and
Shoot our arrows at those who flee.

7

They are leaving, they are fleeing, where is that forest of spears?
Where are those flags of all colours
that floated among them?
No more sparks fly from their bloody weapons.
How many are there? Son, count them well.
Twenty, nineteen, eighteen, seventeen, sixteen,
fifteen, fourteen, thirteen, twelve, eleven, ten, nine,
eight, seven, six, five, four, three, two, one.

8

One! Now none are seen!
This is it, master of the house,
you can leave with your dog
to embrace your wife and your children.
Clean your javelins and keep them with the horn
to later throw yourself down on them to sleep.
At night, the eagles will go to eat
the broken flesh.
And their bones will bleach for all eternity.[37]

37 Michel, Francisque, *Poesías Populares de los vascos*, Auñamendi, Donostia/San Sebastián, 1963, pp. 43-51. Spanish translation by Angel Irigarai. After the English translation in *Gentleman's Magazine* in 1858, the first edition of the original Basque text with an English translation is in Webster, Wentworth; Vinson, Julien, *Basque Legends Collected Chiefly in The Labourd*, Griffith and Farran, London, 1879, pp. 254-257. As mentioned by Wentworth, the poem was published as the copy or transcription of a Medieval chant but was actually a composition of *c.* 1835. When M. Fr. Michel published this, and another song called 'Abarcaren Cantua' in the Gentleman's Magazine, in 1858, as samples of ancient Basque poetry, a letter from Antoine d'Abbadie, 'Membre de l'Institut', subsequently appeared in the number for March, 1859, stating that the song calles 'Abarcaren Cantua' had actually been among the unsuccessful pieces submitted for the prize in the poetical competition at Urrugne, of the previous August; and he adds: 'I am sorry that the Altabiscarraco cantua, mentioned in that same number, is acknowledged as a gem of ancient popular poetry. Truth compels me to deny that it is universally admitted as such, for one of my Basque neighbours has often named the person who, about twenty four years ago, composed it in French, and the other person, who translated it into modern Basque. The latter language, on purely philological ground, stands peerless among the most ancient languages in Europe, and I have felt it my duty to disclaim unfounded pretensions of which it has no need.' In Webster, Wentworth; Vinson, Julien, *Basque Legends Collected Chiefly in the Labourd*, Griffith and Farran, London, 1879, pp. 258-259.

The Battle According to the *Chanson de Roland*

By their very nature, literary works are not historical sources. Nonetheless, it is not always easy to draw a clear line between the brief eighth-century historical chronicles and the literary tradition gathered by the legendary romances [*chansons de geste*]. If the former collect the historical facts, filtering those details that blur the overall image of the narrative, the latter add to the historical events those ingredients that distort reality in order to convert it into legend.

The *Chanson de Roland* is an epic poem of several hundred verses written at the end of the eleventh century—some three centuries after the battle—. The Oxford manuscript attributes its authorship to a Norman monk named Turoldus. It is one of the oldest legendary romances written in a Romance language in Europe. There are several transcriptions of the *Chanson,* the oldest being the *Digby Manuscript 23* of the *Bodleian Library* at Oxford, written in Anglo-Norman between 1140 and 1170.[38] It consists of 4,002 ten-syllable lines distributed in 291 stanzas of unequal length called *tiradas* (*laisses*). Despite the text of the *Digby Manuscript 23* being dated to the end of the twelfth century, the original text could be older, since William of Malmesbury mentions in the *Gesta Regum Anglorum* that the Normans sang stanzas of the *Song of Roland* during the Battle of Hastings on 14 October, 1066.[39]

The *Digby Manuscript 23* is unique because it seems to have been the property of a juggler who used it before or even during public performances, which endows the document with a singular historical interest.[40] This manuscript is one of those documents that Léon Gautier named a *manuscrit de jongleur* (juggler's manuscript), which—as opposed to the *manuscrits de collections* (collection manuscripts)—were instruments for the performance of the *chansons de geste* (songs of gest).[41] The *manuscrits de jonglars* were sometimes provided with sequences of commands to help in memorizing the poem so that it could be recited in public spaces. Very few of these manuscripts have survived, most perishing due to their constant use. As

---

38   *The Bodleian Library record,* vol. 1, J. Johnson., Oxford, 1941, p. 46.

39   Taylor, Andrew, *Textual Situations: Three Medieval Manuscripts and Their Readers,* University of Pennsylvania Press, Philadelphia, 2002, pp. 26-70.

40   Ross, David J. A.; Noble, Peter; Polak, Lucie; Isoz, Claire, *The Medieval Alexander Legend and Romance Epic: Essays in Honour of David J.A. Ros,* Kraus International Publication, Milwood, New York, London, and Nedelin, 1982, pp. 36-42.

41   Gautier, Léon, *Les Epopées Françaises. Etude sur les origines et l'histoire de la littérature nationale,* Victor Palmé Libraire-Edieur, Paris, 1865, pp. 184-185.

Gautier comments, 'I really shudder to think that the Oxford manuscript which contains the famous Chanson de Roland ran such great dangers on the lonely routes of the Middle Ages'.[42] Regarding the latter, the *manuscrits de collections* are luxurious copies generally in good condition given that many of them were kept in libraries, not always to be read but rather 'to be shown to friends, not without some pride'.[43]

While Gautier's assessment was challenged in 1932 by Charles Samarah, author of the first codicological analysis of the document, both authors acknowledged the poor quality of the material used for the preparation of the manuscript, along with its small and manageable size and the signs that it had been used frequently, are features pointing in that direction.[44] In this sense, the enigmatic AOI formula that the Oxford manuscript contains (and which no other Medieval manuscript of the *Chanson* contains) reinforces the view that in fact it was a *manuscrit de jonglar*. AOI, repeated in the margins of the entire poem all over 172 stanzas and absent in the remaining 119 appears at key moments, as if to indicate changes in the mood of the characters or turning points in the course of the story itself. It appears in almost all cases at the end of the last verse of a stanza or *laisse*. But on twenty-one occasions it does not happen that way, and the number of verses between two AOI varies slightly so that, although it has a relatively regular pattern, it does not seem to be permanent or unchanging. All of this suggests that it is a guide to help the juggler sing correctly at the beginning of each melodic or rhythmic phase of the *Chanson*. However, it also could be just a simple abbreviation of *amen*.[45]

The central character of the song is *Rollant li Marchis*, prefect of the March of Brittany who in the *Digby Manuscript 23* version of the *Chanson* appears as Charlemagne's nephew. This fact has given rise to much speculation given the lack of information around the lives of many of the real characters of the time.[46] In general, critics and historians deny that Roland was the

---

42   Gautier, Léon, *Les Epopées Françaises. Etude sur les origines et l'histoire de la littérature nationale*, Victor Palmé Libraire-Edieur, Paris, 1865, pp. 184-185.

43   Gautier, Léon, *Les Epopées Françaises. Etude sur les origines et l'histoire de la littérature nationale*, Victor Palmé Libraire-Edieur, Paris, 1865, pp. 184-185.

44   Samaran, Charles, *La Chanson de Roland. Reproduction Phototypique du Manuscrit Digby 23 de la Bodleian Library d'Oxford*, Société des Anciens Textes Français, Paris, 1933.

45   Storey, Christopher, "AOI in the Chanson de Roland", *Essays Presented to C. M. Girdlestone*, University of Durham, Newcastle upon Tyne, 1960, pp. 311-317. Mandach, André de, "The So Called AOI in the Chanson de Roland", *Symposium: A Quarterly Journal in Modern Literatures*, 11, 2, 1957, pp. 303-315.

46   For example, the minstrel Adenes Le Roy gave rise to the legend of the marriage of Berta and Pepin, parents of Charlemagne, in *Li Romans de Berte aus grans piés* (1270). According to

nephew of the emperor, since Pepin the Short and Bertrada *Regina pede aucae* married between 741 and 745 and had eight children, but only three survived infancy: Carolus, Carloman, and Gisela.[47]

The birthplace of Carolus (*c.* 747-28 January, 814), later known as Charlemagne, is unknown. His birth date is also unknown, although according to the *Annales Pitaviani* he was born in 747.[48] Notwithstanding this reference, according to some authors, available data suggests that his parents married after giving birth to the future emperor, which could explain the fact that the *Annales Pitaviani* post-dated his birth date.[49] In any case, as Janet L. Nelson observes, virtually all historians had accepted 742 as the year of Carolus's birth until Matthias Becher convincingly proposed 2 April, 748 as the emperor's birth date.[50] The latter places the birth of the firstborn in the political context of the power struggles between Pepin and his older brother Carloman—who shared the stewardship of the palace—and later, between him and Childeric, King of the Franks. But Pepin needed an heir to bolster his candidacy to the throne, which would explain his marriage in

this legend, Bertha was the daughter of Cariberto, Count of Laon. Pepin asked for her hand and it was granted to him, but he was convinced that her first marriage would end with a maid like her and that, therefore, she had to be replaced temporarily by her maid Aliste. This was part of a plot to kill Berta, who was taken at night to be murdered in a forest near Le Mans, where, however, those who were going to kill her decided to leave her alive. In the end, her mother, Blancheflore, consort of Flore, King of Hungary, concerned about Bertha, undertook a trip to France to visit her daughter. Upon arrival in Pepin's court, Aliste, fearing that the plot was discovered, pretended to be ill and retired to a dark room. Blancheflore, however, discovered the fraud, finding that the alleged Berta had no big feet. The impostor confesses everything and retires to a convent. Margiste, who had planned all this, is burned alive. A long but fruitless quest to find Bertha, still a virtuous and happy maid, starts. One day Pepin, while hunting, sees a maiden kneeling before a cross at the bottom of a forest. He is wounded and addresses her with ardent love, but in an attempt to defend her honor, the maiden says she is the daughter of a king, *Berthe au grand pied*. Having found her, Pepin then married her and they had six children. See Paris, Paulin (ed.), *Li Romans de Berte aus grans piés*, Techner, Paris, 1836. Also, Dunlop, John C.; Wilson, Henry, *History of Prose Fiction, Volume 1*, George Bell and sons, London, 1906; Feist, Alfred, *Zur Kritik der Bertasage*, Universitats Buchdruckerei, Marburg, 1885.

47   Bertha of Laon (*c.* 720-12 July 783) was named 'big foot' (in Latin *Regina pede aucae* or goose foot and in old French *Berte aus grans pies*) because she had a foot bigger than the other. Bertha was the daughter of Charibert of Laon.

48   In virtue of the birth date (747) given by the *Annales Pitaviani* ('*Et ipso anno fuit natus Karolus rex*'). See Pertz, Georg Heinrich (ed.), *Annales Petaviani*, Monumenta Germaniae Historica (MGH), SS, I, Hannover, 1826, pp. 10-11.

49   Thorpe, Lewis G. M. (ed.), *Einhard and Notker the Stammerer: Two lives of Charlemagne*, Penguin, London, 1969, p. 3.

50   Nelson, Janet L., "Charlemagne, the Man", in Story, Joanna (ed.), *Charlemagne, Empire and Society*, Manchester University Press, Manchester, 2005, p. 26.

744, when he was thirty years old.[51] When, after having deposed Childeric, Pope Stephen II confirmed Pepin's and his descendants' right to the throne in 754, Carloman died, and his sons are not mentioned again in the royal chronicles nor in any other contemporary source.

The chronicles register the date of birth of Carloman (751-4 December, 771), who was 17 when he became king along with his brother Charlemagne.[52] Coinciding with the birth of his second son Carloman and under the usual royal tradition, the Merovingian nobility recognized the rights of Pepin to the throne while named *rex francorum* (king of the Franks) by the bishops, which was a novelty. When in 754 Pope Stephen II confirmed the rights of Pepin and Bertha and their offspring, he likewise established that the future *rex francorum* should be a descendant of the royal marriage.[53]

Gisela (757-810) was the Abbess of the Monastery of Chelles; Einhard makes her the only sister of Charlemagne. According to the chronicler, she had a deep religious vocation since childhood and died as a nun at Chelles.[54] As the *Vita Karoli Magni* records, different literary works referred to her as mother of Roland, whom she would have conceived after having lain with her brother Charlemagne.[55] No children of Carloman have been recorded, and Gisela was cloistered in a convent; therefore, in light of the chronicles, it appears that Charlemagne did not have nephews.

At the same time, it could be risky to deny that Roland was the nephew of the emperor on this basis. It is known that Charles Martel had two wives and an undetermined number of concubines with whom he had

51   Becher, Matthias, *Karl der Grosse*, C. H. Beck, München, 1999, p. 41. En inglés, Becher, Matthias, *Charlemagne*, Yale University Press, New Haven, 2003, pp. 37 & 42.

52   Carloman was born in 751: '*Et fuit natus Karolomannus rex*. Richter, Gustav; Kohl, Horst, *Annalen der deutschen Geschichte im Mittelalter, von der Gründung des fränkischen Reichs bis zum untergang der Hohenstaufen*.' In *Mit fortlaufenden Quellenauszügen und Literaturangaben*, Verlag der Buchhandlung des Waisenhauses, Halle, 1885, vol. 2, P. 29. See also, Becher, Matthias, *Charlemagne*, Yale University Press, New Haven, 2003, p. 42.

53   Fouracre, Paul, "The Long Shadow of the Merovingians", in Story, Joanna (ed.), *Charlemagne, Empire and Society*, Manchester University Press, Manchester, 2005, p. 9.

54   In the original Latin: '*Erat ei unica soror nomine Gisla, a puellaribus annis religiosae conversationi mancipata, quam similiter nt matrem magna coluit pietate. Quae etiam paucis ante obitum illius annis in eo, quo conversata est, monasterio decessit*.' In Holder-Egger, Oswald (ed.), *Einhardi Vita Karoli Magni*, Monumenta Germaniae Historica (MGH), SSRG, Hannover & Leipzig, 1911, p. 23.

55   In the original Latin: '*De hoc nostri cantores multa in carminibus cantant, dicentes eum fuisse filium sororis Karoli regis*.' In Holder-Egger, Oswald (ed.), *Einhardi Vita Karoli Magni*, Monumenta Germaniae Historica (MGH), SSRG, Hannover & Leipzig, 1911, p. 12.

at least seven children, three of whom were illegitimate.[56] We have already mentioned the uncertainties that exist about Pepin's family life and, as the *Vita Karoli Magni* states, Charlemagne married ten times without taking into exact account the concubines he had,[57] the number of children he had with them, or their names.[58] Given all of the above, it appears uncertain whether Charlemagne was either the uncle or the father of Roland.

In any case, the Roland of the *Chanson* goes far beyond the historical character and comes to represent the ideal of the eleventh-century *chevalier errant* (knight errant), and not that of the eighth-century Frankish warrior. The epic hero embodies the physical traits, morality, and beliefs of the Christian society of Turoldus's time, and as such he perishes as a martyr in the context of a crusade that pits Christianity against the Muslim world. Roland lives like a Homeric hero, beyond his own life, in favor of an ideal that will give him immortality in the collective memory through the *chansons de geste*. Thus, Roland persistently refuses to negotiate a truce with the Saracens since he understands victory and war against Islam in terms of a moral obligation. When the enemy offers battle in Errozabal and Oliver announces that they will be attacked, Roland is gratified and says that 'no one will ever sing an action of mine that was not exemplary'.[59]

The Frankish chronicles do not mention Oliver, Roland's inseparable companion-in-arms and brother-in-law, for which reason he seems to be a purely literary character. Roland is courageous and Oliver prudent,[60] the *Chanson* reveals, and while the former does not even conceive of defeat, Oliver understands that it is preferable to call King Charles to secure victory. When the attack begins, Oliver asks Roland to blow his horn three times,

---

56   Fouracre, Paul, "The Long Shadow of the Merovingians", in Story, Joanna (ed.), *Charlemagne, Empire and Society*, Manchester University Press, Manchester, 2005, p. 16.

57   This is not exact. Charlemagne had four wives and an unknown number of heirs. His wives were Desiderata (770–771), Hildegard of Vinzgouw (771–783), Fastrada (784–794) and, Luitgard (794–800). He had five known heirs, Himiltrude, Gersuinda, Madelgard, Regina and Ethelind.

58   Holder-Egger, Oswald (ed.), *Einhardi Vita Karoli Magni*, Monumenta Germaniae Historica (MGH), SSRG, Hannover & Leipzig, 1911, pp. 22-23. See also, Riché, Pierre, *The Carolingians: A Family Who Forged Europe*, University of Pennsylvania Press, Philadelphia, 1993, pp. 368-369.

59   Müller, Theodor, *La Chanson de Roland: nach der Oxforder Handschrift*, Verlag der Dieter-ichschen Buchandlung, Göttingen, 1863, p. 64. See also, Burgess, Glyn S., *The Song of Roland*, Penguin Classics, London, 1990, p. 191.

60   *Rollant est proz e Oliver est sage*, in Müller, Theodor, *La Chanson de Roland: nach der Oxforder Handschrift*, Verlag der Dieterichschen Buchandlung, Göttingen, 1863, p. 69.

which he refuses so that no living man can say that a Christian hero was forced to blow the horn because of the infidels.[61]

Like Oliver, many of the main characters, whether historical figures or not, appear distorted. Such is the case of Charlemagne, who embodies a warrior of unshakable faith, more than two centuries old, who has waged war against impiety guided by James the Apostle. However, unlike Roland, Charlemagne is tired of fighting and wants to return to his homeland. The same can be said as for Bishop Turpin, the image of the warrior cleric and one of the principal and most charismatic figures of the *Chanson*. While the chronicles do not record that he participated in the battle, and the available data indicates that he did not even leave Reims, the archbishop personifies the brave, courageous, and valiant crusader at the core of the eleventh-century militant Church's image.

Duke Neimes appears as the closest and wisest counselor of Charlemagne ('Meillor vassal n'aveit en la curt nul'). This brings to mind the passage from the epitaph of Eggihard (*Aggiardus*), seneschal of the palace, who died in the battle, which records that he was 'the first of the king's court'. Prudence leads Neimes to advise diplomatic negotiations with the Saracens in order to reduce Zaragoza by a pact instead of by the use of force, since he believes it would be a great sin not to accept the pleas of an enemy already defeated.[62]

The circle of warriors closest to the king is completed by the twelve peers or *consilium regio*. Although there was a palatine court subjected to a certain military hierarchy, the twelve peers are never mentioned in the chronicles of the battle. The twelve peers or paladins—*comes palatinus*—constitute a parallel with the twelve apostles of the Arthurian cycle. While the list of the twelve peers varies from one version of the history to another, the *Chanson* includes in the catalog Anseïs *li fiers*, Count Bérengiers, Engelers *li Guascuinz* of Bordeaux, Count Gerins, Count Gerers, Gerart *le veill* of Rossillon, Ivon, Ivoeries, Oliver, Otes, Roland, and Samson. The poet places the twelve peers in care of the rearguard, and they wage battle while killing one by one eleven of the twelve Muslim paladins. At the end of the battle, all of them perish as Christian martyrs.

The list of Frankish heroes is closed with a series of secondary characters. Walter of Hum, 'who conquered Monteagudo, nephew of the old and gray Droün', member of the rearguard of the army, charged with

61   Stanzas or *laisses* 79 to 87, in Müller, Theodor, *La Chanson de Roland: nach der Oxforder Handschrift*, Verlag der Dieterichschen Buchhandlung, Göttingen, 1863, pp. 63-70.

62   Müller, Theodor, *La Chanson de Roland: nach der Oxforder Handschrift*, Verlag der Dieterichschen Buchhandlung, Göttingen, 1863, pp. 14-15.

patrolling the peaks that flank the Zize pass, is the Frank who descends to verify that indeed, all the men are dead. Together with Turpin and Roland, he is one of the last three heroes to die. Duke Ogier, a Danish knight who fights alongside Charlemagne to avenge the death of his Christian peers as well as Thierry, 'li dux d'Argon', who defends Roland's honor at Ganelon's trial facing Pinabel 'of Sorence', his relative. Finally, Aude 'la bele', wife of Roland and Oliver's sister, dies of love upon hearing of the death of Roland.

Ganelon, 'ki la traïsun fist', represents Judas Iscariot. Roland's stepfather and architect of the treachery, Ganelon, is the main cause of the defeat. When Roland proposes that it should be Ganelon who takes the order to King Marsilius to surrender Zaragoza, Ganelon thinks that his stepson plans to kill him and explodes in anger to the point of being willing to betray his people and his religion to kill Roland. While the poet does not offer any other explanation of the cause of Ganelon's deep resentment against his stepson, anger at first and ambition later induce Ganelon to conspire with the Saracens to exterminate the Carolingian rearguard. When news of the attack on the rearguard reaches Charlemagne, he orders Ganelon to be chained, and afterward, on arriving at court, to be tried and executed along with thirty of his relatives, as tradition demanded.

The list of Muslim characters has been created by literary tradition. It appears that the poet did not have contact with the Muslim world, so the names of the characters as well as the weapons they use and their behavior belong to the Christian world. Only the three main heroes seem to be based on historical characters: King Marsilius, Baligant, and Blancandrins of Castel de Valfunde. Marsilius represents Hussain ibn Yahya al-Ansari, wali of Zaragoza in 778, who attended the diet of Paderborn in 777. According to the tradition, Marsilius, father of Jurfaret and faithful nephew of the caliph, was a dishonest man who prepared the trap into which the Franks would fall. Astute but deceitful, when he learns of the death of Baligant and the final defeat of his troops, he turns to the wall and dies of grief 'bearing his sins while demons take his soul'.

Baligant, Emir of Babylon, represents Sulayman ibn al-Arabi, *wali* of Barcelona and Girona, whom Charlemagne took as a hostage and his sons freed somewhere south of Vasconia. Baligant, his son and his brother die in battle. He sees how Muhammad's standard fails on the field of battle and 'his pain is so sharp that he feels he will die'.[63]

---

63 Müller, Theodor, *La Chanson de Roland: nach der Oxforder Handschrift*, Verlag der Dieterichschen Buchandlung, Göttingen, 1863, pp. 245-246.

The emir is presented in the image of a *chevalier errant*, as a vigorous warrior who, in one-on-one combat against Charlemagne, manages to break with his sword the emperor's helmet, cleaving the blade into his scalp and cutting from him an entire palm of flesh, 'or more', exposing the bone. Charlemagne staggers and nearly falls, but God does not want him dead or defeated, so the Archangel Gabriel appears to him and on hearing the holy voice, Charlemagne casts out all fear; he knows that he will not perish on this expedition. He immediately recovers his strength and strikes the emir with the sword of France. He breaks the emir's helmet, upon which gems shine: '[H]e opens his skull, spilling out his brains and after splitting his head all the way to the emir's white beard, knocks him down dead without hope.'[64]

The last of the leading Muslim heroes is Blancandrins of Castel de Valfunde, 'he of the gray hair'. Considering that the current location of Valfonda is about 25 kilometres (15.5 miles) south of Huesca, this hero may well represent Abu Tauer, *wali* of Huesca.[65] Blancandrins stands out among the infidels for being a very wise hero, a good and courageous knight, and a good and noble counselor to his master, King Marsilius. But he is also an impostor who recommends that Marsilius promise Charlemagne that they will embrace Christianity on St. Michael's Day. He even recommends that Marsilius hand over hostages, knowing that they will be put to the sword when the Christians discover the fraud. Blancandrins believes that it is better to sacrifice a few than to lose the fortress and offers his own son as a hostage.

Blancandrins awards Charlemagne bears and lions, hounds broken to the leash, 700 camels, 1,000 molted goshawks, 400 mules laden with gold and silver, and 50 carts full of gold besants with which the emperor could pay as many warriors as he cares to recruit.[66] It is also Blancandrins who—taking advantage of the hatred that gnaws at Ganelon—induces him to commit treason and who, while riding together towards Zaragoza, convinces Ganelon to plot against Roland and his men. After presenting Ganelon to Marsilius, Blancandrins disappears, and the poet never reveals his destiny.

Beyond the suggestive embellishments of the poem, such as the treasure of 700 camels loaded with gold and silver, with which Blancandrins persuades Charlemagne of Marsilius's good faith, and the armies of 400,000 Muslims

---

64 Stanzas 261 and 262. Müller, Theodor, *La Chanson de Roland: nach der Oxforder Handschrift*, Verlag der Dieterichschen Buchandlung, Göttingen, 1863, p. 253.

65 Mandach, André de, *Naissance et développment de la chanson de geste en Europe VI. La Chanson de Roland*, Librairie Droz, Genève, 1993, p. 67.

66 Ancient Byzantine gold or silver coin was also used by Muslims in Western Europe.

facing the 20,000 Franks of the Carolingian rearguard in the Zize pass, the plot is also based on historical facts that, like the characters, have been transformed and endowed with epic overtones by the poet. In any case, it is interesting to contrast legend and reality in order to highlight those aspects that the poet or the popular tradition blurred. It is also interesting to grasp the literary or historical motivations for these distortions of historical facts.

The poem can be divided into two main parts, each one in turn divided into two sections. The first part, which has a strong historical approach, contains stanzas 1 to 176 and is divided into two segments.

Stanzas 1 to 52 describe the negotiation for the surrender of Zaragoza and Ganelon's treason. After seven years of crusade, Charlemagne has conquered Hispania, hitherto occupied by the Muslims. Only Zaragoza, governed by King Marsilius, resists. The Franks receive a suspicious embassy headed by Blancandrins, who proposes to the king the immediate surrender of the fortress and the conversion of the king and his subjects to Christianity. The Frankish war council convinces Charlemagne to accept King Marsilius's terms. Roland proposes that his father-in-law Ganelon be the one to present himself before the Muslim king to accept on the emperor's behalf. He believes that his son-in-law intends to eliminate him, since Marsilius had previously killed two Frankish emissaries and now desires revenge. Along the way, seduced by Blancandrins, Ganelon plans the betrayal and murder of Roland. When Ganelon comes before Marsilius, he advises the king to pledge submission to Charlemagne so that the Carolingian army leaves Hispania, allowing him to attack the rearguard of the imperial legions at the Zize pass. Charlemagne, pleased and well convinced, returns to his homeland and, following Ganelon's advice, leaves his nephew Roland in charge of the rear end of the army.

Stanzas 53 to 176 describe the battle and death of the twelve peers at the Zize pass. Charlemagne crosses the Pyrenees, and Marsilius's numerous troops fall upon the rearguard led by Roland. Cautious Oliver warns Roland three times of the danger and recommends he blow his horn to warn the emperor. However, Roland, fearless to the point of arrogance, refuses to blow the olifant while the emperor and the vanguard of the army has already passed the gorge. Roland, assisted by the best knights of the Frankish army, fights courageously and even repels two Muslim attacks. One by one the Frankish knights fall before an untold number of enemies. Roland finally decides to blow the horn, but this time it is Oliver who, aware that it is too late, suggests not to do it. Nevertheless, Roland blows the horn with such an intensity that his temples burst. After that Oliver dies, and the last two heroes, Turpin and Walter of Hum, also succumb. Alone on the battlefield,

Roland finally perishes, facing the enemy. Before dying he wants to break his sword Durandal—which carries in its hilt one thousand relics—so that it does not fall into enemy hands. But the stone, which he hits his sword against, breaks due to the hard blow. Roland dies as a warrior, his bodied turned toward the western lands occupied by right of conquest. He offers his right glove to God, and St. Gabriel leads his soul to heaven.

The second part, not based on historical events, includes stanzas 177 to 291 and is likewise divided into two sections.

Stanzas 176 to 267 tell of Charlemagne's return to the battlefield, the subsequent defeat of the Muslim army on the shores of the river Ebro, and the capture of Zaragoza. When Charlemagne hears Roland's horn calling for help, he suspects Ganelon's treason and orders him to be chained and immediately returns to Errozabal. He weeps over the bodies of the heroes and orders them to be carried to the sweet lands of France, where they are to be buried. He pursues Marsilius's troops, which are in retreat, and exterminates them on the banks of the river Ebro. In the course of the last battle, Charlemagne confronts the forces of Baligant, Emir of Babylon, who dies at Charlemagne's hands. King Marsilius dies from the wounds that Charlemagne has inflicted on him and demons take his soul, while Chgarlemagne finally takes control of Zaragoza. After burying Roland, Oliver, and Bishop Turpin in the Church of Saint-Romain at Blaye, he returns, discouraged, to Aix-la-Chapelle. Aude, Roland's lover and Oliver's sister, dies of sorrow when she learns of the hero's death.

In stanzas 268 to 291 the poet tells of Charlemagne's return to the palace and Ganelon's trial and execution. Ganelon is indicted, but despite his undeniable betrayal, he alleges having avenged himself against he who had sent him to a certain death. The court rules that the decision should be left to God's judgment in the course of a judicial combat. The champion who defends Ganelon, Pinabel, is defeated by Thierry d'Anjou, who fights for Roland. Ganelon is sentenced to death by dismemberment, and his extremities are tied to four horses. The Archangel Gabriel orders Charlemagne to prepare his armies and undertake a new crusade to rescue King Viviano in Orpah, which has been besieged by the infidels.

While woven into epic fiction, historical references underlie the entire narrative of the poem's first part. The poet offers a literary interpretation of the military campaign waged by Charlemagne in the Ebro valley in 778. The campaign, which from the departure of Charlemagne from Douzy until his arrival at Auxerre, lasted for about seven months, grows into a long seven-year war in the poem. Overall, magnification of the facts is a constant of the *chanson*, which makes extensive use of hyperbole to underline the uniqueness of the story and amplify its epic scale, which must transcend the merely human dimension. Transforming the months into years, the campaign becomes a grueling war of Homeric proportions:

> King Charles, our great emperor,
> Has spent seven entire years in Hispania,
> He has conquered the proud land even unto the ocean.
> Not a single castle has resisted him,
> Neither wall nor city remains to be conquered,
> Except Zaragoza, which is upon a mountain.[67]

The poet avoids making any reference to the Hispanic March and the po-litical and military negotiations with the Muslim walis of the Ebro. Thus, Charlemagne's only purpose when undertaking his campaign is to fight the infidel in the context of a holy war against Islam. But despite the fictitious elements, it is possible to track down historical events such as the difficulties that the Carolingian army faced when trying to capture Zaragoza, which the poem locates 'on a mountain', and therefore inaccessible and almost invulnerable. The poet also refers to the negotiation of the terms of surrender and the taking of hostages.

In any event, and beyond the literary difficulties that mentioning the motivation for the *March* could have caused, a holy war was a more suggestive plot for the eleventh-century public who lived between the First (1096-1099) and Second Crusades (1144-1149). At that time, like today, the audience and their tastes were substantial ingredients for the reputation and notoriety of a literary composition, which had to be recited before the public. Therefore, the Church, patron and mentor of numerous popular hagiographies, which often had the aim of nurturing the flow of pilgrims through various monasteries, would be motivated and even seduced by the disclosure of the exploits of Charlemagne's and Roland's sacrifices. It is therefore not so surprising that the last stanza of the *Chanson* demands from the Christian kings that they undertake new military campaigns under the protection of St. Gabriel.[68]

The geographical setting of the campaign of 778, the Ebro valley, also adopts epic dimensions under Turoldus's hand. The poet transforms it into the entire Iberian Peninsula, from Girona and Pamplona in the east to

---

67 Müller, Theodor, *La Chanson de Roland: nach der Oxforder Handschrift*, Verlag der Dieter-ichschen Buchandlung, Göttingen, 1863, p. 1.
68 Müller, Theodor, *La Chanson de Roland: nach der Oxforder Handschrift*, Verlag der Dieter-ichschen Buchandlung, Göttingen, 1863, p. 1.

Cadiz and Santiago in the west. However, the majority of the place names mentioned in the *Chanson* correspond to identifiable historic sites such as Pamplona and Miranda de Arga, Valtierra and Pina, Balaguer, Tudela, Cortes de Navarra, and the Sierra de Sivil.[69] All these places are located south of Vasconia and on the road that Charlemagne's troops marched in 778 between Pamplona, Zaragoza, and Girona.

The general context of the poem being a holy war forced the poet to turn the Basques into Saracens ('sarrazins') or pagans ('paiens') or simply to avoid any mention of the awkward presence of Christian Basques. Turning Charlemagne's enemies into Saracens allows the depiction of the emperor as a Christian hero leading a religious war planned by St. James himself and under the protection and tutelage of St. Gabriel, who appears to the emperor in dreams and leads Roland's soul to heaven. But while this tradition is collected in the *Historia Caroli Magni et Rotholandi*, the *Chanson* does not mention the episode of St. James' dream. On the contrary, in line with other *chansons de geste* it begins—as in the case of the *Iliad*—*in media res*, at the end of the last year of war, after seven years of conflict.

The adoption of the Christian concept of holy war also turned a war of aggression into a campaign of liberation and restoration. Thus, it is the Saracens and not the Franks who have occupied the ancient Christian land where the remains of St. James the Apostle are buried. The tutelage of St. Gabriel, who speaks by divine intercession, provides the necessary authority to the campaign led by the emperor. The *Chanson de Roland* is one of the first Medieval texts to emphasize that the campaigns of the Christian princes against the emirate were not wars of 'conquest' but rather an endeavor to 'reconquer' or regain lands lost to the Muslims in the past.

However, while the poet rhetorically disguises imperialistic political projects, before an audience eager for military adventures and wild deeds, he

69 Paul Aebischer and Prosper Boissonnade have thoroughly discussed the question of the translation of place names mentioned in the Chanson de Roland. See Boissonnade, Prosper, *Du nouveau sur la chanson de Roland: la genèse historique, le cadre géographique, le milieu, les personnages, la date et l'auteur de poème*, Honore Champion, Paris, 1923, pp. 69-236; Aebischer, Paul, *Rolandiana et Oliveriana: Recueil d'études sur les chansons de geste*, Librairie Droz, Genève, 1967, pp. 235, 243 & 259-260. See also, Aebischer, Paul, *Textes norrois et littérature française de moyen âge*, Librairie Droz, Genève, 1972, p. 54; Sholod, Barton, *Charlemagne in Spain: The Cultural Legacy of Roncesvalles*, Librairie Droz, Genève, 1963, pp. 167-169; Bédier, Joseph (ed. and tr.), *La Chanson de Roland, publiée d'âpres le manuscrit d'Oxford et traduite*, Piazza, Paris, 1937; Lot, Ferdinand, *Études sur les légendes épiques françaises*, Honore Champion, Paris, 1958; Jenkins, Thomas A., *La Chanson de Roland, Oxford version, edition, notes and glossary by T. Atkinson Jenkins*, D. C. Heath, Boston, 1924; Burgess, Glyn S., *The Song of Roland*, Penguin Classics, London, 1990, p. 170.

does not omit telling the story of the siege, destruction, and looting of many fortresses that historically fell or surrendered to the advancing Carolingian troops, among them Pamplona (*Noples*), Tudela and Cortes:

> The emperor is seen to be happy; he is in a good mood,
> He has conquered Cortes and destroyed its walls
> And has thrown down the towers with his catapults.
> His knights have found great booty:
> Gold, silver and precious garments.
> Not a single infidel has been left in the city:
> All died or have been baptized.[70]

The Battle of Errozabal is conceived as an ambush in the Zize pass. The accurate description of the pass and the suggestive mention of the hardships that the Frankish heroes must face in order to pass through the dark and sinister ravines fills the scene with drama:

> High are the mountains and dark the ravines,
> Gloomy the rocks, sinister the gorges.
> With great hardships the Franks cross them that day,
> From fifteen leagues away the clamor is heard.
> When they get to the high-altitude land
> And see Vasconia, the land of their lord,
> They remember their fiefs and their honors,
> And the maidens and their graceful wives.
> There is no one who doesn't cry out of pity.
> More than any other Charles is sorrowful
> He has left his nephew in the passes of Hispania,
> Grief invades him and he can not avoid weeping.[71]

The story requires an explanation of the defeat beyond a prosaic lack of foresight; thus, the poet combines two factors: The advantage that the terrain offered the attackers and the fabulous numerical superiority of the enemy who attempts an ambush with a force twenty times superior, composed of

---

70   Müller, Theodor, *La Chanson de Roland: nach der Oxforder Handschrift*, Verlag der Dieter-ichschen Buchandlung, Göttingen, 1863, p. 6.
71   Müller, Theodor, *La Chanson de Roland: nach der Oxforder Handschrift*, Verlag der Dieter-ichschen Buchandlung, Göttingen, 1863, pp. 51-52.

400,000 soldiers. Defeat is due to the treachery of one man who acts out of his mind, overwhelmed by anger and fueled by greed.

The poet emphasizes that Roland refuseds three times to blow the olifant, even when his friend Oliver insists. The poem explains Roland's attitude in terms of bravery and a certain lack of prudence. But beyond this explanation, Roland's refusal is critical because it explains the absence of Charlemagne from the battlefield. On the other hand, the otherwise uncomfortable presence of the emperor in the Zize pass is reinforced by the fact that the song places the attack on a distant rearguard that has remained under the custody of 20,000 brave warriors. Thus, the defeat falls upon a small—albeit important—portion of the Carolingian army.

Finally, two relevant episodes are included in the song: The recovery of the corpses of the fallen warriors and the defeat of the Muslim army. Both are key points of a *chanson de geste* that required a heroic but at the same time glorious and triumphant ending, especially if we consider that one of the keys of the *Chanson* was to stimulate the popular clamor for a new crusade. The second part of the *Chanson*, heavily dramatized and novelized, elevates the central characters of the plot: Roland and his uncle and lord, Charlemagne. The lament over the lifeless bodies of the 20,000 heroes and the capture of Zaragoza allows the poet to transform defeat into victory and turns those dead in the battle into martyrs who have given their lives for the sake of the Christian ideal.

Each one of these literary elements has an explanation and serves a purpose, but nevertheless the poet composed a unique song whose extraordinary force continues to dazzle the readers of our century with its vigor, dynamism, and marvellous idealism because history can and must be written but art, while it draws on human events, may well transcend historic events, incidents, and time.

The Battle as Described in the *Historia Caroli Magni et Rotholandi*

The *Historia Caroli Magni et Rotholandi*, legendarily attributed to Bishop Turpin of Reims, is a twelfth-century Latin text inspired by Charlemagne's campaign of 778. Although there are more than a hundred copies datable to between the twelfth and thirteenth centuries,[72] the copy preserved in the

---

72 Jones, Cyril M., *Historia Karoli Magni et Rotholandi: ou, Chronique du Pseudo-Turpin*, Slatkine, Genève, 1972, pp. 5-17.

archives of the cathedral of Santiago de Compostela is especially valuable, as it is part of a manuscript entitled *Liber Sancti Jacobi,* known as *Codex Calixtinus.* The *Liber Sancti Jacobi,* compiled between 1140 and 1170, has 225 pages of about 29.5 by 21.4 centimetres, with writing on both sides. Each page generally contains a single column of thirty-four lines, and just a few capital letters are illuminated. The Jesuit Fidel Fita rediscovered the *Codex,* which had been forgotten for at least three centuries, in 1886.

The *Codex,* apocryphally attributed to Pope Callistus II to enhance the credibility and prestige of the narration, includes on the first two pages a letter purportedly written by the abovementioned Pope ('Incipit epistola beati Calixti papa') and addressed to Archbishop Diego of Santiago de Compostela and the holy chapter of the local Clunian abbey. The author claims to have traveled the Iberian Peninsula for years, picking up the traditions of the Way of St. James to keep them in writing. Most authors today argue that the *Codex* was written and transcribed by different authors at different stages and, therefore, its original author is called *Scriptor I.*[73]

Before his election as Pope in 1119, Callistus, Abbot of Cluny, brother of the count of Galicia and son-in-law of King Alfonso VI of Castile, had promoted pilgrimages to Santiago. Later, when he became Pope, he was an ardent promoter of the crusades and elevated the city of Santiago de Compostela to the seat of the archdiocese. As Joseph Bedier points out, the *Liber Sancti Jacobi* was most likely compiled by monks of the Abbey of Cluny, who were encouraged by the idea of promoting throughout all Europe the pilgrimage to the tomb of James the apostle at Compostela.[74] The original manuscript, which could have been the work of a scribe from an abbey near Vézelay, was later moved to Santiago de Compostela by Aymeric Picaud, Chancellor of Pope Callistus II and very likely the author of the fifth and final book of the *Codex,* the *Guía de Peregrinos (Pilgrim's Guide).*

The manuscipt is divided into five books. The first book, *Libro de las Liturgias (Book of the Liturgies),* accounts for almost half of the entire manuscript and includes sermons and homilies that relate to the life and example given by James the apostle, two accounts of his martyrdom, and liturgical services for his veneration. In line with the 'westernizing' policy of Alfonso VI of Castile and with the rituals and practices introduced by the Cluniac order, *Liber I* promotes the universalization of the Roman liturgy over the traditional Mozarabic one that prevailed at the time in the Iberian

---

73   Bedier, Joseph, *La Chanson de Roland commentée,* L'Édition d'Art H. Piazza, Paris, 1927, pp. 12-13.

74   Bedier, Joseph, *La Chanson de Roland commentée,* L'Édition d'Art H. Piazza, Paris, 1927, p. 12.

Peninsula. The liturgical part of this manuscript is particularly relevant for historians of Medieval music since it is one of the most beautiful examples of twelfth-century polyphony.

The second book, *Libro de Santiago Zebedeo, patrón de Galicia, y sus veintidós Milagros* (*Book of James Zebedee, Patron Saint of Galicia, and His Twenty-two Miracles*), is a hagiography that records twenty-two miracles of the apostle allegedly compiled and annotated by Pope Callistus, St. Anselm of Canterbury, St. Bede, and Master Hubert. The book underlines the unique character of St. James and his deeds and emphasizes that pilgrims will purge all their sins and will be saved by faith after having completed the pilgrimage to the tomb of the apostle. The third book of the codex, *Traslación del cuerpo del apóstol a Santiago* (*Transfer of the Body of the Apostle to Santiago*), the shortest of the five volumes, tells the story of the transfer of St. James's body from Palestine to the port of Iria in Galicia in a sailboat guided by an angel.

The fifth book, *Guía del Peregrino* or *Liber Peregrinationis* (*Pilgrim's Guide*) is a breviary for the pilgrim. The author, Aymeric Picaud, describes the four main routes of the Way of St. James (*via Turonensis, via Lemovicensis, via Podiensis,* and *via Tolosana*) that meet in Gares (*Puente la Reina*). Picaud divides the road into generous day-journeys, some of which exceed 70 kilometres (43.5 miles). The author presents the people on the way in a very subjective manner, including references to the food and the quality of the water and wine that the pilgrims may find on their journey. The *Guía* also provides a description of the main churches, hospitals, and relics that pilgrims may visit on the road, highlighting those of Frankish origin. Finally, he depicts the city of Compostela and especially St. James's cathedral, where the remains of the Apostle repose, the final point of the journey.

The *Historia* is the fourth book of the codex. Attributed to Bishop Turpin of Reims, it is an account of Charlemagne's campaign on the Iberian Peninsula, the defeat at Errozabal, and the death of Roland. *Liber IV* is the most decorated of all, with beautiful miniatures and illuminations. Originally known as *Codex Calixtinus Liber IV*, the *Historia* was removed from the codex and bound independently in 1619.[75] During the restoration process between 1964 and 1966, *Liber IV* was again included in the *Codex Calixtinus*.[76]

The attribution of this manuscript to Bishop Turpin of Reims is an indication that the author's actual purpose was to support the veracity of the text

---

75   Jones, Cyril M., *Historia Karoli Magni et Rotholandi: ou, Chronique du Pseudo-Turpin*, Slatkine, Genève, 1972, p. 47.

76   Gabriele, Matthew; Stuckey, Jace, *The Legend of Charlemagne in the Middle Ages: Power, Faith, and Crusade*, Palgrave Macmillan, New York, 2008, p. 128.

and attract the readers to Santiago. Thus, the *Liber IV* begins with a letter from the archbishop in which the author strives to emphasize the true and historical character of the account:

> Forasmuch as you requested me to write to you from Vienne (my wounds being now cicatrized) in what manner the Emperor Charles delivered Spain and Gallicia from the yoke of the Saracens, you shall attain the knowledge of many memorable events, and likewise of his praise-worthy trophies over the Spanish Saracens, whereof I myself was eyewitness, traversing France and Spain in his company for the space of forty years: and I hesitate the less to trust these matters to your friendship, as I write a true history of his warfare. For indeed all your researches could never have enabled you fully to discover those great events in the Chronicles of St. Denis, as you sent me word: neither could you for certain know whether the author had given a true account of those matters, either by reason of his prolixity, or because he was not himself present when they happened. Nevertheless, this book will agree with his history. Health and happiness.[77]

The *Historia* posts certain difficulties when historians try to analyze its content from a historiographical point of view. Its purpose is not only literary or aesthetic; it also aims to attract pilgrims to Compostela through certain places along the way. As a result, some of the places are mentioned by the authors not due exclusively to the oral tradition or to historiographical sources that had vanished at the time, but rather due to other types of motivation, rendering much more complex any attempt to place some of the events described geographically or to locate them chronologically in the story. On the other hand, the manuscript makes occasional references to aspects that are little discussed or even absent from the historical records, such as the encounter that took place in southern Vasconia between Franks, Basques, and Muslims or the events that took place during the siege and capture of Pamplona.

The *Historia* is, in essence, a literary interpretation of Charlemagne's campaign of 778. Despite the title and the author's insistence that it is a historical account of the events that took place before and after the Carolingian campaign in Hispania, the author introduces a number of fantastic

---

77   *History of Charles the Great and Orlando Ascribed to Archibishop Turpin*, T. Rodd, London, 1812, pp. 2-3. See also, Castets, Ferdinand (ed.), *Turpini Historia Karoli Magni et Rotholandi*, Société pour l'Etude des Langues Romanes, Montpellier, 1880, pp. 1-2.

elements. He also uses rhetorical devices such as hyperbole, adjectives, repetition, and parataxis, turning men into giants and magnifying their actions. Also, by virtue of its intentionality and nature, the *Historia* includes religious elements and dogmatic digressions such as the parable of the false executioner (*'De exemplo eleemosynae mortui'*), the spoliation of the dead (*'De qui ad illicita Christianis spolia redierunt'*), and the extensive dialogue between Roland and Ferracutus included in Chapter 17 (*'De Bello et de optimal Gigantis Farracuti Rotholandi Disputatio'*) on some of the central points of Christian doctrine (the Holy Trinity, Mary's virginity and Jesus' death, resurrection and ascension).

Like the *Chanson*, the *Historia* includes many real characters but is strongly fictionalized. Charlemagne, transformed into the emperor of the Romans (*'Rex et Imperator Romanorum Gallorum'*), is the main character. Roland does not play any relevant role until the third and last part of the narrative, when he appears on stage facing the giant Ferracutus in Chapter 17. Chapter 20 (*'De persona et Fortitudine Karoli'*) offers a portrait of Charlemagne in the following terms:

> The emperor was of a ruddy complexion, with brown hair; of a well-made handsome form, but a stern visage. His height was about eight of his own feet, which were very long. He was of a strong robust make; his legs and thighs very stout, and his sinews firm. His face was thirteen inches long; his beard a palm; his nose half a palm; his fore-head a foot over. His lion-like eyes flashed fire like carbuncles; his eye-brows were half a palm over. When he was angry, it was a terror to look upon him. He required eight spans for his girdle, besides what hung loose. He ate sparingly of bread; but a whole quarter of lamb, two fowls, a goose, or a large portion of pork; a peacock, crane, or a whole hare. He drank moderately of wine and water. He was so strong, that he could at a single blow cleave asunder an armed soldier on horseback from the head to the waist, and the horse likewise. He easily vaulted over four horses harnessed together; and could raise an armed man from the ground to his head, as he stood erect upon his band.[78]

The emperor is portrayed as extremely liberal, generous, deeply pious, a great strategist, erudite and learned, and with great fluidity of expression. Thus, when Agolant, King of Africa, surrenders after the taking of Pamplona,

---

78 *History of Charles the Great and Orlando Ascribed to Archibishop Turpin*, T. Rodd, London, 1812, p. 36. See also, Castets, Ferdinand (ed.), *Turpini Historia Karoli Magni et Rotholandi*, Société pour l'Etude des Langues Romanes, Montpellier, 1880, p. 39.

Charlemagne, with the greatest diligence, gathers his troops and proclaims an amnesty for all, under the condition that they join him against the infidels. And 'he freed all the prisoners, made rich the poor, clothed the naked, gave honors to the disinherited, reconciled the malcontents, made enemies become friends, and associated the civilized with the barbarian, uniting all people in those lands through the grace of God in the bond of love'.[79] Turpin, Archbishop of Reims, pardoned their sins and gave his blessing to all of them. According to the author, a solemn assembly was held at court four times a year, on Christmas, Easter, Pentecost, and the feast of St. James. The king would come lavishly adorned with his crown and scepter, in the imperial manner, and was surrounded by great knights and people who admired him and blindly obeyed him.

Roland ('Rotholandus'), Duke of the Carolingian army in command of 4,000 soldiers ('dux exercituum cum quattuor milibus virorum'), is presented as the count of Le Mans ('comes cenomannensis') and lord of Blaye ('Blavii dominus'), brother of Baldwin, son of Milon of Angleris and Bertha, sister of Charlemagne and, consequently, nephew of the king. The Roland of the *Historia* is quite similar to the one of the *Chanson,* a vigorously religious and brave soldier, fearless, tough, smart, and courageous. The *Historia* also mentions Oliver ('Oliverius'), although the character lacks the leadership granted to him by the *Chanson*. Like Roland, Oliver is also a brave knight (*miles acerrimus*), duke of the army in command of 3,000 men, and, as in the *Chanson*, the author depicts Oliver as an expert ('bello doctissimus') and strong warrior ('brachio et mucrone potentissimus').

Facing the Frankish heroes, as in the case of the *Chanson de Roland* and for similar reasons, the author substitutes the Basques for Saracens. Thus the main enemies of the emperor are the various Muslim leaders, such as Agolant, King of Africa; Furra, King of Navarre; Ibrahim, King of Seville; Al-Mansur (*Altimaior* or Almanzor), King of Cordoba; and the Kings Marsir and Beligard, sent by the sultan of Babylon. The *Historia* devotes a large portion of the narrative (Chapters 6 through 14) to the campaign against King Agolant, who according to the story, comes to conquer Agen, halfway between Bordeaux and Toulouse. Mirroring the Marsilius portrayed in the *Chanson*, Agolant is a brave leader, but also deceitful and intriguing, so he does not hesitate to give his word in vain and to break his promises. Therefore, he is shown as a fierce, ruthless, and fanatical Muslim.

79　In Castets, Ferdinand (ed.), *Turpini Historia Karoli Magni et Rotholandi,* Société pour l'Etude des Langues Romanes, Montpellier, 1880, p. 16.

As regards Ganelon (*Ganalon*), he has neither the strength nor the leadership of the antihero in the *Chanson*. He is barely mentioned in the *Historia* until Chapter 21 ('*De proditione Ganaloni et de bello Runciesvallis et de passione pugnatorum Karoli*'), in which the author refers to the betrayal that leads to the defeat in Errozabal. But the *Historia* does not mention the anger that drives Ganelon to betray his king nor the rivalry that pits him against Roland, with whom in this narrative he is not linked by family ties.

The *Historia*, which consists of 32 chapters, can be divided into three parts corresponding to each one of the campaigns launched by Charlemagne to free Hispania from the Muslim yoke.

It begins with the Apostle James' order, which, through divine intercession, entrusts Charlemagne to regain Hispania to boost the pilgrimage to Santiago de Compostela, where the body of the Apostle was buried by divine intersection. The author thus provides authority to the campaign, which the emperor is enforced to undertake.[80] And when in Chapter 12 ('*De datis trebis et de disputatione Karoli et Aigolandi*') Agolant asks Charlemagne what right he has to conquer so many lands that had not belonged to him in the past and to which he has no right, the emperor alludes to the divine plan.[81] And the author affirms, 'for as our Lord and His twelve Apostles subjected the world with their doctrine, so did Charles, King of the Franks and Emperor of the Romans, by recovering Hispania for the greater glory of God'.[82]

Embarked on a crusade that would take him fourteen long years and several military campaigns, the emperor first besieges the fortress of Pamplona, which lies in Muslim hands. However, after three months of siege, the emperor's forces cannot penetrate the impregnable walls that protect the city. The description of the walls coincides with the description that the *De Laude Pampilone* provides.[83] Therefore, one day Charlemagne

---

80   Castets, Ferdinand (ed.), *Turpini Historia Karoli Magni et Rotholandi*, Société pour l'Etude des Langues Romanes, Montpellier, 1880, p. 4.

81   Castets, Ferdinand (ed.), *Turpini Historia Karoli Magni et Rotholandi*, Société pour l'Etude des Langues Romanes, Montpellier, 1880, p. 20.

82   Castets, Ferdinand (ed.), *Turpini Historia Karoli Magni et Rotholandi*, Société pour l'Etude des Langues Romanes, Montpellier, 1880, p. 19.

83   *De Laude Pampilone*, a Latin manuscript that describes Pamplona and its walls. See Larrañaga, Koldo, "Glosa sobre un viejo texto referido a la historia de Pamplona: el De laude Pampilone", *Príncipe de Viana*, 55, No. 201, 1994, pp. 137-148. See also, Elizalde, Ignacio, *Navarra en las literaturas románicas, Edad Media*, Institución Príncipe de Viana, Iruña/Pamplona, 1977, vol. 1, pp. 26 et seq. And also José M. Muruzabal's translation of the text in Muruzabal, José María, "Nuevos datos sobre el origen del reino de Navarra", *Espacio, Tiempo y Forma. Serie III. Historia Medieval*, 7, 1994, pp. 43-44.

begs God that, as he has come to the aid of these Christians moved by faith, He should give them the city, and the walls fall immediately at the hands of James the Apostle.

After recounting Charlemagne's three-year campaign in the Iberian Peninsula, during which he has captured all the cities along his way, the author emphasizes the pious character of the imperial exploits and the divine origin of the Santiago cathedral. Thus, the emperor is shown giving prodigious quantities of gold to kings and princesses to beautify the church of Santiago de Compostela with new bells, books, clothing, and other gifts. He also appoints an abbot and canons of the Order of St. Isidore, martyr and confessor, to attend it.

The second part (chapters 6 to 15) coincides with the second campaign that Charlemagne faces after the conquest of Hispania by the troops of King Agolant coming from Africa. This forces Charlemagne to march once again ahead of his troops, which are now under the command of Duke Milon of Angleris, father of Roland. They confront Agolant's forces near a river, where there is a church in honor of the blessed martyrs Facundus and Primitivus. But upon seeing such a great army, Agolant proposes Charlemagne to decide the battle through a fight between a limited number of warriors. The emperor agrees and leads one hundred of his soldiers against one hundred of the Saracens, who are quickly killed. Then Agolant sends two hundred more men who are also defeated on the spot. And then he sends two thousand, who are also killed at the hands of the Christians, before the rest flee.

Agolant having broken his word, the Christians prepare for battle, and a miracle happens. As the author describes in Chapter eight ('*De bello Sancti Facundus ubi hastae viruerunt*'), those Christians who are to receive the martyr's palm the next day in battle find their spears covered by branches early in the morning. And after the soldiers cut the branches that fell on the ground, large trees spring up and flourish there. Forty thousand Christians perish in that battle along with Milon, Roland's father. Even the king's horse is killed that day, but Charlemagne continues resolutely fighting on foot and, with two thousand Christians, finally defeats Agolant, who retreats to León. Meanwhile, Charlemagne withdraws with his remaining troops to Gaul.

Crossing the Pyrenees, Agolant undertakes a new campaign against Agen with a formidable army composed of troops from fifteen different nations. Charlemagne and six of his men enter the fortress pretending to be part of a diplomatic mission and, having seen the city's defenses, raise an army and besiege the city for six months. In the seventh month, after using battering rams, siege towers, and other machines, the besiegers are ready to storm into the city when Agolant and the rest of the kings flee in the dark of the night through the sewers and, crossing the river Garonne, retreat into Hispania. Charlemagne enters the city the next day and kills ten thousand of the Saracens found in the fortress.

Agolant flees again and seeks refuge in Pamplona, but the emperor besieges the city for the second time and offers to let Agolant surrender it. The former decides to accept the terms and surrenders the fortress. During the meeting between the two kings, he agrees to be baptized only if a certain number of Christians are victorious in combat against an equal number of Moors. But, as he prepares to be born again the following day through baptism, he notices over dinner that there are about thirty men present who are poorly dressed. Agolant asks the emperor who those people are, and when Charlemagne explains to him that those are monks, servants of the Lord, he replies that he refuses to be baptized after seeing how the Christian God treats his servants. He prepares for battle, which is to take place next morning.

This second battle at the gates of Pamplona is depicted in Chapter 14 of the *Historia* ('*De bello Pampiloniae et de norte Aigolandi regis*') as a particularly bloody encounter, in which the Muslim army is completely decimated and Agolant himself killed by the knight Arnaldus of Bellanda.[84] The author avers that Charles fought for his faith and, thus, he triumphed over Agolant 'because everything is possible for those who believe'.[85]

Chapters 16 to 32 narrate how, after the death of Agolant and the 'reconquest' of the entire peninsula, the armies of the emperor face new enemies. Agolant defeated, the emperor faces a new campaign, motivated this time by the insurrection of a king of Navarre called Furra (*De bello Furre contra Karolum*) who has fortified Mount Garzim (most likely Monjardín, atop of which the castle of the kings of Navarre stood at the beginning of the tenth century).[86] Charlemagne prepares for battle again, but this time he asks the Lord to show him who is going to die the next day. The following morning a red cross with the names of the martyrs appears behind the Christian troops. In the battle that takes place later, Furra and three thousand of his soldiers are killed, all of them 'Saracens of Navarre. And Charles made

84 Castets, Ferdinand (ed.), *Turpini Historia Karoli Magni et Rotholandi*, Société pour l'Etude des Langues Romanes, Montpellier, 1880, pp. 24-25.

85 Castets, Ferdinand (ed.), *Turpini Historia Karoli Magni et Rotholandi*, Société pour l'Etude des Langues Romanes, Montpellier, 1880, p. 25.

86 Paris, Gaston B, p.; Meyer, Paul (eds.), *Histoire poétique de Charlemagne*, Librairie Emile Bouillon, Paris, 1905, p. 265.

himself master of the mountain and the castle of Garzim, and subjected the entire country of Navarre.'[87]

It is in this third part that Roland takes the leading role that he lacks in the previous two and in which Ganelon's betrayal is depicted as well as the defeat of Errozabal and the subsequent hero's funeral. Following the events at the castle of Garzim, the king receives news that Admiraldus of Babylon has sent a giant named Ferracutus, of the lineage of Goliath, to Naiara (Nager) with twenty thousand Turks to fight against him. The giant fears neither spear nor javelin and is stronger than forty men. When the Christian army arrives, Ferracutus goes out beyond the gates of the city to oppose any warrior in single combat. One by one Ferracutus defeats Otgerius Dacus; Rainaldus de Alba Spina; Constantine, King of the Romans; Count Oellus; and twenty other warriors. He captures all of them alive and holds them in Naiara.

Facing defeat, Roland asks the emperor to give him permission to confront Ferracutus, and the latter accepts. They fight at the gates of the city. Taking the giant by the beard, Roland manages to throw him from his horse, but he also falls, and they continue the fight on foot. Then Roland aims a blow at the hilt of Ferracutus's sword, causing him to drop it. Enraged, Ferracutus tries to punch Roland, who manages to dodge, but the giant hits Roland's horse on the forehead and kills it. The fight lasts until noon, when Ferracutus demands a truce until the next day, and both fighters retire to their camps.

The next morning, they meet again on the battlefield. The giant this time wields a sword, and Roland a long club to avoid the giant's blows. They continue fighting by throwing stones at each other until at last the giant asks for a second truce and lies down peacefully to sleep on the ground. Roland places a stone as a pillow for the giant and lies down in silence next to him. When Ferracutus wakes up, Roland asks him how he is so strong, and the giant answers that he is only vulnerable if he is wounded in the navel.

After a long argument over religion, both heroes decide to fight under the protection of their respective gods. However, the fight begins advantageously for Ferracutus who, charging his opponent, succeeds in knocking him down. Roland, considering that it may be impossible to escape death, pleads for divine help and is revived by God. Then, he manages to take the giant's sword, stabs him in the navel, and kills him. Mortally wounded, Ferracutus implores Muhammad for help, and a group of Saracens take him into the walls of the city. The Christians then attack and capture Naiara, and Ferracutus and his people are killed to the last man, while all the Christian warriors are released.

---

87   Castets, Ferdinand (ed.), *Turpini Historia Karoli Magni et Rotholandi*, Société pour l'Etude des Langues Romanes, Montpellier, 1880, p. 27.

Shortly after, the emperor receives news that Ibrahim, King of Seville, and Al-Mansur, King of Cordoba, have escaped from Pamplona and have assembled an army of ten thousand Saracens in Cordoba. With six thousand men he goes to the encounter of the Muslim army, but when they are only 4.8 kilometres (3 miles) from the city they find that all the Saracens are disguised with masks and horns on their head, like demons, in such a way that, by making a strange noise with their drums and other instruments, they terrify the horses, which flee before their riders are able to stop them. Thus, prior to engaging combat, the emperor orders that they tie blindfolds over the horses' eyes and cover their ears. Then, assisted by the divine grace, the emperor, wielding a mighty spear and an invincible sword, penetrates the heart of the enemy army, killing as many as eight thousand warriors and Ibrahim, King of Seville. Al-Mansur retreats to the city in panic but surrenders the day after and, after giving his consent to be baptized, pays homage to Charlemagne.

Having thus overcome all his enemies, Charlemagne divides the lands that he has conquered among his soldiers. He gives Navarre and Bearn to the people of Brittany, Castile to the Franks, Naiara and Zara to the Greeks and the Apulians, Aragon to the Pictones, Andalusia to the Teutons, and Portugal to the Dacians and Flemish. Finally, the emperor appoints bishops and prelates in every city and creates a council of dignitaries in Compostela, decreeing that the Church of Santiago would in future be regarded as the Metropolitan See instead of the one of Iria. Turpin, Archbishop of Reims, recounts in the first person that, on the express orders of the king, he along with forty other bishops and prelates have decorated the church and the altar of St. James with extraordinary splendor and magnificence. The author adds, with obvious political intent, that the holy place does not lie under royal jurisdiction.[88]

Immediately after, once the entire Iberian Peninsula has been recovered, the emperor returns to Pamplona and camps there with his army. At that time there are two Muslim kings in Zaragoza, Marsilius (Marsirus) and his brother Baligant (Beligandus), sent by the Sultan of Babylon from Persia. The emperor sends Ganelon to compel them into baptism and to pay homage to him; the brothers, trying to deceive the king of the Franks, agree to be baptized and send him thirty horses laden with gold, silver, and jewels; forty measures of wine for his troops; and one thousand beautiful Saracen women. Meanwhile Marsilius and Baligant reach an agreement with Ganelon

---

88   Castets, Ferdinand (ed.), *Turpini Historia Karoli Magni et Rotholandi*, Société pour l'Etude des Langues Romanes, Montpellier, 1880, pp. 37-38.

to betray the king and pay him twenty horses laden with gold and silver for his treason.

The emperor, who trusts Ganelon, begins his march through the Zize pass and gives command of the rearguard to his nephew Roland and to Oliver, who must safeguard the position with thirty thousand men while Charlemagne marches ahead with the rest of the army: 'But many, who had on the night preceding intoxicated themselves with wine, and been guilty of fornication with the Saracen women, and other women that followed the camp from France, incurred the penalty of death.'[89] Once King Charles has safely passed the narrow strait between the mountains, Marsilius and Baligant, rushing down from the hills with twenty thousand men, attack the Frankish army early in the morning. Some are pierced with lances; some killed with clubs; others beheaded, burnt alive, or suspended on trees. Only Roland, Baldwin, and Tedricus remain. The last two reach the forest and finally manage to escape. After this terrible slaughter, the Saracens retreat.[90]

Here the author includes a new digression explaining that God allowed those who had not lain with women to die as a way to prevent them from committing sin on their return home, giving them a crown of glory in return for their behavior. Those who were guilty of this error expiated their guilt through death. But in this terrible hour, regretting their sins, a merciful God did not forget their last work for the cause of Christ, for whose faith they have given their lives. And the author adds, 'the company of women is evidently baneful to the warrior; those earthly Princes Darius and Mark Anthony were attended by their women, and perished; for lust at once enervates the soul and the body. Those who fell into intoxication and lasciviousness typify the priests that war against vice, but suffer themselves to be overcome by wine and sensual appetites, till they are slain by their enemy the devil, and punished with eternal death.'[91]

Meanwhile, Roland, climbing a high hill, examines the Muslim army, and seeing that many Christians are retreating through the mointain pass, blows his ivory horn. Accompanied by a hundred of them, he faces the enemy, and driven by divine vigor, rushes forward, overcoming all opposition and killing

---

89   Jones, Cyril M., *Historia Karoli Magni et Rotholandi: ou, Chronique du Pseudo-Turpin*, Slatkine, Genève, 1972, p. 39. See also, Castets, Ferdinand (ed.), *Turpini Historia Karoli Magni et Rotholandi*, Société pour l'Etude des Langues Romanes, Montpellier, 1880, p. 42.

90   Castets, Ferdinand (ed.), *Turpini Historia Karoli Magni et Rotholandi*, Société pour l'Etude des Langues Romanes, Montpellier, 1880, p. 42.

91   Jones, Cyril M., *Historia Karoli Magni et Rotholandi: ou, Chronique du Pseudo-Turpin*, Slatkine, Genève, 1972, p. 40. See also, Castets, Ferdinand (ed.), *Turpini Historia Karoli Magni et Rotholandi*, Société pour l'Etude des Langues Romanes, Montpellier, 1880, p. 43.

Marsilius. Beligard retreats from the field with the rest of the Saracens, but Roland is fatally wounded in five places. Tedricus and Baldwin, along with some Christians, make their way to where Roland lies under a tree, next to a marble altar slab. There, in order to prevent Durandal from falling into the hands of the enemy, Roland strikes the slab of marble three times and breaks his sword in two halves.[92]

Immediately afterward, Roland blows the olifant to draw together all the Christians hidden in the adjacent woods and to alert the rest of the army beyond the Zize pass. The hero blows the horn with such vehemence that the veins and nerves of his neck burst. The sound reaches the ears of the king, who is camped in the valley now known under his name, *Valcarlos*, about 12.8 kilometres (8 miles) from the summit. When the emperor hears the horn, he stands up and goes to his aid, but he is stopped by Ganelon, who suggests that Roland is in the habit of blowing his horn even when it is not entirely necessary. At this instant the emperor discovers Ganelon's treason and rushes to help his troops.

Meanwhile, Roland, thirsty, requests water from Baldwin, who, unable to find any, and seeing Roland so close to his end, blesses him and returns to the battle. Immediately thereafter, Tedricus approaches Roland and, weeping bitterly, asks him to strengthen his soul. Roland, who has confessed his sins that same morning and has also received the holy Eucharist before going to battle—as was the custom among crusaders—entrusts his soul to God and dies on the battlefield.

While Bishop Turpin is celebrating Mass in honor of the fallen, a phalanx of terrible beings passes beyond the crowd, dragging Marsilius's soul to hell while a number of angels carry the martyrs' crown to heaven. Baldwin arrives on Roland's horse and reports what has happened and where he has left the hero in his agony. Once back in the battlefield, the emperor discovers the hero's corpse, lying with his arms forming a cross. Charlemagne weeps with eyes and beard wet in tears.

The king solemnly pledges he will pursue the pagans and marches after them with his entire army. The sun stands still for three days until he surprises them on the banks of the river Ebro, near Zaragoza, where he attacks courageously, killing four thousand and dispersing the rest. On his return through Errozabal, the emperor makes inquiries about Ganelon's betrayal. A trial is then held in which Pinabel, defending Ganelon, and Tedricus, defending Roland, meet in single combat. Pinabel is defeated,

92   Castets, Ferdinand (ed.), *Turpini Historia Karoli Magni et Rotholandi*, Société pour l'Etude des Langues Romanes, Montpellier, 1880, p. 45.

treason is revealed, and Ganelon is sentenced to death by dismemberment and quartered by four wild horses.

Once the campaign is over, the emperor orders the consecration of two cemeteries, one in Bordeaux and the other in Arles, where the bodies of the Frankish warriors killed in Errozabal and Naiara are to be buried. Roland's body is placed on a carpet of gold upon two mules, covered with a veil, and is honorably buried in the Church of San Roman, which has been previously built by the emperor. His helmet is put on his head and the ivory horn at his feet. However, the author adds that his body was later transferred to the basilica of Saint Severinus in Bordeaux, the largest city in the province, where he was received with joy. The emperor gives twelve thousand pieces of silver and talents of gold for the repose of their souls and to feed the poor many kilometres around the town of Blaye. Moved by his love for Roland, he also gives rich robes and silver ornaments to the Church and orders that troubadours sing Roland's deeds and that masses and other solemn rituals be celebrated on the anniversary of his death.[93]

Interpretation of the Stained-glass Window of Chartres Cathedral

The city of Chartres belonged to Theobald I, *the Troubadour*, King of Navarre (1234-1253) after the death of his uncle Sancho VII *the Strong*, Lord of Champagne and Brie (1154-1234). In 1234, shortly after the Notre-Dame cathedral was finished, Theobald sold his rights to the city to Louis IX, King of France, who also purchased his domains of Blois, Sancerre, and Châteaudun.[94] Hence, in the tympanum of the right arch of the cathedral's *Portail Royal*, the famous *twins* are hidden behind a shield carved with the coat of arms of the Kingdom of Navarre and not that of France, as would have corresponded to the main entrance of this remarkable cathedral.

Some years earlier, on the night of 10 June, 1194, a fire destroyed the cathedral, which had been newly rebuilt under the direction of Bishop Fulbert. Only the towers, the crypt, and the portico of the new façade of the mid-twelfth century known as *Portail Royal* remained standing.[95] The *Sancta Camisia* or tunic, which according to tradition the Virgin Mary wore

93   Castets, Ferdinand (ed.), *Turpini Historia Karoli Magni et Rotholandi*, Société pour l'Etude des Langues Romanes, Montpellier, 1880, pp. 56-57.
94   Labarge, Margaret W., *Saint Louis: The Life of Louis IX of France*, Eyre & Spottiswoode, London, 1968, p. 58.
95   Houvet, Étienne, *An Illustrated Monograph of Chartres cathedral: Being An Extract of A Work Crowned by The Académie des Beaux-arts*, Étienne Houvet, Chartres, 1925, p. 5.

when she witnessed the crucifixion of her son, and which was donated in 876 to the cathedral by Charles the Bald, grandson of Charlemagne, and kept in the crypt, survived the fire. But the cathedral had to be rebuilt for the fifth time, on this occasion in the brief span of twenty-six years between 1194 and 1220, and not without great economic effort. This undertaking even caused a revolt against the bishop, who was exiled from the city for the space of four years. Finally, on 24 October 1260, the cathedral was consecrated in the presence of Louis IX, Lord of Chartres, under the dedication of the Virgin.[96]

The Notre-Dame cathedral of Chartres is considered one of the jewels of European Gothic architecture; its sculptural iconography as well as its glass windows are likewise considered some of the most beautiful examples of the Gothic artistic expression.[97] Of a total of 186 stained-glass windows from the twelfth and thirteenth centuries, 152 are conserved. More than one thousand different topics are represented on the windows, most of them based on religious themes.[98] From this perspective, although the story of Charlemagne's window registers the subject of the emperor's apocryphal crusades and, therefore, may well be considered a religious theme, together with the zodiac window, it represents an exception to the general rule of narrating the lives of saints or describing biblical episodes.

The master glassmakers were the last craftsmen to work in a cathedral, even after the painters. This allows us to date the stained-glass windows to between 1210 and 1220, when the architectural works of the cathedral were officially finished.[99] According to Marcel Bulteau, most of the 'verrières légendaires de l'étage inférieur' are dated to between 1210 and 1215, but the stained-glass windows of the choir, including the one representing Charlemagne's deeds, were set a little later, in 1220, except for those donated in 1237 by Ferdinand III of Castile and Jeanne Dammartin.[100]

96 Miller, Malcolm B., *Chartres cathedral*, Riverside Book Company, New York, 1996, pp. 12-14.

97 Marriage, Margaret, *Sculptures of Chartres cathedral*, Kessinger Publishing Co., Whitefish (MT), 2003, p. 6. Miller, Malcolm B.; Halliday, Sonia; Lushington, Laura, *Chartres cathedral: Illustrating the Medieval Stained Glass and Sculpture*, Pitkin Pictorials, London, 1992. See also, Miller, Malcolm B., *Chartres cathedral: The Medieval Stained Glass and Sculpture*, Pitkin Pictorials, London, 1980.

98 Snyder, James, *Medieval Art: Painting, Sculpture, Architecture, 4-14th Century*, Pearson Education, Upper Saddle River (NJ), 1989, p. 372. And, Miller, Malcolm B., *Chartres cathedral*, Riverside Book Company, New York, 1996, pp. 75 et seq.

99 Delaporte, Yves, *La cathédrale de Chartres et ses vitraux*, Éditions du Chêne, Paris, 1943, p. 13. See also, Delaporte, Yves; Houvet, Etienne, *Les vitraux de la cathédrale de Chartres*, É. Houvet, Chartres, 1926.

100 Bulteau, Marcel J., *Monographie de la cathédrale de Chartres*, R. Selleret, Chartres, 1887, vol. 1, p. 128. Émile Mâle holds the same opinion. See Mâle, Émile, *Notre-Dame de Chartres*, Flammarion, Paris, 1963, p. 191.

Besides the chemical ingredients to provide colour to the glass pieces, wood and sand were the essential elements to develop the stained glass; therefore, the itinerant glassmaker neighborhoods were generally located between the forest and the city, in places where these elements were abundant.[101] Master glassmakers were usually very highly regarded, and they traveled from city to city in search of well-paid contracts to manufacture or repair the glass windows used to decorate the great Gothic cathedrals of the time. Glass windows were very expensive, and many of them were built with the donations that members of various royal families granted to these cathedrals. This is the case of the rosette window of the north transept, a gift from the French Queen Blanche of Castile, wife of Louis VIII of France.

The stained-glass windows of the twelfth and thireenth centuries were formed of small pieces of glass of different colours assembled by lead strips that defined the figures by isolating fragments of different tones. The themes were initially drawn on cardboard in a sketch called a 'vidimus'. The stories were composed through a series of sequences that were usually read in ascending order, from the early scenes below until the last scenes of the story at the top of the stained-glass window. Once the main theme and the number of scenes or panels was established, the artist decided the order and disposition of the sequences, and a full-scale reproduction of the entire stained-glass window was generated on cardboard. The window was later mounted over the model on a table and was finally placed in one piece in its final location. Generally, the pattern or plan was the same for each of the sections of all stained-glass windows in the cathedral, which provided homogeneity.

As the Benedictine monk Theophilus describes in *De diversis artibus* or *Diversarum artium schedula* (c. 1120), the various pigments (*De diversi vitris coloribus*) were achieved by mixing the unbaked glass dough with different elements such as cobalt oxide for blue, copper oxide or ferrous oxide for green, or ferric oxide mixed with manganese dioxide for red. Depending on the mixture, manganese dioxide could likewise produce a yellow tone. In fact, the result usually was not always as expected, and the tones were not perfectly predictable.[102]

The blue and red tones of the stained glass stand out. In fact, the blue tone known as 'Chartres blue', produced from cobalt oxide extracted from

---

101 Finlay, Victoria, *Colour: A Natural History of The Palette*, Ballantine Books, New York, 2003, p. 314-317.

102 Guichard, Charles (ed.), *Théophile prétre et moine, essai sur divers arts*, Charles de l'Escalopier, Paris, 1843, p. 91 and, in general, pp. 79-118. See an English version in Dodwell, Charles R., *The Various Arts: De Diversis Artibus*, Clarendon Press, Oxford, 1986.

Bohemia and Schneeberg in Saxony, was, according to tradition, the original colour of the *Sancta Camisia* of the Virgin. It was, therefore, a colour with sacred connotations, filtering and unifying (purifying) the sunlight penetrating through the windows. It was also the main background colour in most parts of the cathedral, including Charlemagne's window. Along with blue and red, pale violet, garnet, green, and gold completed the palette, along with paler shades of blue and red, which were achieved by adding calcium fluoride, which whitened or clarified pieces of stronger tones. The final touches—such as robe folds, facial features, details of city walls or palaces used to decorate various scenes, flowers or foliage or muscles—were drawn in black over the colour pieces.

The glass dough pieces resulting from the baking contained bubbles and impurities that enhanced and enriched the original colours, since upon striking these small pieces of iridescent and slightly uneven glass, sunrays produce multiple flashes of different tones. Additionally, the strong tone of the colours enhanced by the sunlight imposed several restrictions that create a deep Medieval ambience and a great appeal. Strong shades of colour combined with the distance from which the observer views them hinders the 'reading' of the windows and, therefore, the drawings must be simple, and the number of characters and details recorded in each scene limited. In sum, the design of the compositions had to be extremely austere and the drawing very precise, designed for color images without depth.

The story of Charlemagne's window is not a written document but a pictorial depiction of the crusades that, according to Medieval legends, were undertaken by the emperor. In essence, the stained-glass window of Chartres, known as *Planche 68*, is a graphic narrative composed of twenty-four vignettes or panels (*pannels*) in which the author represents in ascending chronological order the most representative episodes of the two crusades that, according to the literary tradition, Charlemagne led.[103] It is interesting to note the specific literary sources that feed the narrative of the window and which episodes the glazier artist captured in his work.

The narrative of Charlemagne's stained-glass window is divided into two sections, the second of which is further divided into three sections:

- The first panel at the bottom centre depicts a fur, since the main donor of the window was the city's furriers guild.
- The first group of panels, panels 2 to 7 inclusive, describe the apocryphal crusade of Jerusalem.

103 Durand, Paul, *Monographie de Notre-Dame de Chartres*, BiblioBazaar, LLC, Charleston (SC), 2009, pp. 162-165.

- A second group, contained in panels 8 to 22, describe Charlemagne's expedition of 778 in terms of a crusade against the Muslims, according to the version of the Pseudo-Turpin in the *Codex Calixtinus*. This group is divided again into three sections that correspond to the three expeditions that, according to the *Historia Caroli Magni et Rotholandi*, the emperor undertook in the Iberian Peninsula.
  - Panels 8 to 13: First expedition and the capture of Pamplona.
  - Panels 14 and 15: Second expedition and the defeat of Agolant's troops.
  - Panels 16 to 22: Third expedition, St. Giles's Mass, and the battle of Errozabal.
- Finally, the last two panels (23 and 24) feature two angels who frame the entire work.

As noted by Vétault in 1877, the Charlemagne window of the Chartres cathedral is mainly based on two Medieval chronicles: The *Descriptio qualiter Karolus Magnus clavum et coronam Domini a Constantinopoli Aquisgrani detulerit* for the Crusade of Jerusalem and the *History Caroli Magni et Rotholandi* for the Crusade of 778.[104] Nonetheless, although these are the two main sources, it is clear that the *Chanson de Roland*, as well as the *Karlamagnús saga*, the *Vita sancti Aegidii*, and the oral tradition itself are also literary sources on which the master glassmakers drew to compose the stained glass scenes.

The *Descriptio*, a work datable to the late eleventh century or more probably the beginning of the twelfth century, has traditionally been attributed to a monk from the Abbey of Saint-Denis who was inspired to write it by the First Crusade (1096-1099). The oldest surviving manuscript is conserved in the Bibliothèque Mazarine in Paris listed as *MS 1711*. According to Gerhard Rauschen and Hugo Loersch, publishers of a Latin edition of the text, it is likely that the author of the second part of the text was a monk of the monastery of St. Dionisius (Saint-Denis), owing to a passage (*Descriptio* 123, 18) that includes a digression whose object is promoting the abbey and obtaining benefits for the same.[105] In contrast, Matthew Gabriele suggests that the description is not necessarily linked to Saint-Denis, but that instead

104 Alphonse Vetault was the first author to recognize both the *Historia Caroli Magni et Rotholandi* and the *Descriptio* as the main literary sources for the stained glass window. See Vétault, Alphonse, *Charlemagne*, Alfred Mame et Fils Editeurs, Tours, 1877, p. 545.

105 Rauschen, Gerhard; Loersch, Hugo, *Die Legende Karls des Grossen*, Duncker & Humblot, Leipzig, 1890, pp. 96-100.

it seems likely that someone close to King Philippe I (1060-1108) ordered the writing of the *Descriptio* with the intention of linking his dynasty by blood to the Carolingian one.[106]

The work consists of two parts written by two different authors. The first, depicted in panels 2 to 7 of the Charlemagne window, corresponds to the crusade that, according to legend, the emperor undertook to free Jerusalem and his journey to Constantinople. There he meets with Emperor Constantine, who grants him important relics that Charlemage takes to Aix-la-Chapelle. The author does not forget to mention the establishment of an annual *indictum* that the city should receive for watching over the relics. In the second part, the text relates that upon the death of Charles the Bald and by his own wish, some of the relics and the *indictum* were transferred from Aix-la-Chapelle to Saint-Denis.[107]

As can happen with legends, the tale of the Crusade of Jerusalem was widely circulated and ended up being considered a true story. Around the same time when the *Descriptio* appeared, the poem *Le Pèlerinage de Charlemagne* or *Voyage de Charlemagne à Jérusalem et à Constantinople* was written. The oldest written version of *Le Pèlerinage de Charlemagne* conserved today may be dated to approximately 1140. The text is nourished by the same elements as the *Descriptio*, although it differs in substantial aspects. For instance, unlike *Le Pèlerinage de Charlemagne*, the *Descriptio* narrates the conquest and recovery of Jerusalem.[108] As a matter of fact, the

106 Gabriele, Matthew, "The Provenance of the Descriptio Qualiter Karolus Magnus: Remembering the Carolingians in the Entourage of King Philip I (1060–1108) Before the First Crusade", *Viator*, vol. 39, No. 2, 2008.

107 Rauschen, Gerhard; Loersch, Hugo, *Die Legende Karls des Grossen*, Duncker & Humblot, Leipzig, 1890, p. 97.

108 *Le Pèlerinage* describes how Charlemagne having asked his wife who was the most gallant king of the world she replied to him that it was the Byzantine Emperor Hugo. Therefore, under the pretext of a pilgrimage, Charlemagne and his twelve peers march to the east and come to Jerusalem, where they meet with the patriarch who gives them many relics and confers on Charles the title of emperor. On his return, Charlemagne stops in Constantinople and Emperor Hugo receives and welcomes them in a room in which the king has hidden a spy. At night Charlemagne and the twelve peers drink more than usual and each begins to talk about their extraordinary abilities, such as the ability to sleep with the daughter of King Hugo as many times as they wish in one night. Ashamed for having done so and for having being discovered, they pray before the relics and Charlemagne tells Hugo that in fact he and his twelve peers are capable of the feats they have claimed. Hugo does not believe it, but in virtue of divine intercession, they do perform their tasks and Hugo, impressed, becomes a vassal of Charlemagne. Once back home, Charlemagne forgives his wife and becomes a great king. Burgess, Glyn S.; Cobby, Anne E., *The Pilgrimage of Charlemagne: Le pèlerinage de Charlemagne*, Garland, New York, 1988.

Descriptio includes the conquest of Jerusalem in the context of a holy war that Charlemagne undertook with no more self-interest than to serve the greater interests of the Christian world as a soldier of Christ. Thus, when Constantine offers the emperor rich treasures, he points out that he will only accept relics as gifts.

As noted above, the first panel of the window depicts a master furrier in his workshop showing a beautiful white robe to one who might well be a prosperous buyer fascinated by the skills of the tailor and is willing to pay a good sum for the garment. We owe a debt of gratitude to the generous patrons of the furrier's guild or the *pelletiers fourreurs* of Chartres for this beautiful window. As in the case of companies or individuals that sponsor cultural events today, the window attests for those who visit the cathedral the intensity of their faith and piety and emphasizes the assistance and contribution of the furriers to the interests of their city.

The next set of panels (2-7) focuses on the first part of the *Descriptio*. The second panel depicts Charlemagne seated on his throne and surrounded by two bishops. As in the other scenes, Charlemagne is shown with a long straight hair and furry beard, in contrast to Muslim characters who, as in the case of the defenders of Pamplona, the master glassmaker represented with curled hair and beardless. The emperor appears dressed in a pale-yellow tunic and a cobalt-blue cloak. Charlemagne is doubtlessly the leading figure of the window and, therefore, he appears in fourteen of the twenty-four panels, always dressed in clothing of different colours, predominantly green and garnet, that contrast with the blue background blanketing all the scenes. Except on five occasions (panels 9, 10, 18, 21, and 22), in the scenes showing the emperor the master included at his feet an inscription that reads *Carolus* or *Carrolus* (8, 13) to help the observer to identify him. In six of the panels (8, 9, 11, 13, 18, and 22), the emperor is depicted with a crown and a halo. The halo is always red or green, depending on the background against which it is placed, with the purpose of obtaining a higher contrast. If the background is blue, the halo is red, and if the background is red, the halo becomes green, illustrating the symbolic importance of this detail that does not go unnoticed by the observer.

The second panel depicts the legation of the four bishops whom, according to the *Descriptio*, the Emperor Constantine (272-337) sent to Aix-la-Chapelle with the mission of delivering a letter to Charlemagne. The emperor, slightly tilted to his left, speaks to one of the two bishops. Since only two characters are shown and Charlemagne appears to be speaking with only one of them, Clark Maines suggests that the character seated on his right could well be Bishop Turpin who, according to the

Descriptio, had to read the letter because the emperor himself did not know how to read.[109]

The third panel represents Constantine, leaning on his right arm, asleep in his bed. An angel appears to him in his dream and reveals to him that Charlemagne will liberate Jerusalem. Thus, the master glassmaker depicts Charlemagne on horseback, armed with a spear and a shield, dressed in armor, and wearing a helmet. As Maines notes, the artist made two errors in these first two scenes. On the one hand, the events take place in reverse order to the *Descriptio*'s account, that is, Constantine's dream takes place before he decided to send a legation to visit Charlemagne. On the other hand, the *Descriptio* describes in detail Charlemagne's face in Constantine's dream, while the panel presents Charlemagne with his visor down, in a combative stance.[110]

The fourth panel is dedicated to the battle for Jerusalem. Charlemagne, leading his troops in pursuit of the Muslims, strikes a blow with his sword at the neck of the Muslim king, who dies on his horse in retreat. In line with the tradition of the *chansons de geste*, the illustration of the arms is anachronistic, for it depicts the Christian warriors wearing flat helmets with visors and armed with large triangular shields. Helmets with visors did not become widespread until the twelfth century, and Frankish warriors of the eighth century, even horsemen, preferred round shields and pointed helmets. In any case, the master glassmaker distinguishes the Muslim soldiers from the Christians, representing them according to the fashion of eighth-century Frankish warriors, that is to say, with small round shields (*clipeo rotundo*) and pointed helmets (*pileus*).

The fifth panel shows Constantine receiving Charlemagne at the gates of Constantinople. The emperor amicably extends his right arm over the shoulder of Charlemagne, inviting him to enter the heavily fortified city. In contrast to the blue tones of the background, the bright red light inside the rooms is projected through the open doors and windows (panels 1, 3, 5, 6, 9, 12, and 13). This visual effect generates a feeling of warmth, seclusion, and hospitality in the observer. To the right of Charlemagne stands a figure graciously supporting the panel's frame with his right hand, creating a very artistic illusion of depth.

The sixth panel corresponds to the account of the *Descriptio* in which Constantine offers wonderful treasures to Charlemagne as a reward for his

---

109 Maines, Clark, "The Charlemagne Window at Chartres cathedral: New Considerations on Text and Image", *Speculum*, vol. 52, No. 4, Octubre 1977, pp. 805-806.

110 Maines, Clark, "The Charlemagne Window at Chartres cathedral: New Considerations on Text and Image", *Speculum*, vol. 52, No. 4, Octubre 1977, p. 806.

victorious crusade and the recovery of Jerusalem for Christianity. However, the emperor, who has performed these actions motivated by piety and faith, expresses to Constantine that he will only accept relics as a gift. Thus, the illustration shows Charlemagne supporting his left hand upon Constantine's shoulder as a sign of friendship. He points with his right hand to the three reliquaries and the *Sancta Camisia*, which lies on a stone altar supported by four richly decorated pillars. A *butafumeiro* (censer), symbol of Santiago de Compostela, hangs under one of the arches of the ceiling.

The series of panels of the Crusade of Jerusalem ends with the seventh scene that represents Charlemagne depositing a relic on a richly decorated altar, received by two bishops wearing elegant robes and carrying their staffs. The scene also shows a figure behind the emperor similar to the character of the fifth panel, a beardless and richly dressed young courtier. The presence of an olifant-horn hanging from one of the arches nearest to this character indicates that he may be Roland. Indeed, the figure that accompanies Charlemagne to the gates of Constantinople may also be Roland, main character of the second part of the window. Although the *Descriptio* does not mention the hero of the *Chanson*, it is likely that the tradition impelled the author to introduce this character in the scene and, therefore, to strengthen his identification through the depiction of the ivory horn, symbol of the hero killed at Errozabal.

There are different interpretations of the relics, the temple where the scene is inscribed, and the monks who receive the offering from Charlemagne. Paul Durand argues that Charlemagne offers the reliquaries and the crown of the Muslim king of Jerusalem to the Abbey of Saint-Denis, which would explain the abbot's *crosier* (staff) and the presence of the two monks as well as the absence of Bishop Turpin from the scene.[111] This hypothesis is reinforced by Ernst G. Grimme, who stipulates that the object deposited by Charlemagne is indeed a crown and not a reliquary, and that this scene is based on a forged document from the Abbey of Saint-Denis specifying that all crowns seized from the enemy should be deposited there.[112]

Despite Maines's reluctance to accept this,[113] the whole scene suggests that this is indeed an abbot and not a bishop, and it seems that the object is a crown rather than a reliquary. When comparing this to the reliquaries depicted in

111   Durand, Paul, *Monographie de Notre-Dame de Chartres*, BiblioBazaar, LLC, Charleston (SC), 2009, p. 163.
112   Grimme, Ernst G., "Das Karlsfenster in der Kathedrale von Chartres", *Auhener Kunstblütter des Museumsvereins*, 19-20, 1960-1961, p. 21.
113   Maines, Clark, "The Charlemagne Window at Chartres cathedral: New Considerations on Text and Image", *Speculum*, vol. 52, N° 4, October 1977, p. 807.

the sixth panel, we see clearly that the object that the emperor holds in his hands bears considerable similarity to the crown of the Muslim king whose head Charlemagne cut off in the fourth scene. Among other details, the object of this panel's gable is much smaller than the reliquaries of the previous panel. It has no decorations and has similarities with the pointed crown that the king of Jerusalem wears. On the other hand, the ring of the crown has three encrusted jewels like the rest of the crowns portrayed in window (one central jewel flanked by two smaller). It also lacks the typical *arquería* shown in most decorated reliquaries in the window, including the one in panel six.

The master glassmaker begins the narration of the campaign of 778 in the eighth panel. The scene depicts two scholars of the king's court; one adorned with a bonnet explains to Charlemagne the meaning of the Milky Way or *viam stellarum*, which is found in the sky above all of them. The emperor is found seated on the imperial throne holding the scepter. As in panels 5 and 7, the glassmaker of Chartres artistically represents the monarch's interest by means of a gesture; Charlemagne grabs his necklace with one hand. The symbolic significance of the *viam stellarum* explains why it is present in thirteen out of the twenty-four panels of the window (4, 5, 8, 11, 12, 13, 15, 16, 17, 18, 21, 23, and 24). The Milky Way, known as the Way of St. James according to Medieval legends, is described in the first chapter of the *Historia Caroli Magni et Rothlandi*: 'But observing the starry way in the heavens, beginning at the Friezeland sea, and passing over the German territory and Italy, between Gaul and Aquitaine, and from thence in a straight line over Vasconia, Bearn and Navarre, and through Spain to Gallicia, wherein till his time lay undiscovered the body of St. James.'[114]

The ninth scene represents Charlemagne's dream. The Apostle James appears in dreams to Charlemagne and orders him to march to Galicia following the Milky Way to liberate his grave from the Muslim yoke. Charlemagne, asleep in his bed, is shown—as is Constantine in the third scene—with a halo and a crown, adorned with a tunic and a cloak. This scene is part of the first chapter of the *Historia Caroli Magni et Rothlandi*:

[T]he Milky Way in the sky means that you, with a great army, will enter Galicia fighting against the pagans, and once it has been recovered, you will visit my church and sanctuary, and all people of the borders of the sea, walking in your footsteps, will ask God's forgiveness for their sins,

---

114 *History of Charles the Great and Orlando Ascribed to Archibishop Turpin*, T. Rodd, London, 1812, p. 5. See also, Castets, Ferdinand (ed.), *Turpini Historia Karoli Magni et Rotholandi*, Société pour l'Etude des Langues Romanes, Montpellier, 1880, p. 3.

and will return safely for the celebration of his praise. You recognize the wonders he has done for you throughout your life until the present moment. Proceed then as soon as you are ready, I am your friend and helper, your name will be celebrated for all eternity, and a crown of glory will be your reward in heaven.[115]

The next panel portrays Charlemagne riding with his army toward Galicia. Turpin, Archbishop of Reims, who is behind the emperor, is talking to him. Roland, young and beardless, rides to the right of the emperor holding a staff in his right hand. The artist illustrates two other bearded characters who could well be Milon of Angleris, father of Roland, who is riding alongside him, and Ganelon, who is next to Turpin.

Scenes 11 and 12 reproduce the siege of Pamplona. In the eleventh panel, the artist describes the scene that takes place in the second chapter of the *Historia Caroli Magni et Rothlandi* ('*De muris Pampiloniae per semetipsos lapsis*'). Charlemagne, unable to take the city, whose thick walls have withstood for months the siege of the Carolingian army, kneels in front of his troops and implores God and St. James to intercede for him:

Pamplona was the first city besieged by Charles. He invested three months, but he could not take it because of the invincible strength of its walls. He then made this prayer to God: 'O Lord Jesus Christ, for whose faith I have come here to fight against the pagans, for the love of your glory, give me this city, and you, blessed St. James, if you really appeared to me in dreams, help me to take the city.' And in that moment God and St. James, attending his request, completely destroyed the walls, which fell to the ground. And Charles respected the life of the Saracens who agreed to be baptized, and the rest he put to the sword. The news of this miracle induced the rest of the Saracens to surrender their cities and pay homage and tribute to him, and so were all the lands rapidly subjected.[116]

The twelfth scene shows a Christian warrior on a prancing horse in an attitude of assault, armed with spear and shield, with his helmet's visor down, pursuing a Muslim rider who flees from him unsuccessfully, seeking refuge within the walls of the city. It is the image of the taking of a city after a fight. Taking into

115 Castets, Ferdinand (ed.), *Turpini Historia Karoli Magni et Rotholandi*, Société pour l'Etude des Langues Romanes, Montpellier, 1880, pp. 4-5.
116 Castets, Ferdinand (ed.), *Turpini Historia Karoli Magni et Rotholandi*, Société pour l'Etude des Langues Romanes, Montpellier, 1880, p. 4.

account the resemblance of this scene with the siege of Pamplona represented in the bas-relief of the shrine of Aix-la-Chapelle, built at the beginning of the thirteenth century,[117] in which the artist depicts a guard atop the tallest tower of the city blowing the olifant-horn in alarm, most scholars identify the walled fortress with Pamplona.[118] However, the walls in this panel do not appear to be collapsing, so Maines believes that perhaps this panel should be interpreted as a generic depiction of not just Pamplona, but of all of the cities that Charlemagne took by force.[119] On the other hand, the *Chanson de Roland* mentions in stanza 134 that Roland, disobeying Charlemagne's orders, was the author of a great slaughter in Pamplona (Noples) and that, in order to hide the traces of blood, he had the fields washed with water, as a result of which the *Karlamagnús saga* records that Charlemagne slapped his nephew in the face. All these factors permit us to understand the panel as the capture of Pamplona according to sources other than the *Historia Caroli Magni et Rotholandi*, such as the actual *Chanson* and, most importantly, the *Karlamagnús saga*. The episode of the capture of the city is mentioned only indirectly in the *Chanson* when the poet sings 'he came, then, to conquer Noples without waiting for your orders; the Saracens made a sortie and presented battle to Roland, the good vassal. And he washed the blood-covered meadows to remove the traces of the encounter.'[120]

After the violent action described in the twelfth panel, the master glass-maker reproduced in the thirteenth panel the image of Charlemagne ordering and directing the work of the rebuilding of a church. This panel, crowned with a medallion, groups the six scenes dedicated to the first year of the crusade in Hispania. Thus, the author depicts the contrast between the relentless violence of the war with the emperor's mercy in times of peace, after having achieved victory. In fact, the *Historia Caroli Magni et Rotholandi* records in its fifth chapter ('*De ecclesiis quas Karolus fecit*') how Charlemagne ordered

117 Datable to between 1200 and 1215, and therefore, only slightly older than the window. See Schramm, Percy E.; Mütherich, Florentine, *Denkmale der deutschen Könige und Kaiser: Ein Beitrag zur Herrschergeschichte von Karl dem Grossen bis Friedrich II, 768-1250*, Prestel, Munich, 1962, p. 188 et seq.

118 Mâle, Émile, *L'art religieux du XIIIe siècle en France: étude sur l'iconographie du Moyen Age et sur ses sources d'inspiration*, Ernest Leroux Editeur, Paris, 1898, p. 447. See also, Durand, Paul, *Monographie de Notre-Dame de Chartres*, BiblioBazaar, LLC, Charleston (SC), 2009, p. 164; Maines, Clark, "The Charlemagne Window at Chartres cathedral: New Considerations on Text and Image", *Speculum*, vol. 52, No. 4, October 1977, p. 810.

119 Maines, Clark, "The Charlemagne Window at Chartres cathedral: New Considerations on Text and Image", *Speculum*, vol. 52, No. 4, October 1977, p. 810.

120 Müller, Theodor, *La Chanson de Roland: nach der Oxforder Handschrift*, Verlag der Dieterichschen Buchhandlung, Göttingen, 1863, p. 120.

the expansion and beautification of the church of St. James in order to befit the temple where the sarcophagus of the Apostle would be guarded.[121]

The fourteenth panel describes a battle between Christians riders armed with spears and Muslims carrying swords. This vivid scene shows a Muslim falling dead along with his horse upon being impaled by one of the Christian soldiers, while the rest of the infidels flee, closely pursued by the Christians. If we follow the chronological order of the *Historia Caroli Magni et Rotholandi*, this scene corresponds to the eighth chapter entitled '*De bello Sancti Facundi ubi hastae viderunt*', which is the first battle that takes place after the restoration of St. James' cathedral. This battle marks the beginning of a new military campaign in Iberia after the insurrection of Agolant. The *Historia* narrates in the sixth chapter that once Charlemagne returns to his homeland, a certain pagan king called Agolant defeats all the soldiers left by the emperor in custody of the cities and garrisons and recovers all Hispania with his army, forcing the emperor once again to march in front of his troops, led by Milon of Angleris, Roland's stepfather.

The encounter with the troops of Agolant takes place in front of the church in honor of St. Facundus and St. Primitivus. According to the text, Agolant offers Charlemagne to let the fight be decided by the confrontation between a few Muslim warriors and an equal number of Frankish warriors. The emperor accepts, knowing that the Muslim soldiers are going to be exterminated. And this is the scene illustrated in the panel, which explains why the artist does not show Charlemagne among the Christian paladins.[122]

It is precisely the night before this battle that the miracle of the flowering spears takes place, as represented in the fifteenth panel of the window. The artist shows five Christian warriors fully equipped for battle with swords buckled on and helmets with the visors down, sleeping on their shields.[123] Behind them there are seven flowering spears driven into the ground.

---

121 Castets, Ferdinand (ed.), *Turpini Historia Karoli Magni et Rotholandi*, Société pour l'Etude des Langues Romanes, Montpellier, 1880, p. 9. Maines believes that it could be the scene depicted in the eighth chapter of the *Historia* (*De bello Sancti Facundi ubi hastae viderunt*) in which Charlemagne orders the construction of the abbey in honor of Saint Facundus and Saint Primitivus. See Maines, Clark, "The Charlemagne Window at Chartres cathedral: New Considerations on Text and Image", *Speculum*, vol. 52, No. 4, October 1977, p. 811.

122 Castets, Ferdinand (ed.), *Turpini Historia Karoli Magni et Rotholandi*, Société pour l'Etude des Langues Romanes, Montpellier, 1880, pp. 11-12.

123 The dynamism and realism of the scene is emphasized by representing one of the five sleeping warriors sitting, leaning on his shield rather than holding it, suggesting that it might be a watchman asleep by divine design while the miracle happened. While the window is apparently not representing any hero in particular, among those identified by the divine grace is Milon de Angleris, Roland's putative father.

Above them, the master glassmaker painted the *Milky Way*, which guides the heroes on their crusade. According to the eighth chapter of the *Historia Caroli Magni et Rotholandi*, through the intervention of the saints Facundus and Primitivus, the spears of those who are going to die the next day in the battle are covered with flowers and leaves. At dawn, upon cutting the branches from the spears, large trees spring up in an instant, which—the author of these pages indicates—can still be seen in that place:

> The Christians, who had very carefully prepared their weapons for battle the next day, fixed the bases of their spears at night in the ground in front of the castle, in the meadow, near the river, and they found them in the morning covered with bark and branches. Those, therefore, who were about to receive the crown of martyrdom were very surprised by this event, attributing it to Divine Grace. After cutting the branches off of the spears, on falling to the ground, they quickly rooted and and became lofty trees, which may be still seen flourishing there, chiefly ash. All this denotes the joy of the soul and the loss of the body. And what else? Then the battle began and forty thousand Christians received the martyr's palm along with Duke Milon, father of Roland. The king's horse was also killed, but Charles continued resolutely to fight on foot, and with two thousand Christians courageously broke through the Saracens, cutting many of them in half with his sword, named Gaudiosa.[124]

The sixteenth panel opens the cycle of the third expedition, in which the Battle of Errozabal, central to the *Chanson de Roland*, is inscribed. However, the sixteenth panel representing two warriors fighting against each other that we observe today opening this new phase, was originally placed in the upper apex of the stained-glass window (panel position 22) until 1921.[125] In fact, the stained-glass window, which had been the object of further cleaning and restoration in previous centuries, was newly restored in 1921 in the workshop of the artist glassmaker Jean Gaudin, who had completed similar works in Laon, Soissons, Saint-Quentin, Baye, and Paris.[126] In the opinion of the restorer, both figures were badly placed, so he ordered their relocation.

---

124 Castets, Ferdinand (ed.), *Turpini Historia Karoli Magni et Rotholandi*, Société pour l'Etude des Langues Romanes, Montpellier, 1880, p. 12.

125 Gabriele, Matthew; Stuckey, Jace, *The Legend of Charlemagne in the Middle Ages: Power, Faith, and Crusade*, Palgrave Macmillan, 2008, p. 113.

126 Manhès, Colette; Deremble, Jean-Paul, *Vitraux de Chartres*, Zodiaque, Paris, 2003, p. 108. See also, Bey, Martine C.; Grodecki Louis; Perrot, Françoise, *Les vitraux du Centre et des Pays de la Loire*, Éditions du Centre national de la recherche scientifique, Paris, 1981, pp. 27-28.

The origin and rationale of the Gaudin decision is found in the interpretation of the subject of both panels by Alphonse Vétault at the end of the
nineteenth century, based on the suggestions that Marcel J. Bulteau and the
presbiter of the cathedral Mr. Brou made to the *Société Archéologique d'Eure-
et-Loire* in their work *Monographie de la cathédrale de Chartres.*[127] Bulteau
proposes an interpretation of the window (*Vitrail de saint Charlemagne et
saint Roland*) in his *Description de la cathédrale de Chartres*, according to
which the last panel should be the one representing a priest whom Bulteau
identifies as Turpin. The archbishop offers Mass in memory of those killed in
the Battle of Errozabal, while an angel announces that Roland is in heaven
and Charlemagne, seated, attends the mass, aggrieved by the loss of his
nephew.[128] According to Bulteau, this panel should be placed at the top of
the window as the culmination of the history, and not in the place that it
is found (panel number 16). Paul Durand, concurring with Bulteau in his
work *Monographie de Notre-Dame de Chartres* identifies the original panel
16 as the mass of Archbishop Turpin and, like Bulteau, indicates that the
scene should crown the window.[129]

Vétault proposed to complete the difficult task of reinterpreting the
stained-glass window with the assistance and support of the presbiter
of the cathedral Brou, who had dedicated his life to studying it. And he
concluded that the mass panel (originally panel 16) did not, as Bulteau
argues, depict Turpin, but instead depicted St. Giles, and that what the angel
was announcing not the immortality of Roland's soul but the redemption
of Charlemagne's sin. According to a twelfth-century work entitled *Vie de
Saint Gilles* written by Guillaume de Berneville, the St. Giles Mass was held
after the death of Roland and, therefore, like Bulteau before him, Vétault
concludes that the medallion inserted at the top of the window (panel
22) was not where it should be according to the chronological order of the
narrative. Thus, the chromolithography in his book changes the location
of the panels, placing panel number 16 in place of panel 22 and vice versa,
as corresponds to the chronological order of the events.[130]

Based on these studies, Gaudin in 1921 changed the order of the panels. I
follow here the original Medieval order and, I think, in a future restoration of

127 Bulteau, Marcel J., *Monographie de la cathédrale de Chartres*, R. Selleret, Chartres, 1887.

128 Bulteau, Marcel J., *Description de la cathédrale de Chartres: suivie d'une courte notice sur les
églises de Saint-Pierre, de Saint-André et de Saint-Aignan de la même ville. Avec cinq planches*,
Garnier, Paris, 1850, pp. 237-239.

129 Durand, Paul, *Monographie de Notre-Dame de Chartres. Explication des planches*, BiblioBazaar,
LLC, Charleston (SC), 2009, pp. 162-165.

130 Vétault, Alphonse, *Charlemagne*, Alfred Mame et Fils Editeurs, Tours, 1877, p. 545.

the stained-glass window those panels should be relocated into their original locations, the one that the master glassmaker of Chartres chose 800 years ago for each of these two panels, whether or not they follow the chronological order of the legend. While it is true that the *Vie de Saint Gilles* includes the celebration of the mass after the death of Roland, the *Karlamagnús saga* includes the mass as an event long before the Battle of Errozabal, and also indicates that it was the Archangel Gabriel who ordered the wedding between Milon of Angleris and Gisela. This suggests—considering that the *Karlamagnús saga* is a translation of pre-existing legends—that the chronological organization of the events described in this window was very possibly known by the author. Also, in Vétault's opinion the panel originally placed in position 22 corresponds to the fight of Roland against Marsilius,[131] which in any case does not take place earlier in the narrative than the battle between Roland and Ferracutus (panel 17). Indeed, there is no point in changing the order of the panels by relocating panel 16 in an incorrect chronological order. Finally, I do not believe that based on the interpretations made today, we are in a position to ensure that the glassmaker was wrong when he placed the panels that he himself had conceived, combined, and fixed.

The original panel 16 (today located at the upper end of the stained glass) shows a monk crowned with a halo celebrating mass with a helper holding the Bible, while a king sitting behind them—with crown and halo—appears shocked. The scene shows an angel descending on the officiant and hands him a long scroll. It is very plausible that this panel represents the Mass of St. Giles as recorded in the *Vita sancti Aegidii*, following the tradition included in the *Karlamagnús saga*. According to this legend, the emperor unsuccessfully sought forgiveness for a sin that he did not dare to confess to St. Giles. On a certain day, while the saint was saying mass, an angel placed a letter on the altar in which was described the sin in question. Charlemagne, having lain with his sister Gisela, conceived Roland, who was therefore both the emperor's son and his nephew. After the mass, the letter miraculously disappeared, thus making it known that his sin had been forgiven. The *Ronsasvals* of Provence, which dates from the first half of the twelfth century, also includes this tradition.[132]

Following a narrative logic, through this sixteenth panel the glassmaker opens the last part of the story of the window that represents the third Carolingian expedition in the course of which the Battle of Errozabal occurs. The artist shows Roland in his relationship with the emperor and reveals

---

131 Vétault, Alphonse, *Charlemagne*, Alfred Mame et Fils Editeurs, Tours, 1877, p. 547.
132 Cannone, Belinda; Orcel, Michel, *Figures de Roland*, Klincksieck, Paris, 1998, p. 37.

two key issues of the Rolandian cycle from a high Medieval logic: Roland's death and the relevance of the crusades undertaken by Charlemagne. The hero's death is inherent to his sinful origin, which is redeemed only by a life entirely dedicated to the holy war, ultimately crowned by the palm of martyrdom. Only after a life of sacrifice and the fight against the infidels is Charlemagne absolved of the worst imaginable sin, incest.

The seventeenth panel tells the extraordinary combat at the gates of the city of Naiara (Nager) between Roland and the giant Ferracutus, who was represented by the master glassmaker with a crown. His death is shown when the Christian hero plunges his sword into the navel of the giant. The battle between Roland and the giant Ferracutus, according to the description of the seventeenth chapter of the *Historia Caroli Magni et Rotholandi*, enjoyed great popularity in the Middle Ages and even in the Renaissance, having been endlessly reproduced in miniatures, paintings or even on the facades of religious buildings. The scene corresponds to Chapter 17 (*'De bello Ferracuti gigantis et de optima disputatione Rotholandi'*) of the *Historia Caroli Magni et Rotholandi*.[133]

The eighteenth panel portrays Ganelon, the traitor, riding to the left of Charlemagne through the Zize pass. The glassmaker artistically depicts the depth and narrowness of the pass by stacking various figures in the same image (including two individuals that are not mentioned in the literary sources) as well as some rocks that rise above the horses on top of which many trees grow forming an impenetrable forest. The Milky Way rises on top. Charlemagne is represented gesturing to turn back, while Ganelon tries to persuade him not to by gesturing with his right hand. A third rider wearing a green bonnet like the figure of the eighth panel follows the previous two closely and informs the emperor about the meaning of the Milky Way. The *Historia* only mentions Turpin of Reims riding together with these two characters through the Basque Pyrenees, so even though he lacks a miter, this identification is accepted. By extension, the figure in panel number eight could in turn be identified with the archbishop. Despite the fact that the sources do not mention it, he might well have had knowledge of the religious significance of the Milky Way. This scene corresponds with chapter 23 (*'De sonitu tubae Rotholandi, et de confessione ac transitu eius'*) of the *Historia Caroli Magni et Rotholandi*:

And [Roland] loudly blew the olifant-horn to summon all Christians hidden in the adjacent woods to help him, or to call their friends beyond

---

133 Castets, Ferdinand (ed.), *Turpini Historia Karoli Magni et Rotholandi*, Société pour l'Etude des Langues Romanes, Montpellier, 1880, pp. 29-34.

the mountain pass. The horn was blown with such strength that all other horns were cracked by the sound, and it is said that at that moment Roland blew with such vehemence that his neck's veins and nerves broke. The sound, carried by angels, reached the ears of the king, who had camped in the valley that is still named for Charles, about 12.8 kilometres (8 miles) from Errozabal toward continental Vasconia. Charles would have returned to help him, but he was stopped by Ganelon who, aware of Roland's sufferings, insinuated that he was used to blow the horn on too many occasions. 'He is, perhaps,' he said, 'trailing some wild animal, and the echo of his call spreads through the forest, so it will be useless to go look for him. Oh, traitor, evil man, false like Judas!'[134]

Panel 19 portrays Roland on top of a pile of mutilated Saracen corpses, trying to break the sword Durandal and, in parallel, blowing the olifant for the last time. This scene takes place before the previous one but, by virtue of its symbolic value and relevance in the Rolandian cycle, the glassmaker preferred to place it in the central medallion, in a prominent location, which indicates that the artist gave in this case more importance to the expressive dimension of the scene than to its proper chronological sequence in the narrative of the *Historia*. Besides, the glassmaker did not follow the *Historia* faithfully here since the story tells of how Roland finally managed to break the sword in two. The artist relied instead on the *Chanson* that in stanzas 172 and 173 tells how the sword is of such a strength that the hero is unable to break it. The glass—as the text—is certainly endowed with an inhuman beauty:

> Rollant hath struck the sardonyx terrace;
> The steel cries out, but broken is no ways.
> So when he sees he never can it break,
> Within himself begins he to complain:
> 'Ah! Durendal, white art thou, clear of stain!
> Beneath the sun reflecting back his rays!
> In Moriane was Charles, in the vale,
> When from heaven God by His angel bade
> Him give thee to a count and capitain;
> Girt thee on me that noble King and great.
> I won for him with thee Anjou, Bretaigne,

134 Castets, Ferdinand (ed.), *Turpini Historia Karoli Magni et Rotholandi*, Société pour l'Etude des Langues Romanes, Montpellier, 1880, p. 46.

And won for him with thee Peitou, the Maine,
And Normandy the free for him I gained,
Also with thee Provence and Equitaigne,
And Lumbardie and all the whole Romaigne,
I won Baivere, all Flanders in the plain,
Also Burguigne and all the whole Puillane,
Costentinnople, that homage to him pays;
In Saisonie all is as he ordains;
With thee I won him Scotland, Ireland, Wales,
England also, where he his chamber makes;
Won I with thee so many countries strange
That Charles holds, whose beard is white with age!
For this sword's sake sorrow upon me weighs,
Rather I'ld die, than it mid pagans stay.
Lord God Father, never let France be shamed!'
Rollant his stroke on a dark stone repeats,
And more of it breaks off than I can speak.
The sword cries out, yet breaks not in the least,
Back from the blow into the air it leaps.
Destroy it can he not; which when he sees,
Within himself he makes a plaint most sweet.
'Ah! Durendal, most holy, fair indeed!
Relics enough thy golden hilt conceals:
Saint Peter's Tooth, the Blood of Saint Basile,
Some of the Hairs of my Lord, Saint Denise,
Some of the Robe, was worn by Saint Mary.
It is not right that pagans should thee seize,
For Christian men your use shall ever be.
Nor any man's that worketh cowardice!
Many broad lands with you have I retrieved
Which Charles holds, who hath the great white beard;
Wherefore that King so proud and rich is he.'[135]

The master glassmaker of Chartres accentuates the terrifying scene by illustrating a multitude of bodies severed by Durandal. Thus, the master shows two heads, an arm, and two legs severed from their bodies, as well

---

135 *The Song of Roland: Translated by C. K. [Charles Kenneth] Moncreiff*, Project Gutenberg, 1996. See also, Müller, Theodor, *La Chanson de Roland: nach der Oxforder Handschrift*, Verlag der Dieterichschen Buchhandlung, Göttingen, 1863, p. 158-161.

as a body cut in half from which the intestines hang. On the right side of the panel, Roland, without his helmet, which is at his feet on the ground, blows the olifant-horn ('tuba sua eburnea'), although in this case the artist portrays a surprisingly serene expression on Roland's face. Finally, a divine hand at the apex of the panel descends from the Milky Way over Roland, which gives him a blessing before he dies.

The twentieth panel shows Roland dying with his right arm hanging down, without strength, but still clutching his sword Durandal, which he has not been able to break. The artist represents Roland sitting with his back reclining on his shield, while Baldwin seeks to quench his thirst. This scene corresponds to a line of Chapter 23 (immediately following the narrative of panel 18) of the *Historia*, in which the author emphasizes that good Baldwin, despite his good faith, could not find water to calm the hero's thirst.[136]

The glassmaker of Chartres represents Baldwin with a halo, holding an object with his left arm extended to Roland, while he is extending his right arm toward the hero. Given that the *Historia* expressly states that Baldwin could not find water and, at the same time, it says he gave him his blessing, it is possible that said object, square but difficult to identify, is a Bible. This would explain why he offers it to the hero with his left hand to give him his blessing with his right hand. The fact that Roland is sitting and not lying on the grass is due to the limitations of the scene's frame, which does not permit depicting a lying body but rather a reclining one, taking advantage of the curved edge of the panel. Moreover, the artist once again illustrates the shady and wooded aspect of the Zize pass as represented in the *Chanson*, including an abundance of trees. In this panel, as in the previous one, both characters lack the expression of pain corresponding to the scene. In this case, however, it is obvious that these faces are replacements of the original, which may have been broken or lost, since the lines do not match the rest of the faces of the window.

The twenty-first panel describes Baldwin resting his right arm on the emperor's horse and informing him of Roland's death. Charlemagne, on his horse, raises his left hand, thus letting the emissary speak. This scene corresponds to Chapter 25 ('*De visione Turpini episcopi et de lamentatione Karoli super Rotholandum*') of the *Historia*, according to which, while the battle takes place upon the heights of the Zize pass, Turpin offers mass in Luzaide—that was subsequently to be called *Valcarlos*—not knowing of

136 Castets, Ferdinand (ed.), *Turpini Historia Karoli Magni et Rotholandi*, Société pour l'Etude des Langues Romanes, Montpellier, 1880, pp. 46-47.

what is happening in the battelfield. Turpin has a vision, in which a phalanx of terrible demons drags Marsilius's soul to hell.[137]

In this panel the artist also represents the rocky and wooded aspect of the Zize pass. The fact that the glassmaker did not paint Baldwin on Roland's horse, which would have endowed the scene with a dramatic element, may simply be due to the spatial limitations of the panel. However, unlike in previously discussed images, Baldwin's expression shows profound pain. The figure that stands out behind Charlemagne, on his horse, is most probably Ganelon, whose face is hidden behind the emperor's shoulders. And high above them all, the Milky Way (*via stellarum*) frames the scene.

The final panel, which before the reform of 1921 was located at the apex of the window, represents two warriors with lances facing each other in an encounter on a stony ground. Above them the Milky Way rises. The figure on the left, adorned with a helmet with the visor down, rides a white horse and bears a triangular shield, which indicates that he is a Christian warrior. His opponent, a Muslim king who wears a pointed green crown and carries a round shield, is riding a reddish horse. In the violent collision between the two warriors, the Muslim king's lance breaks against the shield of the Christian hero, who strikes the Saracen's shield with the point of his lance. Although the *Historia* is very explicit on the matter, describing how Roland pulls the giant from his horse by grabbing the giant by the beard, this scene represents the first clash between Roland and Ferracutus.[138]

The image is remarkably like the scene represented on one of the capitols flanking the façade of the ancient marketplace in Lizarra/Estella. Whether it is a reproduction of the capitol or not, it portrays the same first encounter between the two mounted heroes, including the detail of the broken spear. As Roland strikes, Ferracutus staggers back and falls over. The inscriptions *Feragut* and *Rollan* engraved by an artist named Martinus on the upper part of the capitol over each of the figures help us interpret the scene.

Mary J. Schenck maintains that the red-robed figure in panels 12, 14, 16 (current), and 17 is Charlemagne instead of Roland since the window grants the emperor an unmitigated prominence, in some way diminishing the figure of Roland, who only appears as an important element of the emperor's feats.[139] But while several authors have identified this panel as

---

137 Castets, Ferdinand (ed.), *Turpini Historia Karoli Magni et Rotholandi*, Société pour l'Etude des Langues Romanes, Montpellier, 1880, p. 50.

138 Paul Durand holds the same opinion in Durand, Paul, *Monographie de Notre-Dame de Chartres. Explication des planches*, BiblioBazaar, LLC, Charleston (SC), 2009, p. 165.

139 Schenck, Mary J., "Taking a Second Look: Roland in the Charlemagne Window at Chartres", *Société Rencesvals*, vol. 25, No. 1–2, 2006, pp. 371-386.

the fight between Charlemagne and a Muslim chieftain, the fact that the Christian hero does not wear a crown or halo, and lacks the label *Carolus* at his feet (which certainly does not always accompany the figure of the emperor), weakens the legitimacy of this interpretation.

Vétault asserts that this panel depicts Roland fighting against Marsilius, since his round shield and his red horse are mentioned in the *Historia*.[140] But the text of the *Historia* is also restrictive in this respect in describing how, far from confronting Roland in single combat, Marsilius and his troops flee in all directions. The hero, putting his trust in God, chases after them and, overcoming all opposition, kills Marsilius on the spot. On the other hand, in the *Chanson de Roland*, Marsilius does not participate in the Battle of Errozabal and, as he learns his army has been defeated, dies in Zaragoza as a result of the wounds that Charlemagne inflicted on him in the battle on the banks of the river Ebro.

Finally, the hypothesis that this cannot be Roland because this scene breaks with the chronological trajectory of the narrative, cannot be duly sustained either. Panels 18 and 19 do not maintain the sequential order of the narrative either. In fact, the position of this scene at the apex of the window is explained by the importance of the incident and not by the chronology of the event.[141] As Paul Durand explains, the master glassmaker placed the scene of the fight between Roland and Ferracutus in the upper part of the stained glass between two adoring angels (panels 23 and 24) who, hanging from the Milky Way, each hold a *botafumeiro* or censer and a chocolate cup, because the distribution of the panels did not allow him to place it farther down. Indeed, inversions of this sort are very common in works of art of that time.[142]

Thus ends the beautiful narration of the stained-glass window of Chartres, whose excellent conclusion acknowledges the importance of the subject in the overall Rolandian cycle.

140 Vétault, Alphonse, *Charlemagne*, Alfred Mame et Fils Editeurs, Tours, 1877, p. 547.

141 In fact, in strict chronological order, the apex should represent Charlemagne facing Marsilies and avenging the death of Roland according to the narrative of the *Chanson*.

142 Durand, Paul, *Monographie de Notre-Dame de Chartres. Explication des planches*, BiblioBazaar, LLC, Charleston (SC), 2009, p. 165.

Epilogue

Abstract

The last chapter focuses on the general conclusions. Starting from an analysis of the existing sources, both historical and literary, the author includes in this section of the monograph a brief but detailed summary of the most relevant ideas supported throughout it to finish with some final considerations of the figure of King Charles.

Keywords: 778, Rencesvals, Charlemagne, Marca Hispanica, Genocide

In his book *Historical Investigations of the Antiquities of the Kingdom of Navarre*, Joseph Moret, chronicler of the kingdom, opposes his version of the battle to that of Juan de Mariana, which he considers lacking in rigor and even orthodoxy and honesty. In general, Moret criticizes those authors who, like Mariana, use the *Historia Karoli Magni et Rotholandi*, also known as the *Turpin Chronicle*, as a historical source for the study of the battle of Errozabal or any other historical event. According to Moret, far from being an actual chronicle, the *Historia Karoli Magni et Rotholandi* is a beautiful piece of literature that should not be used as a historical source. Moret emphasizes the illicit character of Mariana's chronicle by specifying that, although in the Latin edition of his work the author makes explicit mention of Einhard's *Vita Karoli Magni Imperatoris*, in the Spanish edition he states that the encounter between the Basques and the Franks did not take place because there was no chronicle to register such an encounter, deliberately removing Einhard's *Vita* from the bibliography in that edition. It is certainly difficult to know what Mariana's motivations might have been, but Moret's complaint was legitimate.[1]

Moret also observes that the battle of Errozabal is so recurrent among foreign authors that 'after almost nine hundred years it seems that it happened

---

[1]   Moret, Joseph, *Investigaciones históricas de las antigüedades del Reyno de Navarra*, Editorial de Amigos del Libro Vasco, Bilbao, 1985, p. 225.

Irujo, X., *Charlemagne's Defeat in the Pyrenees: The Battle of Rencesvals.* Taylor & Francis, 2021
DOI 10.5117/9789463721059_EPI

yesterday'.[2] However, the author adds, this historical event had not been studied in detail by native authors to that day, and most of those who had written about the battle had for the most part merely 'repeated the story that they have found disturbed and confused in other author's works'.[3] Moret even considers that this is the effect of a 'very strong and foreign voice', implying that there were still in the seventeenth century political or cultural motivations for altering the historical events.[4]

More than three centuries later, we have not still advanced much.

I started the present book by referring to some of the authors who, in the last fifty years, have advanced the study of this historic episode, and I want to finish it by quoting an article published in Pamplona in August 2015: 'Although it is known as the battle of Rencesvals it seems that historically it was nothing more than a skirmish in which tribes of Basques, perhaps supported by Muslims, attacked the rearguard of the Carolingian army commanded by Roland.'[5] The press release was written by the press office of the Government of Navarre in commemoration of the fiftieth anniversary of the monument to Roland in Errozabal.

Moret probably would have objected and even asked why there were, and still are, two monuments in the battle hill of Ibañeta, one a chapel dedicated to Charlemagne and the other a monument to Roland. On 2 February 1941, during the period of German occupation of the northern Basque Country, a group of officers of the Wehrmacht and members of the Nazi party visited the monument, probably in their search for the Holy Grail and as propaganda to nurture the idea of Aryan supremacy. A storm destroyed the monument in 1934, and a second one was erected on the same spot in 1967, honoring Roland and the Frankish heroes who lost their lives in the battle 1189 years earlier. The remains of it are still visible in Ibañeta.

The Basque historian Arturo Campion explains this in his work *Gartxot, the Bard of Itzaltzu*. Campion describes Gartxot as the custodian of the oral tradition of the Basques, who pervceive the battle of Errozabal as an epic episode of their history. Before the arrival of foreign monks to the monastery of Errozabal, his son Mikelot, who has a privileged voice, sings in his mother tongue the episode

2   Moret, Joseph, *Annales del reyno de Navarra*, Imprenta de Martín Gregorio de Zavala, Pamplona, 1684, p. 209.

3   Moret, Joseph, *Annales del reyno de Navarra*, Imprenta de Martín Gregorio de Zavala, Pamplona, 1684, p. 209.

4   Moret, Joseph, *Annales del reyno de Navarra*, Imprenta de Martín Gregorio de Zavala, Pamplona, 1684, p. 209.

5   "Monumento a Roldán: Medio siglo recordando una batalla legendaria", Diario de Noticias, August 14, 2015.

of the capture and destruction of Pamplona, the main city of the Basques, and Roland's death at the hands of the local warriors in revenge. However, Campion's story has a tragic end, and there is no mention of the Basques until General Franco's death in 1975 when, on the occasion of the 1,200th anniversary of the battle, a monument was erected near the small chapel of Orreaga.

We could refer to the battle of Errozabal as 'the battle that in fact was a battle'. This is one of the first conclusions of this book. The military event that took place in August 778 in the Pyrenees was a battle of great magnitude, a defeat that put in check an entire empire. It was, as documented by the Frankish sources written in Latin, a 'certamen', that is, 'a pitched and decisive battle'. This is deduced from the reading of the historical sources.

It is difficult to know who first referred to Errozabal in terms of a 'skirmish', but the reference does enjoy a great tradition and the term has probably been popularized in the last decades of the twentieth century, primarily in studies of the *Chanson de Roland*. In 1950 Bernardino Llorca, Ricardo García, and Francisco J. Montalban published their *History of the Catholic Church in its Four Great Ages*, in which they argued that 'that event that was no more than a skirmish, then was enlarged by the popular muse'.[6] In 1971 Edilberto Marbán refers to the battle as a 'skirmish' in his work *The Spanish Medieval and Renaissance Theater: A Work for Students of Spanish*.[7] The National University of Cuyo (Argentina) published the proceedings of the Italian Cultural Week, held between 25 and 30 September 1972, in which the editors mention that 'from a rather trivial military event, from a skirmish or an ambush in Rencesvals, the legend arose'.[8] In 1984 Carmenza Neira published an article in the *Medieval Literature* journal of the University of Santo Tomás in which he refers to the battle as a 'skirmish' that the literature has turned into a 'war between East and West', an idea repeated in the *Cuadernos de investigación filológica* in 1987.[9] Years later, Carlos Reyero, in his work *Historical Image of Spain (1850-1900)*,[10] and Jaime del Burgo, in his *General History of Navarre*, make reference to the battle in the context of 'all the skirmishes that the Navarrese disputed against the Muslims',

6   Llorca, Bernardino et al., *Historia de la Iglesia Catolica: en sus cuatro grandes edades: Antigua, Media, Nueva, Moderna*, Biblioteca de Autores Cristianos, Madrid, 1950-1960, p. 106.

7   Marbán, Edilberto, *El teatro español medieval y del Renacimiento: una obra para estudiantes de espanol*, Las Americas, Long Island City, N.Y., [1971], p. 201.

8   Brandenberger, Tobias et al. (eds.), "III. Literatura y Realidad", Revista Iberoromania (2009), 1975 (3), pp. 107-170.

9   Ruiz, Roberto; Aramburu, Francisca, "Substratos míticos en el "Cantar de Roldán", *Cuadernos de investigación filológica*, Vol. 12-13 (1987), p. 7.

10   Reyero, Carlos, *Imagen histórica de España*, Espasa Calpe, Madrid, 1987.

although they do not refer to it as a skirmish but rather as a battle and even a 'glorious deed'.[11] More recently, Manuel Riu, in his *History of Spain*,[12] and Vicente A. Álvarez, in his *History of Spain of the Middle Ages*, have refered to a 'skirmish on the rearguard of the Frankish army'.[13]

None of the aforementioned authors provide any documentation that supports this idea, nor do they explain the basis for their interpretation.

In any case, this is not the most widespread interpretation in either Spanish or in other languages. In Latin, the battle is never referred to as *velitatio* or 'skirmish'. The vast majority of the authors who have written about this historical event in English, French, Basque, and German have referred to it according to the information contained in the sources, in terms of 'certamen' or 'battle'.

The Basques' strategy consisted in ambushing the Carolingian army when it was crossing the narrow passage of Zize. This does not imply that the Basques limited themselves to throwing stones from the mountains on the rear of the Carolingian army. Anyone familiar with the passage from Pamplona to Donibane Garazi, parallel to the present layout of the road to Santiago, will realize that there are very few points from which stones of a certain size can be thrown over an army that marches through it.

As the chronicles relate, the Basques took advantage of higher terrain and launched an attack against the Frankish army, forcing a close combat in which the surprise effect happened to be decisive. The Basque attackers had a critical advantage over the Carolingian army, both because of the panic that the attack generated among the Frankish troops and because the Basques had more appropriate clothing and armament for the terrain in which the battle was taking place.

The Basque 'tribes' represented in the Frankish chronicles were not tribes as such but rather an organized army that defeated the two largest armies in that part of the world at the time, giving rise to the Kingdom of Pamplona only four decades later. The political, economic, and military organization of Vasconia has been duly documented since at least the beginning of the seventh century. The archaeological remains that have been preserved in Pamplona from 778, the dimensions of its walled enclosure, and its urban perimeter in the eighth century suggest that the Basques were more than the 'crowds of nefarious bandits' ('latronum turba nefanda') described by the Frankish amanuensis.[14]

---

11   Del Burgo, Jaime, *Historia general de Navarra: Desde los orígenes hasta nuestros días*, Rialp, Madrid, 1992, p. 249.

12   Riu, Manuel, *Historia de España*, Espasa Calpe, Madrid, 1999, p.93.

13   Álvarez, Vicente A., *Historia de España de la Edad Media*, Ariel, Barcelona, 2008, p. 82.

14   Pertz, Georg Heinrich (ed.), *Annales et chronica aevi Carolini*, Monumenta Germaniae Historica (MGH), SS, I, Hannover, 1826, p. 234.

No historical source refers to the participation of Muslims at Errozabal, and contemporary Arab sources do not even mention it, because it did not concern the Emirate of Cordoba or the *walies* of Zaragoza and other cities along the river Ebro. Only the legend that was forged centuries later, giving rise to one of the most beautiful epics of the European Middle Ages, refers to Muslim warlords in combat against the troops led on the battlefield by Roland and infused the story with religious and political content.

Along the same lines, the aim of the 778 Carolingian campaign was the creation of the *Marca Hispanica*, a buffer state covering a vast area from east to west of the Pyrenees mountains, all along the Ebro valley. Such a political project could only materialize by granting the military control of the main Pyrenean accesses to the Iberian Peninsula, that is, Errozabal in the west and the Summum Pyrenæum or Col de Panissars, a few kilometres west of the present Pertus pass, to the east. In addition, the Frankish troops had to control the main cities on the Ebro valley, from Girona, Barcelona, and Lleida to the east to Zaragoza, Huesca, and Pamplona in the foremost west end of the *Marca*.

Taking advantage of the independence of the Muslim *walies* of the cities of the Ebro valley with respect to the Emirate of Cordoba, Charles invited them to the diet of Paderborn that took place in 777 to seal an agreement of political and military collaboration. This fact is nonetheless transformed into a 'crusade' against Islam by several of the contemporary Frankish chronicles, whose authors endeavor to emphasize the subjugation of the Muslim conurbations to the Carolingian Empire. The chroniclers never mention the settlements agreed between the Frankish king and the Muslim *walies* and never refer to Hussain ibn Yahya al-Ansari's rejection to open the gates of the city of Zaragoza to King Charles.

Although many authors have alluded to the battle of 'Rencesvals' or in the Basque historical tradition to the battle of 'Orreaga', the fighting took place in the plain of Errozabal, which is the original toponym from which the Spanish form 'Roncesvalles' and the French and English 'Rencesvals' derive. Due to the narrowness of the route, the battle took place all along the road that ran, meandering, from Pamplona to Luzaide.

An army consisting of two legions, or roughly 20,000 men and about 800 chariots drawn by 1,600 beasts of burden, stretched along a road as narrow as that of the port of Zize, which, as indicated, would not reach 4 metres at the widest points, and would occupy about 14 kilometres (8.6 miles) in length. If we add to this that the Carolingian army would take about five strenuous days to completing the trek between Pamplona and Donibane Garazi, we have an idea of the dimension of the confrontation.

It has been established that the battle took place on Thursday, 15 August because Eggihard (Aggiardus), 'the first at the king's court', died that day in the battlefield. However, we must not forget that 15 August is only the date of Aggiardus's death, not of the battle itself, and the Frankish sources are very explicit when describing repeated attacks by the Basques along the way, which leads to the conclusion that the battle was fought during the five days' march that the Carolingian army needed to complete the crossing of the Pyrenean pass.

The battle did not consist of an attack on the rearguard. Without disputing that the rearguard and the central part of the Carolingian army must have suffered the effects of the attack more severely than the vanguard, the Frankish chroniclers are unambiguous in claiming that the attack affected the entire Carolingian army. Einhard relates in the *Vita Karoli Magni* that the first attack was launched on 'the back part of the caravan of provisions' ('extremam impedimentorum partem')[15] and on the bulk of the army, and the Saxon poet records this in the *Annales of Gestis Caroli Magni Libri V* when describing the king marching to the head of the vanguard, leaving behind 'the rest of the army' that was affected by the Basque attack.

The battle revolved around the capture and control of the Ibañeta hill, the highest point of the battlefield and the only way out. The possession of the hill allowed the Basques to isolate the rearguard ('novissimum agmen') on the Errozabal plain, to launch an advantegous attack on the central body of the army ('medium agmen') running downhill through the narrow port of Zize, trying to drag 'the back part of the caravan of provisions' ('extremam impedimentorum partem') and avoid a possible counterattack of the vanguard ('primum agmen') headed by the king. As the sources indicate, the main attack was tumultuous, massive, and took the Frankish army by surprise ('subitoque tumultu'). This sudden attack resulted in a close combat in which the Basques had two obvious material advantages: Their personal equipment was much better adapted to the terrain in which the fight was taking place and they had strategic superiority provided by the higher and advantageous position in the terrain ('ex collibus altis'), which generated the panic, as a result of which the battle became a carnage. As Einhard's chronicle reveals, the entire amry was thrown down to the bottom of the gorge and annihilated to the last man ('ad unum omnes interjiciunt').[16]

15   Holder-Egger, Oswald (ed.), *Einhardi Vita Karoli Magni,* Monumenta Germaniae Historica (MGH), SSRG, Hannover & Leipzig, 1911, pp. 12-13.
16   Holder-Egger, Oswald (ed.), *Einhardi Vita Karoli Magni,* Monumenta Germaniae Historica (MGH), SSRG, Hannover & Leipzig, 1911, pp. 12-13.

King Charles never returned to the aid of his ambushed troops. Rather, the Frankish chronicles locate the king in the town of Godinne (Gôdene), about 80 kilometres (50 miles) southwest of Herstal, in October of that year. This means that he covered the approximately 1,270 kilometres (789 miles) separating Ibañeta de Godinne in about fifty days, at a prodigious average speed of more than 25 kilometres (15.5 miles) per day. Moreover, if we consider that the king stopped at Chasseneuil and, as recorded by the Astronomer Limosinus, took a detour through Paris on his way to the *palatium* in Herstal, we must conclude that the king traveled practically alone, without army corps and a caravan of supplies, fleeing after the debacle.

As a result of the defeat, the king lost the *impedimenta* including the royal treasure. As stipulated in the manuals of military strategy used at that time, no king before or after the battle of Errozabal would have transported his treasure in the rear through such a narrow road like that of the Zize pass and on the war path. This fact reinforces the version according to the contemporary historical sources that the attack affected the whole army, including the *centrum agmen* and the backside of the vanguard, which was where the impedimenta and the royal treasury was generally carried.

There is no historical evidence to assert that Roland commanded the rearguard of the Carolingian army. Indeed, Roland was not Roland, nor was Orlando nor Roldán. Despite the suspicions about his paternity, and the legend about the alleged romance between King Charles and his sister, the hero dead in the port of Zize was Hruodlandus or Ruodland, prefect or marquess of the march of Brittany ('brittannici limitis praefectus'). And Charles was not yet Charlemagne when the battle took place.

The battle of Errozabal was extremely violent, and as a result King Charles lost his treasure, but he also lost his army. Roland was not the only paladin killed in battle, nor the chief among the dead, but one of the leaders of the Carolingian army, many of whom were found dead in the Zize pass. The *Einhardi Annales* and the *Annales qui dicuntur Einhardi* are very explicit when recounting that 'most of the paladins that the king had appointed to lead his troops were killed in course of this battle' ('plerique aulicorum, quos rex copiis praejecerat, interfecti sunt').[17]

The very consequences of the battle confirm that it was a historical event of great military and economic consequence, but also of political and even cultural significance. A 'skirmish' does not cause the death of all the main

17   Kurze, Friedrich (ed.), *Annales regni Francorum (741–829) qui dicuntur Annales Laurissenses maiores et Einhardi*, Monumenta Germaniae Historica (MGH), SSRG, VI, Hannover, 1895, pp. 51 & 53.

chieftains of an imperial army, nor the bankruptcy of a kingdom, nor does it generate one of the oldest Medieval epic chants in Europe. In Moret's words, 'such a great pain does not come from a little wound'.[18] Defeat put the empire on the brink of bankruptcy and political and administrative chaos. It would take King Charles two years to fully restore his authority, clean up his ill-fated treasury, and undertake new military adventures.

Mention of the battle was censored during the emperor's lifetime. And Charles would never tread through Vasconia again, nor undertake punitive expeditions against the Basques during the following three decades of his reign. Only in 812 did his son Ludovico Pio, acting as Duke of Vasconia—and the de facto king of the Franks while his father laid affected by serious physical ailments—march his army through the Zize pass for the second time. This attack, which would be known as the Second battle of Errozabal, happened to be a military venture of uncertain consequences, significance, and deontology.

Beyond the actual encounter of the two armies, the battle of 778 is framed in a historical context of a global scale that involved a confrontation among the most outstanding political actors of the time across three different continents: The Caliphate of Baghdad, the Emirate of Cordoba, the independent Muslim kingdoms of the Ebro valley, the Frankish Kingdom, and Vasconia.

One of the direct consequences of the battle was that King Charles was forced to abandon the project idea of forging a *Marca Hispanica* encompassing the whole Pyrenean mountain range. As Joseph Moret argues, Vasconia never became part of the Hispanic *limes* or buffer state, and the Franks did not dominate or govern Vasconia between 778 and 824 when the Third battle of Errozabal took place and the Kingdom of Pamplona was formed in consequence of the Frankish defeat. The historical sources only mention Vasconia three times in the forty-six-year interval; specifically, they narrate the three military campaigns in the years 778, 812 and 824: that is, the campaign of Charlemagne in 778, the campaign headed by his son Ludovico Pio as king of Aquitaine over Pamplona in 812, and, finally, the punitive campaign headed by the counts Aeblus and Aznar in 824. All three had relatively grievous consequences for the Franks. In the words of the chronicler of the Kingdom of Navarre:

> It can be seen that on the occasion of this battle the Franks did not get the dominion over Navarre since Charlemagne was defeated by the natives, and he could never correct this circumstance. The most we can presume

---

18   Moret, Joseph, *Investigaciones históricas de las antigüedades del Reyno de Navarra*, Editorial de Amigos del Libro Vasco, Bilbao, 1985, p. 241.

[form the reading ot the Carolingian chronicles], is that he went and came to and from Zaragoza in full control of the battlefield, taking Pamplona by siege and maybe some other cities, although no other one is named [by the historical sources]. But to run an army through a given territory does not equal establishing a fixed and stable domain over it: this is the main idea where all historical facts converge.[19]

Having abandoned the idea of the creation of a *limes* or buffer state covering the whole of the Pyrenees, in the year eight hundred Charlemagne started new campaigns to secure the eastern *March* which, from 801 until the end of the ninth century, would cover irregularly the cities of Girona and Barcelona and the areas nearby. A territory that broadly coincides with current Catalunya.

The battle of Errozabal constituted a military and political victory for the Basques, but it was also part of the process of deconstruction of the seventh- and eighth-century Vasconia that would gradually disintegrate throughout the ninth century and from whose ashes the Kingdom of Pamplona would sprout in the western margin of the Pyrenees and the territories attached to it.

Finally, Moret includes in his chapter on the battle a small commentary on the prose of the Frankish chroniclers. Einhard mentioned the 'perfidy' of the Basques ('Wasconicam perfidiam'), and the Saxon poet refers to them as 'crowds of nefarious bandits'.[20] In this regard, Moret asks himself, 'Who were the thieves? The Navarrese, who wanted to defend their land or Charlemagne and the Franks who wanted to do away with it by force? Or what perfidy is there in seeking revenge for the grievances produced to them and the ruthless work of pulling Pamplona to pieces [...] leaving it exposed to the Mohammedan invasions?'[21]

The contemporary Frankish chronicles written immediately after the events that took place in Errozabal in 778 were composed by Charlemagne's chroniclers or their sucessors. As a result, they must be interpreted, as they are not objective and do not consider in an objective manner the nations and persons facing the Frankish Kingdom. In contrast to the qualities and attributes of the emperor and other Frankish kings, the Basque and other nations' leaders are usually described in very different and derogatory terms

19   Moret, Joseph, *Investigaciones históricas de las antigüedades del Reyno de Navarra*, Editorial de Amigos del Libro Vasco, Bilbao, 1985, p. 241.
20   Pertz, Georg Heinrich (ed.), *Annales et chronica aevi Carolini*, Monumenta Germaniae Historica (MGH), SS, I, Hannover, 1826, p. 234.
21   Moret, Joseph, *Investigaciones históricas de las antigüedades del Reyno de Navarra*, Editorial de Amigos del Libro Vasco, Bilbao, 1985, p. 241.

('contra Saxones, Frisiones, Alamannos, Baiowarios, Aquitanios, Wascones atque Brittones').[22] Thus, the Frankish chronicles refer continuously to the 'perfidious' Basques—a 'nefarious mob of Basque bandits', according to the Saxon Poet—as a violent, treacherous and barbarous people. The same is true for the Saxons ('Saxoniam plaga magna')[23] Lombards, Bavarians, or in general, any other nation at war with the Frankish Empire and their people.

Regarding the Basques and their leaders, a small sample of the treatment in the chronicles of the seventh and ninth centuries, results in the following:

Year	Source	Text
691	*Annales Mettenses*	*Harum enim gentium duces in contumaciam versi, a Francorum se dominio per desidiam praecedentium principum iniqua se praesumptione abstraxerant*
749	*Annales Mettenses*	*Quibus ille solito more despectis, Wasconiam petiit, et ad Waifarium, Ducem perfidum Aquitaniorum, pervenit*
770	*Vita Hludowici Imperatoris*	*Hunaldo quodam tiranno auctore…*
778	*Vita Hludowici Imperatoris*	*Turbantur, victrix latronum turba nefanda ingentem rapuit praedam, pluresque necavit*
778	*Vita Karoli Magni*	*In ipso Pyrinei iugo Wasconicam perfidiam parumper in redeundo contigit experiri*
816	*Einhardi Fuldensis Annales*	*Wascones gentilitia levitate usi defecerunt, sed duabus expeditionibus ita sunt edomiti, ut tarda eis deditio et pacis impetratio videretur*
816	*Annales Regni Francorum*	*Wascones, qui trans Garonnam et circa Pirineum montem habitant, propter sublatum ducem suum nomine Sigiwinum, quem imperator ob nimiam eius insolentiam ac morum pravitatem inde sustulerat, solita levitate commoti coniuratione facta omnimoda defectione desciverunt*
818	*Chronicon Moissiacense*	*similiter et eius exercitus, quem miserat super Wascones rebelles, cum triumpho victoriae reversi sunt, occisis tyrannibus: et terra quievit*
819	*Einhardi Fuldensis Annales*	*Similiter et Lupus Wasco de perfidia convictus, exilio deportatus est*
824	*Einhardi Annales*	*In ipso Pirinaei iugo perfidia montanorum in insidias deducti ac circumventi*

A good exercise of historical textual interpretation requires avoiding adjectives, but beyond the use of epithets in the present case, the problem is even greater when some sources omit historical events, such as the defeat

---

22 *Annales Mettenses*, in Pertz, Georg Heinrich (ed.), *Annales et chronica aevi Carolini*, Monumenta Germaniae Historica (MGH), SS, I, Hannover, 1826, p. 320.
23 *Annales Sangallenses Majores* [718].

at the battlefield of Errozabal in 778. Among other sources, the *Einhardi Fuldensis Annales* reports that 'Karolus cum exercitu in Hispania usque ad Caesaraugustam venit, Pampilonam urbem destruit, de Ibinalarabi et de Abitauro, praefectis Sarracenorum, obsides accipit, Wasconibus et Nabarris subactis revertitur in Franciam',[24] which, as can be verified by contrasting sources, is substantially contradicted by the facts.

In addition, the Frankish chronicles strive to emphasize the submission of the different nations to the Carolingian Kingdom, particularly after a military episode. After the battle of Errozabal and, in line with what is recorded in the *Einhardi Fuldensis Annales*, the *Annales Regni Francorum* and the *Annales Laurissenses* stress that 'Pampilona destructa, Hispani Wascones subiugatos, etiam et Nabarros, reversus in partibus Franciae'. Again, this is far from what can be confirmed by the facts. In this sense, the repetition of the term 'subiugatos' (subdued) by the chroniclers with reference to Vasconia over three centuries is an indication that the historiographical approach to this and other assessments must be taken with some caution.

Finally, it should also be noted that the writers strive to avoid granting the treatment of 'Rex' to any leader facing the Frankish Kingdom, so that Basque or Saxon leaders are portrayed as dukes ('dux'), or sometimes princes ('princeps'). The Aquitainian case is a good example. The Frankish sources refer to Eudo, Hunald, or Waiofar, who wielded power over Aquitaine until 768, as *Princeps* or *Dux Vasconiae*. However, once the conquest of Aquitaine was consolidated by Pepin the Short after the Eight Years' War (760-768), and after the reversal at Errozabal, Charlemagne rushed to crown his son Ludovico *Rex Aquitaniae* in 778 to appease Aquitainian patriotism and prevent another uprising: '[R]ex Karolus cum filiis et exercitu pacifice Frantiam repetiir filiumque suum Hludouuicum regem regnaturum in Aquitaniam misit.'[25]

In view of the fact that one of the Frankish chroniclers' main purposes was to underline the sublime nature of the king's deeds, they strove to emphasize Charlemagne's piety, and likewise that of his grandfather Charles, his father Pepin, and his son Ludovico, who were portrayed as defenders of the Catholic faith and dispensers of the divine goodness on

24 Pertz, Georg Heinrich (ed.), *Annales et chronica aevi Carolini*, Monumenta Germaniae Historica (MGH), SS, I, Hannover, 1826, p. 349.
25 *Vita Hulowici Imperatoris*, in Tremp, Ernst (ed.), *Astronomus. Das Leben Kaiser Ludwigs (Vita Hludowici imperatoris)*, Monumenta Germaniae Historica (MGH), SSRG, LXIV, Hannover, 1995, p. 294. See also, the *Gesta Hludowici Imperatoris* mentions *Hludouuicus, qui erat rex super Aquitaniam*, in Tremp, Ernst (ed.), *Astronomus. Das Leben Kaiser Ludwigs (Vita Hludowici imperatoris)*, Monumenta Germaniae Historica (MGH), SSRG, LXIV, Hannover, 1995, p. 179.

earth. Chroniclers strongly stress the divine intercession in human affairs and hence the military campaigns of the years 773, 774, 775, 776, 778, 779, 783, 784, 786, 788, and 791 are represented as the result of God's will.[26] The *Annales Petaviani* even compares Charlemagne to John the Baptist in the context of the mass baptisms among Saxon chieftains organized during the diet of Paderborn in 777: '[U]nde in postmodum Karolus rex merito audet cum Iohanne baptista, qui et baptizavit praedicans baptismum in remissionem omnium peccatorum.'[27]

Furthermore, the royal formulas used in official documents and the *Capitularia* accentuate this image of the king by presenting him under the titles *excellentissimus, serenissimus,* and *pacificus.*[28] 'Karolus magnus et praecellentissimus francorum imperator' the *Annales Laurissenses* records, and with respect to his coronation the chronicler states that 'Pope Leo placed the crown upon his head, and at one voice, the people of Rome proclaimed: Charles Augustus, crowned by God magnum and pacific emperor, long life and victory! And after the Lauds, under an ancient apostolic custom, he is worshiped and purified on behalf of the patricians and is entitled Emperor and Augustus.'[29] The author of the anonymous poem in Latin *Karolus magnus et Leo papa* named Charlemagne for the first time Father of Europe: 'King Charles, lord of the world, loved and revered by his people, venerable eminence of Europe, great priest, august hero.'[30]

Although some authors consider Charles one of the patriarchs of the European continent and culture, Raphael Lemkin, promoter of studies of genocide, includes Charlemagne among the leading instigators of genocide in world history and places his reign among one of the twelve more serious cases of genocide in the European Middle Ages.[31] Despite the massacres of

---

26   Ganz, David, "Einhard and the Characterization of Greatness", in Story, Joanna (ed.), *Charlemagne, Empire and Society,* Manchester University Press, Manchester, 2005, pp. 41-42.

27   Pertz, Georg Heinrich (ed.), *Annales et chronica aevi Carolini,* Monumenta Germaniae Historica (MGH), SS, I, Hannover, 1826, p. 16.

28   Duncalf, Frederic; Krey, August C., *Parallel Source Problems in Medieval History,* Harper & Brothers, New York & London, 1912, p. 6.

29   In the original Latin: '*Leo papa coronam capiti eius imposuit, et a cuncto Romanorum populo adclamatum est: Carolo Augusto, a Deo coronato magno et pacifico imperatori Romanorum, vita et victoria! Et post laudes ab apostolico more antiquorum principum adoratus est, adque ablato Patricii nomine, Imperator et Augustus est appellatus.*' Pertz, Georg Heinrich (ed.), *Annales et chronica aevi Carolini,* Monumenta Germaniae Historica (MGH), SS, I, Hannover, 1826, p. 188.

30   '*Rex Carolus, caput orbis, amor populique decusque, Europae venerandus apex, pater optimus, heros Augustus.*' In Rougemont, Denis de, *The Idea of Europe,* World Pub. Co., Cleveland, 1966, p. 46.

31   Jacobs, Steven L., *Lemkin on Genocide,* Lexington Books, Lanham (Md.), 2012, pp. 6 & 18.

civilians or prisoners in Saxony and other corners of the empire and, apart from the military campaigns that took place virtually uninterruptedly throughout Charles's reign, the genocidal essence of the emperor's rule is manifested in the monarch's attempt to exterminate the preexisting forms of life, languages, and religions in the territories conquered by the imperial troops and their replacement by others of the dominant culture through the imposition of severe legal codes and a highly repressive, and in places inquisitorial, administration. It is in this context that the aforementioned deaths took place.

The campaign of 778 brought war and destruction to Vasconia. As recorded by the sources, the pre-battle military operations generated many victims, as did the battle itself and the actions which occurred after it. There is no reference to the wounded on the battlefield in the chronicles, but there must have been many who were never rescued, but rather abandoned to their fate on the battleground. This would torment Charlemagne throughout his life; as recorded by the *Einhardi Annales*, the *Annales Regni Francorum qui dicuntur Einhardi*, and the *Annales de Gestis Caroli Magni*, he believed himself to have lost the favor of God.

Appendix

Historical sources used in the preparation of this book

The main Carolingian chronicles written immediately after the battle of Errozabal are the following:

- *Annales Mettenses* or Annals of Metz, written by an anonymous author in the monastery of Chelles. It is actually two sets of records, one called the *Annales Mettenses Priores* and the second known as the *Annales Mettenses Posteriores*. The *Annales Mettenses Priores* cover a period from 678 (*Anno ab incarnatione domini nostri Iesu Christi DCLXXXVIII*) to the date of writing, in 805 (*Anno dominicae incarnationis DCCCV*). Subsequently the *Annales Mettenses Priores* include an annex extending from 805 to 830 that for the period 805-829 coincides with the *Annales Regni Francorum* (*Anni 806-829 prorsus curn Annalibus regni Francorun concordant*). Written 28 years after the Battle of Errozabal, it is chronologically one of the closest sources to the events, so it is of great interest from a historiographical point of view, although direct reference to the battle is extremely sparse and the defeat of the 778 campaign is described in terms of a military victory.

  The *Annales Mettenses Posteriores* (776-805) represent a timeline or summary of the above, the chronicler having copied passages verbatim from the previous source. In this case, as above, the events of the Battle of Errozabal are discussed only very briefly, with no indication of the defeat. Like most Frankish sources the *Annales Mettenses* lack subjectivity. This lack of accuracy may be explained if we consider that the Carolingian dynasty descended through the paternal line from St. Arnulf, Bishop of Metz, who died in 641. The bishop's son married Begga, daughter of Pepin the Elder, who gave birth to Pepin the Young or Pepin of Herstal, father of Charles Martel and therefore Charlemagne's paternal great-grandfather. Charlemagne's family was closely linked to the monastery to the point that Gisela, sister of Charlemagne – who Alcuin referred to as a *femina verbipotens* -, was Abbess of Chelles, which has raised speculation that she personally participated in the writing of the chronicle.[1]

  In any case, as is the case with other sources of this nature, the *Annales Mettenses* are to a high degree subjective. One of the main objectives

[1] Nelson, Janet L., *The Frankish World (750-900)*, Hambledon Press, London & Río Grande, 1996, p. 191.

of the author was to legitimize the dynastic change that led to the enthronement of the first Carolingian, Pepin the Short, after the deposition of Childric III in 751; therefore, the *Annales Mettenses* conceive the origin of the Merovingian dynasty as the result of a divine resolution. There are several editions easily accessible to the reader, both in the original Latin version and in English translation:

- Latin edition: Simson, Bernhard von (Ed.), *Annales Mettenses Priores*, Monumenta Germaniae Historica (MGH), SSRG, X, Hannover & Leipzig, 1905.
- English edition: Fouracre, Paul; Gerberding, Richard, *Late Merovingian France: History and Hagiography (640-720)*, Manchester University Press, Manchester, 1996, pp. 330-70.
- Also in English: King, P. D., *Charlemagne: Translated Sources*, P. D. King, Lambrigg, Kendal, Cumbria, 1987, pp. 149-66.

— *Annales Laureshamenses* or *Annales Laurissenses* (also known as the annals of the monastery of Lorsch), written by an anonymous monk of the Lorsh monastery *c.* 803 and later copied in 835, covering a period of one hundred years from the early eighth century ('*Anno ab incarnatione Domini 703*') to the early ninth century ('*Anno 803*'). The *Fragmentum (annalium) chesnii* o *chesnianum*, which are also known as the *Annales Laureshamenses Antiquiores*, tell the story of the Frankish Kingdom from 768 to 790. Until 785, the *Fragmentum* are almost identical to the *Annales Laureshamenses* and to the *Annales Mosellani*. As in the previous case, they lack objectivity, but their interest lies in the fact that chronologically they are one of the closest primary sources to the events. With regard to the battle of Errozabal, the *Annales Laurissenses* closely follow the *Annales Mettenses* and, like those, do not mention the defeat at Errozabal.

The original Latin edition and an English edition of the text can be found in:

- Complete Latin edition: Pertz, Georg Heinrich (Ed.), *Annales Laureshamenses, Alamannici, Guelferbytani et Nazariani*, Monumenta Germaniae Historica (MGH), SS, I, Hannover, 1829, pp. 22-39.
- English edition: King, P. D. (Ed.), *Charlemagne: Translated Sources*, P. D. King, Lambrigg, Kendal, Cumbria, 1987, pp. 137-45.

— The *Annales Regni Francorum*,[2] known as the *Royal Frankish Annals* or the *Annals of the Kingdom of the Franks*, formerly known as the

---

2   Name given to this manuscript by the editors of the nineteenth century Latin edition of the *Monumenta Germaniae Historica*.

Annales Laurissenses Maiores, cover the period 741 to 829. There are several copies of this chronicle and one of them has been traditionally attributed to Einhard († 840) although the authorship is still disputed. Everything indicates that the *Annales Regni Francorum* were written in the Carolingian court, so that logically they should be interpreted in light of other sources, given their strong subjectivity.

In any case, the *Annales Regni Francorum* represent one of the fundamental sources for the study of Charlemagne's reign in general and the Battle of Errozabal in particular, although, as noted by Roger Collins, as in the two previous cases, the author does not mention the defeat of the Carolingian army and depicts the campaign of 778 in terms of a military victory.[3]

There are several editions of this manuscript in Latin and in English:

- Latin edition: Kurze, Friedrich (Ed.), *Annales regni Francorum (741–829) qui dicuntur Annales Laurissenses maiores et Einhardi*, Monumenta Germaniae Historica (MGH), SSRG, VI, Hannover, 1895.
- English edition: Scholz, Bernhard Walter (Ed.), *Carolingian Chronicles*, University of Michigan Press, Ann Arbor, 1972, pp. 37-125 (this edition covers the period 741-843).
- English edition: King, P. D. (Ed.), *Charlemagne: Translated Sources*, P. D. King, Lambrigg, Kendal, Cumbria, 1987, pp. 74-107 (King's edition covers the period 768-814).

– The *Annales qui dicuntur Annales Laurissenses Maiores et Einhardi*, so called by the editors of the nineteenth century Latin edition Georg H. Pertz and Friedrich Kurze, cover the same historical period as the *Annales Regni Francorum*, that is, 741 to 829, but their interest lies in the fact that until the year 801 the wording is partially different to the *Annales Regni Francorum*; they are of vital importance as they are the first historical source that literally refers to the defeat at Errozabal and also mentions the reasons that led to the disaster, which makes of them one of the main sources for the study of the battle.

There are several versions of the *Annales qui dicuntur Einhardi* (also known as the *Revised Version Royal Frankish Annals*):

- Latin edition: Kurze, Friedrich (Ed.), *Annales regni Francorum (741–829) qui dicuntur Annales Laurissenses maiores et Einhardi*, Monumenta Germaniae Historica (MGH), SSRG, VI, Hannover, 1895.

---

3   Collins, Roger, *Charlemagne*, University of Toronto Press Ltd., Toronto and Buffalo, 1998, p. 4.

- English edition: Scholz, Bernhard Walter (Ed.), *Carolingian Chronicles*, University of Michigan Press, Ann Arbor, 1972, pp. 37-125 (this edition covers the period 741-801).
- English edition: King, P. D. (Ed.), *Charlemagne: Translated Sources*, P. D. King, Lambrigg, Kendal, Cumbria, 1987, pp. 108-31 (this edition covers the period 768-801).

– The *Vita Karoli Magni Imperatoris* (*Life of the Emperor Charlemagne*) of Einhard or Einhardus (*c.* 814-830), which has also been published under the title *Vita Karoli Imperatoris* (Alfred Holder ed., Freiburg, 1882) or *Vita Karoli Magni* (Wattenbach ed., Berlin, 1876), was written around the year 830, about fifteen years after the emperor's death and about fifty years after the battle. The book is a defense of Charlemagne, dedicated to him by master Einhard who had worked in the service of the emperor for more than twenty years.

The *Vita* is undoubtedly one of the most important sources for the study of the battle, since, as we have had occasion to see, the works written in Charlemagne's lifetime avoided mentioning the battle or any other defeat. Along with the *Annales qui dicuntur Annales Laurissenses Maiores et Einhardi*, it is one of the main sources since, like the latter annals, the chronicle describes very precisely the defeat at Errozabal while the author strives to offer a reasoned explanation to the disaster. Also, the *Vita* includes the first list of names of those killed in the encounter, seneschal Egihardus, Count palatinus Anselmus and Roland [Hruodlandus], Duke of the Breton March ('*Britannici limitis praefectus*').

The *Vita Karoli Magni Imperatoris* was disseminated throughout Europe and over eighty copies of it have been preserved. There are numerous editions in Latin and English:

- Unabridged Latin edition: Holder-Egger, Oswald (Ed.), *Einhardi Vita Karoli Magni,* Monumenta Germaniae Historica (MGH), SSRG, Hannover & Leipzig, 1911 (reprinted in 1965).
- There are different English editions: Dutton, Paul (Ed.), *Charlemagne's Courtier, The Complete Einhard*, Broadview Press, Peterborough (Ont.), 1998, pp. 15-39.
- Collins, John F., *Vita Karoli Magni*, Bryn Mawr Commentaries, Bryn Mawr (PA), 1984.
- Thorpe, Lewis (Ed.), *Two Lives of Charlemagne*, Penguin, Harmondsworth, 1969.
- Firchow, Evelyn Scherabon; Zeydel, Edwin H., *The Life of Charlemagne*, University of Miami Press, Coral Gables (FL), 1972.

- Garrod, Heathcote William; Mowat, Robert Balmain (Eds.), *Einhard's Life of Charlemagne*, The Clarendon Press, Oxford, 1915.
- In French: Halphen, Louis (Ed.), *Eginhard: Vie de Charlemagne*, Belles-Lettres, Paris, 1938.

– *Poetae Saxonis Annalium de Gestis Caroli Magni Imperatoris Libri Quinque* or the *Annals of the Deeds of the Emperor Charles the Great in Five Books* was written by an anonymous author known as the Saxon poet, probably a monk of the Abbey of Saint Gall in the late ninth century, c. 880-890, during the reign of Arnulf of Carinthia to whom the text is addressed.

It is a text that offers many concomitants with the previous two, the *Vita Karoli Magni Imperatoris* and the *Annales qui dicuntur Annales Laurissenses Maiores et Einhardi*. As with these two aforementioned texts, the *Annalium* also makes reference to the battle in terms of a defeat and indicates the causes that could have led to it.

- Unabridged Latin edition: Winterfeld, Paul von (Ed.), *Poetarum Latinorum Medii Aevi,* Monumenta Germaniae Historica (MGH), PLAC, IV, Berlin, 1899, pp. 1-71.
- English edition (part of books 1 and 2): Godman, Peter (Ed.), *Latin Poetry of the Carolingian Renaissance*, University of Oklahoma Press, Norman, 1985.

– Likewise, the *Annales Regni Francorum*, the *Einhardi Annales*, also covers the period from 741 to 829, and includes a reference to the battle that, in the line of the *Vita Karoli Magni Imperatoris* and Poetae Saxonis' *Annalium de Gestis Caroli Magni Imperatoris*, briefly sets out the reasons that led to the catastrophe.

There is an unabridged Latin edition of the text:
- Pertz, Georg Heinrich (Ed.), *Annales et chronica aevi Carolini*, Monumenta Germaniae Historica (MGH), SS, I, Hannover, 1826, p. 135-218.

– In line with the *Annales Mettenses*, the *Einhardi Fuldensis Annales* cover the period of a century and a half from 680 to 838. With regard to the battle of Errozabal the *Einhardi Fuldensis Annales*, closely following the *Annales Mettenses*, do not record it and describe the campaign of 778 as a victorious march through Hispania. As in the *Annales Mettenses*, the source does not mention the diplomatic failure at the gates of Zaragoza.

There is an unabridged Latin edition:
- Pertz, Georg Heinrich (Ed.), *Annales et chronica aevi Carolini*, Monumenta Germaniae Historica (MGH), SS, I, Hannover, 1826, p. 135-218.

–   The *Vita Hludowici Pii Imperatoris* or *Life of Emperor Ludovico Pio* (Louis
    the Pious) was written around the year 840, the final year of Charle-
    magne's reign, by an anonymous author known as the Astronomus
    Limosinus (Limousin Astronomer). As for the battle, the text merely
    states the result of a terrible defeat as a consequence of the rugged
    landscape. However, from the point of view of the content and the
    expression, it is an original manuscript that contrasts with the above
    mentioned descriptions of the battle.
    The *Vita Hludowici Pii imperatoris* was widely spread, hence there are
    several Latin and English editions:
    •   Latin edition: Pertz, Georg Heinrich (Ed.), *Vita Ludowici...*, Monu-
        menta Germaniae Historica (MGH), SS, II, Berlin 1829, pp. 604-48.
    •   Also in Latin: Tremp, Ernst (Ed.), *Astronomus. Das Leben Kaiser
        Ludwigs (Vita Hludowici imperatoris)*, Monumenta Germaniae
        Historica (MGH), SSRG, LXIV, Hannover, 1995, pp. 280-555.
    •   English edition: Cabaniss, Allen (Ed.), *Son of Charlemagne: A
        Contemporary Life of Louis the Pious*, Syracuse University Press,
        Syracuse (NY), 1961.
–   The *Chronicon Moissiacense* (Chronicle of Moissac) is a document
    compiled at the end of the tenth century (*c.* 980) in the monastery of
    Moissac, although there is evidence indicating that this chronicle may
    have been compiled in the Catalan monastery of Ripoll, as it shows
    many similarities with the *Annals of Santa Maria de Ripoll*. Also, both
    manuscripts have a strong resemblance to the *Annales Aniani* or *Annales
    d'Aniane*, so these three documents are often grouped together as the
    Annales Veteres Francorum, although some authors simply identify the
    latter with the *Chronicon Moissiacense*.[4]The chronicon covers the
    period from the early eighth century (*c.* 702) to 828. As in the case of
    some of the sources that we have mentioned, the *Chronicon Moissiacense*
    does not mention the defeat at Errozabal and presents the events that
    took place in 778 as a successful military campaign, as a result of which
    the emperor obtained a rich booty.
    There are several editions of this chronicle in Latin, English and Spanish:
    •   Latin edition: Pertz, Georg Heinrich (Ed.), Monumenta Germaniae
        Historica (MGH), SS, I, Hannover, 1829, pp. 282-313.
    •   Abridged Latin edition: King, P. D. (Ed.), *Charlemagne: Translated
        Sources*, P. D. King, Lambrigg, Kendal, Cumbria, 1987, pp. 145-49.

---

4   Potthast, August, *Wegweiser durch die Geschichtswerke des europäischen Mittelalters bis
    1500*, W. Weber, Berlin, 1896, p. 95.

- • Spanish edition: Lafuente Alcántara, Emilio (Ed.), *Ajbar Machmua (Colección de tradiciones), Crónica anónima del siglo XI*, Real Academia de la Historia, Madrid, 1867.
- – The *Reginionis Abbatis Prumiensis Chronicon*, or *Reginionis Chronicon*, the Chronicon of the Benedictine monk Regino of Prüm († 915) is a compendium of sources composed in the early tenth century. Following the tradition of earlier Medieval chronicles, the chronicon is a history of mankind from Creation to the year 907. Divided into two books, the first covers the period up to the year 741, the date of Charles Martel's death. The second book, of more historic value, covers the period 741 to 906 and was extended to the year 917 by Adalbert, Archbishop of Magdeburg († 981). For the period 741 to 814 Regino mainly based his account on the *Liber historiae Francorum*, but the end of this second book is of more interest in virtue of its originality.
  With regard to the battle of Errozabal, the chronicon follows the *Annales Laurissenses* and therefore does not mention the defeat of the Carolingian army and presents the campaign of 778 as a military victory. The work was first printed in Mainz in the sixteenth century, and there are several editions:
  - • Latin edition: Kurze, Friedrich (Ed.), Monumenta Germaniae Historica (MGH), SSRG, L, Hannover, 1890, pp. 537-612.
  - • English edition: MacLean, Simon (Ed.), *History and politics in late Carolingian and Ottonian Europe. The chronicle of Regino of Prüm and Adalbert of Magdeburg*, Manchester University Press, Manchester, 2009.
- – The *Annales Petaviani* or *Petau Annals* are named so because the first copy was part of the Petau Collection, owned by Alexandre Petau (1610-1672), *conseiller au parlement de Paris*, consequently bearing the ex libris *Alexandri Petavii in Francorum curia consiliarii. Pauli filii*.[5] This chronicle covers the historical period from the year 687 to 799. Divided into three sections, the first part (*pars prima*) extends from the year 687 with the rise of Pepin the Young to power until 740. It is followed by a *continuatio* spanning from 741 until 770. *Pars secunda* begins in 771 when Charlemagne becomes the sole heir of the Frankish Kingdom after the death of his brother Carloman and continues until the year 799, a year before the coronation of the emperor in Rome.
  As in the previous case, the *Annales Petaviani* stick to the *Annales Laurissenses'* account, making no mention of the defeat of the Carolingian

---

5   Hamilton, Walter, *French Book-plates*, George Bell & Sons, London, 1896, p. 68.

army at Errozabal and presenting the campaign of 778 as a victory, as a the result of which Charlemagne obtained a rich booty.

There is an unabridged version of the original manuscript:

- Lartin edition: Pertz, Georg Heinrich (Ed.), *Annales et chronica aevi Carolini*, Monumenta Germaniae Historica (MGH), SS, I, Hannover, 1826, pp. 7-18.

– The *Annales Tiliani*, so called because the manuscript was owned by Jean du Tillet,[6] were written around the year 808 by an anonymous author, covering a period from the year 708 to 807. The chronicle is divided into two parts; the first half encompasses the years 708 to 740 and the second part covers 741 to 807.

The chronicle contains sporadic references to the military events related to Vasconia and specifically mentions the campaign of 778, but it does not provide original information. In particular, concerning the battle of Errozabal, in the line of the *Chronicon Moissiacense*, the *Reginionis Abbatis Prumiensis Chronicon* and the *Annales Petaviani*, it does not mention the defeat and presents the campaign as a triumph.

- Latin edition: Pertz, Georg Heinrich (Ed.), *Annales et chronica aevi Carolini*, Monumenta Germaniae Historica (MGH), SS, I, Hannover, 1826, pp. 6-8 & 219-224.

– The *Codex epistolaris Carolinus*, written in 791, is a compilation of about one hundred letters between various Frankish kings and popes of the years 739 to 791. Unfortunately the compilation collects the letters written in the Papacy. The two letters sent by the Pope in May 778 are extremely interesting for the study of the battle.

There are several editions:

- Latin edition: Dümmler, Ernestus et alia (Eds.), *Epistolae Merowingici et Karolini Aevi,* Monumenta Germaniae Historica (MGH), EPP. III, Berlin, 1892, pp. 469-657.
- Latin edition: Gundlach, W. (Ed.), *Epistolae Karolini*, Monumenta Germaniae Historica (MGH), Epp, III, Berlin, 1892. Pp. 476-653.
- A selection in English of the documents compilled in the *Codex epistolaris Carolinus*: King, P. D., *Charlemagne: Translated Sources*, P. D. King, Lambrigg, Kendal, Cumbria, 1987, pp. 269-307.

– The *Capitularia Regnum Francorum* is a set of legal capitularies passed by Charlemagne, very interesting for all that relates to the laws on

---

6   Halphen, Louis, *Études critiques sur l'histoire de Charlemagne: les sources de l'histoire de Charlemagne, la conquête de la Saxe, le couronnement impérial, l'agriculture et la propriété rurale, l'industrie et le commerce*, Felix Alcan, Paris, 1921, p. 37.

military matters and also by virtue of the references in the documents to the new pieces of legislation adopted after the battle of Errozabal. There are several editions:

- Latin edition: Boretius, Alfredus, *Capitularia Regnum Francorum*, Hannover, Impensis Bibliopolii Hahniani, Hannover, 1883.
- Abridged edition in English: Loyn, Henry Royston; Percival, John, *The Reign of Charlemagne: Documents on Carolingian Government and Administration*, St. Martin's Press, New York, 1976.

- The *Gesta Karoli Magni imperatoris* or *Deeds of the Emperor Charles the Great* was written by the Franciscan monk of the Abbey of Saint Gall Notker Balbulus the Stammerer or Monachus Sangallensis († 912). It is estimated that the author finished the manuscript in 883 or in 884 because it was dedicated to Charles the Fat, great-grandson of Charlemagne, who visited Saint Gall in 883.

  In general, the text shares the same limitations and inadequacies as the rest of the Carolingian sources, i.e., a lack of objectivity and the inclusion of legendary elements. In the present case the chronicler emphasizes the glory of the ancestors of Charles the Fat. Concerning the battle of Errozabal itself, the text makes no reference to it.

  There are several editions of the *Gesta Karoli Magni imperatoris* in the original Latin version and in English:

  - Unabridged Latin edition: Pertz, Georg Heinrich (Ed.), *Gesta Karoli Magni imperatoris*, Monumenta Germaniae Historica (MGH), SS, II, Berlin, 1829, pp. 726-63.
  - Also: Haefele, Hans F. (Ed.), Monumenta Germaniae Historica (MGH), SSRG, NS, XII, Berlin, 1959.
  - In English: Thorpe, Lewis (Ed.), *Two Lives of Charlemagne*, Penguin, Harmondsworth, 1969, pp. 93-172.

There are also literary sources for the study of the impact of the battle in Medieval Europe, very interesting but lacking historical reliability:

- The *Chanson de Roland* (Song of Roland) is an epic song of the eleventh century. There are several versions of the original poem datable between the twelfth and the fourteenth centuries, which reveals the popularity that the poem enjoyed in the Middle Ages. This is one of the oldest European epic songs. The oldest manuscript known of the Song of Roland is listed as MS Digby 23 in the Bodleian Library at Oxford University. Dated to around 1140 and 1170 and consisting of 4,004 verses it has traditionally been attributed to the minstrel Turoldus (Thorvald). There are numerous editions and versions of the work in many different languages as well as several online editions. Among the most important we can mention the following:

- In the original version: Segre, Cesare; Tyssens, Madeleine; Guidot, Bernard, (Eds.), *La chanson de Roland*, Librairie Droz, Genève, 2003.
- In English: Duggan, Joseph J. (Ed.), *La chanson de Roland: The Song of Roland*, Brepols, Turnhout, 2005.
- In English: Short, Ian; Pearcy, Roy (Eds.), *La Chanson de Roland = The Song of Roland: The French corpus*, Anglo-Norman Text Society, London, 2000.
- The English edition translated by Glyn Sheridan Burgess includes excerpts from the original version: Burguess, Glyn Sheridan (Ed.), *The Song of Roland*, Penguin Classics, London, 1990.
- In French: Short, Ian (Ed.), *La Chanson de Roland*, Librairie générale française, Paris, 1997.
- The reader may access a complete reproduction of the original manuscript Digby 23 preserved in Oxford: http://image.ox.ac.uk/show?collection=bodleian&manuscript=msdigby23b

– The *Historia Caroli Magni et Rotholandi* or *Liber IV* del *Liber Sancti Iacobi* (*History of the Life of Charlemagne and Roland*) written by Pseudo Turpin is part of the *Codex Calixtinus*. The manuscript, also known as *Historia Turpini* (Turpin's History), was written in Latin in the twelfth century and contains many fantastic references to the military campaign of 778. While the *Historia Caroli Magni et Rotholandi* recorded that it had been written by Turpin, Archbishop of Reims, it is now considered that such authorship is not legitimate. The book was widely disseminated, serving as a basis for further literary and musical works on the life of Charlemagne. The *Historia Caroli Magni et Rotholandi* was first printed in Frankfurt in 1566.

Among other available editions we may cite:

- Latin edition: Castets, Ferdinand (Ed.), *Turpini Historia Karoli Magni et Rotholandi*, Paris, 1880.
- English edition: Rodd, Thomas (Ed.), *History of Charles the Great and Orlando Ascribed to Turpin*, London, 1812.

– The *Ephytaphium Aggiardi* or Einhard's epitaph is a brief but very interesting poem about the death of the seneschal of Charlemagne's palace who died in the battle of Errozabal.[7] This text is especially relevant because it provides an accurate date for Einhard's death and, consequently, provides the exact day of the battle, that is, 15 August 778.

7　Also recorded as *Aggiardus, Einhard, Eginhard, Eginardo* and *Egiardo*.

There is an edition of the original Latin version:

- Dümmler, Ernst; Strecker, Karl; Traube, Ludwig, *Poetae Latini aevi Carolini*, Monumenta Germaniae Historica (MGH), Berlin, 1881, vol. 1, pp. 109-10.

– The *De Gestis Regnum Anglorum* (*Chronicle of the Kings of England*) by William of Malmesbury (*c.* 1080/1095 – *c.* 1143) records that during the battle of Hastings in 1066 Taillefer sang verses of the *Chanson de Roland* to rouse King William's troops, which illustrates the notoriety of the events that occurred in Errozabal nearly three centuries earlier.

There are several editions of *De Gestis Regnum Anglorum*, among them we may mention the following:

- English edition: Bowra, Cecil Maurice, *Heroic Poetry*, Macmillan, London, 1964, pp. 414.
- A second English edition of the referred passage: Stubbs, William (Ed.), *Willelmi Malmesbiriensis Monachi De gestis regnum Anglorum. Libri Quinique, Historiae Novellae Libri III*, Her Majesty's Stationery Office (HMSO), London, 1887-89, p. 302.
- Also: Mynors, Roger A. B.; Thomson, Rodney M.; Winterbottom, Michael (Eds.), *William of Malmesbury, Gesta Regum Anglorum. The History of the English Kings*, Oxford University Press, Oxford, 2002.
- There is an older edition edited by J. A. Giles and translated by the Rev. John Sharpe in 1815: William of Malmesbury, *Chronicle of the Kings of England*, George Bell and Sons, London, 1904.

– The *Roman de Rou* by Wace is an epic chronicle in verse of the history of Normandy from the reign of Duke Rollo (or Rolf) *c.* 911 until the battle of Tinchebray in 1106. Wace used Malmesbury's *History of the Kings of England* for his work, so that, as in the previous case, it is of interest because of the allusion to the events that took place in 778 (verses 8013 to 8018).

There are several editions of the poem:

- English edition by Glyn Sheridan Burgess and Anthony J. Holden: Wace, *The Roman du Rou*, Société jersiaise, Jersey, 2002.
- There is a previous edition by Anthony J. Holden: Wace, *Le Roman du Rou*, A. & J. Picard, Paris, 1965.

Historical sources for the study of the history of Vasconia in the period 711 to 778:

– The *Liber historiae Francorum* (*Book of the History of the Franks*), probably written in the monastery of Saint Médard *c.* 727, is the continuation of the *Fredegarii et aliorum chronica* until 721. Among the existing editions of the work we can mention the following:

- Unabridged Latin edition: Krusch, Bruno (Ed.), *Liber historiae francorum*, Monumenta Germaniae Historica (MGH), SSRM, II, Hannover, 1888, pp. 241-328.
- English edition: Bernard S. Bachrach (Ed.), *Liber historiae Francorum*, Coronado Press, Lawrence (KS), 1973. Includes the last eleven chapters of the book in the English translation.
- Also in English: Fouracre, Paul; Gerberding Richard A. (Eds.), *Late Merovingian France: History and Hagiography (640-720)*, Manchester University Press, Manchester, 1996, pp. 79-96.

- The *Fredegarii Scholastici libri IV cum Continuationibus* (*Chronicle of Fredegar with Continuations*) records the events that took place in the Frankish Kingdom from 584 to 641. Subsequent authors continued the chronicle by adding fragments until the year 768 when Charlemagne and his brother Carloman were crowned emperors. It is one of the largest preserved chronicles and therefore one of the primary sources for the study of this period.

There are several Latin and English editions:

- Latin edition: Krusch, Bruno (Ed.), *Fredegarii Scholastici libri IV cum Continuationibus. Fredegarii et aliorum chronica. Vitae sanctorum* (*generis regii*), Monumenta Germaniae Historica (MGH), SSRM, II, Hannover, 1888, pp. 1-193.
- English edition: Wallace-Hadrill, J. M. (Ed.), *The Fourth Book of the Chronicle of Fredegar with its Continuations*, Greenwood Press, Connecticut, 1960.

- The *Annales mosellani* o *mosellenses*, or simply *Moselle Annals* are a number of Frankish annals covering the years 703 to 798 probably written in the monasteries of Metz and Gorze in the upper reaches of the river Moselle. Until 785 the *Annales Mosellani*, the *Annales Laurissenses* (beginning in also in the year 703), and the *Fragmentum Chesnii* (beginning in 768) are entirely concurrent. The copyist of the *Annales Mosellani* most likely based his writing on a copy of the *Annales Laurissenses* but lost an entry, namely the one for the year 786 and, therefore, the dating given by the author after that date is wrong.

Among the existing editions we may mention the following:

- Latin edition: Lappenberg, J. M. (Ed.), Monumenta Germaniae Historica (MGH), SS, XVI, Hannover, 1859, pp. 491-99.
- English edition (abridged): King, P. D., *Charlemagne: Translated Sources*, P. D. King, Lambrigg, Kendal, Cumbria, 1987, pp. 132-7.

- The *Annales Guelferbytani* or *Wolfenbüttel Annals*, composed in the early ninth century, cover the years 741 to 805, to which later authors added extracts referring to the years 817 and 823. The *Annales Guelferbytani* share with the *Annales Nazariani* and the *Annales Alamannici* the period 708 to 789 and in turn served as the main source for the *Annales Laurissenses*, the *Annales Mosellani* and the *Fragmentum Chesnii*. There are several editions in Latin and English:
  - Latin edition: Pertz, Georg Heinrich (Ed.), *Annales et chronica aevi Carolini*, Monumenta Germaniae Historica (MGH), SS, I, Hannover, 1826, pp. 23-31 & 40-46.
  - English edition: King, P. D., *Charlemagne: Translated Sources*, P. D. King, Lambrigg, Kendal, Cumbria, 1987, pp. 149-66.
- The *Annales Nazariani* cover the eighth century. As already noted, they share with the *Annales Guelferbytani* the period between the years 708 and 789. The *Annales Nazariani* are divided into two parts; the first one covers the period 708-768, until the death of Pepin the Short. The second part starts from the beginning of the reign of Charlemagne until 791. There are several editions:
  - Latin edition: Pertz, Georg Heinrich (Ed.), Monumenta Germaniae Historica (MGH), SS, I, Hannover, 1926, pp. 19-31 & 40-44.
  - English edition (abridged): King, P. D., *Charlemagne: Translated Sources*, P. D. King, Lambrigg, Kendal, Cumbria, 1987, pp. 155-57.
- The *Annales Loiseliani* or *Annals of Loisel*, named for being part of Antoine Loisel's library, are also known as the *Annales Regum Francorum Loiseliani* or *Annales Regum Francorum a) Eginhardi, b) Loiseliani, c) Bertiniani.*
  - Latin edition: Bouquet, Martin, *Annales rerum Francicarum, quae a Pippino et Carolo M. regibus gestae sunt, dicti Loiseliani*, 1744.
  - There is also a newer edition: Bouquet, Martin, *Recueil des historiens des Gaules et de la France*, Victor Palmé, Paris, 1871.

Arab sources:
- *Manuscript 127* of the Bodleian Library of Oxford by Abd al-Malik ibn Habib (*c.* 796-853). As mentioned by Larry J. Simon, 'by his own account, his works number over one thousand, but only two fragments survive. One is Manuscript 127 of the Bodleian Library (Oxford); its Arabic text is unedited but Melchor M. Antuña obtained a photocopy of the portion referring to the conquest and translated it into Spanish. Sánchez-Albornoz, in an introduction to the translation, observed that the manuscript is not Ibn Habib's original but a greatly altered excerpt

by Ibn Habib's pupil, Ibn Abi Rika. The excerpt is full of much fabulous and some absurd material. The second fragment of Ibn Habib's work to survive exists in the anonymous eleventh-century *Fatho-l-Andalus*.[8] There is a commentary on the work in Spanish in:

- Sánchez Albornoz, Claudio; Antuña, Melchor M., "Notas de Ibn Abi Rika de las lecciones de Ibn Habib acerca de la conquista de España por los árabes", *Cuadernos de Historia de España*, 1-2, 1944, pp. 248-268.

– *Ta'rikh iftitah al-Andalus* or simply *Ifitah* (History of the Conquest of al-Andalus) by Ibn al-Kutiya. *Ta'rikh iftitah al-Andalus* is a choricle on the history of al-Andalus until the government of Abd al-Rahman III (912-961). There are few editions of the chronicle in Spanish:

- Ibn al-Kutiya, *Iftitah: Ta'rikh iftitah al-Andalus*, P. de Gayangos, E. Saavedra & F. Codera, Madrid, 1868.
- There is a second edition by Julián Ribera: Ibn al-Kutiya, *Iftitah: Ta'rikh iftitah al-Andalus*, Madrid, 1926.
- There is an English edition by David James: *Early Islamic Spain: The History of Ibn al-Qutiya: A Study of the Unique Arabic Manuscript in the Bibliothèque Nationale de France, Paris, with a Translation, Notes, and Comments*, Routledge, London and New York, 2011.

– The *Ajbar Machmua* or *Collection of Traditions* is an eleventh-century anonymous chronicle covering the historical period between 711 and 929, the date of the foundation by Abd al-Rahman III of the independent Caliphate of Cordoba. There are few editions of this book.

- First Spanish edition: Lafuente Alcántara, Emilio (Ed.), *Ajbar Machmua (Colección de tradiciones), Crónica anónima del siglo XI*, Real Academia de la Historia, Madrid, 1867.
- There is a newer edition also in Spanish: Lafuente Alcántara, Emilio (Ed.), *Ajbar Machmua (Colección de tradiciones), Crónica anónima del siglo XI*, El Bibliófilo, Madrid, 1984.

– *Kitab Al-Muqtabis fi Tarikh al-Andalus*, or the chronicle of Abu Marwán Hayyán Ibn Jalaf Ibn Hayyan al-Qurtubi (987-1075), which has been preserved incomplete, intermittently covers the history of al-Andalus between 796 and 942. It includes interesting references to Vasconia, but is primarily important for the immediate aftermath of the battle of Errozabal. The chronicle is particularly interesting because the author was the son of the secretary of Al-Mansur Ibn Abi Aamir, known as

---

8   Simon, Larry J., "Jews, Visigoths, and the Muslim Conquest of Spain", *UCLA Historical Journal*, 4, 1983.

Almanzor or Al-Mansur, from which it follows that he possibly handled very reliable data. There are two editions:

- Spanish edition: Lévi-Provençal, Évariste; García Gómez, Emilio (Eds.), *Textos inéditos del Muqtabis de ibn Hayyan sobre los orígenes del reino de Pamplona, Al-Andalus. Revista de las Escuelas de Estudios Árabes de Madrid y Granada*, vol. 19, 2, 1954, pp. 295-316.
- Abridged Spanish edition (years 796-847): Corriente, Federico (Ed.), *Crónica de los Emires Alhakam I y Abdarrahman II entre los años 796 y 847*, Instituto de Estudios Islámicos y del Oriente Próximo, Zaragoza, 2001.

- *Al-Kamil fi al-Tarikh (The Complete History)* written by Abu al-Hassan Ali ibn Muhammad ibn Muhammad (known as Ali 'Izz al-Din Ibn al-Athir al-Jazari) (1160-1233), written c. 1231, is a key work of the Muslim historiography, primarily for the study of the Crusades.
  - This work was translated into French by Edmond Fegnan: Ibn al-Athir, *Annales du Maghreb & de l'Espagne traduites et annotées par Edmond Fagnan*, Typographie Adolphe Jourdan, Alger, 1898.
  - There is a new edition from 2001: 'Izz al-Din Ibn al-Athir, *Annales du Maghreb & de l'Espagne traduites et annotées par Edmond Fagnan*, Adamant Media Corporation, 2001.
  - There is also an English translation by D. S. Richards: *The Chronicle of Ibn Al-athir for the Crusading Period from Al-kamil Fi'l-ta'rikh: The Years 491–541/1097–1146, the Coming of the Franks and the Muslim Response*, Ashgate, Aldersot, 2006.

- *Kitab al-bayan...* or *Book of the Amazing Story of the History of the Kings of Al-Andalus and Morocco* is a history of the Maghreb (including Morocco and Algeria) and al-Andalus written in 1312. Despite being written at a later date, it is valuable to recover or reinterpret prior written sources. Among the editions of this work we may mention the following:
  - Ibn Idhari al-Marrakushi, *Kitab al-bayan al-mughrib fi akhbar muluk al-Andalus wa'l-Maghrib*, R. Dozy, Leiden, 1848-51.
  - In French: Fagnan, Edmond (Ed.), *Histoire de l'Afrique du Nord et de l'Espagne intitulée Al-Bayano'l-Mogrib*, vol. 2, Imprimerie Orientale, Argelia, 1904.
  - G. S. Colin and E. Lévi Provençal edited the book under the title: Ibn Idhari al-Marrakushi Ahmad b. Muhammad, *Kitab al-bayan al-mughrib, fi akhbar al-Andalus wa'l-Maghrib*, G. S. Colin and E. Lévi-Provençal, Leiden, 1948-51.
  - There is a Spanish edition: Huici Miranda, A. (Ed.), *Colección de crónicas árabes de la Reconquista*, Tetuán, 1953-54 (vols. 2 and 3).

- Also a recent edition of the latter: Huici Miranda, A. (Ed.), *Al-Bayán al-Mugrib, Nuevos fragmentos almorávides y almohades*, Anubar Ediciones, Valencia, 1963.
- Also: Ibn 'Idari Al-Marrakusi, *Historias de Al-Andalus Por Aben-Adhari de Marruecos*, BiblioBazaar, LLC, Charleston (SC), 2008, vol. 1.

Other sources:
- *Liber Pontificalis* (*Book of the Popes*) is a collection of biographies of popes from Saint Peter to Pope Stephen the fifth in 885-891. The book was later extended by one or more anonymous authors until the Papacy of Pius II in the fifteenth century.
  - French edition: Duchesne, Louis (Ed.), *Le Liber pontificalis. Texte, introduction et Commentaire*, 2 vols. Rome, 1886-92.
  - A newer edition of the latter: Duchesne, Louis (Ed.), *Le Liber pontificalis. Texte, introduction et Commentaire*, 3 vols., Paris, 1955-57.
  - English edition: Raymond Davis, *The Lives of the Eighth Century Popes*, University of Liverpool Press, Liverpool, 1995 (the various editions of this work cover the period 715-817.)
- The Crónica Mozárabe de 754 (o Continuatio Hispana) also known as *Crónica de Isidoro de Beja* or *Isidori Pacensis Episcopi Chronicon* (Chronicle of Isidore of Beja), is one of the main historical sources for the study of the Muslim conquest of al-Andalus, as virtually all the Arab sources so far discovered do not record the events that took place immediately after the invasion of 711. Composed by a Mozarabic chronicler in Toledo or Cordoba the book was written in Latin and covers the period between 610 and 754. This chronicle was published for the first time in its entirety in Iruñea/Pamplona in 1615.
  - Spanish edition: Flórez, Enrique, *España sagrada*, Vol. 8, Real Academia de la Historia, Madrid, 1869, pp. 282-325.
  - There is also a new critical edition of the book in Spanish: López Pereira, José Eduardo (Ed.), *Crónica Mozárabe de 754*, Anubar, Zaragoza, 1980.
- *Chronicon sine Breviarium chronicorum de sex mundi aetatibus de Adamo usque ad ann. 869* or Universal Chronicle of Saint Adon or Adonis Viennensis (799-875),[9] Archbishop of Vienne in Lotharingia, covers the eighth and ninth centuries in the Frankish Kingdom, interspersing written sources and oral traditions or legends.

---

9   Also registered as *Ado, Adon,* o *Adonis Viennensis.*

- Latin edition: Bouquet, Martin, *Recueil des historiens des Gaules et de la France*, Victor Palmé, Paris, 1871, 2 vols.
- There is also an abridged Latin edition: Pertz, Georg Heinrich (Ed.), *Annales et chronica aevi Carolini*, Monumenta Germaniae Historica (MGH), SS, I, Hannover, 1826, pp. 315-323.

— *Historia arabum* (*History of the Arabs*) by the Navarrese Bishop Rodrigo Ximenez de Rada or Rodericus Ximenes (*c.* 1170-1247). Based on earlier sources, Ximenez de Rada records various events related to the history of al-Andalus from a Christian perspective.

- Latin edition: Erpenius, Thomas (Ed.), *Historia saracenica qua res gestae Muslimorum inde a Muhammede Arabe*, Iohannem Maire & Elzevirios, 1625, pp. 1-75 and 373-448.
- A newer Latin edition: Fernández Valverde, Juan; Estévez Sola, Juan A. (Eds.), *Roderici Ximenii de Rada opera omnia*, Brepols Editores Pontificii, Turnhout, 1999.

Bibliography

Abadal, Ramón, "La expedición de Carlomagno a Zaragoza: el hecho histórico. Su carácter y significación", *Coloquios de Roncesvalles*, Institución Príncipe de Viana, Iruñea/Pamplona, 1956.

Aebischer, Paul, *Préhistoire et protohistoire du Roland d'Oxford*, Editions Francke, Berne, 1972.

Aebischer, Paul, *Rolandiana Borealia. La "Saga af Runzivals bardaga" et ses dérivés scandinaves comparés à la Chanson de Roland. Essai de restauration du manuscrit français utilisé par le traducteur norrois*, Université de Lausanne. Publications de la Faculté des Lettres XI, Lausanne, 1954.

Aebischer, Paul, *Rolandiana et Oliveriana: Recueil d'études sur les chansons de geste*, Librairie Droz, Genève, 1967.

Aebischer, Paul, *Textes norrois et littérature française de moyen âge*, Librairie Droz, Genève, 1972.

Aebischer, Paul, *Textes norrois et littérature française de moyen âge*, vol. 1, Librairie Droz, Genève, 1954.

Allen, J. H.; Allen, W. F.; Hudson, Henry P. (eds.), *Caesar's The Gallic War*, Ginn & co., Boston, 1891.

Alonso, Dámaso, *La primitiva épica francesa a la luz de una nota emilianense*, Consejo Superior de Investigaciones Científicas, Madrid, 1954.

Alonso, Dámaso, *La primitiva épica francesa a la luz de una nota emilianense*, Revista de Filología española, No. 37, Madrid, 1953.

Álvarez, Vicente A., *Historia de España de la Edad Media*, Ariel, Barcelona, 2008.

Arbeloa, Joaquín, *Los orígenes del Reino de Navarra (710-925)*, Auñamendi, Donostia/San Sebastián, 1969. 3 vols.

Bachrach, Bernard S. (ed.), *Liber historiae Francorum*, Coronado Press, Lawrence (KS), 1973.

Bachrach, Bernard S., *Armies and Politics in the Early Medieval West*, Variorum, London, 1993.

Bachrach, Bernard S., *Early Carolingian Warfare: Prelude to Empire*, University of Pennsylvania Press, Philadelphia, 2001.

Bachrach, Bernard S., *Merovingian Military Organization (481-751)*, University of Minnesota Press, Minneapolis, 1972.

Bachrach, Bernard S., "Animals in Warfare in Early Medieval Europe", *Septimane*, vol. XXXI, 1983, pp. 707-764.

Barbero, Alessandro, *Charlemagne, Father of a Continent*, University of California Press, Berkeley and Los Angeles, 2000.

Bard, Rachel, *Navarra: The Durable Kingdom*, University of Nevada Press, Reno, 1982.

Becher, Matthias, *Charlemagne*, Yale University Press, New Haven, 2003.

Becher, Matthias, *Eid und Herrschaft: Untersuchungen zum Herrscherethos Karls des Grossen*, Thorbecke, Sigmaringen, 1993.

Becher, Matthias, *Karl der Grosse*, C. H. Beck, München, 1999.

Bédier, Joseph (ed. and tr.), *La Chanson de Roland, publiée d'âpres le manuscrit d'Oxford et traduite*, L'Édition d'Art H. Piazza, Paris, 1937.

Bedier, Joseph, *La Chanson de Roland commentée*, L'Édition d'Art H. Piazza, Paris, 1927.

Bennett, Matthew; Bradbury, Jim; DeVries, Kelly, *Fighting Techniques of the Medieval World: Equipment, Combat Skills and Tactics*, Macmillan, London, 2006.

Berganza, Francisco, *Antigüedades de España, propugnadas en las noticias de sus reyes, en la crónica del real monasterio de San pedro de Cerdeña, en historias, cronicones y otros instrumentos, manuscritos, que hasta ahora no han visto la luz pública*, Francisco de Hierro, Madrid, 1721.

Bhote, Tehmina, *Charlemagne: The Life and Times of an Early Medieval Emperor*, The Rosen Publishing Group, New York, 2005.

Blázquez, José María, *Mosaicos romanos de Navarra*, Instituto Español de Arqueología del Consejo Superior de Investigaciones Científicas, Madrid, 1985.

Böhmer, Johann F.; Mühlbacher, Engelbert, *Die Regesten des Kaiserreichs unter den Karolingern, 751-918*, Innsbruck Wagner'schen Universitätsbuchhandlung, Innsbruck, vol. 1, 1908.

Boissonnade, Prosper, *Du nouveau sur la chanson de Roland: la genèse historique, le cadre géographique, le milieu, les personnages, la date et l'auteur de poème*, Honore Champion, Paris, 1923.

Boretius, Alfredus (ed.), *Capitularia Regum Francorum*, Monumenta Germaniae Historica (MGH), Leges, Hannover, 1883.

Bouquet, Martin, *Annales rerum Francicarum, quae a Pippino et Carolo M. regibus gestae sunt, dicti Loiseliani*, 1744.

Bouquet, Martin, *Recueil des historiens des Gaules et de la France*, Victor Palmé, Paris, 1871.

Bouquet, Martin, *Recueil des historiens des Gaules et de la France*, Gregg International Publishers Ltd., Farnborough, 1968.

Bouthillier, Denise (ed.), *Petri Cluniacensis Abbatis De miraculis libri duo*, Brepols, Turnhout, 1988.

Bowra, Cecil Maurice, *Heroic Poetry*, Macmillan, London, 1964.

Braunfels, Wolfgang (ed.), *Karl der Grosse, Lebenswerk und Nachleben*, L. Schwann, Dusseldorf, vol. 1, 1965.

Buckler, Francis W., *Harunu'l-Rashid and Charles the Great*, The Mediaeval Academy of America, Cambridge (Mass.), 1931.

Bulteau, Marcel J., *Description de la cathédrale de Chartres: suivie d'une courte notice sur les églises de Saint-Pierre, de Saint-André et de Saint-Aignan de la même ville. Avec cinq planches*, Garnier, Paris, 1850.

Bulteau, Marcel J., *Monographie de la cathédrale de Chartres*, R. Selleret, Chartres, 1887.

Burger, André, "Le champ de bataille de Roncevaux dans la Chanson de Roland", *Coloquios de Roncesvalles*, Institución Príncipe de Viana, Iruñea/Pamplona, 1956.

Burgess, Glyn S.; Cobby, Anne E., *The Pilgrimage of Charlemagne: Le pèlerinage de Charlemagne*, Garland, New York, 1988.

Burguess, Glyn S. (ed.), *The Song of Roland*, Penguin Classics, London, 1990.

Bury, John B.; Brooke, Zachary N., *The Cambridge Medieval History*, Macmillan, vol. 2, 1913.

Cabaniss, Allen (ed.), *Son of Charlemagne: A Contemporary Life of Louis the Pious*, Syracuse University Press, Syracuse (NY), 1961.

Cabaniss, Allen, *Charlemagne*, Twayne Publishers, New York, 1972.

Cameron, Averil, *The Later Roman Empire (284-430)*, Harvard University Press, Cambridge, 1998.

Cannone, Belinda; Orcel, Michel, *Figures de Roland*, Klincksieck, Paris, 1998.

Capitulare de Villiis, in *Introduction to Contemporary Civilization in the West*, Columbia University Press, London & New York, 1961, pp. 326-334.

Castets, Ferdinand (ed.), *Turpini Historia Karoli Magni et Rotholandi*, Paris, 1880.

Castets, Ferdinand (ed.), *Turpini Historia Karoli Magni et Rotholandi*, Société pour l'Etude des Langues Romanes, Montpellier, 1880.

Cawthorne, Nigel, *Military Commanders: The 100 Greatest Throughout History*, Enchanted Lion Books, New York, 2004.

Codera, Francisco, *Estudios críticos de historia árabe española*, Editorial Maxtor, Valladolid, 2005.

Colas, Louis, "La voie romaine de Bordeaux à Astorga dans sa traversée des Pyrénées", RFA, No. 14, 1912.

Collins, John F., *Vita Karoli Magni*, Bryn Mawr Commentaries, Bryn Mawr (PA), 1984.

Collins, Roger, "The *Vaccaei*, the *Vaceti*, and the Rise of *Vasconia*", in, Collins, Roger, *Law, Culture and Regionalism in Early Medieval Spain*, Aldershot, Hampshire, 1992.

Collins, Roger, *Charlemagne*, University of Toronto Press Ltd., Toronto and Buffalo, 1998.

Collins, Roger. *The Basques*, Blackwell Publishing, London, 1990.

Connolly, Peter, *Greece and Rome at War*, Prentice-Hall Inc., Englewood Cliffs (NJ), 1981.

Contamine, Philippe, *War in the Middle Ages*, Basil Blackwell, Oxford, 1984.

Corriente, Federico (ed.), *Crónica de los Emires Alhakam I y Abdarrahman II entre los años 796 y 847*, Instituto de Estudios Islámicos y del Oriente Próximo, Zaragoza, 2001.

Cutts, Edward L., *Charlemagne*, Society for Promoting Christian Knowledge, London, 1882.

D'Abadal i de Vinyals, Ramon, *Catalunya Carolingia. El Domini Carolingi a Catalunya*, Barcelona, 1986.

Dabbs, Jack A., *Dei Gratia in Royal Titles*, Mouton, The Hague, 1971.

Del Burgo, Jaime, *Historia general de Navarra: Desde los orígenes hasta nuestros días*, Rialp, Madrid, 1992.

Delaporte, Yves, *La cathédrale de Chartres et ses vitraux*, Éditions du Chêne, Paris, 1943.

Delaporte, Yves; Houvet, Etienne, *Les vitraux de la cathédrale de Chartres*, É. Houvet, Chartres, 1926.

Delbouille, Maurice, *Sur la genèse de la Chanson de Roland*, Palais des académies, Bruselas, 1954.

Delbrück, Hans, *History of the Art of War within the Framework of Political History: The Middle Ages*, Greenwood Press, Westport (CT), 1982.

Dennis, George T., *Maurice's Strategikon: Handbook of Byzantine Military Strategy*, University of Pensilvannia Press, Philadelphia, 1984.

DeVries, Kelly, *Medieval Military Technology*, University of Toronto Press, Toronto, 1992.

DeVries, Kelly; Smith, Robert D., *Medieval Weapons: An Illustrated History of their Impact*, ABC-CLIO, Santa Barbara (Ca.), 2007.

Dodwell, Charles R., *The Various Arts: De Diversis Artibus*, Clarendon Press, Oxford, 1986.

Duchesne, Louis (ed.), *Le Liber pontificalis. Texte, introduction et Commentaire*, 2 vols. Rome, 1886-92.

Duchesne, Louis (ed.), *Le Liber pontificalis. Texte, introduction et Commentaire*, 3 vols., Paris, 1955-57.

Duggan, Joseph J. (ed.), *La chanson de Roland: The Song of Roland*, Brepols, Turnhout, 2005.

Duggan, Joseph J., *A Guide to Studies on the Chanson de Roland*, DS Brewer, London, 1976.

Dulaurier, Édouard (ed.), *Histoire générale de Languedoc avec des notes et les pièces justificatives*, Édouard Privat Librairie Éditeur, Toulouse, 1876.

Dümmler, Ernestus; Perels, Ernst; Kehr, Paul F. (eds.), *Epistolae Merowingici et Karolini Aevi*, Monumenta Germaniae Historica (MGH), EPP. III, Berlin, 1892.

Dümmler, Ernst; Strecker, Karl; Traube, Ludwig, *Poetae Latini aevi Carolini*, Monumenta Germaniae Historica (MGH), Berlin, 1881.

Duncalf, Frederic; Krey, August C., *Parallel Source Problems in Medieval History*, Harper & Brothers, New York & London, 1912.

Dunlop, John C.; Wilson, Henry, *History of Prose Fiction, Volume 1*, George Bell and sons, London, 1906.

Durand, Paul, *Monographie de Notre-Dame de Chartres. Explication des planches*, BiblioBazaar, LLC, Charleston (SC), 2009.

Dutton, Paul (ed.), *Charlemagne's Courtier: The Complete Einhard*, Broadview Press, Peterborough (Ont.), 1998.

Dyboski, R.; Arend, Z. M., *Knyghthode and bataile: A 15th Century Verse Paraphrase of Flavius Vegetius Renatus' Treatise "De re militari"*, The Early English Text Society, London, 1935.

Einhard, *Vita Karoli Magni*, Harper and Brothers, New York, 1880.

Einhard; Notker the Stammerer, *Two Lives of Charlemagne*, Penguin Classics, London, 2008.

Elizalde, Ignacio, *Navarra en las literaturas románicas, Edad Media*, Institución Príncipe de Viana, Iruña/Pamplona, vol. 1, 1977.

Erbe, Michael, *Quellen zur germanischen Bekehrungsgeschichte (5.-8. Jahrhundert)*, G. Mohn, Gütersloh, 1971.

Erpenius, Thomas (ed.), *Historia saracenica qua res gestae Muslimorum inde a Muhammede Arabe*, Iohannem Maire & Elzevirios, 1625.

Estornés Lasa, Bernardo, *Historia general de Euskal Herria. 476-824 época vascona*, in *Enciclopedia General Ilustrada del País Vasco*, Auñamendi, Donostia, 1981.

Estornés Lasa, Bernardo; Lévi-Provençal, Évariste, *Eneko "Arista", fundador del reino de Pamplona y su época: un siglo de historia vasca, 752-852*, Ekin, Buenos Aires, 1959.

Evans, Stephen S., *The Lords of Battle: Image and Reality of the Comitatus in Dark Age Britain*, Boydell Press, Woodbridge, 1998.

Fagnan, Edmond (ed.), *Histoire de l'Afrique du Nord et de l'Espagne intitulée Al-Bayano'l-Mogrib*, vol. 2, Imprimerie Orientale, Argelia, 1904.

Falque Rey, Emma; Estévez Sola, Juan A. (eds.), *Chronica Hispana Saeculi XII: Pars II: Chronica Naierenesis*, Brepols Publishers, Turnholt (Belgium), 1990.

Fawtier, Robert, *La Chanson de Roland: étude historique*, E. de Boccard, Paris, 1933.

Feist, Alfred, *Zur Kritik der Bertasage*, Universitats Buchdruckerei, Marburg, 1885.

Ferdinand, Walter (ed.), *Corpus iuris germanici antiqui*, Impensis G. Reimeri, Berlin, vol. 2, 1824.

Fernández Valverde, Juan; Estévez Sola, Juan A. (eds.), *Roderici Ximenii de Rada opera omnia*, Brepols Editores Pontificii, Turnhout, 1999.

Fernández Valverde, Juan; Estévez Sola, Juan A. (eds.), *Roderici Ximenii de Rada opera omnia*, Brepols Editores Pontificii, Turnhout, 1999.

Finlay, Victoria, *Colour: A Natural History of The Palette*, Ballantine Books, New York, 2003.

Firchow, Evelyn Scherabon; Zeydel, Edwin H., *The Life of Charlemagne*, University of Miami Press, Coral Gables (FL), 1972.

Fita y Colomer, Fidel; Vinson, Julien, *Le codex de saint-Jacques-de-Compostelle*, Maisonneuve et Cie, Paris, 1882.

Flórez, Enrique, *España sagrada*, vol. 8, Real Academia de la Historia, Madrid, 1869.

Fouracre, Paul; Gerberding Richard A. (eds.), *Late Merovingian France: History and Hagiography (640-720)*, Manchester University Press, Manchester, 1996.

Francke, Kuno, *Social Forces in German Literature: A Study in The History of Civilization*, Henry Holt & Co., New York, 1899.

Frappier, Jean, *Les Chansons De Geste Du Cycle De Guillaume D'orange: Le Couronnement De Louis, Le Charroi De Nîmes, La Prise D'orange*, Société d'Edition d'Enseignement Supérieur, Paris, 1955.

Gabriele, Matthew, "The Provenance of the Descriptio Qualiter Karolus Magnus: Remembering the Carolingians in the Entourage of King Philip I (1060–1108) Before the First Crusade", *Viator*, vol. 39, no. 2, 2008.

Gabriele, Matthew; Stuckey, Jace, *The Legend of Charlemagne in the Middle Ages: Power, Faith, and Crusade*, Palgrave Macmillan, 2008.

Ganshof, François-Louis, "Une crise dans le règne de Charlemagne. Les années 776 et 779", in, Roth, Charles; Gilliard, Charles (eds.), *Mélanges d'histoire et de littérature offerts à Monsieur Charles Gilliard, professeur honoraire de l'Université de Lausanne, à l'occasion de son soixante-cinquiéme anniversaire*, F. Rouge & Cie., Lausanne, 1944.

Ganshof, François-Louis, "L'armee sur les carolingiens", *Ordinamenti Militari in Occidente nell'alto medioevo*, Settimane di Studio del Centro Italiano di Studi sull'alto medioevo 15, Spoleto, 1968, pp. 109-130.

Ganshof, François-Louis, *The Carolingians and the Frankish Monarchy*, Longman, London, 1971.

García de Cortázar y Ruiz de Aguirre, José Ángel, *Introducción a la historia medieval de Álava, Guipúzcoa y Vizcaya en sus textos*, Txertoa, Donostia/San Sebastián, 1979.

Garrod, Heathcote W.; Mowat, Robert B. (eds.), *Einhard's Life of Charlemagne: The Latin Text*, Clarendon Press, Oxford, 1925.

Garrod, Heathcote William; Mowat, Robert Balmain (eds.), *Einhard's Life of Charlemagne*, The Clarendon Press, Oxford, 1915.

Gautier, Léon, *L'Entrée en Espagne: chanson de geste inédite, renfermée dans un manuscrit de la Bibliothèque de Saint-Marc à Venise*, Techener, Paris, 1858.

Gautier, Léon, *Les Epopées Françaises. Etude sur les origines et l'histoire de la littérature nationale*, Victor Palmé Libraire-Edieur, Paris, 1865.

Gerritsen, Willem P.; Van Melle, Anthony G., *A Dictionary of Medieval Heroes: Characters in Medieval Narrative Traditions and Their Afterlife in Literature, Theatre and the Visual Arts*, The Boydell Press, Woodbridge, 2000.

Gil Fernández, Juan, *Crónicas asturianas: Crónica de Alfonso III (Rotense y "A Sebastián"). Crónica albeldense (y "Profética")*, Universidad de Oviedo, Oviedo, 1985.

Godman, Peter, *Latin Poetry of the Carolingian Renaissance*, University of Oklahoma Press, Norman, 1985.

Goldsworthy, Adrian K., *The Roman Army at War 100 B.C.-A.D. 200*, Clarendon Press, Oxford, 1996.

Grimm, Wilhelm, *Ruolantes liet*, Göttingen 1838.

Guichard, Charles (ed.), *Théophile prétre et moine, essai sur divers arts*, Charles de l'Escalopier, Paris, 1843.

Gundlach, W. (ed.), *Epistolae Karolini*, Monumenta Germaniae Historica (MGH), Epp, III, Berlin, 1892.

Gundlach, W., *Codex epistolaris Carolinus. Epistolae merowingici et karolini aevi*, MGH Epp. III., W. Gundlach, Hanover, 1892.

Hack, Achim Thomas, *Codex Carolinus: Päpstliche Epistolographie im 8. Jahrhundert*, A. Hiersemann, Stuttgart, 2007.

Haefele, Hans F. (ed.), Monumenta Germaniae Historica (MGH), SSRG, NS, XII, Berlin, 1959.

Haldon, John F., *Warfare, State and Society in the Byzantine World, 565-1204*, Routledge, London, 2003.

Haller, Johannes, *Die Quellen Zur Geschichte der Entstehung des Kirchenstaates*, Druck und Verlag von B. G. Teubner, Leipzig & Berlin, 1907.

Halphen, Louis (ed.), *Eginhard: Vie de Charlemagne*, Belles-Lettres, Paris, 1938.

Halphen, Louis, *Études critiques sur l'histoire de Charlemagne: les sources de l'histoire de Charlemagne, la conquête de la Saxe, le couronnement impérial, l'agriculture et la propriété rurale, l'industrie et la commerce*, Felix Alcan, Paris, 1921.

Halsall, Guy, *Warfare and Society in the Barbarian West (450-900)*, Routledge, London & New York, 2003.

Hamilton, Walter, *French Book-plates*, George Bell & Sons, London, 1896.

Hanson, Victor (ed.), *Hoplites: The Classical Greek Batle Experience*, Rotledge, London & New York, 1989.

Heather, Peter J., *The Fall of the Roman Empire: A New History of Rome and the Barbarians*, Oxford University Press, New York, 2006.

Higounet, Charles, *Bordeaux pendant le haut moyen age*, Fédération historique du Sud-Ouest, Bordeaux, 1963.

Hincmar, *Epistola De Ordine Palatii*, F. Vieweg Librairie Éditeur, Paris, 1883.

Holder-Egger, Oswald (ed.), *Einhardi Vita Karoli Magni,* Monumenta Germaniae Historica (MGH), SSRG, Hannover & Leipzig, 1911 (reprinted in 1965).

Holmes, Thomas R., *Caesar's Conquest of Gaul*, Macmillan, London, 1903.

Horrent, Jules, *La Chanson de Roland dans les littératures française et espagnole au moyen âge*, Bibliothèque de la Faculté de Philosophie et Lettres de l'Université de Liége, Paris, 1951.

Horrent, Jules, *Roncesvalles. Etude sur le fragment de cantar de gesta conservé à l'Archivo de Navarra (Pampelune)*, Société d'Edition 'Les Belles Lettres', Paris, 1951.

Houvet, Étienne, *An Illustrated Monograph of Chartres cathedral: Being an Extract of a Work Crowned by the Académie des Beaux-arts*, Étienne Houvet, Chartres, 1925.

Huici Miranda, A. (ed.), *Al-Bayán al-Mugrib, Nuevos fragmentos almorávides y almohades*, Anubar Ediciones, Valencia, 1963.

Huici Miranda, A. (ed.), *Colección de crónicas árabes de la Reconquista*, Tetuán, 1953-54.

Hutton, Edward, *The Cities of Lombardy*, Macmillan Co., New York, 1912.

Ibn 'Idari Al-Marrakusi, *Historias de Al-Andalus Por Aben-Adhari de Marruecos*, BiblioBazaar, LLC, Charleston (SC), 2008.

Ibn al-Athir, *Annales du Maghreb & de l'Espagne traduites et annotées par Edmond Fagnan*, Typographie Adolphe Jourdan, Alger, 1898.

Ibn al-Kutiya, *Iftitah: Ta'rikh iftitah al-Andalus*, Madrid, 1926.

Ibn al-Kutiya, *Iftitah: Ta'rikh iftitah al-Andalus*, P. de Gayangos, E. Saavedra & F. Codera, Madrid, 1868.

Ibn Idhari al-Marrakushi Ahmad b. Muhammad, *Kitab al-bayan al-mughrib, fi akhbar al-Andalus wa'l-Maghrib*, G. S. Colin and E. Lévi-Provençal, Leiden, 1948-51.

Ibn Idhari al-Marrakushi, *Kitab al-bayan al-mughrib fi akhbar muluk al-Andalus wa'l-Maghrib*, R. Dozy, Leiden, 1848-51.

'Izz al-Din Ibn al-Athir, *Annales du Maghreb & de l'Espagne traduites et annotées par Edmond Fagnan*, Adamant Media Corporation, 2001.

Jacobs, Steven L., *Lemkin on Genocide*, Lexington Books, Lanham (Md.), 2012.

James, David (ed.), *Early Islamic Spain: The History of Ibn al-Qutiya: A Study of the Unique Arabic Manuscript in the Bibliothèque Nationale de France, Paris, with a Translation, Notes, and Comments*, Routledge, London and New York, 2011.

James, Georg P. R., *France in the Life of Her Great Men: The History of Charlemagne*, J & J Harper, New York, 1833.

Jaurgain, Jean de, *Vasconia. Estudio histórico crítico (S. VI-XI)*, Auñamendi, Donostia/San Sebastián, 1976. 2 vols.

Jaurgain, Jean de, *Vasconie. Étude historique et critique sur les origines du royaume de Navarre, du Duché de Gascogne, des comtés d'Aragon, de Foix, de Bigorre, d'Alava & Biscaye, de la vicomté de Béarn et des grands fiefs du duché de Gascogne (première partie)*, Pau, 1898.

Jenkins, Thomas A., *La Chanson de Roland, Oxford Version, Edition, Notes and Glossary by T. Atkinson Jenkins*, D. C. Heath, Boston, 1924.

Jiménez de Rada, Rodrigo, *Historia de los hechos de España*, Alianza, Madrid, 1989.

Jimeno Jurio, José María, *¿Dónde fue la batalla de Roncesvalles?*, Pamiela, Iruñea/Pamplona, 2004.

Jimeno Jurio, José María, *¿Dónde fue la batalla de Roncesvalles?*, Institución Príncipe de Viana, Iruñea/Pamplona, 1974.

Jimeno Jurio, José María, *Historia de Pamplona y de sus lenguas*, Txalaparta, Tafalla, 1995.

Jimeno Jurio, José María, *Nafarroako toponimia eta mapagintza / Toponimia y cartografía de Navarra*, vol. 35, Nafarroako Gobernua, Iruñea, 1996.

Jones, Arnold H. M., *The Later Roman Empire, 284-602: A Social Economic and Administrative Survey*, John Hopkins University Press, Baltimore, 1986.

Jones, Cyril M., *Historia Karoli Magni et Rotholandi: ou, Chronique du Pseudo-Turpin*, Slatkine, Genève, 1972.

King, P. D., *Charlemagne*, Methuen and Co. Ltd., London, 1986.

King, P. D., *Charlemagne: Translated Sources*, P. D. King, Lambrigg, Kendal, Cumbria, 1987.

Krusch, Bruno (ed.), *Fredegarii Scholastici libri IV cum Continuationibus. Fredegarii et aliorum chronica. Vitae sanctorum (generis regii)*, Monumenta Germaniae Historica (MGH), SSRM, II, Hannover, 1888.

Krusch, Bruno (ed.), *Liber historiae francorum*, Monumenta Germaniae Historica (MGH), SSRM, II, Hannover, 1888.

Kurze, Friedrich (ed.), *Annales regni Francorum (741–829) qui dicuntur Annales Laurissenses maiores et Einhardi*, Monumenta Germaniae Historica (MGH), SSRG, VI, Hannover, 1895.

Kurze, Friedrich (ed.), *Monumenta Germaniae Historica* (MGH), SSRG, L, Hannover, 1890.

Labarge, Margaret W., *Saint Louis: The Life of Louis IX of France*, Eyre & Spottiswoode, London, 1968.

Lacarra, José María, *Historia del Reino de Navarra en la Edad Media*, Caja de Ahorros de Navarra, Iruñea/Pamplona, 1975.

Lacarra, José María, *Vasconia medieval, historia y filología: conferencias pronunciadas los días 10 y 11 de enero de 1956*, Seminario Julio de Urquijo, Donostia, 1957.

Lafuente Alcántara, Emilio (ed.), *Ajbar Machmua (Colección de tradiciones), Crónica anónima del siglo XI*, Real Academia de la Historia, Madrid, 1867.

Lafuente Alcántara, Emilio (ed.), *Ajbar Machmua (Colección de tradiciones), Crónica anónima del siglo XI*, El Bibliófilo, Madrid, 1984.

Lafuente Alcántara, Emilio (ed.), *Ajbar Machmua (Colección de tradiciones), Crónica anónima del siglo XI*, Real Academia de la Historia, Madrid, 1867.

Lamb, Harold, *Charlemagne: The Legend and the Man*, Bantam Biography, New York, 1968.

Lamb, Harold, *Charlemagne: The Legend and the Man*, Doubleday, New York, 1954.

Lappenberg, J. M. (ed.), Monumenta Germaniae Historica (MGH), SS, XVI, Hannover, 1859.

Larrañaga, Koldo, "Glosa sobre un viejo texto referido a la historia de Pamplona: el De laude Pampilone", *Príncipe de Viana*, 55, N° 201, 1994.

Lee, Guy C., *Historical Jurisprudence: An Introduction to the Systematic Study of the Development of Law*, Macmillan, London, 1911.

Lejeune, Rita, "La naissance du couple littéraire 'Roland et Olivier'", *Mélanges Henri Grégoire, Annuaire de l'Institut de philologie et d'histoire orientales et slaves*, Brussels, 1950.

Leonis imperatoris Tactica, Typis Regiae Universitatis Scientiarum Budapestinensis, Budapest, 1922.

Lester, Geoffrey (ed.), *The Earliest English Translation of Vegetius' De re militari*, Carl Winter Universitätsverlag, Heidelberg, 1988.

Lévi Provençal, Évariste, "Du nouveau sur le Royaume de Pampelune au IXe Siècle", *Bulletin Hispanique*, 55, 1953.

Lévi Provençal, Évariste, *Histoire de l'Espagne musulmane*, Maisonneuve & Larose, Paris, 1950. 3 vols.

Lévi-Provençal, Évariste; García Gómez, Emilio (eds.), *Textos inéditos del Muqtabis de ibn Hayyan sobre los orígenes del reino de Pamplona, Al-Andalus. Revista de las Escuelas de Estudios Árabes de Madrid y Granada*, vol. 19, no. 2, 1954, pp. 295-316.

Lévi-Provençal, Évariste; García Gómez, Emilio, "Textos inéditos del Muqtabis de Ibn Hayyan sobre los orígenes del Reino de Pamplona", Al-Andalus, 19, 1954.

Lewis, Archibald R., *The Development of Southern French and Catalan Society, 718–1050*, University of Texas Press, Austin, 1965.

Lewis, David L., *God's Crucible: Islam and the Making of Europe, 570 to 1215*, W. W. Norton & Company, New York, 2008.

Limentani, Alberto, *L'"Entrée d'Espagne" e i signori d'Italia*, Antenore, Padua, 1992.

Livingstone, Arthur, "The Carmen de Prodicione Guenonis Translated into English, with Textual Notes", *The Romanic Review, a Quarterly Journal*, vol. 2, Columbia University Press, New York, 1911, pp. 61-79.

López Pereira, José Eduardo (ed.), *Crónica mozárabe de 754*, Anubar, Zaragoza, 1980.

Lot, Ferdinand, *Études sur les légendes épiques françaises*, Honore Champion, Paris, 1958.

Lot, Ferdinand, *L'art militaire et les armées au Moyen Age en Europe et dans le Proche Orient*, Payot, Paris, 1946.

Loyn, Henry Royston; Percival, John, *The Reign of Charlemagne: Documents on Carolingian Government and Administration*, St. Martin's Press, New York, 1976.

Loyn, Henry Royston; Percival, John, *The Reign of Charlemagne: Documents on Carolingian Government and Administration*, St. Martin's Press, New York, 1976.

MacLean, Simon (ed.), *History and Politics in Late Carolingian and Ottonian Europe: The Chronicle of Regino of Prüm and Adalbert of Magdeburg*, Manchester University Press, Manchester, 2009.

Maines, Clark, "The Charlemagne Window at Chartres cathedral: New Considerations on Text and Image", *Speculum*, vol. 52, No. 4, October 1977.

Mâle, Émile, *L'art religieux du XIIIe siècle en France: étude sur l'iconographie du Moyen Age et sur ses sources d'inspiration*, Ernest Leroux Editeur, Paris, 1898.

Mâle, Émile, *Notre-Dame de Chartres*, Flammarion, Paris, 1963.

Mandach, André de, "The So-Called AOI in the Chanson de Roland", Symposium: A Quarterly Journal in Modern Literatures, vol. 11, no. 2, 1957, pp. 303-315.

Mandach, André de, *Naissance et développment de la chanson de geste en Europe VI. La Chanson de Roland*, Librairie Droz, Genève, 1993.

Marbán, Edilberto, *El teatro espanol medieval y del Renacimiento: una obra para estudiantes de espanol*, Las Americas, Long Island City, N.Y., [1971].

Marca, Pierre de, *Histoire du Béarn*, Paris, 1640.

Marca, Pierre de, *Marca Hispanica sive Limes Hispanicus, hoc est geographica & historica descriptio cataloniae, ruscinonis, & circumiacentium populorum*, ed. É. Baluze, Paris, 1688.

Marriage, Margaret, *Sculptures of Chartres cathedral*, Kessinger Publishing Co., Whitefish (MT), 2003.

Martínez Txoperena, Juan Mari, "La batalla de Orreaga y la participación de los nativos", *Megalitos Pirenaicos. Arqueología y megalitismo en el Pirineo Occidental*, August 2014.

McKitterick, Rosamond, *Charlemagne: The Formation of a European Identity*, Cambridge University Press, Cambridge, 2008.

McMahon Sheehan, Michael (ed.), "Aging and the Aged in Medieval Europe", *Papers in Mediaeval Studies*, 11, PIMS, 1990, p. 92.

Melczer, William (ed.), *The Pilgrim's Guide to Santiago de Compostela*, Italica Press Inc., New York, 1993.

Menéndez Pidal, Ramón, "Roncesvalles, un nuevo cantar de gesta español del siglo XIII", Revista de Filología Española, IV, Madrid, 1917.

Menéndez Pidal, Ramón, *La Chanson de Roland et la tradition épique des Francs*, Librairie Picard, Paris, 1960.

Menéndez Pidal, Ramón, *La Chanson de Roland y el neotradicionalismo*, Espasa-Calpe, Madrid, 1959.

Michel, Francisque, *La Chanson de Roland: ou de Roncevaux, du XIIe siècle*, Chez Silvestre libraire, Paris, 1837.

Michel, Francisque, *Poesías Populares de los vascos*, Auñamendi, Donostia/San Sebastián, 1963.

Migne, Jacques P., *Patrologiae cursus completus. Operum beati Caroli Magni Imperatoris*, Paris, 1862.

Migne, Jacques-Paul (ed.), *Patrologiae cursus completus*, Garnier, Paris, vol. 71, 1879.

Miller, Malcolm B., *Chartres cathedral*, Riverside Book Company, New York, 1996.

Miller, Malcolm B., *Chartres cathedral: The Medieval Stained Glass and Sculpture*, Pitkin Pictorials, London, 1980.

Miller, Malcolm B.; Halliday, Sonia; Lushington, Laura, *Chartres cathedral: Illustrating The Medieval Stained Glass And Sculpture*, Pitkin Pictorials, London, 1992.

Mombert, Jacob Isidor, *A History of Charles the Great (Charlemagne)*, D. Appleton & Co., New York, 1888.

Monin, Louis H., *Dissertation sur le roman de Roncevaux*, L'Imprimerie Royale, Paris, 1832.

Monlezun, Jean Justin, *Histoire de la Gascogne depuis les temps les plus reculés jusqu'à nos jours*, E. Repos, Paris, 1864.

Moret, Joseph, *Annales del reyno de Navarra*, Imprenta de Martín Gregorio de Zavala, Pamplona, 1684.

Moret, Joseph, *Annales del reyno de Navarra*, Institución Príncipe de Viana, Pamplona, 1988.

Moret, Joseph, *Investigaciones históricas de las antigüedades del Reyno de Navarra*, G. Martínez, Iruñea/Pamplona, 1665.

Moret, Joseph, *Investigaciones históricas de las antigüedades del Reyno de Navarra*, Editorial de Amigos del Libro Vasco, Bilbao, 1985.

Mortier, Raoul (ed.), *La Chronique de Turpin en les grandes chroniques de France, Carmen de Prodicione Guenonis, Ronsansvals*, Éditions de la Geste Francor, Paris, vol. 3, 1941.

Müller, Theodor, *La Chanson de Roland: nach der Oxforder Handschrift*, Verlag der Dieterichschen Buchandlung, Göttingen, 1863.

Muruzabal, José M., "Nuevos datos sobre el origen del reino de Navarra", *Espacio, Tiempo y Forma. Serie III. Historia Medieval*, 7, 1994.

Mynors, Roger A. B.; Thomson, Rodney M.; Winterbottom, Michael (eds.), *William of Malmesbury, Gesta Regum Anglorum: The History of the English Kings*, Oxford University Press, Oxford, 2002.

Narbaitz, Pierre, *Le matin basque ou, histoire ancienne du peuple vascon*, Librairie Guénégaud, Paris, 1975.

Narbaitz, Pierre, *Orria, o la batalla de Roncesvalles. 778*, Elkar, Donostia, 1979.

Nelson, Janet L., *The Frankish World (750-900)*, Hambledon Press, London & Río Grande, 1996.

Nicholson, Helen, *Medieval Warfare: Theory and Practice of War in Europe 300-1500*, Palgrave Macmillan, London & New York, 2004.

Nicolle, David, *Carolingian Cavalryman AD 768-987*, Osprey Publishing, Oxford, 2005.

Nicolle, David, *God's Warriors: Crusaders, Saracens and the Battle for Jerusalem*, Osprey Publishing, Oxford, 2005.

Ogg, Frederic A., *A Source Book of Mediaeval History: Documents Illustrative of European Life and Institutions from the German Invasion to the Renaissance*, American Book Company, New York, 1908.

Oihenart, Arnaud, *Notitia utriusque Vasconiae, tum Ibericae, tum Aquitanicae, qua praeter situm regions et alia scitu digna, Navarrae Regum, Gasconiae Principum, caeterarumque, iniis, insignium vetustae et dignitate familiarum stemmata ex probatis authoribus et vetustis monumentos exhibentur*, Eusko Legebiltzarra/Parlamento Vasco, Gasteiz/Vitoria, 1992.

Orella, José Luis, *Historia de Euskal Herria*, Volume 1, Txalaparta, Tafalla, 2003.

Paris, Gaston B. P. (ed.), "Carmen de Prodicione Guenonis et la légende de Roncevaux", *Société des amis de la Romania*, XI, 1882.

Paris, Gaston B. P., *De pseudo-Turpino*, A. Franck, Paris, 1865.

Paris, Gaston B. P.; Meyer, Paul (eds.), *Histoire poetique de Charlemagne*, Librairie Emile Bouillon, Paris, 1905.

Paris, Paulin (ed.), *Li Romans de Berte aus grans piés*, Techner, Paris, 1836.

Pérez de Laborda, Alberto, *Guía para la historia del País Vasco hasta el siglo IX: fuentes, textos, glosas, índices*, Txertoa, Donostia/San Sebastián, 1996.

Perry, Walter C., *The Franks: From their First Appearance in History to the Death of King Pepin*, Longman, Brown, Green, Longmans, and Roberts, London, 1857.

Pertz, Georg Heinrich (ed.), *Annales et chronica aevi Carolini*, Monumenta Germaniae Historica (MGH), SS, I, Hannover, 1826.

Pertz, Georg Heinrich (ed.), *Annales Laureshamenses, Alamannici, Guelferbytani et Nazariani*, Monumenta Germaniae Historica (MGH), SS, I, Hannover, 1829.

Pertz, Georg Heinrich (ed.), *Monumenta Germaniae Historica* (MGH), SS, I, Hannover, 1829.

Pertz, Georg Heinrich (ed.), *Vita Ludowici...*, Monumenta Germaniae Historica (MGH), SS, II, Berlin 1829.

Pfaffe, Konrad der, *Das Rolandslied*, F. A. Brockhaus, Leipzig, 1874.

Plumptre, Edward H., *The Commedia and Canzoniere of Dante Alighieri: Life of Dante. Hell. Purgatory*, W. Isbister Ltd., London, 1886.

Porter, Pamela J., *Medieval Warfare in Manuscripts*, University of Toronto Press, Toronto, 2000.

Powel, Thomas, *Ystorya de Carolo magno, from the Red Book of Hergest*, Honourable Society of Cymmrodorion, London, 1883.

Prestwich, Michael, *Armies and Warfare in the Middle Ages: The English Experience*, Yale University Press, New Haven, 1999.

Rabanis, Joseph F., *Les Mérovingiens d'Aquitaine: essai historique et critique sur la charte d'Alaon*, Durand, Paris, 1856.

Rauschen, Gerhard; Loersch, Hugo, *Die Legende Karls des Grossen*, Duncker & Humblot, Leipzig, 1890.

Raymond Davis, *The Lives of the Eighth Century Popes*, University of Liverpool Press, Liverpool, 1995.

Reich, Emil, *Select Documents Illustrating Mediaeval and Modern History*, P.S. King & Son, London, 1905.

Remie Constable, Olivia (ed.), *Medieval Iberia: Readings from Christian, Muslim, and Jewish Sources*, University of Pennsylvania Press, Philadelphia, 1997.

Reuter, Timothy, "The Recruitment of Armies in the Early Middle Ages: What Can We Know?". In, Nørgård Jørgensen, Anne; Clausen, Birthe L. (eds.), *Military Aspects of Scandinavian Society in a European Perspective AD 1-1300*, Copenhagen, 1997.

Reyero, Carlos, *Imagen histórica de España*, Espasa Calpe, Madrid, 1987.

Rialle, Girard de; Vinson, Julien (eds.), *Revue de Linguistique et de Philologie Comparée*, vol. 15, Maisonneuve de Cie, Libraires-éditeurs, 1882.

Ribera, Julián, *Historia de la conquista de España del abenalcotía el Cordobés seguida de fragmentos históricos de Abencotaiba...*, Revista de Archivos, Madrid, 1926.

Richards, D. S. (ed.), *The Chronicle of Ibn Al-athir for the Crusading Period from Al-kamil Fi'l-ta'rikh: The Years 491–541/1097–1146, the Coming of the Franks and the Muslim Response*, Ashgate, Aldersot, 2006.

Riché, Pierre, *The Carolingians: A Family Who Forged Europe*, University of Pennsylvania Press, Philadelphia, 1993.

Riché, Pierre; McNamara, Jo Ann (eds.), *Daily Life in the World of Charlemagne*, University of Philadelphia Press, Philadelphia, 1978.

Richter, Gustav; Kohl, Horst, *Annalen der deutschen Geschichte im Mittelalter, von der Gründung des fränkischen Reichs bis zum untergang der Hohenstaufen: mit fortlaufenden Quellenauszügen und Literaturangaben*, Verlag der Buchhandlung des Waisenhauses, Halle, 1885.

Riquer, Martín, *Chanson de Roland. Cantar de Roldán y el Roncesvalles Navarro*, Acantilado, Barcelona, 2003.

Riu, Manuel, *Historia de España*, Espasa Calpe, Madrid, 1999.

Robinson, James Harvey (ed.), *Readings in European History*, Ginn & Co., Boston, 1904.

Rodd, Thomas (ed.), *History of Charles the Great and Orlando Ascribed to Turpin*, London, 1812.

Roques, Mario (ed.), "Ronsasvals, poème épique provençal", *Société des amis de la Romania*, LXV, 1940-41.

Roques, Mario (ed.), "Ronsasvals, poème épique provençal", *Société des amis de la Romania*, LVIII, 1932.

Roques, Mario (ed.), "Ronsasvals, poème épique provençal", *Société des amis de la Romania*, XLVIII, 1922.

Ross, David J. A.; Noble, Peter; Polak, Lucie; Isoz, Claire, *The Medieval Alexander Legend and Romance Epic: Essays in Honour of David J.A. Ros*, Kraus International Publication, Milwood, New York, London, and Nedelin, 1982.

Roth, Jonathan P., *The Logistics of the Roman Army at War (264 BC – AD 235)*, E. J. Brill, Leiden, 1999.

Rougemont, Denis de, *The Idea of Europe*, World Pub. Co., Cleveland, 1966.

Sage, Michael M., *The Republican Roman Army: A Sourcebook*, Routledge, New York, 2008.

Salrach i Marés, Josep M., *El procés de formació nacional de Catalunya: (segles VIII-IX)*, Edicions 62, 1978.

Samaran, Charles, *La Chanson de Roland. Reproduction Phototypique du Manuscrit Digby 23 de la Bodleian Library d'Oxford*, Société des Anciens Textes Français, Paris, 1933.

Sánchez Albornoz, Claudio; Antuña, Melchor M., "Notas de Ibn Abi Rika de las lecciones de Ibn Habib acerca de la conquista de España por los árabes", *Cuadernos de Historia de España*, 1-2, 1944, pp. 248-268.

Schenck, Mary J., "Taking a Second Look: Roland in the Charlemagne Window at Chartres", *Société Rencesvals*, vol. 25, No. 1–2, 2006, pp. 371-386.

Schlyter, Kerstin, *Les énumérations des personnages dans la Chanson de Roland: étude comparative*, C.W.K. Gleerup, Lund, 1974.

Scholz, Bernhard Walter (ed.), *Carolingian Chronicles*, University of Michigan Press, Ann Arbor, 1972.

Schramm, Percy E.; Florentine Mütherich, Florentine, *Denkmale der deutschen Könige und Kaiser: Ein Beitrag zur Herrschergeschichte von Karl dem Grossen bis Friedrich II, 768-1250*, Prestel, Munich, 1962.

Schutz, Herbert, *Tools, Weapons and Ornaments: Germanic Material Culture in Pre-Carolingian*, Brill Academic Publishers, Leiden, 2001.

Scott, A. Brian; Martin, Francis X. (eds.), *Expugnatio Hibernica*, Royal Irish Academy, Dublin, 1978.

Seeck, Otto (ed.), *Notitia dignitatum. Accedunt notitia urbis Constantinopolitanae et latercula provinciarum*, Berlin, 1876.

Segre, Cesare; Tyssens, Madeleine; Guidot, Bernard, (eds.), *La chanson de Roland*, Librairie Droz, Genève, 2003.

Segura Murguía, Santiago, *Mil años de historia vasca a través de la literatura greco-latina. De Aníbal a Carlomagno*, Universidad de Deusto, Bilbao, 2001.

Settipani, Christian, *Noblesse du Midi Carolingien: Études Sur Quelques Grandes Familles d'Aquitaine et de Languedoc du IXe au XIe Siècles*, Prosopographica et Genealogica, Oxford, 2004.

Sholod, Barton, *Charlemagne in Spain: The Cultural Legacy of Roncesvalles*, Librairie Droz, Genève, 1963.

Short, Ian (ed.), *La Chanson de Roland*, Librairie générale française, Paris, 1997.

Short, Ian; Pearcy, Roy (eds.), *La Chanson de Roland = The Song of Roland: The French corpus*, Anglo-Norman Text Society, London, 2000.

Simson, Bernhard von (ed.), *Annales Mettenses Priores*, Monumenta Germaniae Historica (MGH), SSRG, X, Hannover & Leipzig, 1905.

Snyder, James, *Medieval Art: Painting, Sculpture, Architecture, 4-14th Century*, Pearson Education, Upper Saddle River (NJ), 1989.

Southern, Pat, *The Roman Army: A Social and Institutional History*, ABC-CLIO, Santa Barbara (Cal.), 2006.

Spiegel, Gabrielle M., *The Past as Text: The Theory and Practice of Medieval Historiography*, The Johns Hopkins University Press, Baltimore (MD), 1999.

Stelten, Leo F. (ed.), *Flavius Vegetius Renatus Epitoma rei militaris*, Peter Lang, New York, 1990.

Storey, Christopher, "AOI in the Chanson de Roland", *Essays Presented to C. M. Girdlestone*, University of Durham, Newcastle upon Tyne, 1960, pp. 311-317.

Story, Joanna (ed.), *Charlemagne, Empire and Society*, Manchester University Press, Manchester, 2005.

Strayer, Joseph R., *Dictionary of the Middle Ages*, Charles Scribner's Sons, New York, 1982-89.

Stubbs, William (ed.), *Willelmi Malmesbiriensis Monachi De gestis regnum Anglorum. Libri Quinique, Historiae Novellae Libri III*, Her Majesty's Stationery Office (HMSO), London, 1887-89.

Taylor, Andrew, *Textual Situations: Three Medieval Manuscripts and Their Readers*, University of Pennsylvania Press, Philadelphia, 2002.

Thatcher, Oliver J.; Schevill, Ferdinand, *Europe in the Middle Age*, Charles Scribner's Sons, New York, 1911.

Thompson, James W., *The Dissolution of the Carolingian Fisc in The Ninth Century*, University of California Press, Berkeley, 1935.

Thorpe, Lewis (ed.), *Einhard and Notker the Stammerer: Two Lives of Charlemagne*, Penguin, London, 1969.

Torrey, Charles C. (ed.), *The History of the Conquest of Egypt, North Africa and Spain, Known as the Futuh Misr of Ibn 'Abd al-Hakam*, Yale University Press, New Haven, 1922.

Tremp, Ernst (ed.), *Astronomus. Das Leben Kaiser Ludwigs (Vita Hludowici imperatoris)*, Monumenta Germaniae Historica (MGH), SSRG, LXIV, Hannover, 1995.

Tudanca, Juan M., *Evolución socioeconómica del alto y medio Valle del Ebro en época bajoimperial romana*, Gobierno de La Rioja, Instituto de Estudios Riojanos, Logroño, 1997.

Tyler, Elizabeth Stearns, *La Chançun de Williame*, Oxford University Press, New York, 1919.

Ubieto, Antonio, "La derrota de Carlomagno y la Chanson de Roland", *Hispania*, 23, Madrid, 1963.

Ubieto, Antonio, *La Chanson de Roland y algunos problemas históricos*, Anubar, Zaragoza, 1985.

Vegetius Renatus, Flavius, *Epitoma rei militaris*, Peter Lang, New York, 1990.

Verbruggen, Jan F., *The Art of Warfare in Western Europe During the Middle Ages: From the Eighth Century to 1340*, The Boydell Press, Woodbridge, 2001.

Vétault, Alphonse, *Charlemagne*, Alfred Mame et Fils Editeurs, Tours, 1877.

Vic, Claude de; Vaissette, Joseph, *Historie Générale du Languedoc avec les notes et des pièces justificatives*, J. B. Paya Propriétaire Éditeur, Toulouse, 1872-92. 15 vols.

Vielliard, Jeanne (ed.), *Le guide du pèlerin de Saint-Jacques de Compostelle: texte latin du XIIe siècle*, Librairie Philosophique J. Vrin, Paris, 2004.

Wace, *Le Roman du Rou*, A. & J. Picard, Paris, 1965.

Wace, *The Roman du Rou*, Société jersiaise, Jersey, 2002.

Wallace-Hadrill, J. M. (ed.), *The Fourth Book of the Chronicle of Fredegar with its Continuations*, Greenwood Press, Connecticut, 1960.

Watson, William E., "The Battle of Tours-Poitiers Revisited", *Providence: Studies in Western Civilization*, 2, 1993.

Webster, Graham, *The Roman Imperial Army of the First and Second Centuries A.D.*, University of Oklahoma Press, Norman, 1998.

Webster, Wentworth, "Altabiskarco Cantua", *Boletín de la Academia de la Historia*, Madrid, vol. 3, 1883.

Webster, Wentworth; Vinson, Julien, *Basque Legends Collected Chiefly in The Labourd*, Griffith and Farran, London, 1879.

Werner, Karl F., "Heeresorganisation und Kriegsführung im Deutschen Königreich des 10 und 11 Jardhunderts", *Ordinamenti Militari in Occidente nell'alto medioevo*, Settimane di Studio del Centro Italiano di Studi sull'alto medioevo 15, Spoleto, 1968, pp. 791-856.

William of Malmesbury, *Chronicle of the Kings of England*, George Bell and Sons, London, 1904.

Williams, Robert, "The History of Charlemagne: A Translation of *Ystorya Carolo Magno* with a Historical and Critical Introduction", *Y Cymmrodor*, 20, 1907.

Wilson, Derek A., *Charlemagne*, Random House, Inc., New York, 2006.

Winterfeld, Paul von (ed.), *Poetarum Latinorum Medii Aevi*, Monumenta Germaniae Historica (MGH), PLAC, IV, Berlin, 1899.

Yanguas y Miranda, José (ed.), *Crónica de los reyes de Navarra escrita por Carlos, Príncipe de Viana*, Imprenta de Teodoro Ochoa, Pamplona, 1843.

Zink, Michel, *Medieval French Literature: An Introduction*, Medieval & Renaissance Texts & Studies, Binghamton, N.Y., 1995.

Index

For Product Safety Concerns and Information please contact our EU
representative GPSR@taylorandfrancis.com
Taylor & Francis Verlag GmbH, Kaufingerstraße 24, 80331 München, Germany

www.ingramcontent.com/pod-product-compliance
Lightning Source LLC
Chambersburg PA
CBHW071513110726
47908CB00003B/828